Simulation Foundations, Methods and Applications

AF173097

More information about this series at http://www.springer.com/series/10128

Bernard P. Zeigler · Hessam S. Sarjoughian

Guide to Modeling and Simulation of Systems of Systems

Second Edition

With contributions by Raphaël Duboz and Jean-Christophe Soulié

 Springer

Authors
Bernard P. Zeigler
University of Arizona
Tucson, AZ
USA

Hessam S. Sarjoughian
Faculty of Computer Science
  and Computer Systems Engineering
Arizona State University, School of
  Computing, Informatics, and Decision
  Systems Engineering
Tempe, AZ
USA

With contributions by
Raphaël Duboz
CIRAD
Montpellier
France

Jean-Christophe Soulié
CIRAD
Montpellier
France

ISSN 2195-2817   ISSN 2195-2825   (electronic)
Simulation Foundations, Methods and Applications
ISBN 978-3-319-87731-0   ISBN 978-3-319-64134-8   (eBook)
DOI 10.1007/978-3-319-64134-8

Printed on acid-free paper

This Springer imprint is published by Springer Nature
The registered company is Springer International Publishing AG
The registered company address is: Gewerbestrasse 11, 6330 Cham, Switzerland

Preface

Systems of systems are at the root of this century's global challenges of economy, climate, and energy. We are accustomed to building such systems directly in the real world, yet it is becoming increasingly too dangerous, costly, unethical, or risky to do so. In such cases, the only workable alternative is to build and test within virtual reality. System of systems virtual build and test can be supported by a discrete-event systems specification (DEVS) simulation modeling formalism and a system entity structure (SES) simulation model ontology.

This book guides the reader in the use of software tools based on DEVS and SES to tackle a wide variety of systems of systems problems ranging from artificial systems based on cloud information technology to living systems such as agricultural food crops. Commercial and open-source DEVS Modeling and Simulation Environments are covered in depth.

This book is the first to provide an approach to integrating both energy and information processing requirements into system design. This approach, based on activity concepts that are intrinsic to DEVS-based system design, allows us to virtually build and test systems that are capable of emulating biological systems in their ability to balance their information processing functionalities against the energy and resource expenditure incurred in their use.

This edition adds a new chapter covering DEVS Support for Markov Modeling and Simulation. The new chapter provides some concepts and applications for the related facility that has been developed in MS4 Me since the first edition. The edition also augments Chapters 8 and 16 with material intended to enhance guide to modeling and simulation of systems of systems. We want to take the opportunity to recognize Raphaël Duboz and Jean-Christophe Soulié as co-authors for their authorship of Chapter 17.

Acknowledgement The authors would like to acknowledge the numerous developers and users whose efforts contributed to this project. Specifically, we thank Doohwan Kim, Chungman Seo, Robert Coop, Ranjit Singh, Robert Flasher, Ting-Shen Fu, Weilong Hu, Vignesh Elamvazhuthi, Soroosh Gholami,

Abdurrahman AlShareef, Mostafa Fard, Phillip Hammonds, Miguel Soto, Raphaël Duboz, and Jean-Christophe Soulié for their dedication, hard work, and expertise that brought the DEVS concept to its realization in environments including MS4 ME™, DEVS-Suite, CosMoS, and VLE.

Potomac, USA   Bernard P. Zeigler
Tempe, USA   Hessam S. Sarjoughian

Contents

Part I
Basic Concepts

Modeling and Simulation of Systems of Systems

1

This book is about modeling and simulation in support of "virtual build and test" for Systems of Systems (SoS), which include complex information-technology-based business, engineering, military systems, as well as the societal infrastructures they support. Such systems are at the root of this century's global challenges of interacting economic crises, world-wide crop failures, extreme effects of climate change, and out-of-control viral epidemics. We are accustomed to building such systems directly in the real world and letting subsequent use and Mother Nature tell us how good they are. Increasingly, however, it is becoming too dangerous, costly, unethical, or risky to do so. "Build and test within virtual reality" is more often the only workable alternative—where by "virtual" we include a wide range of representations of the eventual fielded reality either wholly within a single computer or as networked distributed simulations, often enhanced with physically analogous and immersive environments.

Following are a few representative examples of problems needing the systems of systems concept. We briefly look at motivating objectives, why current approaches are not adequate to meet these objectives, and how the SoS concept and supporting virtual build and test environments can overcome conventional limitations.

Controlling National Health Care Costs

- *Objective*: coordinate the various health-related systems including hospitals, doctors, pharmacists, and insurers, which are currently largely uncoordinated, so as to improve patient care and greatly reduce its cost.
- *Key Conventional Limitation*: it is not feasible to experiment in reality with alternative systems for coordinating the interactions of the medical, pharmaceutical, and insurance subsystems.
- *System of Systems Approach*: model the national health care system as a system of systems formulating architectures of coordination and measures of quality for health care delivery.

© Springer International Publishing AG 2017

B.P. Zeigler and H.S. Sarjoughian, *Guide to Modeling and Simulation of Systems of Systems*, Simulation Foundations, Methods and Applications, DOI 10.1007/978-3-319-64134-8_1

- *Virtual Build and Test*: develop a family of coordinating architectures which employ net-centric information technology and can be evaluated in a simulated environment of providers and clients for their effectiveness in improving care while reducing cost.

Cloud System Architectures

- *Objective*: develop simulation models that can capture software and hardware parts of service-oriented computing systems and their integration.
- *Key Conventional Limitations*: understanding of cloud system architectures using software-centric simulation approaches are inadequate. In particular, simulation-based architectural designs with heavy emphasis on software are not suitable for capturing cloud system dynamics.
- *System of Systems Approach*: introduce co-design concepts commonly used in embedded system simulation for cloud systems.
- *Virtual Build and Test*: formulate domain-neutral software system model abstractions that account for SOA principles (i.e., elevating component simulation to simulation-as-a-service concept). Develop hardware system simulation models that can be integrated with software system simulation models in a systematic fashion.

Failing Agricultural Food Crops

- *Objective*: develop crops (for example, rice is the world's food staple) that are robust enough to survive in the extreme and variable environments increasingly prevalent under climate change.
- *Key Conventional Limitations*: can't experiment with large enough numbers of variations of plant genetics and growing conditions to find the sought for plant varieties.
- *System of Systems Approach*: model plants as systems with dynamic linkages among component traits to understand their combined impact on the whole plant system depending on genotypes and weather and soil conditions.
- *Virtual Build and Test*: develop a family of plant model architectures to simulate plant growth and its regulation in a wide range of genetic and environmental parameters, focusing on sensitivity to resource availability.

Catastrophic Forest Wild Fires

- *Objective*: improve forest fire fighting systems to be capable of dealing with the increasingly challenging wild fires that cause millions of dollars in destruction of natural resources and increasingly homes and possessions.
- *Key Conventional Limitation*: too dangerous and costly to create artificial fires of the magnitude and intensity needed to understand dynamics of spread and develop effective containment methods.

- *System of Systems Approach*: model forest topography, weather, and fuel characteristics with embedded sensor networks, connected prediction and decision-making components, and agent models of human and robotic fire fighters.
- *Virtual Build and Test*: develop a family of model architectures to simulate forest fire spread and its suppression by a range of tactics and strategies involving prediction of spread and allocation of human and artificial resources.

Lagging Drug Development

- *Objective*: Develop new effective drugs for wide spread diseases and chronic illnesses that reduce the enormous cost of treatment.
- *Key Conventional Limitations*: high capital investment required to develop new drugs in current laboratory environments and numerous sources of error due to poor understanding of the biology of drug action.
- *System of Systems Approach*: model the biology of drug action at the molecular level with reusable components and their interactions.
- *Virtual Build and Test*: develop a virtual environment that allows simulating the effects of drugs on disease analogs thereby moving the search for drugs from the wet laboratory to a higher speed and more flexible equivalent.

1.1   Virtual Build and Test

Addressing challenges such as the ones just enumerated requires taking a System of Systems approach supported by Virtual Build and Test methodology. *Discrete-Event Systems Specification* (DEVS) is a simulation modeling formalism that provides the basis for simulating systems of systems in a virtual environment. DEVS has both system theoretic and information theoretical roots. Just as arithmetic underlies addition, multiplication, and other calculation, so DEVS underlies simulation of discrete-event models. DEVS Simulation is performed by an engine that implements a technology-agnostic Abstract DEVS Simulator algorithm. In addition, *System Entity Structure* (SES) is a high level ontology framework targeted to modeling, simulation, systems design, and engineering. An SES is a formal structure governed by a small number of axioms that provide clarity and rigor to its models. The structure supports hierarchical and modular compositions allowing large complex structures to be built in stepwise fashion from smaller, simpler ones.

Simulation models typically employ different formalisms for state and time advance, depending on whether discrete or continuous mechanisms are used. DEVS provides a common programming model of the simulation process that allows a composition of heterogeneous models to dynamically evolve on a common time base in a distributed simulation environment. In such a dynamic composition, each component model generates outputs and consumes inputs produced by others in the proper temporal relationship. This book discusses DEVS-based interoperation through standardizing data distribution and time-management functionalities, implemented over data distribution services middleware such as Web services.

1.2   Modeling and Simulation Intrinsic to Virtual Build and Test

Before homing in on the details of the modeling and simulation process itself, we will look at the virtual built and test system development process in more detail. As illustrated in Fig. 1.1, the process typically starts with a phase in which the requirements are developed for the system to be built. However, in the SoS context, this system will not be built from scratch but will be a combination of already existing components and new ones to be constructed. Thus, the end goal must be addressed to both implementing new components and integrating them with existing components to meet the desired functional and performance requirements.

The relative portion of new-to-existing components offers a way to distinguish different types of SoS problems. For example, designing energy efficient buildings represents a high new-to-existing component ratio where components are manufactured from raw materials and assembled into new structures. On the other hand, designing policies to achieve greater crop yields is characterized by the fact that the new components implementing the policies constitute a relatively small part of the overall agricultural system. Nevertheless, the full range of interventions on reality, from limited management to full scale engineering, are included in the concept of virtual build and test. Most importantly, in all cases there is a need for valid computer representation of the reality in terms of simulation models to support the integration with new components that will enable testing the alternatives before actual implementation and fielding.

Fig. 1.1 Centrality of modeling and simulation within system of systems development

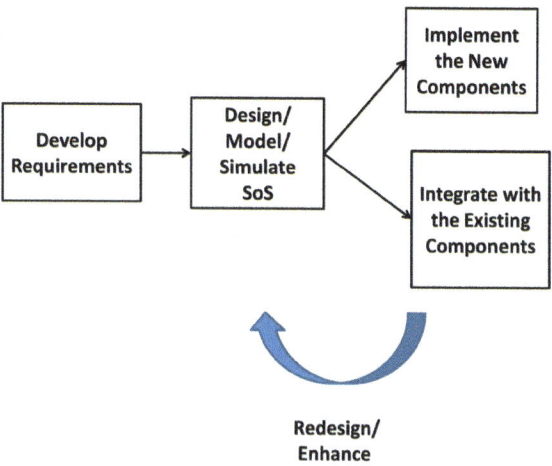

In a conventional approach, once we are done designing, modeling, and simulating the proposed system we would then construct the new components and integrate them with the existing ones. This follow on phase is like taking a blue print or abstract system specification and implementing it with actual hardware and software. However, this kind of separation between design and implementation does not make full use of the models that have developed in the simulation phase. So there is likely to be a lot of duplicated effort and error that creeps into the implementation. Instead, the modeling and simulation (M&S) environment should help to transfer the models as smoothly as possible from their simulation guises to forms in which they change as little as possible but only the engine in which they are executed changes. Similarly, the integration of new components with existing components should be initially addressed within the simulation phase in a way that does not require starting from scratch later in the implementation phase. This requirement is attainable to the extent that the middleware platform for integrating the components is also the compatible with the engine for executing the new components. The DEVS environment to be discussed in this book offers a solution to meet this requirement by allowing the models developed for simulation to be executed by a real-time engine and interfaced through data distribution middleware to other existing components. In this DEVS-based approach, the new components are designed, developed, and tested as DEVS models within a virtual environment while existing components are represented by stubs or abstractions that provide sufficient fidelity to enable adequate simulation-based testing of the new system. Then the same DEVS models are transferred to the DEVS-based distributed simulation environment with extensions in their message structures to allow them to exchange information in, as well as being time-managed by, the distributed environment. Interfacing to the existing components also occurs by means of the middleware where these real components replace the stubs in the system composition as it was represented in the simulation.

As a consequence of this DEVS-based approach, there is an added benefit to the redesign and enhancement that inevitably occurs within the system's life cycle. Whenever such a modification of the SoS is needed, it can first be expressed and tested within the original simulation environment and then transferred to actual operation in the same way that original implementation was performed. There would be no need to start from scratch to develop a simulation model of the existing system to support the design, development, and testing of the modifications before fielding them.

1.3 Multi-disciplinary Collaboration Using Multi-formalism Modeling

A characteristic property of SoS is that the component systems are typically associated with different disciplines and are constructed by expert developers trained in these disciplines. As a consequence, model components reflect diverse world views and heterogeneous formalisms that must be integrated together in the composite model of the SoS. As a universal computational basis for systems theory, DEVS offers a single common framework for accommodating a limitless variety of domain-specific modeling formalisms. A DEVS-based environment offers a practical means of supporting interdisciplinary team or community-developed libraries of heterogeneous model components that can be integrated together to construct the virtual models. Moreover, the System Entity Structure offers a structured means of organizing such model repositories to help compose the right combinations of alternatives to satisfy the particular objectives of the moment.

In a truthful disclaimer, the vision of a DEVS-based environment with all the functionality just depicted is still on the way toward full realization. Nevertheless, progress has been made and environments exist that show the feasibility of the approach and suggest where further research and development is needed in more specifics.

We discuss three DEVS modeling and simulation environments for SoS virtual build and test in this book.

MS4 Me™ is a modeling and simulation environment developed as the first in a commercial line of DEVS products (http://ms4systems.com). MS4 Me is aimed at a variety of users such as students, managers, modelers, developers, and programmers enabling them to work at the level for which they are most comfortable and productive. MS4 Me employs a DEVS simplification, Finite Deterministic DEVS (FDDEVS), as the basis for a simplified syntax/content assisted language that beginners and non-programmers can employ to quickly and easily construct basic DEVS models. These models of component systems can then be coupled together to create a simulation with a few natural language statements for the System Entity Structure. Once the basic outlines of the model have been established, the environment features a structured approach for DEVS experts and Java programmers to enhance the FDDEVS descriptions with the depth needed to actually simulate real systems of systems. A notable feature intended to accelerate such a development process is the Sequence Designer tool which automatically creates both FDDEVS models and an SES to couple them together from a simple sequential diagram input. Chapters 2 through 12 of the book are devoted to DEVS concepts as implemented in MS4 Me with the remaining chapters devoted to expositions of how these concepts apply to SoS. The following DEVS modeling environments are discussed in depth to illustrate their powerful features in this regard.

Component-Based System Modeler and Simulator (CoSMoS) offers an integrated platform for developing component-based, modular, hierarchical families of models. It is grounded in a unified logical, visual, and persistent perspective on models. It supports specifying families of parallel DEVS, Cellular Automata, and XML Schema models. Its unique features are storing models in relational databases, model complexity metrics, and separating simulatable and non-simulatable models from one another. Systems of systems may be modeled as separate software and hardware systems which can be then used together to model alternative system architectures. The CoSMoS lifecycle process affords basic capabilities starting from model conceptualization and ending with simulation execution. It integrates *DEVS-Suite* simulator, which supports developing and execution of hierarchical parallel

DEVS models. The simulator is built using DEVSJAVA and DEVS Tracking Environment with configurable synchronized control for simulation execution and viewing. It supports automating design of experiments in combination with animation of simulation execution, viewing time-based data trajectories at run-time, and storing simulation data for post-processing. Model libraries for Semiconductor Supply-Chain Manufacturing, Service-Oriented Computing, MIPS32 Processors, Network-on-a-chip, Swarm Net, UML design patterns, and Household Agents have been developed. The simulator is in use in academic institutions in many countries and several research centers in government agencies and commercial entities. CoSMoS and DEVS-Suite are featured in Chaps. 14 through 16.

Virtual Laboratory Environment (VLE) is aimed at collaborative development of simulation models for Living Systems of Systems. The environment employs DEVS to combine traditional continuous models with discrete-event and other modern formalisms to encourage collaborative development, validation, replication, and experimentation within a virtual laboratory context. The goal is to support decision making in SoS applications such as control of epidemic outbreaks among animals (remember the avian flu?) and reengineering of rice varieties to withstand loss of viability. The French National Institute for Agricultural Research (INRA), one of the world's elite agricultural institutes, chose VLE to integrate its stock of existing agriculture models and to develop new simulation capabilities using DEVS. As discussed in Chap. 17, the RECORD project documented why INRA chose DEVS and VLE to support model reuse and collaboration among its model developers. The DEVS/VLE combination was preferred among many commercial and academic contenders based on VLE's implementation of DEVS's formal support for coupling and integration of models in the diverse formalisms being employed in the agricultural domain.

1.4 Background in the Literature

Since the appearance of one of the author's (Zeigler) "Theory of Modeling and Simulation" in 1976, the DEVS approach to modeling and simulation it introduced has taken root in academia and is emerging into common research and industrial use. Since it is aimed at more of a guide to the use of DEVS concepts and tools, this book cannot replicate the background theory in full within the space available. Thus, we refer you, the reader, to consider acquiring the background from some of the following books:

- Systems of Systems—Innovations for the 21st Century, Edited by Mo Jamshidi, Wiley, 2008.
- Object Oriented Simulation with Hierarchical, Modular Models: Intelligent Agents and Endomorphic Agents, by Bernard P. Zeigler, Academic Press, Orlando, 1990.

- Multifaceted Modeling and Discrete-Event Simulation, by Bernard P. Zeigler, Academic Press, London, 1984.
- Theory of Modeling and Simulation: Integrating Discrete-Event and Continuous Complex Dynamic Systems, by Bernard P. Zeigler, Herbert Praehofer, and Tag Gon Kim, 2nd Edition, By, Academic Press, NY, 2000.
- Modeling and Simulation-Based Data Engineering: Introducing Pragmatics into Ontologies for Net-Centric Information Exchange, by Bernard P. Zeigler and Phillip E. Hammonds, Academic Press, NY, 2007.
- Discrete-Event Modeling and Simulation Technologies: A Tapestry of Systems and AI-Based Theories and Methodologies, Editors: Hessam S. Sarjoughian and François E. Cellier Springer-Verlag Publishers, 2001.
- Discrete-Event Modeling and Simulation: A Practitioner's Approach (Computational Analysis, Synthesis, and Design of Dynamic Systems) by Gabriel A. Wainer, CRC Press, 2009.
- Discrete-Event Modeling and Simulation: Theory and Applications (Computational Analysis, Synthesis, and Design of Dynamic Systems), Editors: Gabriel A. Wainer, Pieter J. Mosterman, CRC Press, 2010.
- Building Simulation Software: Theory, Algorithms, and Applications, by James Nutaro, Wiley Publishers, NY, 2010.
- DEVS Net-Centric System of Systems Engineering with DEVS Unified Process. CRC-Taylor & Francis Series on System of Systems Engineering, by Saurabh Mittal and José L. Risco-Martín (to appear).
- Agent-Directed Simulation and Systems Engineering Editors: Levent Yilmaz and Tuncer Ören, Wiley, 2009.

1.5 Guide to Modeling and Simulation of Systems of Systems

The present book builds upon the material in the earlier books but goes beyond them in several critical ways. It centers on the unifying theme of "virtual build and test" as a means of integrating and providing context to the various technical concepts and tools discussed. In doing so, it provides an inclusive exposition of the many aspects of DEVS-based concepts and tools, all relating back to the "virtual build and test" theme. In particular, Chaps. 2–8 offer a step-by-step introduction to DEVS concepts and corresponding MS4 Me features that enable you to gain hands-on experience with the concepts to build sophisticated SoS models. A User Reference to the features of MS4 Me accompanies this book and is also sold by the publisher. The software itself is available from MS4 Systems (http://ms4systems. com). Chapters 9–12 develop more advanced concepts for modeling and simulation of SoS and illustrate them with MS4 Me features developed earlier. Chapters 13–18 discuss applications of the concepts to virtual build and test for a variety of SoS application domains using the capabilities of CoSMoS/DEVS-Suite and VLE as well as MS4 Me. The software packages are available at http://acims.asu.edu

(CoSMoS/DEVS-Suite) and http://vle-project.org (VLE). Exercises to reinforce the concepts, to encourage using the three sets of tools, and to compare their capabilities are provided throughout the book.

The primary target for this book is both practitioners and academics (professors and students). Practitioners include simulation software developers supporting system development, systems engineers designing and architecting systems, and managers of such projects. The technical level targeted at first-or-second year graduate students is augmented with introductory and summary sections written at a more general level so that managers and others can skim over technical parts.

Hopefully, the advances described here will inspire continued research and development of the DEVS framework that builds upon the concepts and tools we present.

DEVS Integrated Development Environments

2

In this chapter, we discuss basic DEVS and SES concepts and tools to support working with these concepts in the context of an actual modeling and simulation environment, the MS4 Modeling Environment. To address the different perspectives that stakeholders bring to the modeling and simulation world, we provided three different introductions aimed at three different types of users. For the general M&S user, we provided a description of the concepts supported by MS4 Me™ through the immediate application of its most basic tools. For the M&S Developer, we provided a more advanced introduction to MS4 Me™'s underlying DEVS concepts and theory and the tools that support them. For the M&S Expert Professional, we offered a glimpse into MS4 Me™'s features in more depth as well as the theory that supports them. This book is divided into three parts. In the first part, we discuss basic DEVS and SES concepts and tools to support working with these concepts in the context of an actual modeling and simulation environment, called MS4 Modeling Environment (MS4 Me™). Then in Part II, we discuss more advanced concepts that such tools can support, and in Part III, we discuss some actual applications that throw light on the kinds of System of Systems problems that can be addressed with such concepts and tools.

2.1 The MS4 Me Is a Modeling and Simulation (M&S) Environment

MS4 Me is a modeling and simulation (M&S) environment developed as the first in a commercial line of DEVS products (ms4systems.com). MS4 Me is aimed at a variety of users such as managers, modelers, developers, and programmers enabling them to work at the level for which they are most comfortable and productive. With this variety in mind, this chapter offers three different introductions aimed at three different types of users. Let's call these types of users Drivers, Designers, and Racing Pros. Drivers want to know what basic things cars can do and how they can

© Springer International Publishing AG 2017   13
B.P. Zeigler and H.S. Sarjoughian, *Guide to Modeling and Simulation of Systems of Systems*, Simulation Foundations, Methods and Applications, DOI 10.1007/978-3-319-64134-8_2

make cars do those things. Drivers are not interested in the car per se—only how well it gets them to where they want to go. Designers want to know how to make better cars—so they need to know what things are under the hood and how those things work together to make a car do what it does. Racing Pros want to exploit the car to its extreme. They want to get familiar with all its features and how to use them to the fullest extent. So like a Driver, you might want to know what MS4 Me does as a tool in your tool box. Let's call you the M&S User in this case. Or like a Designer, you might be an M&S Developer and want to open the hood so as to get into MS4 Me's underlying DEVS concepts and theory. Or like a Racing Pro, you are an M&S Expert Professional and want to know MS4 Me's features in depth as well as the theory that supports them.

You can skip to the introduction that best characterizes your needs and roles. However, since each introduction is written with a different perspective, you might be better served if you skimmed each one looking for nuggets that might help you understand your own focus and also how it interacts with others.

2.1.1 Introduction for the M&S User

For the modeling and simulation general user, the MS4 Me modeling environment offers a restricted English language interface to generate models and then simulate the behavior graphically in real time. With minimal training, an M&S user such as a systems engineer or manager can take a need expressed in common English into a restricted, but clearly stated, set of English statements that are checked and automatically transformed into graphical models on the fly; then these individual models can be coupled to other models and presented to the stakeholder to ensure that the need is expressed as intended and that it fits a standardized process.

If the need expressed in the model is deficient or incorrect, the user and the stakeholder can negotiate immediately where intent and model have diverged iteratively arriving at a very precise statement that is formal and adheres to a standard process and language.

MS4 Me is capable of expressing very simple processes, such as workflows, as well as extremely complex, and precise timing and mathematical functions, including complex functions required to coordinate activities of components.

Coordination Example: Jazz Band Leader Much of today's work is done in teams, and team coordination is becoming ever more required. Coordination can be very scripted in the way a playwright determines the flow and actions of the actors. Or it can be very loose as in a Jazz combo where individual players have a large role in determining the outcome. And as we will see in many examples through the book, coordination may have to be implemented at many levels of organization of systems to enable loosely coupled or semi-autonomous components to work toward common goals.

Let's consider an example where coordination lies somewhere in between very scripted and very loose in which a band leader coordinates the sections (rhythm, woodwind, horns) of a jazz band. We will focus on how the leader starts the

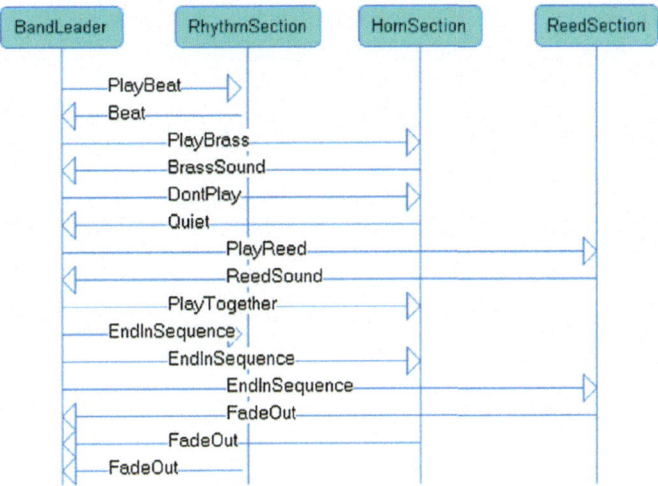

Fig. 2.1 Sequence diagram interface example for the Jazz Band

sections playing, changes the lead from one section to another, and brings the piece
to a close in which sections fade out in a sequence. Using the sequence diagram
interface of MS4 Me, you can easily lay out this kind of coordinated interaction.

As illustrated in Fig. 2.1, the BandLeader, Rhythm, Horn, and Reed sections are
actors in the diagram, each with its own lifeline descending down the page. Message transmissions from a sender to a receiver are shown as labeled arrows and
presented in the order in which they occur as time advances down the page. For
example, the BandLeader starts the piece by telling the Rhythm section to provide
the beat. The Rhythm section responds by providing the beat to the BandLeader
(We could complicate the diagram by also drawing arrows labeled by PlayBeat to
the other sections, to indicate that they also hear the beat being played). From this
input, you can automatically generate a model where you can see the actors
interacting and events occurring as prescribed. This model can be viewed in the
Simulation Viewer as shown in Fig. 2.2.

Watching the flow in the Simulation Viewer, you can check whether the
structure and behavior are as you would like them to be, and if not, you can change
the input at two levels:

- You can go into the files generated and change some of the times in the actor
  models, to change the times at which events occur—corresponding to what we
  call a change in behavior.
- You can go back and change the sequence diagram to alter the flow of events.
  This is a more radical change in the model—corresponding to what we call a
  change in structure.

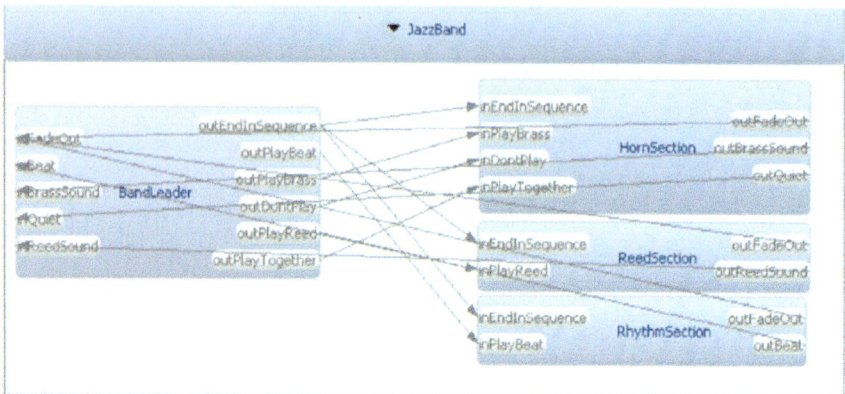

Fig. 2.2 The Jazz Band Model generated from the sequence diagram

We will show how the model generated by the sequential diagram interface leads to more advanced uses after presenting the remaining introductions.

2.1.2   Introduction for the M&S Developer

For the modeling and simulation developer, MS4 Me offers a powerful, adaptable platform designed to develop DEVS models and simulations quickly. It includes constrained natural language (NL) interface which greatly speeds the development of models and their dynamic simulations to near real time. The graphical simulations can be run immediately upon input of the model. The NL interface and animation capability lend themselves well to capture requirements concisely, but rigorously. The tool is easy to use with only limited training. It is this combination of linguistic and dynamic graphical display of a need that will allow stakeholders and system engineers to visualize and negotiate the capabilities and behaviors expressed.

The vision of a DEVS Modeling and Simulation Environment is to provide an integrated development environment dedicated to the creation of DEVS models and their simulation. Such an environment makes developers feel they are working with a complete set of tools that are able to support all the functions needed to create DEVS models and simulate them within, or externally to, the environment. Such a vision has become feasible with the advent of the Eclipse open source community (www.eclipse.org) and its support of extensible language development and other programming frameworks. One such framework, Xtext, provides a set of domain-specific languages and tools (parsers, type-safe abstract syntax tree, interpreter, etc.) to create a programming language and automatically generate its implementation in the Java Virtual Environment.

MS4 Me employs Xtext, its Extended Bachus-Naur Form (EBNF) grammar within the Eclipse Modeling Framework on the Rich Client Platform, and the

Fig. 2.3 Part of MS4 ME
initial user interface

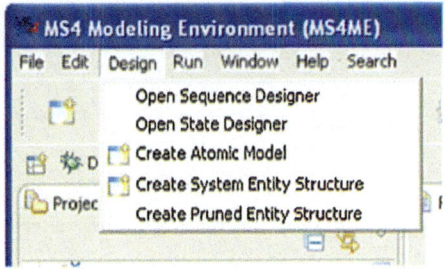

Fig. 2.4 Constrained natural
language for creating atomic
models

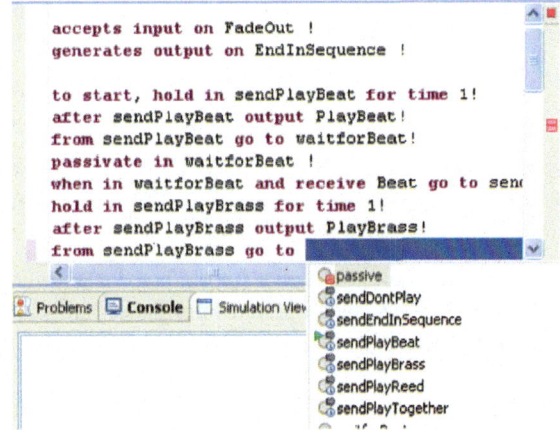

Graphical Modeling Project to provide a full blown IDE specifically tailored to a
DEVS development environment.

Figure 2.3 illustrates how the MS4 Modeling Environment user interface sets the
look and feel for access to tools dedicated to DEVS modeling and simulation. The
Design drop-down menu displays items that open files for the three main types of
object: (1) Finite Deterministic DEVS (FDDEVS) that creates atomic models,
(2) System Entity Structures that create families of hierarchical coupled models, and
(3) pruned entity structure scripts that make choices from the available alternatives
to specify a particular hierarchical coupled model. These objects represent and
extend basic system concepts—atomic models, coupled models, and hierarchical
(or nested) coupled models. The environment is concerned with providing tools to
construct such models, test them for correctness, modify them until satisfactory, and
simulate or animate them.

By using Eclipse's Xtext EBNF grammar development facility, MS4 Me provides a constrained natural language to define FDDEVS models. As illustrated in
Fig. 2.4, there are seven basic sentence types with variable slots that together define
a FDDEVS model. These sentence types define such elements as input and output
ports, states (including initial state), time advances, internal transitions, external
transitions, and generated outputs. As the modeler writes the text, the editor parses
it and creates an outline shown on the right of the figure that displays the structure

```
☐ MS4 ME Launch Page   📄 *ProcessorOfJobs.dn  ✕   Ⓙ ProcessorOfJobs.java

    from sendJob go to waitForJob !

    accepts input on Job with type WorkToDo !
    generates output on Job with type WorkToDo !

    use count with type int and default "0"!
    use storedJob with type WorkToDo and default "new WorkToDo()

      external event for waitForJob with Job
   <%
   if (input.hasMessages(inJob)) {
   ArrayList<Message<WorkToDo>>
    messageList = inJob.getMessages(input);
    storedJob =     RegularJobMessageList.get(0).getData();
    holdIn("sendJob",storedJob.getProcessingTime());
   %>!
   output event for sendJob
   <%
       output.add(outJob, storedJob);
   %>!
```

Fig. 2.5 Tagged blocks for extending FDDEVS models to full-fledged DEVS models

that has been defined. Besides providing instant visualization, and click-access to source definitions, the captured information is available for model processing, as discussed earlier.

As text is entered, the parser provides syntax checking and sentence completion assistance. Such assistance is also content-based in that permissible entries are shown on request—the example in Fig. 2.4 illustrates that the parser is expecting a state and suggests states that have been entered earlier as candidates.

Although FDDEVS models have the essential properties of DEVS models, they form a subclass of all DEVS models (hence of all discrete-event systems). Figure 2.5 shows how the MS4 Me provides constructs to enable extending a FDDEVS model to become a full-fledged DEVS model implemented in Java. The linguistic support allows modelers to specify the types of DEVS messages accepted by input ports and generated by output ports, interpretation of inputs and generation of outputs, state variables and their types, new types as required, and especially operations on state variables invoked by internal and external transitions. The grammar recognizes tagged blocks for internal and external transitions in which Java code that executes the desired transition can be placed. The modeler can inspect and test the generated Java model, returning always to the FDDEVS file to make changes. Thus, consistency is always maintained between the high level specification (FDDEVS) and the implementation (Java). The approach realized by the tagged blocks also maintains traceability back from the resulting Java code to its block source.

The natural language interface for constructing System Entity Structures (SES) is illustrated in Fig. 2.6. The most fundamental statement here is the one in the modeler provides a decomposition of a system in terms of components from a certain perspective. The couplings associated with this perspective can then be defined and linked with this perspective. Hierarchical construction is done by

```
ProcessorOfEntities.dnl        *ProcessorOfJobs.dnl        *SimpleWorkFlow.ses  ×
  From the top perspective, SimpleWorkFlow is made of GeneratorOfJobs,
                            ProcessorOfJobs, and Transducer!
  From the top perspective, GeneratorOfJobs sends Job to ProcessorOfJobs!
  From the top perspective, GeneratorOfJobs sends outJob to Transducer as ariv!
  From the top perspective, ProcessorOfJobs sends outJob to Transducer as solved!
  From the top perspective, Transducer sends Stop to GeneratorOfJobs !
```

Fig. 2.6 Constrained natural language for System Entity Structure specification

recursive decomposition of a component to the depth desired. Both external and internal couplings are easily specified. The modeler may adopt any number of perspectives for decomposing a system or component according to the modeling objective and level of resolution needed.

The SES formalism supports a powerful extension of hierarchical system concepts that we briefly touch on here (Wymore 1967). For an in-depth survey of Wymore's system theory and its relation to model-based system engineering (Friedenthal et al. 2009), see Ören (1984), Ören and Zeigler (2012). Figure 2.7 illustrates an SES for an unmanned air vehicle testing environment, which illustrates both decompositions (single line icons) and specializations (double line icons), where a specialization offers a choice of alternatives to plug into a component slot.

For example, SensorPackage can be decomposed, from the experiment perspective, into various sensor components such as FeedBack Sensor, Observation Sensor, MotionSensor, and WeaponSensor. In addition, TestAgent has a specialization, labeled by Scenario, into alternatives such as Baseline, Observational, or Attack—selection of one will configure the TestAgent appropriately. MS4 Me provides a user interface to support pruning of choices (i.e., pruning of decom positions and specializations) with the selections recorded in the files for pruned entity structures. Automatic transformation of such structures into simulation models affords a system design environment for investigating a family of possible

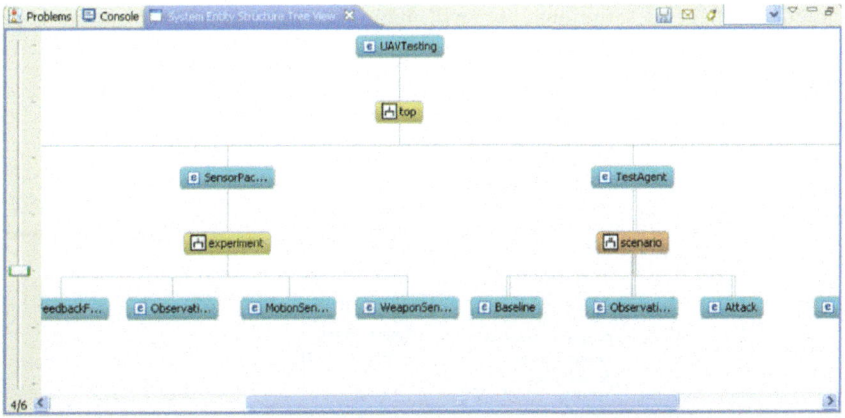

Fig. 2.7 System Entity Structure tree showing decomposition and specialization icons

architectural models through simulation. Reaccessing such files for subsequent copying and modification as desired supports reuse and extensibility.

2.2   Introduction for the M&S Professional

Around the time of the emergence of DEVS as the computational basis for systems simulation, another important trend took hold. Object orientation (OO) was first introduced in simulation and later spread to programming in general. It is fair to say that OO is at the heart of current information technology, so much so, that its presence is often taken as a given. For simulation modeling, DEVS and OO formed an ideal marriage. DEVS brought the formal and conceptual framework of dynamic systems while OO provided a rapidly evolving wealth of implementation platforms for DEVS models and simulations—first in languages such as Java and C++, and later in network and Web infrastructures, and today continuing in the future toward Cloud information technologies (Wainer and Mosterman 2009). The first implementation of DEVS in object orientated form was described in Zeigler (1987), and there are currently numerous such implementations, some of which are listed in DEVS (2012). In the next section, we discuss how Wymore's concepts take computational form in today's information technology implementations of the DEVS formalism.

2.2.1   System Structure and Behavior

As illustrated in Fig. 2.8, MS4 Me employs the essential system concepts of structure and behavior to generate simulation models. The modeler provides the structural description, essentially the hierarchical coupled model, by writing the System Entity Structure in natural language form. The modeler provides the behavioral description by writing the lowest level component atomic models in natural language form. After discussing the basics of these concepts and their natural language descriptions, we will return to the sequence diagram input

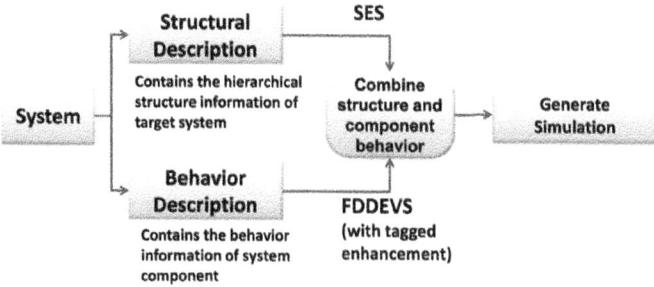

Fig. 2.8 MS4 Me's approach to specifying structure and behavior

interface (recall the Jazz Band example) that writes the natural language coupled and atomic specifications for you.

2.2.2 Finite Deterministic DEVS (FDDEVS)

We begin with a brief introduction to the contained natural language and Finite Deterministic DEVS (FDDEVS).

States A state can either be a "hold state" or a "passive state." A hold state is one that the model will stay in for a certain amount of time before automatically changing to another state (via an internal transition). A passive state is one that the model will remain in indefinitely (or until it receives a message that triggers an external transition).

Passive States To define a passive state, use the following syntax:

```
passivate in STATE_NAME!
```

Hold States To define a hold state, use the following syntax:

```
hold in STATE_NAME for time 5.7!
```

Initial States One state in the model must be designated as the initial state. To do this, the state description must start with "to start." For example, if we wanted to make the previous state the initial state, we would use this syntax:

```
to start passivate in STATE_NAME!
```

or

```
to start hold in STATE_NAME for time 5.7!
```

Internal Transitions Every hold state in the model must have one and only one internal transition defined in order to specify the state to which the model should transition after the specified amount of time. Internal transitions use the following syntax:

```
from CURRENT_STATE go to NEXT_STATE!
```
```
<add extra line>
```

Output Any state that has an internal transition can also have one output message that is generated before that internal transition occurs. The syntax for this is:

```
after STATE_NAME output OUTPUT_MESSAGE!
```
```
<add extra line>
```

External Transitions Any state can have one or more external transitions defined. An external transition defines an input message that the model might receive when in a given state and the state to which the model should transition in reaction to that input message. The syntax is:

```
when in STATE_NAME and receive INPUT_MESSAGE go to NEXT_STATE!
```

2.2.3 System Entity Structure (SES)

Let's continue with the second concept, the System Entity Structure (SES). One of the powerful capabilities of the MS4 Me tool is the ability to couple multiple models into a larger and more complete system. The SES language is used to describe how a system is decomposed into subsystems when viewed from a certain perspective, different specializations of a system that might occur, messages sent from one system to another, and variables that a system might have. A SES is made up of:

Aspects describing subsystems that make up a system when that system is viewed a certain way.
Example: A car has an engine, a transmission, and a chassis when one considers the structural components of the car, but it also has a manufacturer, model, and license plate when one considers the physical description of the car.
Specializations that describe different subsystems that perform the duties of some system.
Example: Continuing the car example from above, the engine might be an electrical engine, a gasoline engine, or a natural gas engine.
Couplings that describe how systems interact with each other.
Example: The car's engine can send rotation to the transmission, and the transmission can send motion to the chassis (by actually turning the wheels).
Similarities that can be used to indicate that one system is similar to another in some way.
Example: When considering the structural components of a truck, it's easier to say that a truck is like a car instead of describing the same components.
Variables that a system might have which affect its behavior.
Example: An engine might have a variable called "HoursRun" that keeps track of the total number of hours that the engine has been operating, and this variable might affect the performance or reliability of the engine.

The SES and FDDEVS are specified in logical and mathematical form (see Mittal and Douglass 2011, for background on FDDEVS and Zeigler and Hammonds 2007 for in-depth discussion of the SES). A complete theory of DEVS is given in Zeigler et al. (2000) with key formal properties of well definition, closure under coupling, universality and uniqueness summarized in the Appendix. While the details of the mathematics are transparent to users, it is important to point out that the tool is based on a rigorous mathematical specification with more than thirty years of scrutiny and application. It is this rigor which will provide confidence to stakeholders and engineers that a need expressed in this format is syntactically and formally correct. The formal properties summarized in the Appendix give DEVS checks and balances that allow other models created in the specification to be coupled together correctly. The tool actually prevents users from making logical and syntactical mistakes that might otherwise propagate through to requirements.

In the DEVS formalism, *atomic* DEVS captures the system behavior, while *coupled DEVS* describes the structure of system. The MS4 ME natural language interface automatically generates the mathematics demonstrated here, freeing the system engineer to capture needs quickly yet rigorously. The specification forces you to extract information from the stakeholder in a very efficient manner and distills any need into its fundamental components. In practically, any behavior or function the elements of the specification are required. A well defined need of any kind will contain these atomic elements. In essence, to capture a DEVS model forces you to ask the questions:

- What are the inputs?
- If nothing external happens, what does the system do and when?
- If there is an external input, what does the system do?
- What are the outputs?

In addition, creating a DEVS' **atomic** model forces you to ask questions like:

- What are the possible states?
- In the absence of input, how long does the system stay in each of its states?
- When an input event occurs, how does the system change state?
- After the system finishes its time in a state, what output does it produce and what state does it go to?

Creating a DEVS' **coupled** model forces you to ask questions like:

- What are the components?
- How are the components connected internally?
- How are the components connected externally?
- What are the sub-components?
- What are the interfaces?

2.3 Jazz Band Continued

The model generated by the Jazz Band sequence diagram of Fig. 2.1 is a coupled model that has as components the actors appearing in the diagram, namely, the BandLeader, Rhythm, Horn, and Read sections. The SES that is generated is given in natural language form:

From the music perspective, JazzBand is made of BandLeader, RhythmSection, HornSection, and ReedSection!

From the music perspective, BandLeader sends PlayBeat to RhythmSection!

From the music perspective, RhythmSection sends Beat to BandLeader!

From the music perspective, BandLeader sends PlayBrass to HornSection!

From the music perspective, HornSection sends BrassSound to BandLeader!

From the music perspective, BandLeader sends DontPlay to HornSection!

From the music perspective, HornSection sends Quiet to BandLeader!

From the music perspective, BandLeader sends PlayReed to ReedSection!

From the music perspective, ReedSection sends ReedSound to BandLeader!

From the music perspective, BandLeader sends PlayTogether to HornSection!

From the music perspective, BandLeader sends EndInSequence to RhythmSection!

From the music perspective, BandLeader sends EndInSequence to HornSection!

From the music perspective, BandLeader sends EndInSequence to ReedSection!

From the music perspective, ReedSection sends FadeOut to BandLeader!

From the music perspective, HornSection sends FadeOut to BandLeader!

From the music perspective, RhythmSection sends FadeOut to BandLeader!

Note that the first sentence lists the components of the model while the remaining sentences describe the message flow broken down into a set of coupling specifications. Each such specification sets up the possibility for a message transmission. For example, the second sentence sets up a coupling of the output port outBeat of BandLeader to the input port inBeat of RhythmSection. There is no intrinsic order to the coupling statements of an SES—any permutation will result in the same set of couplings. These couplings are shown as grey lines in the simulation view of Fig. 2.2. In contrast to the sequence of message transmissions specified by the sequence diagram, they describe routing patterns. Indeed, this places the burden on the component behaviors to enact a sequence of transmission events, accordingly, each of the four components, BandLeader, RhythmSection, HornSection, and ReedSection in the Jazz Band needs an atomic model to provide the behavior in the manner shown in Fig. 2.2. The FDDEVS natural language forms for these atomic models are automatically generated. That of the RhythmSection is shown here:

```
to start,passivate in waitforPlayBeat!
```

```
when in waitforPlayBeat and receive PlayBeat go to sendBeat!
```

```
hold in sendBeat for time 0!
```

```
after sendBeat output Beat!
```

```
from sendBeat go to waitforEndInSequence!
```

```
passivate in waitforEndInSequence!
```

```
when in waitforEndInSequence and receive EndInSequence go to
sendFadeOut!
```

```
hold in sendFadeOut for time 0!
```

```
after sendFadeOut output FadeOut!
```

```
from sendFadeOut go to passive!
```

```
passivate in passive!
```

FDDEVS models expressed in natural language have an alternative description in the form of state diagrams. The state diagram for RhythmSection is shown in Fig. 2.9. In this graphical depiction, states are shown as rectangles, each state has a time advance and may have external transitions (input arrows with "?") and internal transitions with or without outputs (arrows with "!"). The modeler can work in either of the natural language and state diagram equivalent representations and switch between them at will.

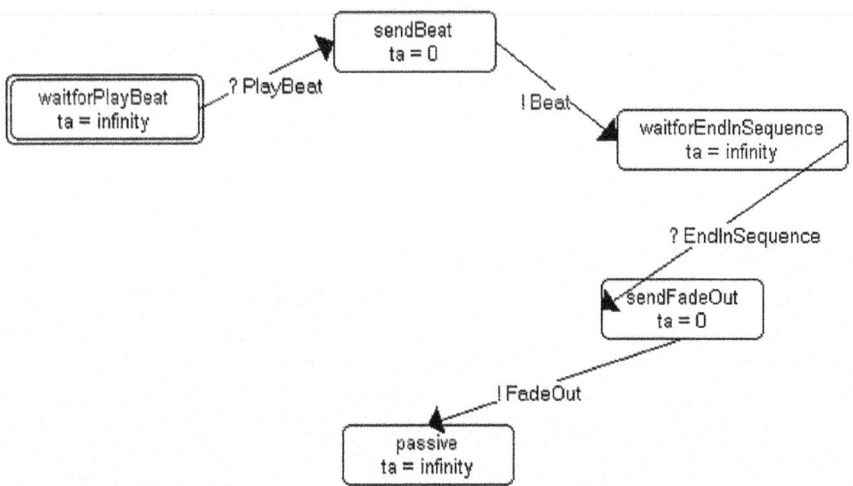

Fig. 2.9 State Diagram view of RhythmSection

The SES is automatically generated as a *.ses file and deposited in the Models. ses folder while the FDDEVS models are generated as *.dnl files and deposited in the Models.dnl folder. This makes them available to work with further as you wish to continue to develop the model. For example, the standard hold time for the sendFadeOut state is 0. But we can change the value in the RhythemSection.dnl file to the duration that the component should hold for while fading out, as in:

hold in sendFadeOut **for time** 20!

2.4 Summary

In this chapter, we discussed basic DEVS and SES concepts and tools to support working with these concepts in the context of an actual modeling and simulation environment, the MS4 Modeling Environment (MS4 Me) (ms4systems.com). To address the different perspectives that stakeholders bring to the modeling and simulation world, we provided three different introductions aimed at three different types of users. For the general M&S user, we provided a description of the concepts supported by MS4 Me through the immediate application of its most basic tools. For the M&S Developer, we provided a more advanced introduction to MS4 Me's underlying DEVS concepts and theory and the tools that support them. For the M&S Expert Professional, we offered a glimpse into MS4 Me's features in more depth as well as the theory that supports them.

To summarize, there are two main pillars to the DEVS-based modeling and simulation for Systems of Systems (SoS), the DEVS formalism itself and the SES that enables composition of DEVS models as components. For the composition of components required in the SoS context, the most relevant pillar to start with is the SES. Thus, the next chapter will start the exposition of the SES and its features mentioned above. We will then return to consider the FDDEVS formalism in its natural language form and the enhancements that can be made to be incorporated into Java models in Chap. 4.

Appendix: Key Formal Properties of DEVS

This appendix summarizes some key formal properties of DEVS as given in Zeigler et al. (2000). These include well definition, closure under coupling, universality and uniqueness. The fact that DEVS stands for Discrete-Event System Specification becomes more apparent from examining Fig. 2.10.

Here, we see an apparent distinction between Atomic DEVS and Dynamic Systems. The set of all Dynamic Systems is taken as a well-defined class in which each system has a set of input time segments, states, state transitions, and output time segments (Zeigler et al. 2000). Although the class of Dynamic Systems is well defined, it is too encompassing and mathematical a concept to allow directly constructing a particular member system. A DEVS atomic model contains the sets (input, states, output) and functions (transition and output) that take the right form

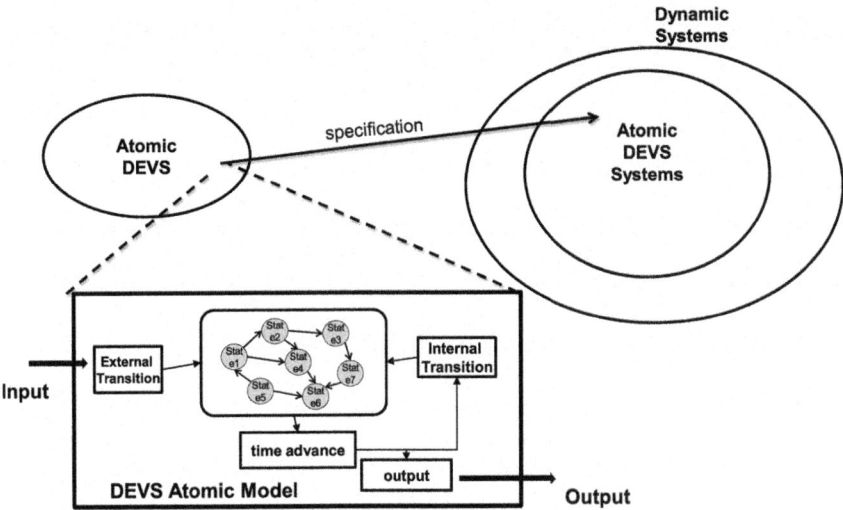

Fig. 2.10 DEVS Atomic Models as system specifications

to provide such a construction. The theory shows how the sets and functions should be interpreted to specify a dynamic system and establishes the conditions under which such a specification is well defined, i.e., where there is one, and only one, dynamic system that can be constructed from an Atomic model. In Fig. 2.11, the set of Atomic DEVS Dynamic Systems is the subset of Dynamic Systems that are specified by the set of Atomic Models.

Indeed, the theory shows how DEVS provides a computational framework for working with Dynamic Systems as computational models of real world Systems of Systems. This is further clarified in Fig. 2.11 which shows that DEVS coupled models also define a subclass of Dynamic Systems.

A DEVS Coupled Model constructs a Dynamic System by specifying its components and couplings. The theory shows how the components and couplings should be interpreted to specify a well-defined system. In Fig. 2.11, the set of Coupled DEVS Dynamic Systems is the subset of Dynamic Systems that are specified by the set of Coupled Models. Actually, the theory shows that the subset of Coupled DEVS Systems is contained within the subset of Atomic DEVS Systems. This property is called closure under coupling and states that the dynamic system specified by a coupled model can be represented as (more technically, is behaviorally equivalent to) an Atomic DEVS System. Closure under coupling is important for two reasons: (1) it provides the basis for the Abstract DEVS Simulator, i.e., a simulator is the computational device that carries out the rules by which the components carry out state transitions and send messages to each other through the couplings. (2) It justifies hierarchical composition in which a coupled model (treated as its behaviorally equivalent atomic model) can become components themselves in larger coupled models.

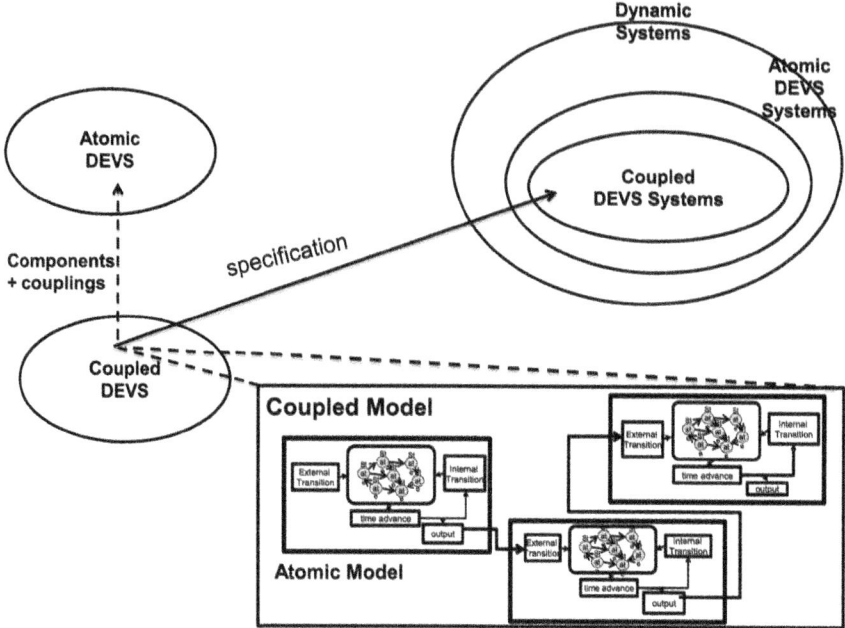

Fig. 2.11 DEVS Coupled Models as system specifications closed under coupling

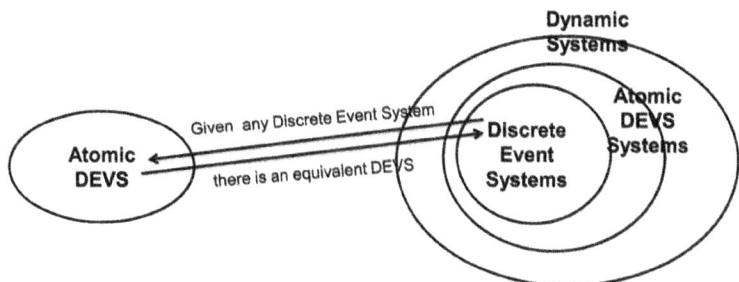

Fig. 2.12 DEVS Universality and Uniqueness for Discrete-Event Systems

The properties of well definition and closure under coupling give you confidence that the models that you construct using a DEVS Modeling Environment are backed up by a solid mathematical and logical foundation. The properties of universality and uniqueness, illustrated in Fig. 2.12, support the claim that any discrete-event model you are likely to want to build, can be done in a DEVS Modeling Environment. First, let's define a Discrete-Event Dynamic System as a Dynamic System with discrete-event input and output segments. The theory shows that DEVS is universal in the sense that any such Discrete-Event Dynamic System is behaviorally equivalent to a DEVS Dynamic System. Moreover, uniqueness says, that there is a

DEVS equivalent system which has the smallest number of states and is essentially contained within any other such equivalent. This means that you are not limited in the range of discrete-event models that you build in a DEVS Modeling Environment. Indeed, you can build any discrete-event model you could build in some other environment. Moreover, if you do not include extraneous and redundant features in it, then it will be the most efficient representative of all the models that could give the same behavior.

References

DEVS. (2012). DEVS Standardization Group. http://cell-devs.sce.carleton.ca/devsgroup/?q=node/8.

Friedenthal, S., Moore, A., & Steiner, R. (2009). *A practical guide to SysML: the systems modeling language* (1st ed.). San Mateo: Morgan Kaufmann.

Mittal, S., & Douglass, S. A. (2011). From domain specific languages to DEVS components: application to cognitive M&S. SpringSim (TMS-DEVS), pp. 256–265.

Ören, T. I. (1984). GEST—a modelling and simulation language based on system theoretic concepts. In T. I. Ören, B. P. Zeigler, & M. S. Elzas (Eds.), *Simulation and model-based methodologies: An integrative view* (pp. 281–335). Heidelberg: Springer.

Ören, T. I., & Zeigler, B. P. (2012). System theoretic foundations of modeling and simulation: A historic perspective and the legacy of A. Wayne Wymore. Simulation.

Wainer, G. A., & Mosterman, P. J. (2009). *Discrete-event modeling and simulation: Theory and applications*. London: Taylor & Francis.

Wymore, A. W. (1967). *A mathematical theory of systems engineering: The elements*. New York: Wiley.

Zeigler, B. P. (1987). Hierarchical, modular discrete-event models in an object oriented environment. *Simulation J., 49*(5), 219–230.

Zeigler, B. P., Kim, T. G., & Praehofer, H. (2000). *Theory of modeling and simulation: integrating discrete-event and continuous complex dynamic systems* (2nd ed.). Boston: Academic Press.

Zeigler, B. P., & Hammonds, P. (2007). *Modeling & simulation-based data engineering: Introducing pragmatics into ontologies for net-centric information exchange*. Boston: Academic Press, 448 pages.

System Entity Structure Basics

3

In this chapter, you will see how the System Entity Structure (SES) can help you construct models for Systems of Systems. In fact, we will use the SES to better understand the process for constructing such models. Modeling and Simulation (M&S) refers to a set of activities that are undertaken for a variety of reasons—to enable better decisions by testing out alternative policies using simulation models, to build simulators of complex technology systems for use in training, and to provide environments to support virtual build and test of Systems of Systems, as discussed in Chap. 1. It will be helpful to get a sense of the activities involved in M&S from a bird's eye perspective before we dive down into DEVS-based tools for simulation model construction, the focus of this book.

A good starting point, although somewhat simplistic, is to visualize the activities as a process or sequence of steps to accomplish a task in some ways similar to a software development process. The kind of M&S task under discussion here is to enable better decisions by testing out alternative choices using simulation models. The process as often formulated has the following steps:

1. Clarify your objectives for this modeling and simulation task—there may be many objectives motivating model development for decision making.
2. Gather relevant data.
3. Construct your model.
4. Execute the model.
5. Interpret the results of simulation.

One thing to notice immediately is that, while constructing and simulating a model are central to the process, other activities that lay the groundwork (Steps 1 and 2) and interpret the results (Step 5) can't be ignored. Indeed your success as a modeling and simulation developer may strongly depend on your understanding of these peripheral activities and your ability to collaborate with others to assure their success.

© Springer International Publishing AG 2017   31
B.P. Zeigler and H.S. Sarjoughian, *Guide to Modeling and Simulation of Systems of Systems*, Simulation Foundations, Methods and Applications, DOI 10.1007/978-3-319-64134-8_3

3.1 Modeling and Simulation as a Simple Workflow

In its simplest form, the M&S process can be shown as a "waterfall" in the sense that it proceeds from beginning to end without ever returning to early steps (Fig. 3.1).

We'll consider this formulation of M&S activities to introduce the System Entity Structure and DEVS modeling supported by MS4 Me. Later in Chap. 13, we'll return to consider how MS4 Me supports a much more realistic and flexible M&S process formulation.

M&S process portrayed in Fig. 3.1 will be formulated with the help of a System Entity Structure (SES) using relevant tools of the MS4 Me environment. Figure 3.2 shows an outline of the M&S process portrayed in Fig. 3.1. We see that in this representation the process is considered to be an entity, MSProcessSystem, which is decomposed into the steps of Fig. 3.1, each represented as an entity with a corresponding name.

Formulating the process in this way will introduce you to activities involved in modeling and simulation, while at the same time probe the SES in its most basic form. As an additional outcome, you can generate an animation of the process that allows you to see the successive activation of the modules representing the process steps together with the information flow among these modules.

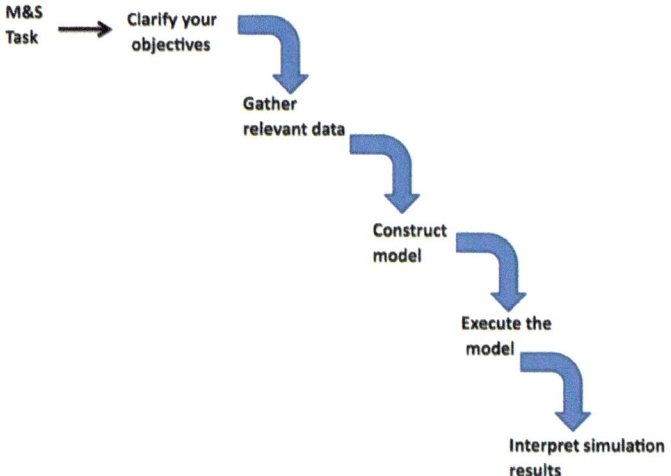

Fig. 3.1 The M&S Process as waterfall sequence of steps

Fig. 3.2 Outline of the
MSProcess SES

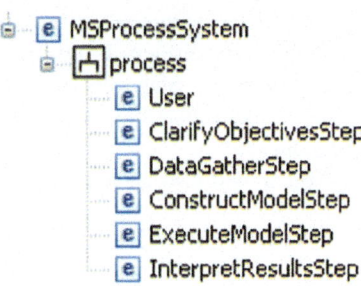

3.2 Decomposition and Coupling

Two unique features of the SES are decomposition and coupling. Decomposition tells how to decompose or breakdown an entity into entities. These entities later can represent components in a model constructed for the original entity. Coupling tells how information can flow among the components in the constructed model. Let's see how the MS4 Me environment helps you specify the SES under consideration. The first step is to indicate the top entity of the SES and its subentities as follows:

From the process **perspective,** MSProcessSystem **is made of**
User, ClarifyObjectivesStep, DataGatherStep,
ConstructModelStep, ExecuteModelStep, **and**
InterpretResultsStep!

Note that the subentities are listed (the order doesn't count) after the "is made of" phrase. These are components in a particular decomposition labeled as "process" in the "From the … perspective" phrase. The constant parts of the statement are in bold font—the parts that convey user information are in ordinary font. The "process" label for the perspective serves to allow us to provide coupling information for the components. For example, the sentence:

From the process **perspective**, User **sends** InitialObjectives **to**
ClarifyObjectivesStep!

states the User component *is capable of sending a message* called InitialObjectives to the ClarifyObjectivesStep component. Whether or not a model actually outputs InitialObjectives at any time depends on the model itself. Of course, entities included in such a coupling statement must have been included in the "made of" statement. The next statement:

from the process perspective, ClarifyObjectivesStep sends ClearObjectives
to DataGatherStep!

states the ClarifyObjectivesStep component sends a message called ClearObjectives to the DataGatherStep. From these two coupling statements, we can see that the ClarifyObjectivesStep gets as input, InitialObjectives, and processes this input to produce the ClearObjectives output. This agrees with the name given to the component.

You should now be able to interpret the following coupling statements:

```
from the process perspective, DataGatherStep sends
ValidData to ConstructModelStep!
from the process perspective, ConstructModelStep sends
ValidModel to ExecuteModelStep!
from the process perspective, ExecuteModelStep sends
ExperimentSummaries to InterpretResultsStep!
from the process perspective, InterpretResultsStep sends
RankedAlternatives to user!
```

Couplings defined by the above statements appear in the outline of the SES: This display of couplings may be easier to scan through than the original natural language text.

The following statement is also a coupling statement but it relates the overall process to one of the components:

```
From the process perspective, MSProcessSystem sends StartUp to User!
```

This states that the encompassing model, MSProcessSystem sends a StartUp message to the User component.

The semantics of above statements are evident in the following display generated by the MS4 Me simulation (Fig. 3.3).

Fig. 3.3 Outline of the MSProcess SES showing coupling

Exercise

Review the statements discussed above and check whether they agree with Table 3.1 of inputs and outputs.

Input/output tables such as Table 3.1 play a role in the animation that is generated from an SES by MS4 Me. The analyzing program derives input/output relations for each the entities in the way we have discussed just now and creates models for each of the components that behave according to these tables. If it has a single input and output, when a model receives the input, it responds by generating the output. If the model has several inputs and outputs, unless modified, the model will output all the outputs when receiving any input. This is because the SES portrays couplings, or possible information flows, but cannot say exactly which ones will occur. In other words, we can only infer the possible input/output relation (that any identified input can produce any identified output) associated with an entity not the actual one that a model for the entity would produce. This looseness in behavior is unlikely to be what you intend so you have to eliminate undesired pairings in the model's input/output relation. For example, in the MSProcessSystem SES, the User model has two inputs: StartUp and RankedAlternatives and one output, InitialObjectives. Table 3.1 lists the output of the User component as "No output" since we are not concerned with how the User handles the RankedAlternatives (whether to make a decision or return to revisit the M&S process). However, in the table generated from the SES both inputs produce the same output. So we need to remove the pair (RankedAlternatives, InitialObjectives) to make the model behave as we intend.

Let us say that a model is *compatible* with an entity if the model is capable of receiving inputs and producing outputs inferred from the SES coupling involving that entity. Since the SES analyzer only examines the couplings involving an entity, it can resolve the selection of models for an entity to those compatible with it but no further.

Exercise

Provide a counterexample to the claim that it is always possible from an analysis of the SES alone to infer which model a developer intends to replace as a component

Table 3.1 Input/output relation to components

Component	Input	Output
User	StartUp	InitialObjectives
User	RankedAlternatives	—No output—
ClarifyObjectivesPhase	InitialObjectives	ClearObjectives
DataGatherPhase	ClearObjectives	ValidData
ConstructModelPhase	ValidData	ValidModel
ExecuteModelPhase	ValidModel	ExperimentSummaries
InterpretResultsPhase	ExperimentSummaries	RankedAlternatives

for the entity. Hint: write an SES containing an entity which receives two distinct input messages and produces two distinct output messages. Suggest at least two models that are compatible with the entity's coupling but have different input/output tables.

3.3 Hierarchical Construction

Let's examine the M&S process in somewhat more detail. Consider breaking down the steps of Figs. 3.1 and 3.2 along the following lines:

- *Clarifying your objectives* breaks down into clarifying requirements (specifying the decisions that modeling should support), values (how to measure the model outputs), and weights (how to weight the measures).
- *Gathering relevant data* involves finding the right data and validating it to make sure it is representative of the system being modeled.
- *Constructing a model* first requires defining the model, then implementing it, calibrating it with data gathered in the previous step, and validating the model against unused data or newly gathered relevant data.
- *Executing the model* involves formulating alternative decisions and running simulation experiments to get the model's evaluation of these alternatives.
- *Interpreting the results of simulation* involves evaluating alternatives and ranking them for the user's examination.

This more detailed description of the M&S Process can be expressed in the SES so that it has more than one level and generates hierarchical models. In contrast to the "flat" model in Fig. 3.4, a *hierarchical* model contains at least one component that itself is composed of subcomponents. To show how the SES can make this

Fig. 3.4 Simulation Viewer showing the DEVS coupled model generated from the SES

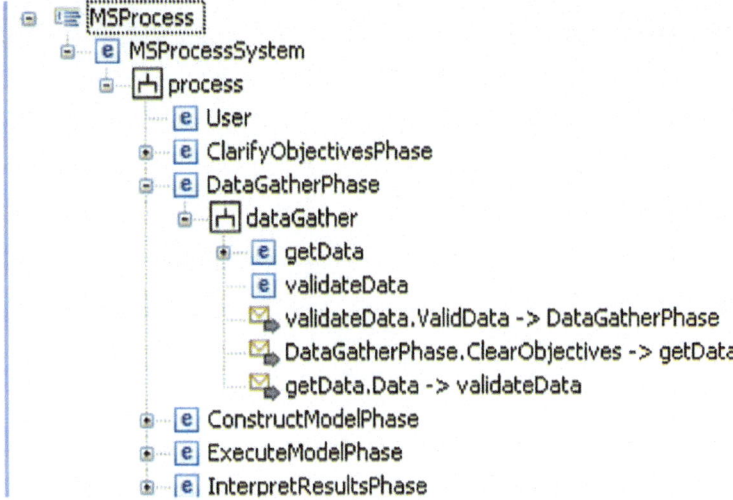

Fig. 3.5 The outline of the SES as extended by the decomposing DataGatherPhase

happen, we'll start with the description of data gathering. Let's consider that the DataGather Phase contains two components, getData and validateData. Notice that we use the term "Phase" instead of "Step" to avoid a conflict where the two types of models, atomic and coupled, resulting from transformation will have the same name. As with the MSProcessSystem, we express this composition as follows:

From the dataGather perspective, DataGatherPhase is made of getData and validateData!

The effect of this statement is to add entities below the DataGatherPhase entity. Consider the following coupling statements (and compare with Fig. 3.5).

From the dataGather perspective, DataGatherPhase sends ClearObjectives to getData!
From the dataGather perspective, validateData sends ValidData to DataGatherPhase!
From the dataGather perspective, getData sends Data to validateData!

The first two statements mention DataGatherPhase while the third mentions only its subentities. The first is an example of *external input coupling,* it says that the DataGatherPhase is capable of sending an input ClearObjectives to its subcomponent, getData. The second is an example of *external output coupling*, which says that the subcomponent, validateData is capable of sending validData to its parent entity, DataGatherPhase. The third is an example of *internal coupling* that describes a coupling involving subentities, getData and validateData.

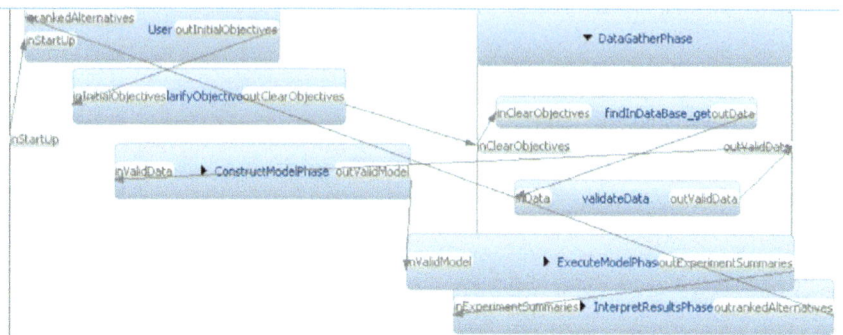

Fig. 3.6   The DataGatherPhase model as an expanded component of MSProcessSystem

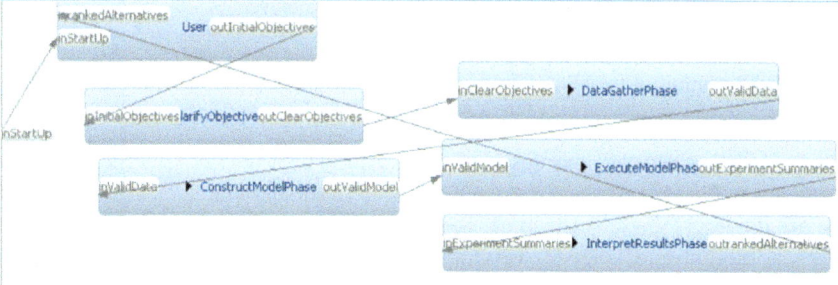

Fig. 3.7   The hierarchical model for MSProcessSystem (showing the component coupled models in black box form)

The resulting hierarchical coupled model for MSProcessSystem is shown in Fig. 3.6. It shows the new coupled model for the generated substructure under DataGatherPhase. Note that the couplings involving DataGatherPhase when it is a subcomponent (of the MSProcessSystem) and those (just discussed) that relate DataGatherPhase to its subcomponents, agree on names of messages. This allows a ClearObjectives message sent to DataGatherPhase to be relayed downward to its getData subcomponent. Similarly, the component validateData sends validData upward to its parent, DataGatherPhase.

This discussion leads to an important *coupling rule for decomposition*: When we decompose an entity we have to remember to make the external input and external output couplings consistent with the internal couplings of the **parent** entity.

The hierarchical model for MSProcessSystem is shown in Fig. 3.7.

Exercise

Extend the SES for MSProcessSystem to include the decomposition of its remaining components. Add the following segments to the original SES, prune, and generate the Simulation Viewer and animation. Compare your Simulation Viewer display for each component with the Simulation Viewer displays below. Also compare the Simulation Viewer display for the top level model with the one given at the end of the section. In each case, follow the message flow given by the animation and try to explain how the couplings make this happen. Give reasons why the couplings have been specified the way they have and experiment with alternatives to see how the information flow is affected.

Decomposing Clarify Objectives

From the clarifyObjectives perspective, ClarifyObjectivesPhase is made of clarifyRequirements, clarifyValues, and clarifyWeights!

From the clarifyObjectives perspective,ClarifyObjectivesPhase sends InitialObjectives to clarifyRequirements!

From the clarifyObjectives perspective,ClarifyObjectivesPhase sends InitialObjectives to clarifyValues!

From the clarifyObjectives perspective,ClarifyObjectivesPhase sends InitialObjectives to clarifyWeights!

From the clarifyObjectives perspective,clarifyRequirements sends ClearObjectives to ClarifyObjectivesPhase!

From the clarifyObjectives perspective,clarifyValues sends ClearObjectives to ClarifyObjectivesPhase!

From the clarifyObjectives perspective,clarifyWeights sends ClearObjectives to ClarifyObjectivesPhase!

This gives rise to the view in Fig. 3.8.

Decomposing Model Construction

From the constructModel perspective, ConstructModelPhase is made of defineModel,implementModel,calibrateModel,and validateModel!

From the constructModel perspective, ConstructModelPhase sends ValidData to defineModel!

From the constructModel perspective, defineModel sends ModelDefinition to implementModel!

From the constructModel perspective, implementModel sends ImplementedModel to calibrateModel!

From the constructModel perspective, calibrateModel sends CalibratedModel to validateModel!

From the constructModel perspective, validateModel sends ValidModel to ConstructModelPhase!

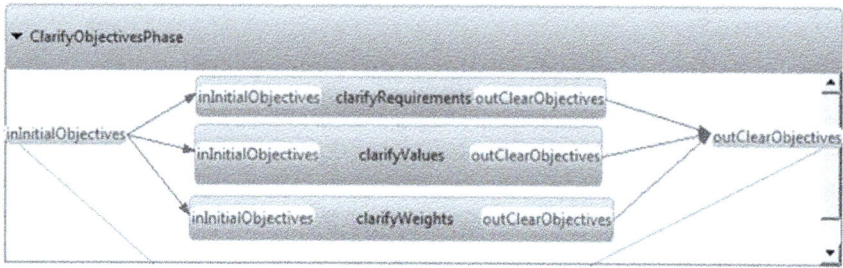

Fig. 3.8 Decomposition of ClarifyObjectivesPhase

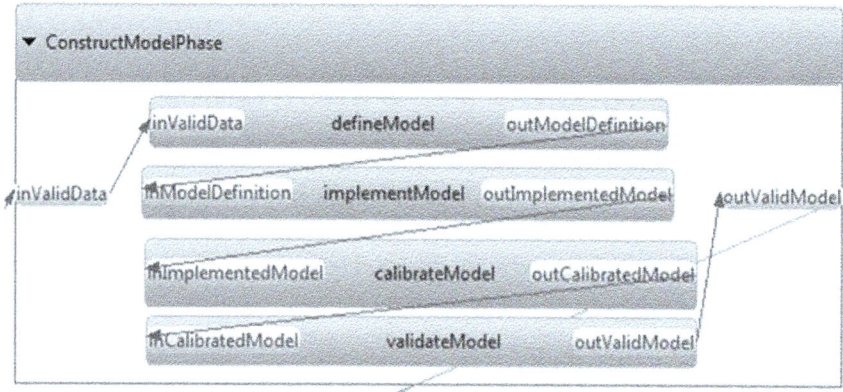

Fig. 3.9 Decomposition of ConstructModels

This gives rise to the view in Fig. 3.9.

From the executeModel perspective, ExecuteModelPhase is made of generateAlternatives and runExperiments!

From the executeModel perspective, ExecuteModelPhase sends ValidModel to generateAlternatives!

From the executeModel perspective, generateAlternatives sends Alternatives to runExperiments!

From the executeModel perspective, runExperiments sends ExperimentSummaries to ExecuteModelPhase!

This gives rise to the view in Fig. 3.10.

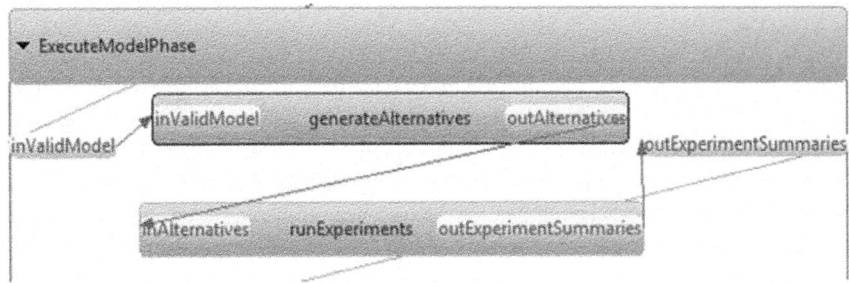

Fig. 3.10 Decomposition of ExecuteModelPhase

Decomposing Results Interpretation

From   the   interpretResults   perspective,
InterpretResultsPhase is made of evaluateAlternatives and
rankAlternatives!

From   the   interpretResults   perspective,
InterpretResultsPhase sends ExperimentSummaries to
evaluateAlternatives!

From the interpretResults perspective, evaluateAlternatives
sends EvaluatedAlternatives to rankAlternatives!

From the interpretResults perspective, rankAlternatives
sends rankedAlternatives to InterpretResultsPhase!

This gives rise to the view in Fig. 3.11.

Components in a process often require more than one input from other component to work properly. For example in the M&S process, a correct model construction phase needs to receive both the gathered data and the clarified objectives of the earlier stages. This idea is explored in the following:

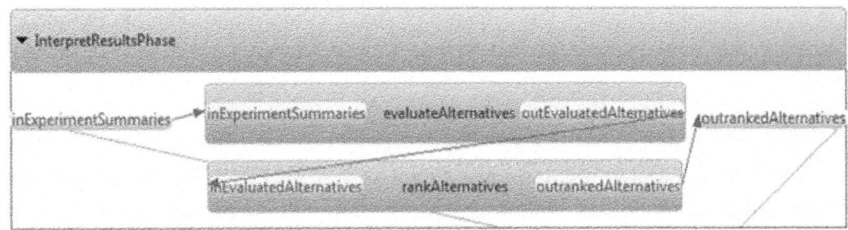

Fig. 3.11 Decomposition of InterpretResults Phase

Add a coupling to the SES for MSProcessSystem to represent the transfer of clarified objectives from the ClarifyObjectivesPhase to the ModelConstructionPhase. Generate the animation for the amended SES and observe the effect of the new coupling on the information flow. (You will notice that ClarifiedObjectives arrives at ModelConstructionPhase first it triggers model construction to complete too early.) Correct the problem by amending the input/output table for ModelConstructionPhase so that it allows only the ValidData input to trigger its output. Should the user's objectives also inform other stages in the process? If so, add appropriate couplings and take care of any premature outputs in the animation.

Many activities in the real world can be organized into processes similar to the modeling and simulation process discussed in this chapter. For example, wine making can be decomposed into growing grapes, harvesting, crushing, destemming, and fermentation.

(a) Using MS4 Me, develop an SES for the wine-making process including top level components and couplings. Check that the message flow is as you expect by using the automation capability.
(b) Extend your SES to capture next level decompositions. For example, for wine making, the fermentation sub-process can be broken down into separation, holding in a barrel, and blending.

3.4   Summary

We formulated some of the basic activities in modeling and simulation as a process or sequence of steps that can be represented with a System Entity Structure. Besides conveying some familiarity with M&S activities, we used the example to discuss two unique features of the SES, decomposition, and coupling. Decomposition tells how to breakdown an entity into subentities that can represent model components. Coupling tells how information can flow among the components in the constructed model. Hierarchical construction occurs when one or more entities are further decomposed into subentities. We saw that the coupling between the parent and its child entities (called external input, and external output, coupling) must be consistent with the coupling involving the parent with its siblings at the next level. We also saw that while an SES defines the inputs and outputs of any model that will represent an entity, the SES cannot specify which of the possible input/output pairs is actually used by the model. In the next chapter, we will examine the decompositions and other features of the SES in more depth.

DEVS Natural Language Models and Elaborations

4

At this point, you have a basic understanding of how the System Entity Structure contains entities that can direct the retrieval of components drawn from a repository. The SES also contains coupling information that enables components to exchange messages and execute their state transitions. In MS4 Me, the default repository used by the SES is a folder of Java class files for atomic models. Although the SES is agnostic as to how these models came to populate this folder, the environment provides a primary means of creating such models through transformation of Finite Deterministic DEVS (FDDEVS) specifications. This chapter aims to provide an understanding first, of the FDDEVS models in *.dnl files, and second that how these files get transformed into DEVS atomic models expressed in Java. However, such models are limited in capability since the FDDEVS representation is limited in its expression of messages that can be processed and states that can be established. So the second goal of this chapter is to show how you can enhance dnl files to enable them to automatically generate DEVS atomic models in Java that have full capability to express messages and states. We also show how hierarchical models can be created using the Sequence Designer and then be enhanced using the FDDEVS elaboration process.

4.1 FDDEVS Model for Generating Jobs in a Time Sequence

We begin by illustrating how a model that generates instances of a class of jobs can be developed from a simple FDDEVS model as a starting point. The natural language specification has the following form:

© Springer International Publishing AG 2017
B.P. Zeigler and H.S. Sarjoughian, *Guide to Modeling and Simulation of Systems of Systems*, Simulation Foundations, Methods and Applications, DOI 10.1007/978-3-319-64134-8_4

```
to start hold in generate for time 10!
after generate output Job!
from generate go to generate!
when in generate and receive Stop then go to passive!
passivate in passive!
```

When saved as a GeneratorOfJobs.dnl file in MS4 Me an outline appears as in the top portion of Fig. 4.1.

The outline shows that there is an input port, Stop and an output port, Job. There are two states, *generate* and *passive* where *generate* transitions back to itself as an internal transition (after 10 units of time), outputting a Job just before completing the transition. Therefore, an output is generated periodically with period 10. A second view of the same model is the state diagram at the bottom of Fig. 4.1. It shows the same information with graphical elements. Note the use of exclamation points for outputs and question marks for inputs. The state diagram is generated from the dnl file. Conversely, there is an interface for entering data into the state diagram and reflecting it back into the file.

When you save this dnl file you automatically generate a Java atomic model class file, and an extract of this file is shown here:

Fig. 4.1 Outline and state diagram of generator of jobs

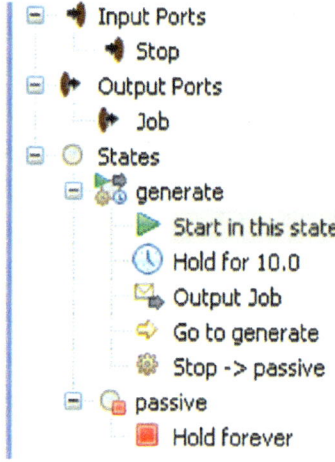

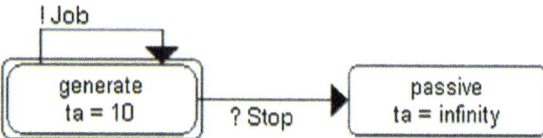

```
// Declare state variables
String phase = "generate";
Double sigma = 10.0;
// End state variables
// Input ports
public final Port<Serializable> inStop =
addInputPort("inStop", Serializable.class);
// Output ports
public final Port<WorkToDo> outJob =
addOutputPort("outJob", WorkToDo.class);
// End output ports
//Constructor
public GeneratorOfJobs() {
this("GeneratorOfJobs");
}
public void initialize() {
holdIn("generate", 10.0);
}
public void internalTransition() {
if (phaseIs("generate")) {
holdIn("generate", 10.0);
return;
}
passivate();
};
public void externalTransition(double timeElapsed,
MessageBag input) {
        sigma -= timeElapsed;
// Fire state transition functions
if (phaseIs("generate")) {
if (input.hasMessages(Stop)) {
passivateIn("passive");
return;
}
}
};
public Double getTimeAdvance() {
return sigma;
};
public MessageBag getOutput() {
MessageBag output = new MessageBagImpl();
if (phaseIs("generate")) {
output.add(outJob, null);
}
return output;
}
```

When you select the Run in Simulation Viewer menu item, an instance of this class is displayed in the Simulation Viewer as in Fig. 4.2. By pressing the step button, you can verify that generated model displays the behavior you expect.

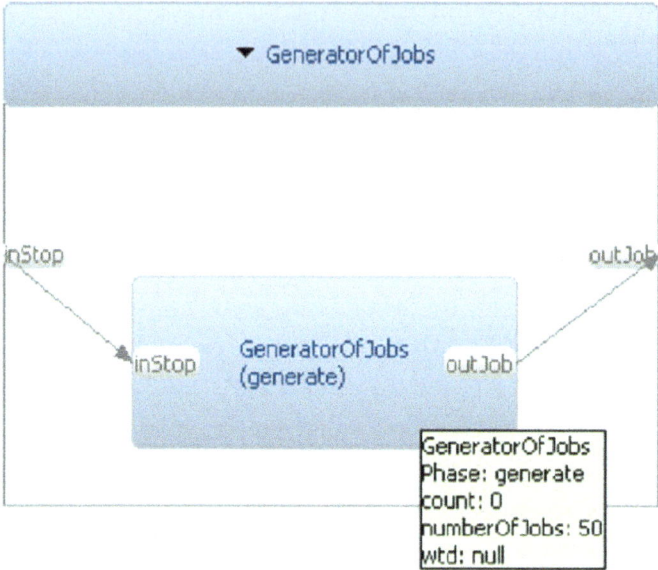

Fig. 4.2 GeneratorOfJobs in Simulation Viewer

4.2   FDDEVS Model for Processing Jobs

We continue with a model that processes instances of a class of jobs that is developed from a simple FDDEVS model. The natural language specification differs somewhat from that of the Generator and has the following form:

```
to start, passivate in waitForJob!
when in waitForJob and receive Job then go to sendJob!
hold in sendJob for time 50!
after sendJob output Job!
from sendJob go to waitForJob!
```

When saved as a ProcessorOfJobs.dnl file in MS4 Me the outline is shown in Fig. 4.3.

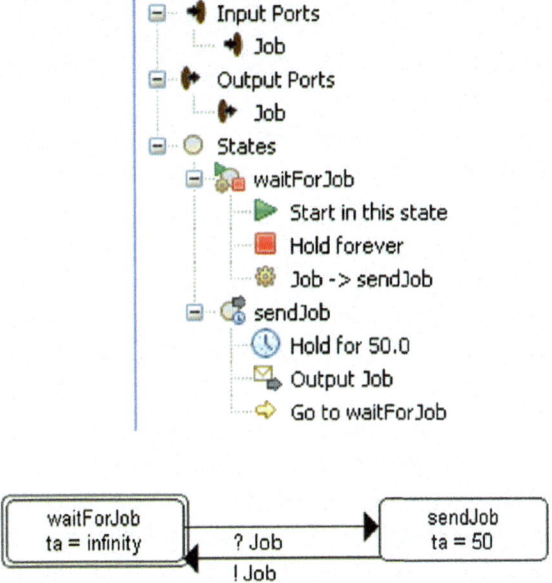

Fig. 4.3 Outline and state diagram of ProcessorOfJobs

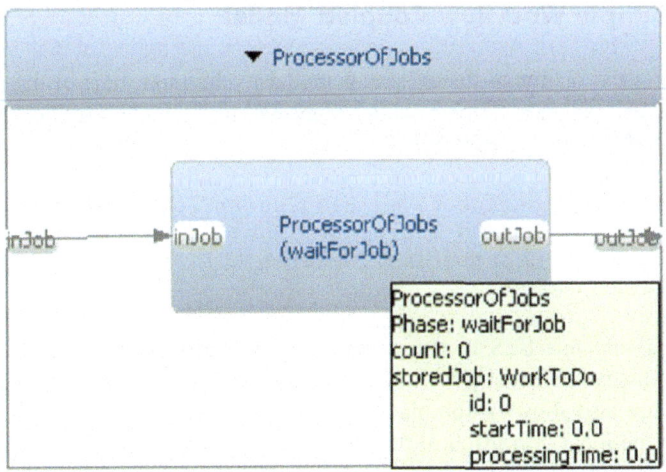

Fig. 4.4 ProcessorOfJobs in Simulation Viewer

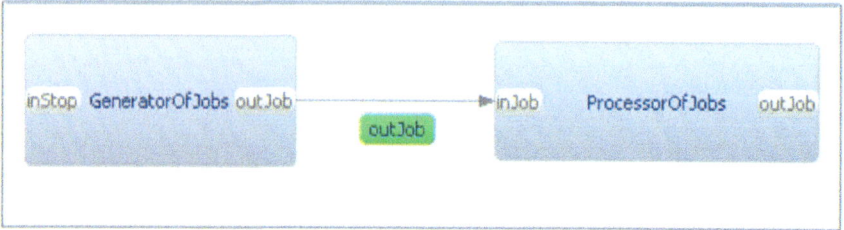

Fig. 4.5 Simple workflow model in the Simulation Viewer

The outline shows that there are both input and output ports for Job—when mapped to Java, these ports become inJob and outJob, respectively. There are two states, *waitForJob* and *sendJob*, where if the model receives a Job while waiting in waitForJob it transitions to state sendJob. After holding in sendJob for 50 units of time, the model outputs a Job just before transitioning back to waitForJob. When you select the Run in Simulation Viewer menu, you automatically generate a Java atomic models class and an instance of it is displayed in the Simulation Viewer as in Fig. 4.4. By injecting a Job from the input menu of inJoh, and pressing the step button, you can verify that the generated model displays the behavior you expect.

4.3   A Simple Workflow Coupled Model

By coupling the output of the generator model to the input port of the processor model, we can create a coupled model representing a simple workflow. You can accomplish this with a simple SES:

```
From the top perspective, SimpleWorkFlow is made of
GeneratorOfJobs and ProcessorOfJobs!
From the top perspective, GeneratorOfJobs sends Job to
ProcessorOfJobs!
```

After passing this SES to the pruning and transformation process, a coupled model results can be executed in the Simulation Viewer as in Fig. 4.5.

The figure also shows a Job placed on the output port outJob by the generator flowing to the input port inJob of the processor. The job is contained in a message traveling along the coupling from outJob to inJob.

Exercise

Add external output coupling to the SimpleWorkFlow SES so that jobs coming out of the processor can flow externally. Similarly, add external input coupling to the SES so that when pruned and transformed the model can be stopped externally.

4.4   Elaborating FDDEVS into Fully Capable Models in Java

Before proceeding, we will review some concepts of DEVS messages that will be needed to understand and employ the enhancement facility of MS4 Me. Figure 4.6 illustrates the roles of input and output ports in DEVS Models. Each port has an associated type (class) which governs the values that can appear on that port.

In more detail, we have the following concepts:

- Port—an instance of a class that implements the Port interface. Ports are typed. For example, to add an output port outJob with associated class WorkToDo, use

```
addOutputPort("outJob", WorkToDo.class);
```

- Data (or value)—an instance of a Java class that implements Serializable and is associated with a Port, for example, WorkToDo wtd = new WorkToDo();
- Message—a pairing of a Port and a value that is an instance of the class associated with the Port.

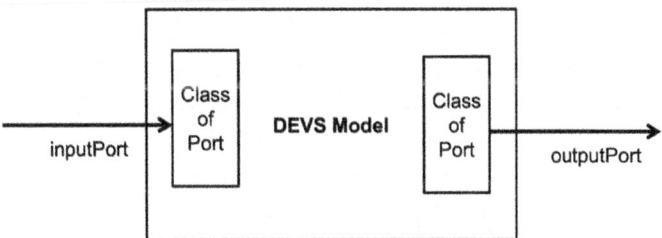

Fig. 4.6 Illustrating input and output ports in DEVS models

- MessageBag—a collection that allows multiple occurrences of the message instances (such a collection is called a bag). An empty MessageBag is made with a constructor:

```
MessageBag output = new MessageBagImpl();
```

Then message instances are added as in

```
output.add(outJob, wtd);
```

The mapping of FDDEVS into Java treats message bags as containing at most one message. For example, in the statement

```
when in waitForJob and receive Job go to Processing!
```

The input message that the model is looking for is on port inJob with the value on the port being an instance of the associated class, WorkToDo. The messages arriving on an input port are available by processing a variable called messageList, specifically for that port. Then to get the first value on that port, we get the first message and its data. For example,

```
WorkToDo job = messageList.get(0).getData();
```

Likewise, in the statement,

```
after Processing output Job!
```

The message generated is added to the output

```
output.add(Job, wtd);
```

MS4 Me supports the ability to elaborate the generated source code by adding additional definitions and java source code to FDDEVS natural language files. For an example, let's consider the elaboration of GeneratorOfJobs.dnl file in such a way that we actually specify the type of jobs being generated.

Figure 4.7 shows a state diagram view of the DEVS model with the addition of callouts that suggest how to define the code fragments that are embedded in the FDDEVS source to implement the required Job generation.

To elaborate the GeneratorOfJobs model, we can define code for some or all of the tagged code blocks, which will then be copied and inserted into the GeneratorOfJobs class source file. There are also additional statements that support elements in such code. The following text shows the augmented GeneratorOfJobs.dnl file with captions that are keyed to the callouts in Fig. 4.7.

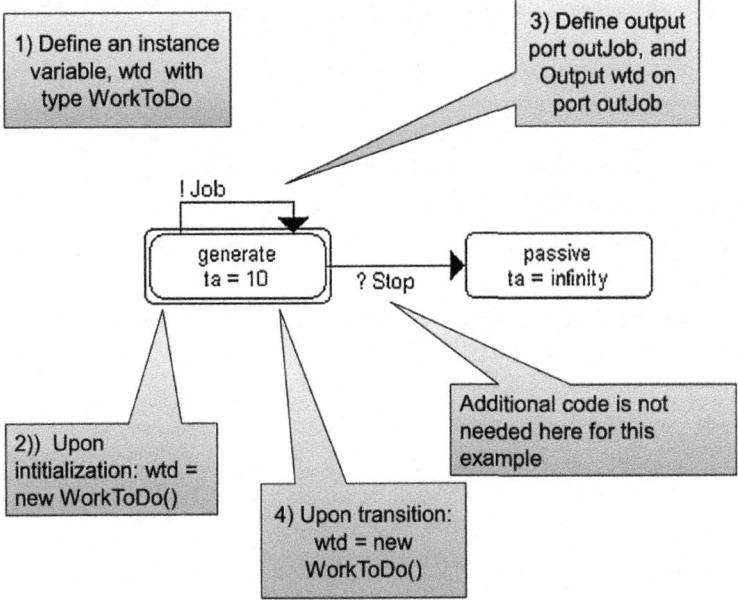

Fig. 4.7 State diagram depiction of the GeneratorOfJobs

0) Define Class WorkToDo

A WorkToDo has id, processingTime, and startTime!
the range of WorkToDo's id is int!
the range of WorkToDo's processingTime is double!
the range of WorkToDo's startTime is double!

1) Declare State (instance) Variables

use count with type int and default "0"!
use wtd with type WorkToDo!

2) Instantiate the instance variables

Initialize variables
```
<%
count =0;
wtd = new WorkToDo();
wtd.setId(count);
```

```
wtd.setprocessingTime (20+count);
%>!
```

3) Define output port outJob

```
generates output on Job with type WorkToDo!
```

Generate output in the internal transition of generate

```
output event for generate
<%
output.add(outJob, wtd);
%>!
```

4) On the transition for generate, create a new job to output

```
Internal event for generate
<%
count ++;
wtd = new WorkToDo();
wtd.setId(count);
wtd.setprocessingTime(20+count);
%>!
```

Java source files for the WorkToDo and GeneratorOfJobs classes are automatically generated when you save the dnl file. Snippets of these files are shown below with comments that indicate where the code fragments are inserted into the source code. Then you can verify that the model is as you desire by running it in the Simulation Viewer.

```
public class WorkToDo implements Serializable {
  //the class is public so is available for use beyond this
file
  int id;
  double startTime;
  double processingTime;
public WorkToDo(int id, double startTime, double
processingTime) {
        this.id = id;
        this.startTime = startTime;
        this.processingTime = processingTime;
    }
  //setters and getters are generated for each instance
variable

public void setId(int id) {
this.id = id;
}
public int getId() {
return this.id;
}
```

```
...
}
public class GeneratorOfJobs extends AtomicModelImpl {
    // Declare state variables
    protected int count = 0;
    protected int numberOfJobs = 5;
    protected WorkToDo wtd;
    String phase = "generate";
    Double sigma = 1.0;
    // End state variables

    // Input ports
public final Port<Serializable> inStop =
addInputPort("inStop",
             Serializable.class);
    // End input ports

    // Output ports

public final Port<WorkToDo> outJob =
addOutputPort("outJob", WorkToDo.class);

    // End output ports

public GeneratorOfJobs() {
this("GeneratorOfJobs");
}
...

public void initialize() {
super.initialize();

// Default state variable initialization
count = 0;
numberOfJobs = 5;

holdIn("generate", 10.0);

// Initialize Variables

wtd = new WorkToDo();
wtd.setId(count);
wtd.setProcessingTime(20 + count);
// End initialize variables
    }

public void internalTransition() {
if (phaseIs("generate")) {
holdIn("generate", 1.0);
//ENDID
// Internal event code
count++;
```

```
if (count >= numberOfJobs)
passivateIn("passive");
else {
wtd = new WorkToDo();
wtd.setId(count);
wtd.setProcessingTime(20 + count);
}
// End internal event code

return;
}
passivate();
};

public void externalTransition(double timeElapsed,
MessageBag input) {
Subtract time remaining until next internal transition (no
effect if sigma == Infinity)
sigma -= timeElapsed;

// Fire state transition functions
if (phaseIs("generate")) {
if (input.hasMessages(Stop)) {
ArrayList<Message<Serializable>> messageList = Stop
                                    .getMessages(input);
passivateIn("passive");
return;
}
}
};

public MessageBag getOutput() {
MessageBag output = new MessageBagImpl();
if (phaseIs("generate")) {
// Output event code

output.add(outJob, wtd);
// End output event code
        }
return output;
    }
...
}
```

Note that the instance variables and methods in such a file are directly related to the sets and functions defined in the DEVS formalism (see the Appendix to Chap. 12 for this correspondence).

Exercise

Use the MS4 Me enhancement process to enable the GeneratorOfJobs to generate jobs at random times.

Hint: Build upon the following

```
use rand with type Random and default "new Random()"!
use period with type double and default "10"!
  internal event for generate
  <%
period = 10 * rand.nextDouble();
%>!
  add Library
  <%
import java.util.*;
  %>!
```

Exercise

Continue elaborating the GeneratorOfJobs to create Jobs with random processing times.

4.5   Elaborating ProcessorOfJobs into a Java Model

We now have a generator of jobs which are instances of class WorkToDo. We can now extend the ProcessorOfJobs to be able to accept such instances.

The corresponding state transition diagram with callouts for the transitions to extend the ProcessorOfJobs is shown in Fig. 4.8.

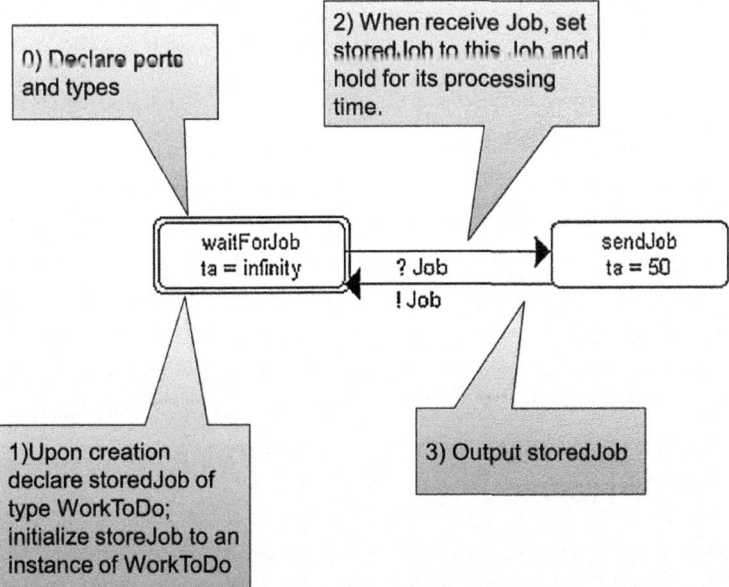

Fig. 4.8 State diagram for ProcessorOfJobs

As with GeneratorOfJobs, we augment the ProcessorOfJobs.dnl files with the following text, keyed to Fig. 4.8.

0) Declare ports and types;

```
accepts input on Job with type WorkToDo!
generates output on Job with type WorkToDo!
```

1) Declare an instance variable with type WorkToDo

```
use storedJob with type WorkToDo and default "new
WorkToDo()"!
```

2) In the initialize method of the model, instantiate the instance variable

```
//this will be automatically done by setting the default as
shown in 1)
// storedJob = new WorkToDo();
```

3) When receive Job, decode it and store it

external event for waitForJob **with** Job

```
<%
storedJob = messageList.get(0).getData();
System.out.println("Received WorkToDo with id "+
storedJob.getId());
holdIn("sendJob",storedJob.getProcessingTime());
%>!
```

4) Output stored job

output event for sendJob

```
<%
output.add(outJob, storedJob);
%>!
```

The class file, ProcessorOfJobs.java, is automatically generated when you save the corresponding.dnl file.

Exercise

Using the code fragments just given, follow the approach given for GeneratorOfJobs to complete the definition of the extended java source for ProcessorOfJobs. Test your model using Simulation Viewer.

4.6   Transducer: Model to Measure Job Completion Time and Throughput

A transducer keeps track of jobs and computes turnaround (completion) time and throughput. Transducer.dnl has the following content:

```
use jobsArrived with type HashSet!
use jobsSolved with type HashSet!
use observationTime with type double!
use totalTa with type double!
use clock with type double!

accepts input on Ariv with type WorkToDo!
accepts input on Solved with type WorkToDo!
generates output on Stop!

to start hold in observe for time 100!
after observe output Stop!
from observe go to done!

when in observe and receive Ariv then go to observe
eventually!
when in observe and receive Solved then go to observe
eventually!
passivate in done!
```

The code elaboration for Transducer is given in the Appendix. The Transducer can be coupled into the SimpleWorkFlow model to provide turnaround time and throughput measurements. The SES below provides such a coupling:

```
From the top perspective, SimpleWorkFlow is made of
GeneratorOfJobs, ProcessorOfJobs, and Transducer!
From the top perspective, GeneratorOfJobs sends Job to
ProcessorOfJobs!
From the top perspective, GeneratorOfJobs sends outJob to
Transducer as inAriv!
From the top perspective, ProcessorOfJobs sends outJob to
Transducer as inSolved!
From the top perspective, Transducer sends Stop to
GeneratorOfJobs!
```

After pruning and transformation, the extended SimpleWorkFlow model appears in the Simulation Viewer. When you press Step or View you can see messages with their content flow among components as in Fig. 4.9.

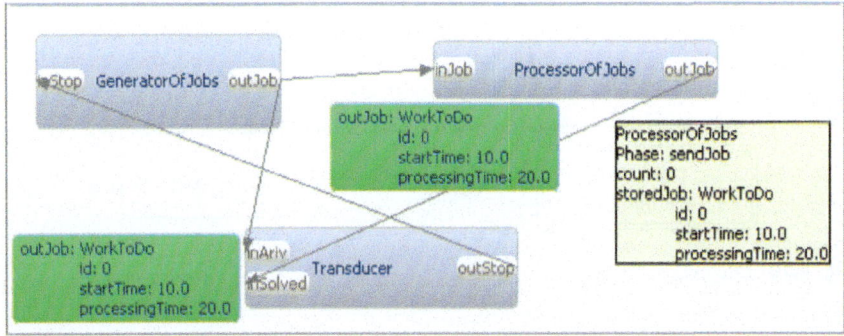

Fig. 4.9 Extended SimpleWorkFlow model in Simulation Viewer

By hovering your mouse over a model icon you can bring up a view of the current phase and values of other state variables of the model, as shown for ProcessorOfJobs.

Exercise

Using MS4 Me, complete the development of the Transducer and implement the extended SimpleWorkFlow. Perform simulations for combinations of Period and processingTime (see Chap. 5).

Exercise

Use MS4 Me to model the life cycle of a book as it is loaned from a library as shown below (Fig. 4.10). Start with FDDEVS and note that the accumulated fine uses the elapsed time in OverDue until returned. This requires you to elaborate the model using a tagged expression for the external transition of OverDue with return.

Exercise

An SES for a simple representation of the reaction of Hydrogen and Oxygen to form water is shown below (Fig. 4.11) along with FDDEVS models of the reaction process and the reactants (O and H) and product (Water). The ReactProcess requests that Hydrogen and Oxygen release two and one molecules, respectively, each time step. When they do so, the process requests that water accepts one

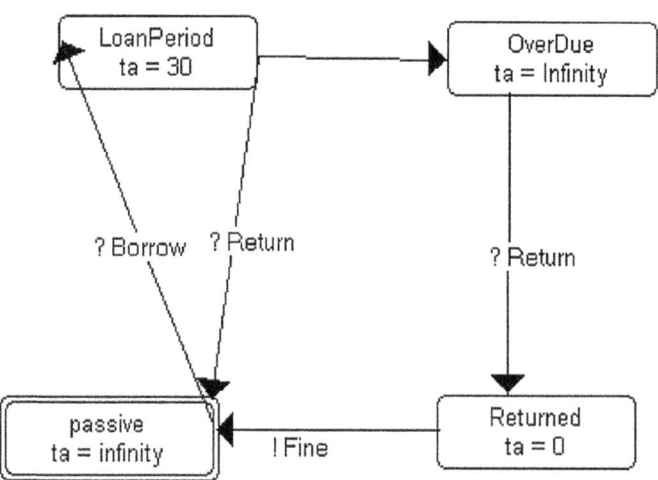

Fig. 4.10 Life cycle of a book

molecule. This iteration in time continues until one or both of the reactants have no molecules left. Using MS4 Me enhance the given FDDEVS models to work with the SES and pruning to produce coupled models with the described behavior.

Hint: use a state variable to keep track of the number of molecules in each of the components. Arrange it so the initial number of molecules is set by the choice of High or Low in the SES. Have the reactants decrease their molecule count each time they do a release and emit a negative number when the level falls below zero.

ReactProcess

```
to start passivate in waitForInput!
when in waitForInput and receive StartUp go to sendRelease!
when in waitForInput and receive Release go to sendRelease!
hold in sendRelease for time 1!
from sendRelease go to waitForInput!
after sendRelease output Release!
```

Hydrogen

```
to start passivate in waitForInput!
when in waitForInput and receive ReleaseTwoMolecules go to
sendRelease!
hold in sendRelease for time 1!
from sendRelease go to waitForInput!
after sendRelease output MoleculesOfHydrogen!
```

Oxygen

```
to start passivate in waitForInput!
when in waitForInput and receive ReleaseOneMolecule go to
sendRelease!
hold in sendRelease for time 1!
from sendRelease go to waitForInput!
after sendRelease output MoleculesOfOxygen!
```

Water

```
to start passivate in waitForInput!
when in waitForInput and receive AcceptOneMolecule go to
sendRelease!
hold in sendRelease for time 1!
from sendRelease go to waitForInput!
after sendRelease output MoleculesOfWater!
```

Exercise

Boyle's Law states that Pressure * Volume is a constant. Incrementally, this states that ChangeInVolume = ChangeInPressure * Volume/Pressure. Write an enhanced FDDEVS whose inputs change in pressure and outputs change in volume. Hint: use Pressure, Volume, deltaP, and deltaV as state variables of type double with ChangeInPressure and ChangeInVolume of type DoubleEnt, where

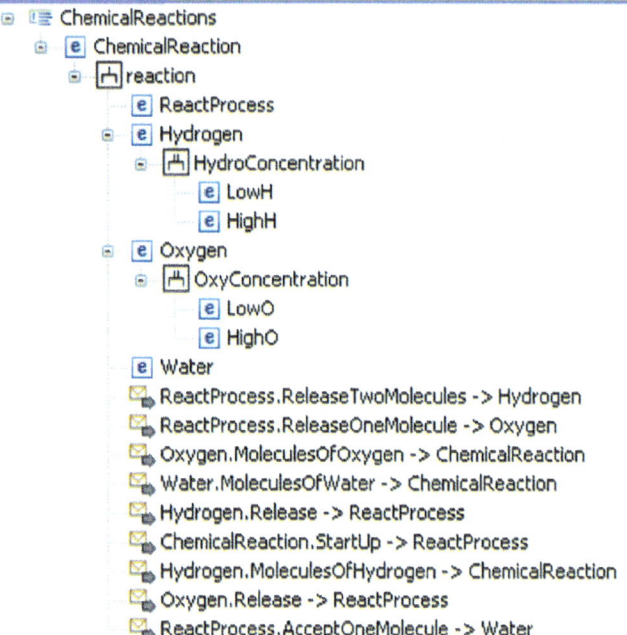

Fig. 4.11 Outline of reaction process SES

```
DoubleEnt has a value!
the range of DoubleEnt's value is double with default "0.1"
```

(This allows you to inject pressure changes of .1 in Simulation Viewer testing.)

4.7 Using Elaboration to Handle Non-deterministic State Transitions

FDDEVS, Finite *Deterministic* DEVS, is indeed deterministic. This means that there is at most one internally caused transition to another state from any state. There is no transition for a passive state. In mapping to Java, however, the FDDEVS state becomes the phase instance variable and other instance variables can be added to increase the state vector of the model. You can use the enhancement facility to take advantage of this enhanced state to specify internal transitions to states other than the one that FDDEVS specifies. Indeed, the next state and its duration become the default that you can override by writing a tagged code block for the associated transition.

For example as it stands, the only way to stop the GeneratorOfJobs is to inject an external Stop input into the inStop port. The enhancement process allows you to specify the conditions under which generation should stop under control of the model's own autonomous decision making. In the code of Sect. 4.1, we already keep a count of jobs generated so far. Let's add an instance variable as a parameter to limit the number of jobs:

```
use numberOfJobs with type int and default "5"!
```

Now we can compare the current count with the maximum allowed and halt generation when that number is reached. This is done in the tagged block for the transition from generate:

```
Internal event for generate
<%
count ++;
if (count>=numberOfJobs)
passivateIn("passive");
else{
wtd = new WorkToDo();
wtd.setId(count);
wtd.setProcessingTime(20+count);
}
%>!
```

As you see below, this code is inserted after the transition statement generated by the hold in specified in the natural language. The passivateIn ("passive") statement which is executed only after the iteration limit has been reached sets the phase to "passive" rather than to "generate" and so overrides the FDDEVS generated default.

```
holdIn("generate", 1.0);
count++;
if (count >= numberOfJobs)
passivateIn("passive");
else {
wtd = new WorkToDo();
wtd.setId(count);
wtd.setProcessingTime(20 + count);
}
```

Exercise

Suppose that half way through generating its allocated number of jobs, the generator pauses and waits for an input to resume generation of the rest. Extend the FDDEVS natural language specification to include an external Resume input, which causes resumption of generation when the phase is Paused. Augment the tagged block for the internal event for generate so that the transition to Paused occurs mid-way through the assigned number of jobs.

Tagged blocks for external transitions are also placed after the hold in statement associated with an FDDEVS "when receive.." statement. This allows you to override the default transition for external events just as with internal events.

Exercise

The current ProcessorOfJobs ignores a Job arriving while it is in sendJob. Extend the FDDEVS natural language specification to specify a transition back to sendJob when a Job is received while in sendJob. Add a tagged code block for this transition that stores the new Job in a queue unless this queue is full, in which case it transitions to a phase QueueOverflow.

4.8   Using Elaboration to Handle Multiple Simultaneous Inputs

FDDEVS is defined so as to accept a single input through an external event. Often however, multiple inputs arrive at the same time to a model component. For example, in typical models derived from differential equations, all components are updated at the same clock time each time step. This means that at each time step, a component may receive inputs from multiple components. In particular, the reaction example of an earlier exercise, the ReactProcess receives simultaneous inputs on port inRelease from Oxygen and Hydrogen. Even in models in which transitions are not synchronized, simultaneous events may occur to produce multiple inputs to a component. Also it is often convenient to combine multiple outputs in the same output message (see below) and send it to another component. In Java, an incoming message representing multiple inputs contains multiple content elements (port-value pairs). The FDDEVS natural language translation to Java looks at only the first content element of an incoming message even when more than one such content are present.

To preclude errors that could arise in such circumstances, you can elaborate external event tagged blocks to examine each content element in an incoming message. Java provides several alternatives to do so. One standard way is to iterate through the message using the pattern illustrated for job arrival in the Processor OfJobs, as in:

```
external event for waitForJob with Job
<%
HashSet<WorkToDo> Jobs = new HashSet<WorkToDo>();

for (int j = 0;j < messageList.size(); j++){
WorkToDo wtd = messageList.get(j).getData();

Jobs.add(wtd);
}
%>!
```

4.9   Using Elaboration to Generate Multiple Simultaneous Outputs

As suggested above, an atomic model can generate a message with multiple content elements to another component. An example arises naturally in the ProcessorOfJobs just discussed when it finishes more than one job from the jobs it has stored in the external event just discussed. Here is how to generate multiple content elements for the same output message:

```
output event for sendJob
<%
for (WorkToDo job:Jobs){
  output.add(outJob,job);
}
  %>!
```

The examples for ProcessorOfJobs illustrate multiple inputs and outputs all on the same port. You also can handle multiple inputs and outputs with different ports. For example, you could extend the model to allow jobs to arrive simultaneously on two ports, "inHighPriorityJob" and "inLowPriorityJob" and to emerge on two ports, "outHighPriorityJob" and "outLowPriorityJob."

The way to do this is get accessed to the messages on the ports of interest in the external event for any one of these ports, e.g.,

```
external event for waitForJob with Job
<%
if (input.hasMessages(inJob)) {
ArrayList<Message<WorkToDo>>
RegularJobMessageList = inJob.getMessages(input);
// then get data from this list e.g.
RegularJobMessageList.get(0).getData();
}

if (input.hasMessages(inHighPriorityJob)) {
ArrayList<Message<WorkToDo>>
HighPriorityMessageList =
inHighPriorityJob.getMessages(input);
// then get data from this list e.g.
HighPriorityMessageList.get(0).getData();
}

if (input.hasMessages(inLowPriorityJob)) {
ArrayList<Message<WorkToDo>>
  LowPriorityMessageList =
inLowPriorityJob.getMessages(input);
  // then get data from this list e.g.
LowPriorityMessageList.get(0).getData();
}

%>!
```

To generate messages on different output ports in the same message bag is easier. It just involves using the add method to add ports and associated values to the output message. For example,

```
output event for sendJob
<%
for (WorkToDo job:Jobs){
    output.add(outJob,job);
}
for (WorkToDo job:HighPriorityJobs){
    output.add(outHighPriorityJob,job);
}
%>!
```

Note: Remember to declare any ports being used using the "accepts" or "generates" statement as appropriate.

4.10 Model Development Accelerated by the Sequence Diagram

The Sequence Designer (SD) serves as a model development tool accelerates model development when combined with the other tools in the DEVS modeling environment. You can use the SD to generate atomic and coupled models that can be integrated together to create complete hierarchical models. Furthermore, you can elaborate the natural language *.dnl and *.ses files generated in the process to enhance the component models and the SES to generate the family of models that you had in mind. We illustrate this process with an example of testing of Unmanned Autonomous Systems.

In this example, the top level model will be called UASSystemTesting and its components include an Unmanned Autonomous System (UAS), a sensor package carried by the UAS, and test instrumentation that controls the UAS and the sensor package attached to it. In our development process, we will use the SD twice: first, to develop the top level model of the components and their interaction and second, to elaborate the sensor package into a coupled model with sensors and data handlers.

We start with a sequence diagram for the top level model developed with the SD tool as shown in Fig. 4.12.

The generation capability of the MS4 Me environment writes the *.dnl files and creates the coupled model is shown in Fig. 4.13.

As discussed in Chap. 3, to elaborate the SensorPackage, we need to replace the atomic model illustrated in Fig. 4.9 by a coupled model with the same interface—the same input and output ports. Here, we can use the SD to generate the required coupled model. To do so, we use the SD to change the type of the SensorPackage from atomic to coupled and open a sequence diagram for this coupled model. As shown in Fig. 4.14, note the automatic addition of an actor with the underlined

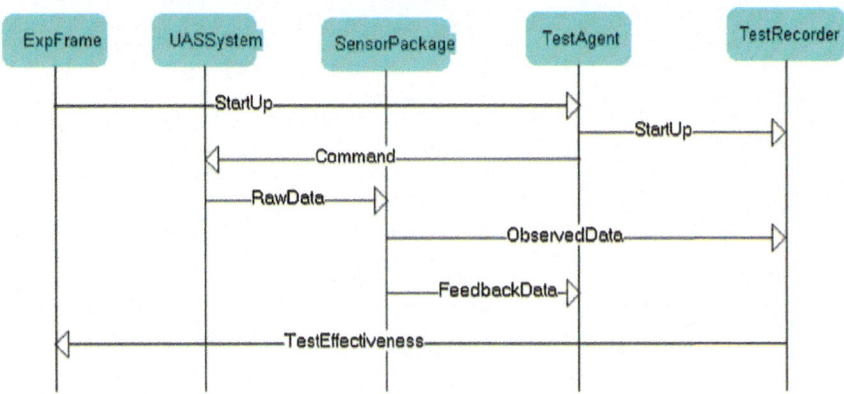

Fig. 4.12 Sequence diagram for testing of unmanned autonomous systems

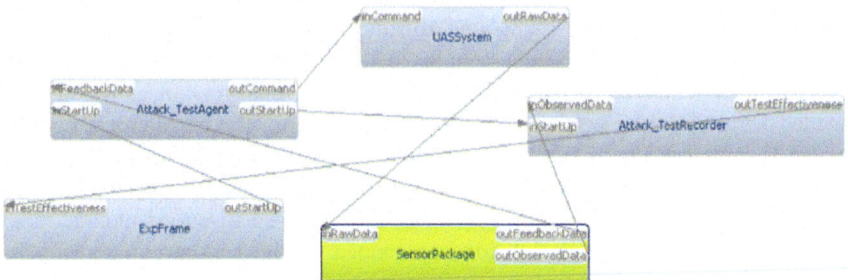

Fig. 4.13 Testing of unmanned autonomous systems. Coupled model

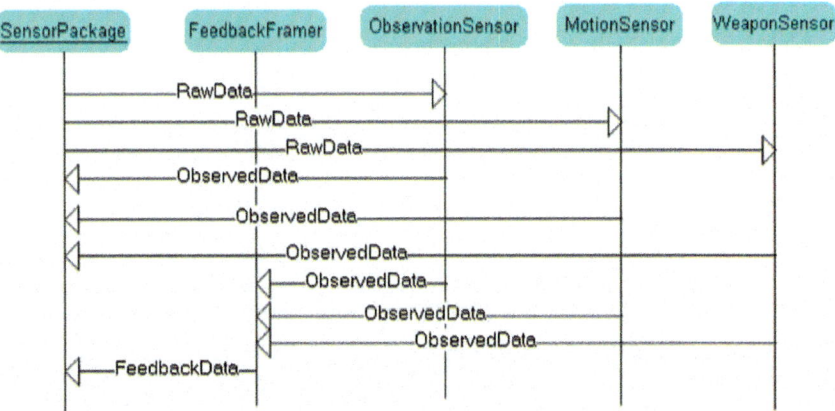

Fig. 4.14 Using the SD to elaborate the sensor package

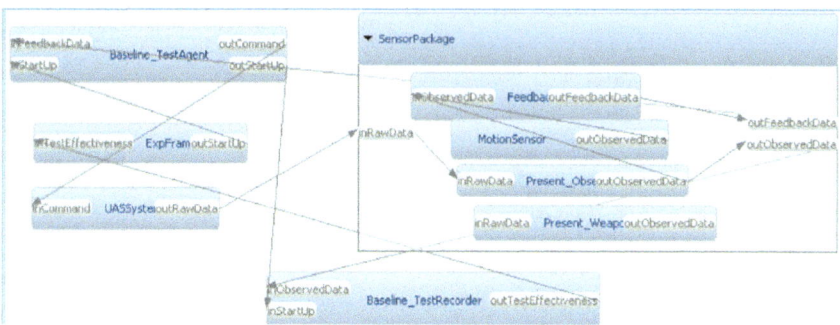

Fig. 4.15 Hierarchical model for testing of unmanned autonomous systems

name of the SensorPackage. This actor plays the role of the SensorPackage coupled
model as far as its interactions with its components.

Now we can add actors to the sequence diagram and describe the information
exchanges among sensors and a data handler within the SensorPackage. The
messages sent and received by this underlined SensorPackage actor create the right
couplings in the overall SES generated by the SD tool. Furthermore, the collection
of *.dnl files generated in the process populates the repository of atomic models
needed to provide the behavior of the overall system. The hierarchical coupled
model is shown in Fig. 4.15.

In addition to using the SD to construct and integrate models into a hierarchical
composition, you can enhance the resulting SES with specializations and additional
aspects. For example, specializations are added to the sensor components for
presence/absence and electromagnetic type as depicted in the outline of Fig. 4.16.

Also, you can extend the atomic models by enhancing the *.dnl files as discussed
earlier in this chapter. For example, you can define a class for the Command
message sent from the TestAgent to the UASSystem, as in:

```
A Command has a Mode and Duration!
The range of Command's Mode is String!
The range of Command's Duration is TimeInterval with
default "new TimeInterval()"!

A TimeInterval has a startTime and an endTime!
The range of TimeInterval's startTime is double with
default "0"!
The range of TimeInterval's endTime is double with default
"10"!
```

Then you can add a tagged block for the output generated by
the sendCommand:

output event for sendCommand
```
<%
Command c = new Command("Hover",new TimeInterval(100,130));
output.add(outCommand,c);
%>!
```

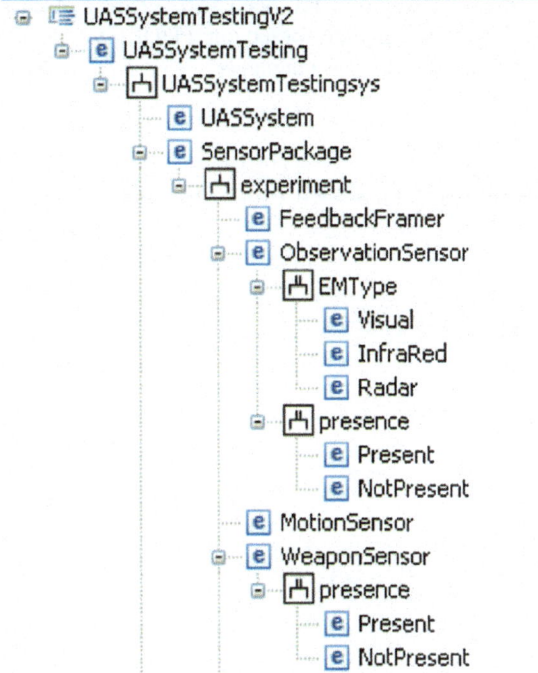

Fig. 4.16 Enhancing the SES with specializations

In this way, you can develop a fully-fledged hierarchical coupled model starting from the initial version created using the SD tool.

Exercise

Enhance the UASSystem FDDEVS model so that it can process the Command message sent to it by the Test Agent.

4.11   Summary

This chapter aimed at giving you an understanding of FDDEVS models expressed in dnl files, how these files get mapped into DEVS atomic models expressed in Java, and how you can enhance dnl files to enable to them to automatically generate DEVS atomic models in Java that have full capability to express messages and states. The discussion touched on aspects of the model definition process and presented numerous examples to illustrate these aspects. We also showed how hierarchical models can be created using the Sequence Designer and then enhanced using the FDDEVS elaboration process. See Chap. 12 for a discussion of how the approach to creating DEVS models based on FDDEVS elaboration fits into a broader view of DEVS specification languages.

Appendix: Transducer FDDEVS File (Transducer.dnl)

```
to start hold in observe for time 100!
after observe output Stop!
from observe go to done!
when in observe and receive Ariv then go to observe
eventually!
when in observe and receive Solved then go to observe
eventually!
passivate in done!

use jobsArrived with type HashSet!
use jobsSolved with type HashSet!
use observationTime with type double!
use totalTa with type double!
use clock with type double!

accepts input on Ariv with type WorkToDo!
accepts input on Solved with type WorkToDo!
generates output on Stop !

Initialize variables
<%
jobsArrived = new HashSet();
jobsSolved = new HashSet();
observationTime = 200;
totalTa = 0;
clock = 0;
holdIn("observe",observationTime);
%>!

external event for observe with Ariv
<%
clock = clock +timeElapsed;
WorkToDo job = messageList.get(0).getData();
job.setStartTime(clock);
System.out.println("Start job " + job.getId() + " @
startTime = " + clock);
jobsArrived.add(job);
%>!

external event for observe with Solved
```

```
<%
    clock = clock + timeElapsed;
    WorkToDo job = messageList.get(0).getData();
    WorkToDo arrived = null;
for (Object o : jobsArrived) {
    WorkToDo j = (WorkToDo) o;
    if (j.getId() == job.getId()) {
        arrived = j;
        break;
                            }
                }
totalTa += (clock - arrived.getStartTime());
System.out.println("Finish job " + arrived.getId()
                            + " @ startTime = " + clock);
job.setStartTime(clock);
    jobsSolved.add(job);
%>!

internal event for observe
<%
clock = clock + getTimeAdvance();
double throughput;
double avgTaTime;
if(jobsSolved .size() > 0) {
    avgTaTime = totalTa / jobsSolved .size();
    if (clock > 0.0)  throughput = jobsSolved .size()  /
    clock;
    else throughput = 0.0;
}
else {
    avgTaTime = 0.0;
    throughput = 0.0;
}
System.out.println("End time: " + clock);
System.out.println("jobs  arrived  :  "  +  jobsArrived.size
());
System.out.println("jobs solved : " + jobsSolved .size());
System.out.println("AVERAGE TA = " + avgTaTime);
System.out.println("THROUGHPUT = " + throughput);

%>!
add library
<%
import java.util.HashSet;
%>!
```

Specialization and Pruning

5

At this point, you learned how to decompose a system into components and couplings and how to use the System Entity Structure to express such a composition. You also learned that the decomposition process can be applied to the components as well. For example, for the M&SProcessSystem (Chap. 3) we continued to decompose each of the top level components using the same kinds of statements that we used for top level model itself. In addition, we noted that the coupling rule of decomposition offers guidance to assure information flow from a component into its subcomponents and conversely, from the subcomponents to the parent. However, with the approach taken so far, the SES generates one hierarchical model rather than a family of such models. Another construct, besides decomposition, will allow you to expand the alternatives for selection, so as to generate multiple possible pruned entity structures. This construct is *specialization* and we will introduce its use now.

5.1 Specializations

Returning to the discussion of the M&S Process, recall that the gathering of relevant data involves finding the right data and validating it to make sure it is representative of the system being modeled. We formulated this idea by decomposing the Data-GatherPhase into getData and validateData. Now suppose that we want to capture some distinct ways in which finding the right data can be accomplished. For example, we might have some data immediately available, or we might find it by searching some data bases. Alternatively, we might have to undertake a research program to acquire the data from experiments. A specialization statement can express this idea as:

```
getData can be immediateAccess, findInDataBase, or
startResearch in meansToGetData!
```

© Springer International Publishing AG 2017
B.P. Zeigler and H.S. Sarjoughian, *Guide to Modeling and Simulation of Systems of Systems*, Simulation Foundations, Methods and Applications, DOI 10.1007/978-3-319-64134-8_5

Fig. 5.1 The SES for
MSProcessSystem showing
the meansToGetData
specialization

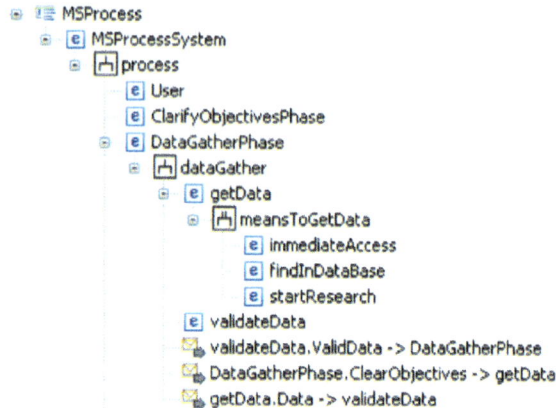

When added to the SES for MSProcessSystem, the outline that is generated is
shown in Fig. 5.1. We see an icon below getData that shows that a specialization of
getData is labeled meansToGetData and has the entities attached to it: immediateAccess, findInDataBase and startResearch. In words, meansToGetData is a
specialization for getData and we can select one of the entities immediateAccess,
findInDataBase, startResearch as an alternative to find the data.

To illustrate further, let us add the following specializations to the SES. The first
captures alternatives for implementing a model; the second captures options for
ranking alternatives produced by executing the model.

```
implementModel can be startFromScratch,
reuseFromRepository, or buildFromComponents in
 constructionApproach!
rankAlternatives can be downSelect, satisfice, or optimize
in evaluationMode!
```

Exercise

Add the above specializations to the *.ses file describing the SES for MSProcessSystem and display the outline generated. For each specialization, list its
entities, and identify the parent entity.

5.2 Pruning of Specializations

The presence of specializations in an SES sets up a family of possibilities for
selection since the specializations can, unless constrained, combine in all possible
ways. For example, in the SES for the M&SProcessSystem, each of the 3 specializations has 3 choices so there are 3 * 3 * 3 = 27 resulting combinations.

(a)

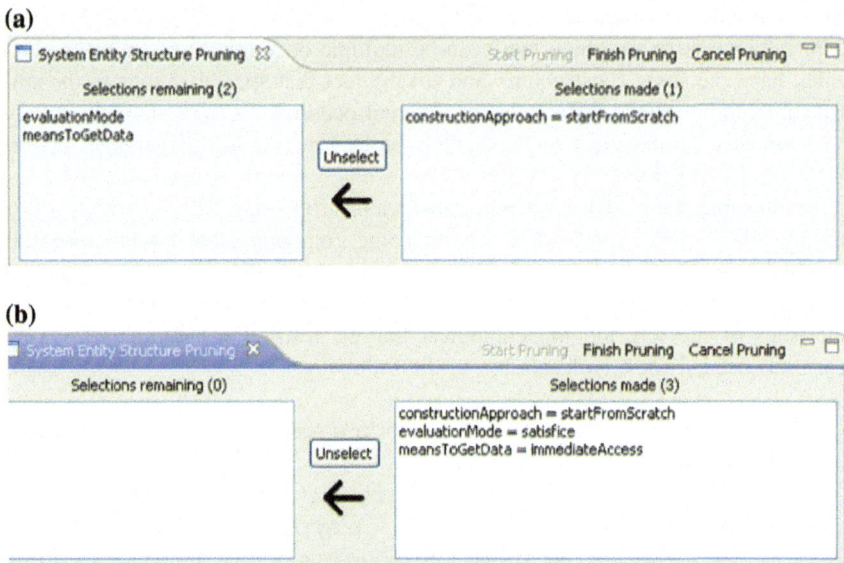

(b)

Fig. 5.2 Pruning from initial choice to completion

Figure 5.2a shows the MS4 Me display for pruning the SES after a selection of startFromScratch has been made from the constructionApproach specialization. At this stage, we have a partially pruned entity structure since two specializations have yet to be dealt with. Figure 5.2b shows a completely pruned entity structure (PES) where selections have been made for all specializations. Such a PES represents a single structure that embodies the information needed to automatically construct a specific hierarchical simulation model.

Exercise

Add some specializations to the SES that you constructed for the exercise at the end of Chap. 3. For example, "on hill sides" and "on flat land" are different ways to grow grapes. Use the pruning interface of MS4 Me to produce a completely pruned entity structure. How many such PESs are there?

5.3 Multiple Occurrences of Specializations

A fundamental characteristic of the real world seems to be the constant interplay of uniformity and diversity. There are recognizable classes of things—atoms, genes, cars, planets, etc., with numerous replications of some basic defining pattern, yet differing in other properties in ways that make these replications distinctive.

Such "diversity through uniformity" is represented in the SES through (a) its *uniformity* property, in which there can be multiple occurrences of an entity all of which have the same substructure, and (b) the fact that specializations in the substructure can be pruned differently for different occurrences. In a physics analogy, the symmetry (uniformity) of the SES is broken in pruning to generate diverse pruned entity structures.

To illustrate these ideas, we will consider the following SES in which a processing job is represented together with some computers that could process it. Eventually, we will want to associate the right choice of computer for the job according to its size. The SES can be easily elaborated to represent various characteristics of the job and the computers but we restrict this complexity to the essentials needed for this discussion in the following:

> From the top perspective, JobContext is made of Job and
> Computer!
> Job can be small, medium, or large in size!
> Computer can be EeeFamily, HP, or Apple in brand!
> From the compute perspective, EeeFamily is made of CPU and
> IO!
> From the compute perspective, HP is like EeeFamily!
> From the compute perspective, Apple is like EeeFamily!
> CPU can be miniPower, mediumPower, or maxPower in
> computePower!

In the outline of this SES in Fig. 5.3a, we see that computers are distinguished by manufacturer (the brand specialization) and that each computer contains a CPU which can vary in processing power (the computePower specialization). Note that the SES makes explicit the interplay of decomposition (the compute aspect) and alternatives (the brand and computePower specializations) that are difficult to represent in other ontology frameworks and would otherwise be buried in the simulation code.

Now, in pruning, we might start with a selection of size for job such as medium. Then the selection of appropriate computing power might depend on which brand is selected as shown by the multiple occurrences of the computePower specialization in Fig. 5.3b. We can select the brand first and then make a choice from the computePower specialization in its substructure. Alternatively, we can make the choice from a computePower specialization and this will automatically make the selection of brand—the reason is that making a selection in the substructure of one of the brand selections implies selecting that brand choice as well.

Exercise

Use MS4 Me to define the above SES and try pruning (1) top down (i.e., brand first) and (2) bottom-up (compute Power first). Do you get the same PES in the end?

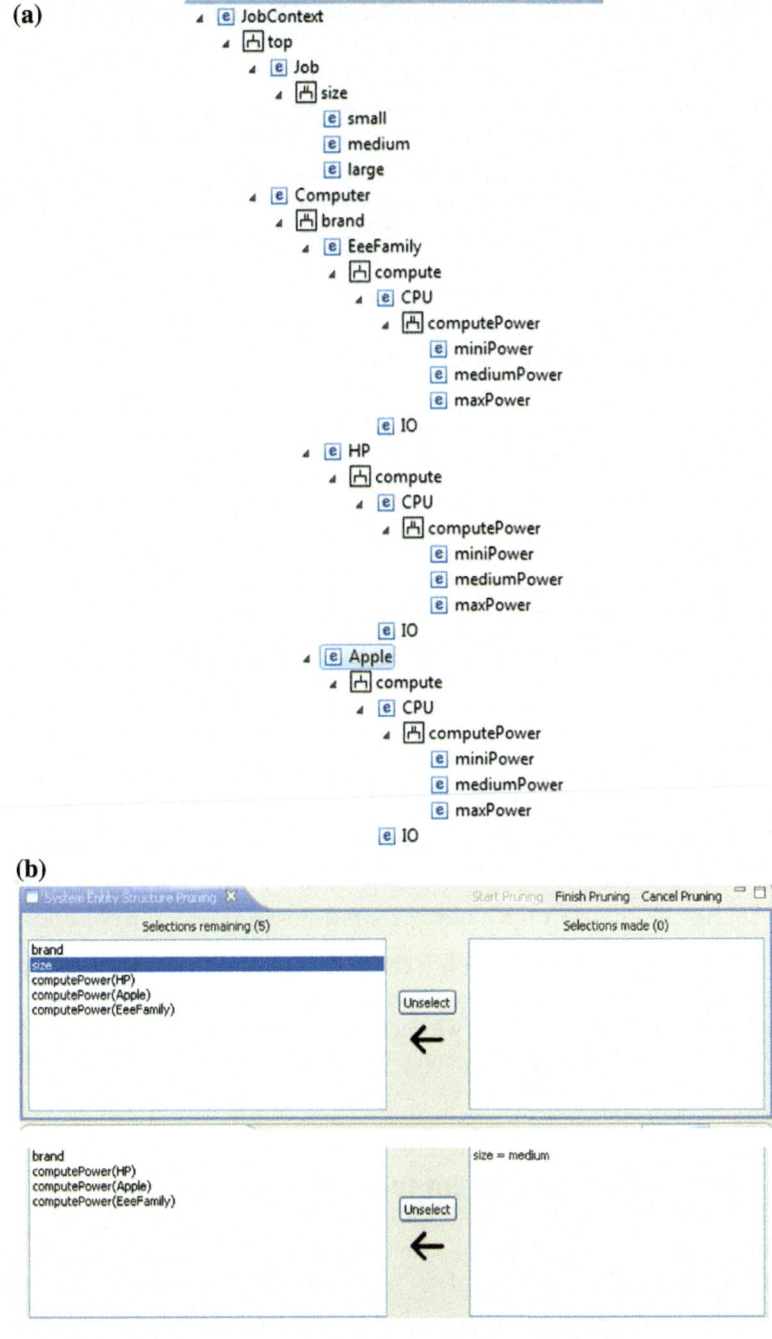

Fig. 5.3 Outline of SES with multiple occurrences and view through pruning interface

5.4   Rules for Adding Specializations: There Are None

A specialization can be added below any entity in an SES, irrespective of whether the entity is the root entity (top entity in the SES), entity in an aspect (i.e., a component in decomposition) or is in a specialization (i.e., a entity representing an alternative). Moreover, an entity may have any number of specializations under it and the same specialization may occur multiple times in the SES. Using the SES for MSProcessSystem as an example, we will discuss the effect of a specialization in each of these contexts.

5.4.1   Specialization Under Root Entity

An entity selected from the specialization modifies the root entity. For example, consider the specialization:

MSProcessSystem can be timeConstrained or
timeUnconstrained in timeliness!

Selecting timeConstrained from timeliness requires that the process be accomplished within certain deadlines in real time. On the other hand, the other choice specifies that deadlines do not exist and allows the process to seek accuracy over timeliness.

5.4.2   Specialization Under Entity Under Aspect

An entity selected from the specialization modifies the entity in an aspect. For example, consider the specialization

DataGatherPhase can be Present or NotPresent in presence!

Here the presence specialization is a child of the parent DataGatherPhase entity which is under the process aspect. The presence specialization has a special meaning in the SES. It determines whether the parent entity appears in the pruned entity structure. For example, selecting NotPresent from presence removes the DataGatherPhase from the PES.

5.4.3   Specialization Under Entity Under Specialization

An entity selected from the specialization modifies the entity under another specialization. This make it part of a taxonomy. For example, consider the specialization

reuseFromRepository can be local or internet in location!

Since reuseFromRepository is an entity under constructionApproach, the just added location specialization forms part of a taxonomy for constructionApproach. In this case, internet is a choice for reuseFromRepository itself a choice for constructionApproach.

Exercise

Add the location specialization under reuseFromRepository to the SES for MSProcessSystem. Then use the pruning interface of MS4 Me to prune the resulting SES to confirm that the two step taxonomy is created. Further, add specializations under the other entities startFromScratch and buildFromComponents to broaden the taxonomy. Consider adding additional specializations to deepen the taxonomy.

5.4.4 Specialization Under Entity Besides Another Specialization

The specializations combine in combinatorial fashion under the entity. For example, consider the specialization

```
reuseFromRepository can be open or restricted in
accessRights!
```

Having just added the location specialization, reuseFromRepository now has two specializations which combine to give four combinations (open, local), (open, internet), (restricted, local) and (restricted, internet).

Exercise

Add the above specializations to the SES for MSProcessSystem. Use the pruning interface of MS4 Me to produce a completely pruned entity structure. How many such PESs are there?

For the SES you created for Exercise 2 at the end of Chap. 3, add at least one specialization from each of the categories outlined above.

Exercise

Figure 5.4 is the outline of an SES for a Car. Write a natural language specification using MS4 Me that matches this SES.

Use the pruning interface of MS4 Me to produce a completely pruned entity structure. How many such PESs are there for this SES?

Fig. 5.4 Outline of an SES
for a car

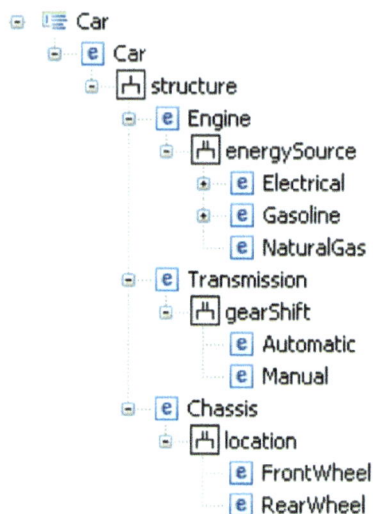

5.5   Variables and Specializations

Variables attached to entities in the SES make it possible to assign numeric and other data values in the interpretation of the pruned entity structure (PES). For example, the following assigns variables height and weight to the entity boy.

A boy has height,weight, and eyeColor!

To constrain the possible values that can be assigned, we can indicate the data type and range of values, e.g.,

The range of a boy's height is double with values [20, 72]!

Specializations can be combined with variables to allow you to constrain the range of values via pruning. For example, we can add a specialization labeled Height for the boy entity:

A boy can be short, average, or tall in Height!

Then ranges can be assigned to the selections, e.g., as:

Set short_boy's height to [20, 40]!
Set average_boy's height to [41, 59]!
Set tall_boy's height to [60, 72]!

Now in pruning, the selection of short for Height under boy (for example) will convey to the interpreter of the PES that the values must be constrained to the range [20, 40]. The interpreter might sample values randomly from the given range, providing a sweep through a short category. Discrete values can be assigned as well. For example, if there were a correlation between height and eye color we might have

```
Set short_boy's eyeColor to grey!
Set average_boy's eyeColor to blue!
Set tall_boy's eyeColor to brown!
```

More than one specialization can be introduced to constrain values:

A boy can be underweight, normal, or overweight in Weight!

and for example,

```
Set underweight_boy's weight to [50,110]!
```

When there are multiple variables attached to an entity (e.g., height, weight, eye color, ...) and multiple entities having such variables, the effect is to be able to generate a large number of instances with numerical and other data values consistent with the pruning specifications.

5.6 Summary

A major strength of the SES is that it generates a family of hierarchical models rather than single composition. To understand how this is accomplished, we discussed a second main construct called specialization to complement and interact with the earlier introduced operation of decomposition. Specialization enables you to expand the alternatives, or options, for selection. We showed how a pruning interface supports understanding the combinatorial space of possible selections. You need not make all available selections at one session and can return later to amend and add to a pruning file. This allows you to generate multiple possible pruned entity structures that can be transformed into simulation models (selections not made are filled in randomly in this transformation.) In the next chapter, you will see that more than one decomposition can be associated with an entity—which further enriches the variety of possible structures prunable from an SES.

Aspects and Multi-aspects

6

So far we have encountered different aspects that are present in the same System Entity Structure. However, these aspects were under *different* entities so that no entity had more than one aspect. When an entity has only one aspect, this allows you to decompose the model it represents in one way (as well as provide couplings for the associated composition). In the next section, you will see how there can be different aspects for the *same* entity and how this allows you to decompose a system in different ways. After that, we will discuss the concept of multi-aspect which provides a uniform way to associate an unlimited number of related aspects with the same entity. Each multi-aspect effectively opens up a large space of simulation models with an unbounded variety of possibilities for coupling their components. So, finally, we discuss how coupling of components can be specified for such multi-aspects in uniform ways that greatly reduce the amount of data entry required.

6.1 Multiple Aspects (Decompositions)

6.1.1 Expressing Different Aspects for Same Entity

Consider adding the following to the SES for MSProcessSystem (Chap. 3).

```
From the fastProcess perspective, MSProcessSystem is made
of User, ClarifyObjectivesPhase, getModelFromRepository,
ExecuteModelPhase, and InterpretResultsPhase!
```

Here, we add a second aspect to the SES which has a different label, "fastProcess," to distinguish it from the first which was labeled "process." The newly added aspect represents a decomposition of the modeling and simulation process in which the gathering data phase is skipped and, rather than being constructed, a model is

© Springer International Publishing AG 2017   81
B.P. Zeigler and H.S. Sarjoughian, *Guide to Modeling and Simulation*
of Systems of Systems, Simulation Foundations, Methods and Applications,
DOI 10.1007/978-3-319-64134-8_6

retrieved directly from a repository. This foreshortening of the process is consistent with the label "fastProcess" and would be suitable when the M&S development process is constrained by time and resource availability. Because we are skipping the data-gathering phase, the output of the clarifying objectives phase now has to drive the model retrieval. This is implemented in the coupling:

```
From the fastProcess perspective, ClarifyObjectivesPhase
sends ClearObjectives to getModelFromRepository!
```

Also, the output of the model must be sent to start the model execution:

```
From the fastProcess perspective, getModelFromRepository
sends ValidModel to ExecuteModelPhase!
```

After adding the fastProcess aspect and the above couplings to the SES, its outline appears in Fig. 6.1. Note that there are now two aspects under the MSProcessSystem entity. To produce a specific DEVS model, eventually one of these aspects must be selected.

Exercise

Fill in the rest of the couplings for this decomposition in the SES for the M&S process. Use the MS4 Me tool to generate the outline and compare with Fig. 6.1.

6.1.2 Pruning of Aspects

Recall that an aspect represents decomposition and that at most one decomposition per entity can give rise to a simulation model. Therefore, you must select a single aspect whenever there are more than one aspect under an entity. Returning to the pruning interface of MS4 Me with the amended SES, you will now see MSProcessSystem included in the list of prunable items on the left-hand side. Highlighting that entity will now allow you to select one of its two aspects. Since aspects combine with specializations, each selection of an aspect will enable pruning of all items in the substructure (specializations or multiple aspects under entities). Accordingly, there are now two families of pruned entity structures for the M&S Process SES—one for the original process aspect and one for the fastProcess aspect.

Exercise

Using the MS4 Me interface, create at least two completely pruned entity structures stemming from the selection of the aspects under MSProcessSystem.

Fig. 6.1 Outline of the SES for MSProcessSystem after fastProcess addition

6.1.3   Aspects: Perspectives and Abstractions

As the name implies, the SES concept of aspect allows you to represent taking different perspectives on the same real-world system or process and including them within the same structure. The great benefit of viewing the same thing from different perspectives is that this may well lead to simplifications or idealizations that allow dispensing with a lot of the complexity inherent in the real world. System abstractions derived from different perspectives often can be treated in a stand-alone or quasi-independent manner. Unfortunately, although an effective abstraction enables you to get into the right ballpark from that particular point of view, its assumptions tend to conflict with those of other abstractions when pushed beyond its limits. The advantage of including multiple aspects in the same structure (a single SES) is that we can work with them all together as a whole when we need to.

Consider, for example, modeling multi-person games on the Internet. The Internet can foster the illusion of a virtual space such that players may focus on the rules of the game no matter where they are geographically located in the real world. Thus, modeling such a game from the player's perspective can represent the constraints of the game and the players' strategies for dealing with them. From the game host's point of view however, supporting a menu of several games does not critically depend on a particular game but only on their general characteristics that relate to providing the speed of response necessary to maintain the illusion that players are not separated by distances between them. Let's recognize that these different abstractions are driven by different objectives—the player's goals of working out winning strategies and the host's objectives in providing the virtual world's illusion. And while initially self-contained, they may interact at important junctures. For example, a player may realize that he enjoys a slight speed advantage and capitalize on it in making a play. Likewise, the game developer may realize that a particular game may stress the network more than average and so require special treatment. A third aspect which includes the combined entities in both aspects can be added to take account of the interactions that arise under circumstances where the original assumptions fail.

Exercise

Develop an SES for the game/network scenario that has three aspects under its root entity. In the game aspect, players A and B vie to be the first to recognize an object that appears (virtually) simultaneously on their separate screens. In this abstraction, there are the players, their screens, and the game-serving computer. The focus is on the pattern recognition skills of the players, and no Internet representation is present. In the second aspect, the game server and players' computers are modeled as nodes on the Internet with a representation of the latencies experienced by packets sent from node to node. The goal is to assure that despite such latencies, the game software assures the virtual simultaneity of screen displays. The third aspect allows players to perceive breakdowns in the simultaneity of screen displays and includes players to exploit such perceptions.

Exercise

You can obtain some descriptions of building architectures drawn from Wikipedia http://en.wikipedia.org/wiki/Architectural_style as well as particular house styles and building materials http://en.wikipedia.org/wiki/Townhouses. Develop an SES for a house that will allow you to design a particular house by pruning. The SES should be such that you could prune it to obtain any one of several house styles. For example, from the sentence, "Townhouses usually consist of multiple floors and have their own outside door as opposed to having only one level and an interior hallway access," you can infer that different aspects might exist for single level and multi-level styles and that outside door is an option.

6.2 Multi-aspects—Multiple Related Decompositions of an Entity

6.2.1 Limitations of Aspects

So far you have learned that you can express several decompositions of an entity using one aspect for each decomposition. However, there is a limitation that we now address. This limitation arises from the fact we need to provide a finite list of entities for each aspect. This is awkward when we want to let an aspect have an indefinite number of entities. For example,

```
From the top perspective, the People are made of Alice,
Bill, and Charlie!
```

States that the entity, People, is composed of specifically three entities with names: Alice, Bill, and Charlie.

To increase the number of entities to four, we need to explicitly add a fourth named entity, say David. This means changing the SES, replacing the above sentence by this one:

```
From the top perspective, the People are made of Alice,
Bill, Charlie, and David!
```

Alternatively, we can use place both aspects with different names in the same SES:

```
From the topThree perspective, the People are made of
Alice, Bill, and Charlie!
From the topFour perspective, the People are made of Alice,
Bill, Charlie, and David!
```

Although this approach allows us to select aspects of the same entity with different numbers of entities, we have to list the decompositions explicitly. Besides being tedious and error prone, the choice is always limited by the finite set of aspects actually defined.

6.2.2 Multi-aspect Restructuring

The concept of *multi-aspect* is intended to address the limitation of having to explicitly declare decompositions having different numbers of entities. To illustrate, consider the following pair of statements:

```
From the top perspective, the World is made of People and
Environment!
From the multiPerson perspective, People are made of more
than one Person!
```

The second statement generates a multi-aspect in the SES. A multi-aspect is a special case of an aspect except that it has only one child called its *multi-entity*—which can generate a specified number of copies (Zeigler and Hammonds 2007). In the above example, People is the entity that has the multi-aspect labeled by multiPerson and Person is its multi-entity of multiPerson.

To *expand* a multi-entity (i.e., to generate copies), you add a specialization to it, for example:

```
Person can be id in index!
```

Then in a pruning file, you include two statements such as:

```
restructure multiaspects using index!
set multiplicity of index as [3] for Person!
```

Where the first statement tells the pruner to expand using the specialization labeled by index, and the second tells how many copies to make. The specialization

Fig. 6.2 Multi-aspect restructuring

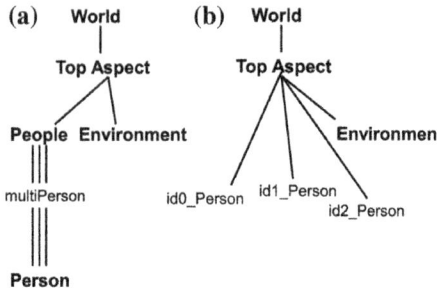

entity, id, is used to identify the copies—for example, id0_Person, id1_Person, id2_Person, are generated. These new entities are added to the (ordinary) aspect under the grandparent entity, and the multi-aspect is removed from the SES. For example, the new SES after the given restructuring can be described by

```
From the top perspective, the World is made of Environment,
id0_Person, id1_Person and id2_Person!
```

Figure 6.2 illustrates this restructuring where the original SES is depicted in Fig. 6.2a, and the restructured SES is depicted in Fig. 6.2b. Note that the multi-aspect multiPerson has been eliminated, and the copies of the multi-entity Person are added to the aspect under World. Note that originally, Person was the grandchild of World, and now, the copies of Person are the children of World.

6.2.3 Pruning Multi-aspects

The multi-entity of a multi-aspect can have a sub-SES below it. For example, we might have

```
Person can be short, medium, or tall in height!
```

Here, each of the copies inherits this sub-SES, and during pruning, each these copies can be pruned independently. This can be visualized as equivalent to replacing the specialization for Person by the same specialization added to each new entity:

```
id0_Person can be short, medium, or tall in height!
id1_Person can be short, medium, or tall in height!
id2_Person can be short, medium, or tall in height!
```

The pruning file can then specify pruning selections for none, some, or all the entities. For example,

```
select medium from height for id1_Person!
```

Selects medium height for the person with identity id1. As general is the case, selections not made explicitly in the pruning file are made randomly.

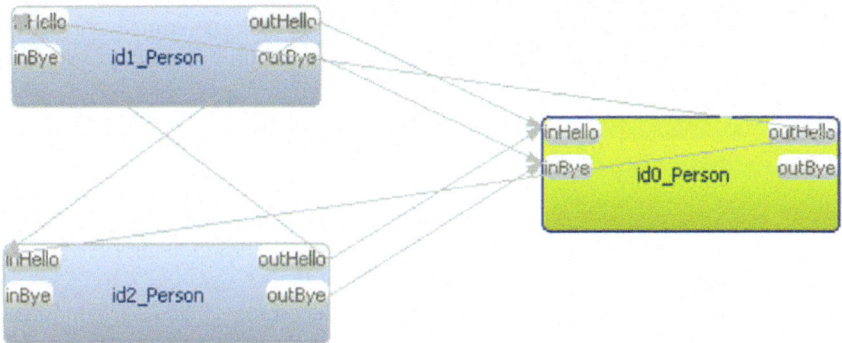

Fig. 6.3 Illustrating all-to-all coupling pattern

6.2.4 Multi-aspect Uniform Coupling

After restructuring, the entities of a multi-aspect can be coupled by referring to them by name. For example,

```
From the top perspective, id0_Person sends Bye to
id1_Person!
```

Creates a coupling from outBye of id0_Person to inBye of id1_Person. Such individualized coupling can be tedious and error prone as the numbers of entities increases. Therefore, we need the capability to create couplings that can be uniformly stated similarly to the logic quantifier, *for all*. For example,

```
From the top perspective, World is made of People and
Environment!
From the multiPerson perspective, People are made of more
than one Person!
Person can be id in index!
From the top perspective, all Person sends Bye to
id0_Person!
From the top perspective, all Person sends Hello to all
Person!
```

This creates the coupling pattern shown in the Simulation Viewer capture of Fig. 6.3. Here, every Person's output port outBye is coupled to id0_Person's input port inBye. Every Person's output port outHello is coupled to every Person's input port inHello (the exception that there is no self-coupling, i.e., no output port of a component is coupled to any of its input ports).

Uniform coupling can be employed to couple entities between different restructured multi-aspects. For example, in the following SES, all boys say Hello to each other, all girls say Hello to each other, and all girls greet all boys.

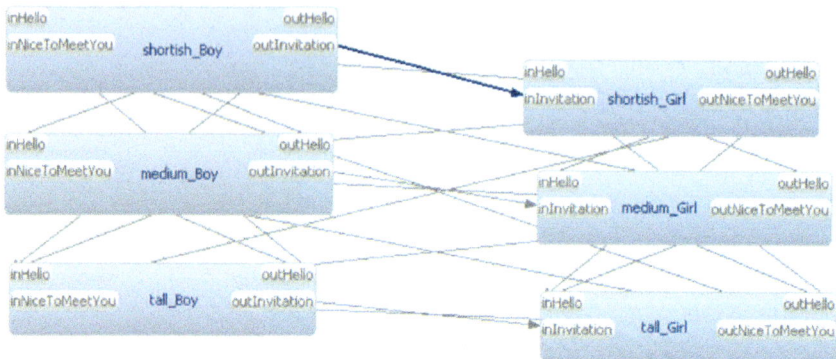

Fig. 6.4 Coupling based on matching

```
From the dating perspective, the DatingGame is made of Boys
and Girls!
From the boy perspective, Boys are made of more than one
Boy!
Boy can be shortish, medium, or tall in height!
From the girl perspective, Girls are made of more than one
Girl!
Girl can be shortish, medium, or tall in height!
From the dating perspective, all Boy sends Hello to all
Boy!
From the dating perspective, all Girl sends Hello to all
Girl!
From the dating perspective, all Girl sends NiceToMeetYou
to all Boy!
```

Here, note that restructuring is based on the height specialization. This will work
in a straightforward manner provided you don't use height as the basis for identifying multi-entity copies (in other words, "set multiplicity of height ..." does not
appear in the pruning file).

We introduce another form of uniform coupling with the *each-to-each* construct
shown in the following:

```
From the dating perspective, each Boy sends Invitation to
each Girl!
```

As illustrated in Fig. 6.4, this results in each boy having its output port
outInvitation coupled to the inInvitation port a girl having the same height.
Matching is done on the basis of having the same prefix in the pruned name of an
entity (e.g., tall in tall_boy). Couplings are not added for matches that cannot be
made—for example, if the numbers of boys and girls are not equal. Other coupling
types, such as all-to-each, are supported.

6.2.5 One-to-All and All-to-One Coupling

Coupling any entity to the entities of a multi-aspect can be specified in using the one-to-all form as in:

```
From the dating perspective, short_Boy sends Greeting to
all Girl!
```

This will work provided that the entity to be coupled is in the same coupled model as the multi-entities. For example, if MatchMaker were added to the Dating Game, then one could specify:

```
From the dating perspective, MatchMaker sends
MakeInvitation to all Boy!
```

The source entity can also be the coupled model that contains the multi-entities, so that we can specify:

```
From the dating perspective, DatingGame sends
MakeInvitation to all Boy!
```

All-to-one coupling works in a predictably similar manner to one-to-all coupling. For example,

```
From the dating perspective, all Boy sends Preference to
MatchMaker!
```

Exercise

Extend the following SES text so that every person sends a Sit instruction to his/her own dog, and every dog can Bark so that it is heard by the whole world. Write a pruning file so that there are five People and three Dogs.

```
From the top perspective, World is made of People and Dogs!
From the person perspective, People are made of more than
one Person!
From the dog perspective, Dogs are made of more than one
Dog!
Person can be id in index!
Dog can be id in index!
```

Exercise

A proposed satellite system architecture contains relay satellites and image-taking satellites. Imaging requests from a single ground station are sent to relay satellites which can pass on the requests to all imaging satellites. After taking an image, an imaging satellite can send it to all relay satellites which can relay it back to the ground station. Develop an SES with multi-aspects for each type of satellite that employs one-to-all, all-to-all, and all-to-one coupling. Write a pruning file that specifies two relay and ten imaging satellites (see Chap. 13).

More on "all" and "each" coupling appears in Chap. 9 in the context of DEVS distributed simulation and in Chap. 15 on Cloud systems.

6.2.6 Hierarchical Construction with Multi-aspects

Multi-aspect restructuring, pruning, and coupling paradigms apply to hierarchical construction as well. For example, when a multi-aspect is expanded into entities, each entity may itself have a multi-aspect in need of expansion. This leads to hierarchical construction where the components at one level are constructed from components at the next lower level. A global situation awareness database system consisting of multiple geographically distributed enclaves offers an example. Each enclave contains a database server that serves any number of clients. There is no direct connection among clients. Database servers are connected to each other in an all-to-all fashion so that a client's update in one enclave is propagated to all the others.

To express this system in MS4 Me, we create multi-aspects for multiple enclaves and for multiple clients within each enclave which leads to an SES description:

```
From the overall perspective, MultiEnclaveNet is made of
Enclaves!
From the multiEnclave perspective, Enclaves are made of
more than one Enclave!
//sharing of updates among enclaves
From the overall perspective, all Enclave sends DBUpdate to
all Enclave!
Enclave can be enclaveid in index!
From the enclave perspective, Enclave is made of DBServer
and Clients!
From the multclient perspective, Clients are made of more
than one Client!
Client can be clientid in index!
//interaction of clients and servers within an enclave
From the enclave perspective, all Client sends DBQuery to
DBServer!
From the enclave perspective, all Client sends DBUpdate to
DBServer!
From the enclave perspective, DBServer sends DBResponse to
all Client!
//connecting the server within an enclave to the enclosing
enclave
From the enclave perspective, DBServer sends DBUpdate to
Enclave!
From the enclave perspective, Enclave sends DBUpdate to
DBServer!
```

Fig. 6.5 Outline for
MultiEnclaveNet

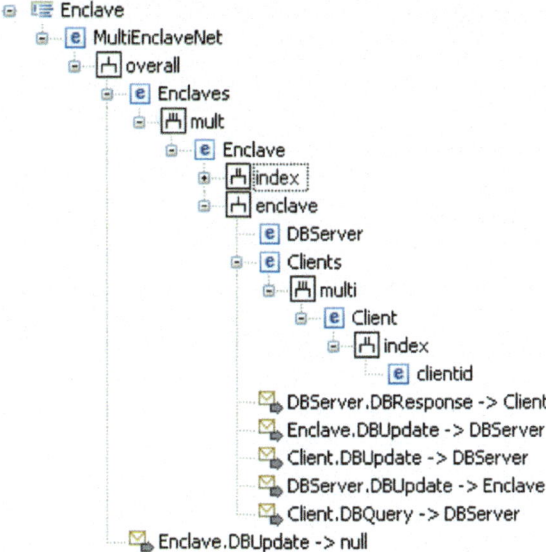

The outline in Fig. 6.5 shows the outline for the MultiEnclaveNet SES. After
pruning and transformation, MultiEnclaveNet will become a coupled model that
contains one or more Enclaves, each of which becomes a coupled model that
contains a DBServer and multiple clients.

The numbers of Enclaves and Clients can be specified in a pruning file containing statements such as:

```
restructure multi-aspects using index!
set multiplicity of index as [2] for Enclave!
set multiplicity of index as [3] for Client!
```

Note that it is permissible, and desirable, to use the same specialization (here
index) for different multi-aspects in the SES, where the multiplicity can be differentially specified in the pruning file. If different names are used, e.g., enclaveIndex
and clientIndex, then a bottom-up order must be given for restructuring, as in

```
restructure multi-aspects using clientIndex then
enclaveIndex!
```

Note that the number of clients in each enclave is the same since we can't
specify them individually. This is a limitation on the expressiveness of the current
version of MS4 Me which can be removed by supporting specification of multiplicity using context.

Exercise

Using MS4 Me, enter the above SES and test it using the animation feature. Try specifying different numbers of enclaves and clients per enclave. How might it become possible to specify different numbers of clients in each enclave?

Exercise

In the space system in Exercise xx, the imaging and relay satellites are composed of modules where some of the modules are different for each type of satellite. For example, imaging satellites have cameras whereas relay satellites have more powerful transceivers able to communicate with the earth. Elaborate on your SES for Exercise xx by attaching a multi-aspect for modules under the multi-entity of the relay as well as the imaging satellite.

Exercise

A relation is a set of pairs, where each pair has a left element and a right element. Here, the left element belongs to a domain set and the right element belongs to a range set. This structure can be generated by an SES described by:

```
From the rel perspective, Relation is made of pairs!
From the mult perspective, pairs is made of more than one
pair!
pair can be id in index!
From the pr perspective, pair is made of left and right!
left can be key in domain!
right can be value in range!
```

To specify a particular relation, you can write a pruning file starting with the following (as an example):

```
restructure multi-aspects using index!
set multiplicity of index as [4] for pair!
set multiplicity of domain as [6] for left!
//creates elements key0, key1,...., key5 for selection
from domain
set multiplicity of range as [3] for right!
```

Using context sensitive pruning (Chap. 8), add selection statements to define a particular relation compatible with the above statements. Hint: to specify a pair (key5, value0), for the first pair, write:

```
select key5 from domain for left under id0_pair!
select value0 from range for right under id0_pair!
```

6.2.7   Uniform Pairwise Coupling

So far we have used multi-aspects to specify compositions with components that are derived from the same entity and whose particulars are decided while pruning. We have also been able to specify couplings among these components that are uniform in the sense of applying to all in the same manner (see Sect. 6.2.3). However, there are important kinds of coupling patterns that don't fit this mold. For example, cellular automata connect up their components in a mesh pattern based on a geometrical coordinate grid (Wainer et al. 2010; Muzy and Hu 2008). Tree automata lay out their components on a tree structure where starting from the root, each non-leaf node has, say two, children, and there are no couplings other than between parents and children. Indeed, there are numerous such connection schemes, and variations thereof, of possible interest to modelers. To bring each of these schemes within the framework of multi-aspects presents a challenge since it is not possible to specify them all in advance. Instead, we can provide a mechanism that allows modelers to specify their own patterns.

To explain this approach, we can envision a coupling scheme which consists of two parts: (1) specification of network connectivity, and (2) the coupling of ports between connected components. The network connectivity can be described by a mathematical graph of elements called nodes, and pairs of nodes, called edges. Furthermore, in our context, the graph is a directed graph, or digraph, meaning that the pairs are ordered. In an ordered pair, the left-hand node can be called the sender, and right-hand node is the receiver. The nodes of the graph are in one-one correspondence with the components, and the form of the graph is given by specifying a subset of edges. Such a subset can be regarded as being selected from all the available ordered pairs using a pruning process. Each pair corresponds to a direct connection between associated components. In summary, a directed graph sets up the pairwise connections for the network connectivity

This leaves the port-to-port coupling to be specified for each connection in the directed graph of a coupling scheme. Recall that in general different pairs of components can have different port-to-port couplings. However, to simplify the coupling specification and in the spirit of uniformity, we will force the port-to-port coupling to be the same across all such pairs.

To see how this *uniform coupling* rule works, consider the coupling example in Sect. 6.2.3,

```
From the top perspective, id0_Person sends Bye to
id1_Person!
```

This creates a coupling from outBye of id0_Person to inBye of id1_Person. Here, the ordered pair of components is (id0_Person, id1_Person), or for short (id0, id1), and the port-to-port coupling is (outBye, inBye). The uniform coupling requirement dictates that all edges in the network digraph have the same port-to-port coupling. So for example, if (id2, id3) is a connected pair, then a port-to-port coupling (outBye, inBye) is assigned to this pair. The corresponding natural language statement would be:

```
From the top perspective, id2_Person sends Bye to
id3_Person!
```

To make the uniform coupling rule operational, we need a way to specify network connectivity and then a way to specify port-to-port coupling. For network connectivity, the question is: How can you select a set of pairs of nodes to form a directed graph? To answer this question, suppose the following appears in an SES file:

```
From the topsys perspective, MonorailSystem is made of EF,
MonorailStations, and circleCouplingSpecification!
From the multiStation perspective, MonorailStations is made
of more than one MonorailStation!
MonorailStation can be id in index!
```

Note the presence of a special entity, circleCouplingSpecification that has been added as a sibling to MonorailStations which contains the multiStation multi-aspect. When the pruner interprets this file, the suffix, CouplingSpecification, will be recognized, and the pruner will expect to see further detail in the pruning file. The prefix, circle, is the name of the set of pairs intended to form the digraph for the network of MonorailStations. To explicitly specify such a set of pairs, you can write, for example:

```
add coupling circlepair from id0 to id1 in index!
add coupling circlepair from id1 to id2 in index!
add coupling circlepair from id2 to id3 in index!
add coupling circlepair from id3 to id0 in index!
```

Which creates the pairs (id0, id1), (id1, id2), (id2, id3), (id3, id0) forming a cycle in the graph with nodes id0, ..., id3.

Next, you can attach port-to-port couplings to these pairs. For example, to associate couplings with the circleCouplingSpecification, you can write

```
for circle leftnode sends Car to rightnode!
for circle rightnode sends GoAhead to leftnode!
```

Where we note that since the pairs are ordered, there is a node on the left (called leftnode), and a node on the right (called rightnode). Furthermore, by the uniform coupling rule, the first statement specifies that each left node sends car to its paired right node, and each right node sends GoAhead to its paired left node.

Viewed in the Simulation Viewer (Fig. 6.6), we can see the network connectivity cycle digraph together with the port-to-port coupling specified by the pairs.

Finally, to provide the right context for all the information needed in the pruning file to allow such couplings to be properly interpreted, we add the statement:

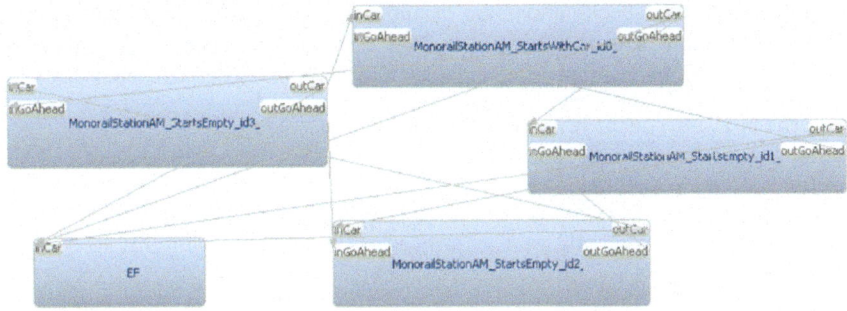

Fig. 6.6 Monorail composition

write coupling specification for MonorailStation and index
based on circle!

This identifies the name of the multi-entity in the multi-aspect (MonorailStation), and the specialization (index) to be used in the coupling specification named by the circle.

6.2.8 Predefined Coupling Specifications

At this point, we see that separating the node-to-node network connectivity from the port-to-port coupling specification using uniform coupling rule greatly reduces the number of items to be specified because you avoid having to separately give the couplings for each node pair. Nevertheless you still have to explicitly list all the node pairs to specify the network connectivity, and this part still can be tedious and error prone. To provide further support, MS4 Me provides some predefined forms of network digraphs that you can put to use. For example, replacing the general "write coupling specification" just mentioned with the following statement in the pruning file will create a cycle of nodes to be associated with the circleCouplingSpecification:

write cyclic specification for MonorailStation and index
based on ~circle!

Such a specification effectively selects a subset pairs forming a cycle of size specified in the multiplicity statement. So in the end, instead of explicitly listing all couplings, you can use the following compact set of statements in the pruning file:

restructure multi-aspects using index!
set multiplicity of index as [4] for MonorailStation!
write cyclic specification for MonorailStation and index
based on ~circle!
for circle leftnode sends Car to rightnode!
for circle rightnode sends GoAhead to leftnode!

This file will create the same coupled model illustrated in Fig. 6.6.

Cellular and tree specifications are examples of other forms of predefined coupling specifications available for use in MS4 Me. Cellular specification offers an example of multidimensional space expansion for a multi-aspect. Consider the SES:

```
From the cell perspective, cellspace is made of cells,
cellEWCouplingSpecification, and
cellNSCouplingSpecification!
From the mult perspective, cells are made of more than one
cell!
cell can be x or y in location!
```

A pruning script to create a standard Moore neighborhood (immediate North, South, East, West neighbors) is:

```
restructure multiaspects using location!
set multiplicity of location as [10,10] for cell!
for cellEW leftnode sends East to rightnode!
for cellEW rightnode sends West to leftnode!
write cellular specification for cell and location based on
cellEW!
for cellNS leftnode sends South to rightnode!
for cellNS rightnode sends North to leftnode!
write cellular specification for cell and location based on
cellNS!
```

Exercise

Write an atomic model to provide the behavior of a Monorail station that sends a car to the next station in a cycle but only after it has received a GoAhead from that station indicating that no car currently occupies it (the car it previously hosted has moved ahead). A station must wait until the car it sends to the next station actually reaches there before sending a GoAhead to the previous station. (See Hwang and Zeigler (2009) for a representation and analysis of a Monorail system in FDDEVS).

Exercise

In the previous exercise, instead of the atomic model, write a coupled model for a Monorail station that explicitly decomposes the station into a platform and the track to the next station. This will allow a station to send a GoAhead to the previous station as soon as the car it is releasing is on the track to the next station.

Exercise

Add a specialization that allows a choice between the atomic and coupled models you have constructed.

Exercise

Add another specialization that allows pruning each station to start empty or with a car.

6.3 Summary

This chapter started with a discussion of how different aspects can be associated with the same entity and how this allows you to decompose a system in different ways. This led to a consideration of the concept of multi-aspect which provides a uniform way to associate an unlimited number of related aspects with the same entity. Pruning a multi-aspect involves setting its multiplicity and restructuring it into an ordinary aspect with the specified number of components. We saw that pruning of multi-aspects effectively opens up a large space of simulation models with an unbounded variety of possibilities for coupling their components. Unfortunately, unless properly managed, this variety can also entail enormous amounts of detailed data entry which can be tedious and error prone. This led to development of a uniform coupling rule which separates node-to-node network connectivity (specified by a directed graph) and port-to-port coupling which is forced to be uniform across all network connections. Some commonly employed schemes such as cyclic, cellular, and tree compositions have well-defined digraphs with uniform couplings so they fit this mold.

References

Hwang, M. H., & Zeigler, B. P. (2009). Reachability graph of finite & deterministic DEVS networks. *IEEE Transactions on Automation Science and Engineering, 6*(3), 454–476.

Muzy, A., & Hu, X. (2008). Specification of dynamic structure cellular automata & agents. In *Proceeding of the 14th IEEE Mediterranean Electrotechnical Conference, MELECON2008* (pp. 240–246).

Wainer, G., Liu, Q., Dalle, O., & Zeigler, B. P. (2010). Applying cellular automata and DEVS methodologies to digital games: A survey. *Simulation & Gaming, 41*(6), 796–823.

Zeigler, B. P., & Hammonds, P. (2007). *Modeling simulation-based data engineering: Introducing pragmatics into ontologies for net-centric information exchange.* Boston: Academic Press, 448 pp.

Managing Inheritance in Pruning

7

Recall that pruning a System Entity Structure involves selecting aspects from entities as well as entities from specializations. In particular, selecting an entity (the child) from a specialization under another entity (the parent) results in a combination of child and parent that can inherit some of the properties of the parent or child. MS4 Me allows flexibility in how you want this inheritance to be carried out. This chapter discusses the mechanism for expressing inheritance and how to control its execution and outcomes.

7.1 Creating Instances with Underscore

The primary means of denoting inheritance in the SES is through underscores embedded in names. In its simplest form, the underscore serves to create instances of an entity. We have already encountered the use of underscore to name copies of a multi-entity in Chap. 6. In MS4 Me, the underscore can be used to create instances of any component model class within an SES. This feature will be illustrated by modifying the SES for SimpleWorkFlow that you first encountered in Chap. 4:

From the top perspective, SimpleWorkFlow is made of First_GeneratorOfJobs, Second_GeneratorOfJobs, and ProcessorOfJobs!

Here, two instances of GeneratorOfJobs are created as components of SimpleWorkFlow. For coupling purposes, you can treat these names in the same way as ordinary names. For example,

From the top perspective, First_GeneratorOfJobs sends Job to ProcessorOfJobs!

© Springer International Publishing AG 2017
B.P. Zeigler and H.S. Sarjoughian, *Guide to Modeling and Simulation of Systems of Systems*, Simulation Foundations, Methods and Applications, DOI 10.1007/978-3-319-64134-8_7

creates a coupling from First_GeneratorOfJobs's output port outJob to ProcessorOfJobs's input port inJob. Let's see how the underscore actually creates instances as a byproduct of its support for inheritance.

7.2 Specifying the Base Class for Inheritance

In MS4 Me, the Java class subclass/superclass relationship is indicated using underscores that are interpreted in the process of model generation according user specification. For example, A_B can mean that the model class A_B will be a derived class of class A or of class B depending on specifications in the pruning file. The underscore connector usually arises automatically in pruning of specializations in which A is the child, and B is the parent. For example, in the SES just mentioned, MS4 Me allows the model class arising from Slow_GeneratorOfJobs to be generated as a subclass of either Slow, the child, or GeneratorOfJobs, the parent. Here, since we have already constructed GeneratorOfJobs, it is natural to want Slow_GeneratorOfJobs to inherit from GeneratorOfJobs, the parent. If nothing else is specified, this will happen by default, and Slow_GeneratorOfJobs will be generated as a subclass of GeneratorOfJobs. Its source code has the form:

```
public class Slow_GeneratorOfJobs extends GeneratorOfJobs{
public Slow_GeneratorOfJobs(){
this("Slow_GeneratorOfJobs");
}
public Slow_GeneratorOfJobs(String nm) {
super(nm);
}
}
```

Actually, since the SES allows a hierarchy of specializations, the name of a pruned entity can be a concatenation of names of children and the parent. For example, Random_Slow_GeneratorOfJobs might be the result of selecting Random and Slow from specializations under GeneratorOfJobs. In such concatenated names, the default specification is to select the last name in the sequence—which is the parent.

7.3 Configuring the Base Class

The standard method of employing Java inheritance is to override methods of the superclass as appropriate for the derived class. This is the appropriate approach when a child is the source of inheritance. When the parent is the source of inheritance, the appropriate approach is to let the superclass (parent) behavior be configured from information it gets from the subclass (child). This can be done by noting that the single argument constructor, Slow_GeneratorOfJobs(String nm), passes on its string argument to the superclass, GeneratorOfJobs. This makes the derived class name available for use in configuring the superclass's behavior. To see how this happens, we note that the single argument constructor of AtomicModelImpl sets its name field to the incoming string argument.

```
public AtomicModelImpl (String modelName) {
name = modelName;
...
}
```

and this behavior is invoked by the call to super from a derived class. For example, in the code for GeneratorOfJobs:

```
public GeneratorOfJobs(String modelName) {
super(modelName);
...
}
```

the call to super (which is AtomicModelImpl) sets the name field to modelName. But we have seen that the name coming from a derived class such as Slow_GeneratorOfJobs class is the string "Slow_GeneratorOfJobs." Thus, you can use this transmitted name to tell the superclass how to configure itself to suit the derived class that is "calling" it. For example, let's add the following to the source code of GeneratorOfJobs:

```
private double Period;
public void interpretNameAsPeriod() {
    if (name.startsWith(''Slow'')) {
       Period = 50;
    } else if (name.startsWith(''Fast'')) {
       Period = 10;
    } else {
       Period = 20;
    }
}
```

and modify the initialize method:

```
public void initialize() {
...
interpretNameAsPeriod();
...
holdIn("generate", Period);
}
```

as well as similarly modifying the holdIn() argument in the deltint method. Here, during initialization, the Period will be set according to the incoming name and cause the model to generate jobs at higher or lower rates as specified. Note that these additional code fragments can be implemented using the tagged code blocks within the originating FDDEVS *. dnl file (Chap. 4).

Exercise

Distribute the above additional code fragments within the GeneratorOfJobs *. dnl file in Chap. 4 to obtain the effect of configuring the GeneratorOfJobs model from the incoming model name. Hint: Include the definition for interpretNameAsPeriod() in the "add additional code" block.

7.4 Inheritance in Pruning

As indicated above, inheritance using underscores can arise from specialization selections during pruning of an SES. For example, we add specializations for the generator and processor in the SimpleWorkFlow SES:

```
From the top perspective, SimpleWorkFlow is made of GeneratorOfJobs and
ProcessorOfJobs!
GeneratorOfJobs can be Slow or Fast in frequency!
ProcessorOfJobs can be Short or Long in processingTime!
From the top perspective, GeneratorOfJobs sends Job to ProcessorOfJobs!
```

Then, the pruning file can contain pruning selections as in:

```
select Fast from frequency for GeneratorOfJobs!
select Short from processingTime for ProcessorOfJobs!
```

When you run the model in the Simulation Viewer, as in Fig. 7.1, the effect will be to generate Fast_GeneratorOfJobs and Short_ProcessorOfJobs as subclasses of their respective superclasses. You can then configure GeneratorOfJobs and

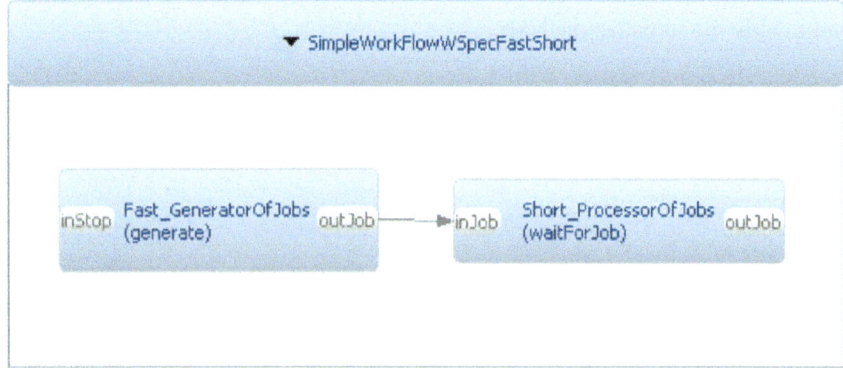

Fig. 7.1 Pruned and transformed SimpleWorkflow

ProcessorOfJobs to support inheritance appropriately. The coupling for the constructed models is automatically derived from the original coupling specification.

Exercise

Define an SES that has three aspects for SimpleWorkFlow: (1) decomposition into generator and processor without any inheritance, (2) decomposition into generator and process which have underscores to indicate desired subclasses, and (3) decomposition with specializations as just discussed. Write pruning files that select these aspects, respectively.

7.5   Specifying Inheritance from a Child

As suggested above, MS4 Me let's you specify that the class generated by A_B should be a subclass of either the parent class B or child class A. When, as in Slow_GeneratorOfJobs, the child is best viewed as modifying, or configuring, the parent, subclassing the parent is in order. On the other hand, subclassing of the child is more appropriate when the child provides most of the functionality, and the parent is mostly a placeholder. For example, in the specification,

```
Player can be Reactive or Proactive in strategy!
```

Consider combinations of the form, Reactive _Player and Proactive _Player that arise in pruning. If Reactive and Proactive are distinct behaviors that already are implemented as different models, then the combinations are best derived from these children. In such cases, you can override the default inheritance from the parent by specifying the desired inheritance in the pruning file:

```
inherit from Reactive!
inherit from Proactive!
```

The following exercise concerns alternative behaviors, compliance, and non-compliance with commands that players acquire through subclassing.

Exercise

SimonSays is a children's game in which Simon issues commands that may or not be obeyed by the players. If the command starts with the string "SimonSays," then it must be obeyed. Otherwise, it must not be obeyed. If the player fails to comply in either case, he/she leaves the game. Here is an SES for such a game:

```
From the game perspective, the SimonSaysGame is made of Simon and Players!
From the player perspective, Players is made of more than one Player!
Player can be Alice, Bill, or Charlie in name!
Player can be Compliant or NonCompliant in compliance!
```

The messages exchanged between Simon and the players are: SimonSays, Command, Comply, and YouAreOut. Assume that FDDEVS specifications for Compliant and NonCompliant behaviors are described as follows:

Compliant Behavior

```
to start, hold in waitForSimonSays for time 2!
from waitForSimonSays go to waitForAssessment!
when in waitForSimonSays and receive SimonSays go to waitForCommand!
passivate in waitForCommand!
when in waitForCommand and receive Command go to executeCommand!
hold in waitForAssessment for time 10!
from waitForAssessment go to waitForSimonSays!
when in waitForAssessment and receive YouAreOut go to outOfGame!
hold in executeCommand for time 1!
after executeCommand output Comply!
from executeCommand go to waitForAssessment!
passivate in outOfGame!
```

Non-Compliant Behavior

```
to start, hold in waitForSimonSays for time 2!
from waitForSimonSays go to waitForAssessment!
when in waitForSimonSays and receive SimonSays go to waitForSimonSays
eventually!
when in waitForSimonSays and receive Command go to executeCommand!
hold in executeCommand for time 1!
after executeCommand output Comply!
from executeCommand go to waitForAssessment!
```

(a) Generate the Java class files from these specifications.
(b) Write a FDDEVS specification for Simon.
(c) Write a pruning file for the SES that ensures that players derive their behaviors from the Compliant and NonCompliant classes.
(d) Add uniform couplings (Chap. 6) to the SES so that the message exchange between Simon and the players (SimonSays, Command, Comply, and YouAreOut) is correctly specified.
(e) Elaborate Simon and the player models using the code blocks approach of Chap. 4 to amend any behaviors in need of correction.

7.6 Summary

Selecting an entity (the child) from a specialization under another entity (the parent) results in a combination of child and parent for which there is some flexibility in how its inheritance is to be carried out. In the default case, the parent becomes the base class for the combination. You can write the Java model generated from the parent to be configured to the particular child selected by making use of the name transmitted through the constructor. Otherwise, if you specify inheritance from a child, then you can write the Java model for the child so that it provides the behavior for the combination. The inheritance specifications are added to the pruning script and control the hierarchical model generated by transforming the system entity structure.

Automated and Rule-Based Pruning and Experimental Execution

8

The main features of the System Entity Structure, its specializations and aspects, as well as pruning and model generation have now been introduced. Such concepts provide a wealth and variety of potential hierarchical structures with which to tackle complex Systems of Systems problems. However, the rapidly growing combinatorial spaces that are set up by specialization and aspect selections can outstrip human capacity to do the manual pruning discussed in Chap. 5. Accordingly, this chapter discusses automated pruning—concepts and tools for pruning that can reduce, and sometimes, eliminate, the manual pruning that is otherwise required.

The complex models generated by automated pruning require effective simulation executives to control the experimentation for scanning through alternatives and collecting data from multiple runs for analysis. To conclude this chapter, we discuss a methodology and supporting concepts that make such experimentation control more straightforward, reliable, and less time consuming. It can be implemented on sequential computers as well as parallel and distributed platforms.

8.1 Automated Pruning

Recall that when you save your selections after pruning, MS4 Me produces a script file with the *.pes extension as distinct from the *.ses extension for the original SES. A pruning script that provides decisions for all selections—for both specializations and aspects—specifies a unique pruned entity structure (PES). However, you may not always want to provide such a complete specification. For one reason, you may be pruning a large SES and want to see some results along the way toward complete pruning. For another, when you stop short of making all selections, MS4 Me produces a partial pruning script that can be thought of as a template to generate a family of related PESs. This family consists of all PESs which satisfy the selections that have been made but which differ in choices made randomly for selections that were left open. Such a family can be referred to as a *solution space*.

© Springer International Publishing AG 2017
B.P. Zeigler and H.S. Sarjoughian, *Guide to Modeling and Simulation of Systems of Systems*, Simulation Foundations, Methods and Applications, DOI 10.1007/978-3-319-64134-8_8

In this light, an empty pruning file can be regarded a partial script with its solution space being the whole space, i.e., the family of all PES generated by the SES. MS4 Me can work from any such pruning file to generate the complete space by enumeration, or it can sample from this space randomly. In the following sections, we discuss such automated pruning in the form of such enumerative and random pruning. After describing these generation approaches, we consider various forms of pruning rules that constrain how automated pruning works. Chapter 13 discusses an illustrative application to fractionated satellite system architectures, a prototypic system of systems.

8.1.1 Enumerative Pruning

Enumerative pruning generates completely pruned entity structures one after another in some order making sure that each family member is produced once and only once (see Zeigler et al. 2000). This "brute force" method is good for relatively small solution spaces—recall that the family size grows geometrically with number of choices. For example, consider the SES:

```
From the sys perspective, SendReceivePair is made of Sender and
Receiver!
From the sys perspective, Sender sends Hello to Receiver!
Sender can be Slow or Fast in speed!
Receiver can be Ready or NotReady in preparedness!
```

Here, sender and receiver are entities that have specializations, speed, and preparedness, respectively, each with two choices. In enumerative pruning, all four combinations are generated successively with no repetitions. For instance, enumerative pruning first generates a coupled model with a selection of Slow from speed for sender and a selection of NotReady from preparedness for receiver. This results in the class SendReceivePair.java with the following body:

```
Slow_Sender Slow_Sender = new Slow_Sender();
addChildModel(Slow_Sender);
NotReady_Receiver NotReady_Receiver = new NotReady_Receiver();
addChildModel(NotReady_Receiver);
addCoupling(Slow_Sender.outHello,NotReady_Receiver.inHello);
```

Enumerative pruning continues to generate three more coupled models with the three remaining pairs of selections (Slow, Ready), (Fast, NotReady), and (Fast, Ready). Each coupled model appears in its own distinctly named class file with the Java code configured appropriately, to the selection pair—the right components appear and the couplings are adapted to them.

8.1.2 Random Pruning

Random pruning samples from the family of pruned entity structures rather than generate them all in some order. As mentioned earlier in the book, a choice with uniform probability is made wherever the pruning file has not given the pruner a basis for decision. The pruner iterates through a loop to generate a complete pruned entity structure the number of iterations you specify. By starting from a different initial seed for its pseudo-random number generator at each iteration, the pruner draws different random samples (instance PESs) from the solution space. This process is constrained by a set of rules. In the next section, we discuss such rules in detail.

8.2 Context-Free and Context-Sensitive Pruning

A pruning script in a file with *.pes extension can contain rules that direct the pruning process as well as other statements concerning pre- and post-processing of the pruning results. Now, the rules that specify pruning of specializations in a pruning script, take two forms, context sensitive and context free, with the latter being a special case of the former. To explain the difference, let us return to the SES in Chap. 5, replicated here in Fig. 8.1.

Note that there are three occurrences of the CPU entity corresponding to the three entities of the brand specialization under computer. Each of these occurrences has the computePower specialization under it. So a selection from computePower could be different for different occurrences. In other words, a choice of which computing power matches a particular type of task might well depend on the computer brand. This is an example of context sensitivity

For example, after pruning the just mentioned SES, the following is part of a pruning script:

```
select HP from brand for Computer!
select medium from size for Job!
select mediumPower from computePower for CPU under HP under Computer
under JobContext!
```

An example of a context-free rule is the first in the above script:

```
select HP from brand for Computer!
```

This makes a selection of HP from the brand specialization for the computer entity. There is only one occurrence of the brand specialization so there is no question about context sensitivity.

Fig. 8.1 Outline of
JobContext SES

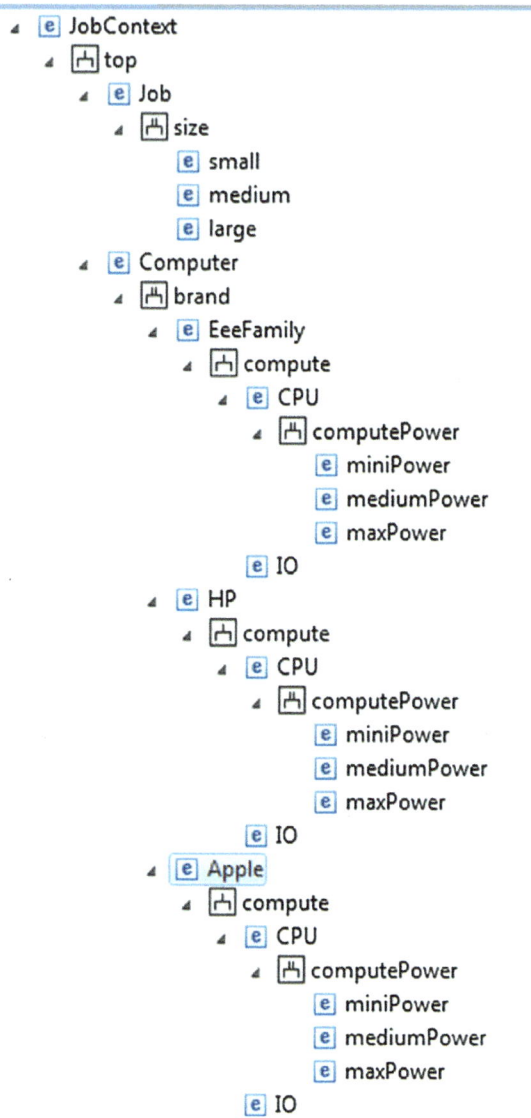

Contrast this statement with the last one in the above pruning script:

```
select mediumPower from computePower for CPU under HP under Computer
under JobContext!
```

Here, selection of mediumPower from the computePower specialization for the
CPU is made in the context of the CPU entity—this is the path from this entity to
the root entity of the SES enumerated through the succession of the intermediate
entities: "under HP under Computer under JobContext."

In general, the context for an entity provided in a rule can be *partial*, i.e., it can range from none (an empty path) to the full path to the root entity such as just mentioned. Where none of the path is provided, we have a *context-free* rule. For example,

```
Select miniPower from computePower for CPU!
```

Here, the selection of miniPower from the computePower specialization is applied to every occurrence of the CPU entity.

In contrast, the following is a *context-sensitive* rule:

```
Select mediumPower from computePower for CPU under HP!
```

Here, the selection of mediumPower from the computePower specialization is applied to any occurrence of CPU satisfying the partial context specification: "under HP"—in fact, in this SES, there is only one such occurrence.

We see that specifying a partial context enables a rule to be applied to every occurrence of the entity satisfying that partial context. However, in general, there may be more than one rule, and concomitantly, more than one partial context may apply to an entity. So an algorithm that implements the pruning operation must be able to make a decision on which selection to enforce in such ambiguous circumstances.

8.2.1   Pruning Algorithm for Context-Sensitive Selection

To understand how the pruning algorithm in MS4 Me manages rule-context conflicts, consider a pruning script that has the two statements mentioned above:

```
Select miniPower from computePower for CPU!
Select mediumPower from computePower for CPU under HP!
```

Here, the rules appear to be contradictory since they advocate different choices for the CPU under HP. However, there is a straightforward conflict resolution rule that resolves this situation.

Conflict Resolution Method:

If several rules apply to the same specialization:

always choose the selection corresponding to the most specific partial context that matches the entity occurrence.

A partial context *matches* an entity occurrence if the partial context is an initial segment of the path from the entity occurrence to the root entity. In particular, if the partial context is an empty string (i.e., no context is specified), then a match occurs. Indeed, if there are no other matching selections, then the choice will default to such a context-free rule.

To see how this works, consider applying the pair of rules above applied to each of the CPU occurrences in the SES, using the conflict resolution method when needed.

The CPU occurrences under both EeeFamily and Apple satisfy only the first, context free, selection. So they get the miniPower selection for computePower. In contrast, the CPU under HP satisfies both partial contexts. However, the second is more specific and so its selection is enforced. So while the default selection (miniPower) applies to the other brands, the HP brand gets the mediumPower choice.

The algorithm implemented in MS4 Me orders partial contexts by length, longest first—on the basis that longer paths are more specific than shorter paths. For each entity occurrence that it encounters, the algorithm finds the longest (most specific) partial context that matches the occurrence under consideration and applies the associated rule to it. We will discuss this algorithm in more detail in Sect. 8.2.5. But this is a good place to note that not all entity occurrences need to have a selection rule that dictates which choices to make. The choices not so specified can be made manually in the pruning script, or rules to make these choices can be generated from conditional rules as discussed next.

Exercise

Consider the following SES:

```
from the bilateral perspective, body is made of leftArm and rightArm!
from the physical perspective, leftArm is made of muscle and bone!
from the physical perspective, rightArm is like leftArm!
muscle can be strong or weak in strength!
muscle can be large, normal, or small in size!
```

Write a pruning script that selects a large, strong muscle for the right arm and a small, weak muscle for the left arm. Make these selections in the MS4 pruner, and compare the *.pes file that it produces with your script. Do the same comparison, where both arms have the same size and strength of muscle.

Exercise

Add the following to the above SES:

```
from the pair perspective, couple is made of husband and wife!
from the whole perspective, husband is made of body and soul !
from the whole perspective, wife is like husband!
```

Write a pruning script in which all right and left arms have the same muscle size and strength.

Write a pruning script in which husband's right and left arms have the same muscle size and strength but differ from those of the wife's.

8.2.2 Conditional Rule-Based Pruning

Often selections for one entity depend on choices made for another entity. Different approaches to such constrained pruning are discussed in Zeigler and Hammonds (2007). MS4 Me supports rule-based pruning, where rules are the form:

If condition then action

where condition and action are selection statements such as discussed above. Consider, for example,

```
if Select small from size for Job
then Select miniPower from computePower for CPU!
```

Here, the selection of small from the specialization size constrains the choice of miniPower from the computePower specialization for CPU. In other words, this links the choice of computer power to the size of the task given to it. Note that these if-then rules are added to the SES specification file (*.ses). This is because they constrain pruning choices but do not actually make them.

Further, the selections in conditions and actions of rules can be context sensitive including the special case of context free. For example, the following is a set of context-free rules that relate the size of the job to choice of compute power required —note that each of the three sizes is covered.

```
if Select small from size for Job then Select miniPower from
computePower for CPU!
if Select medium from size for Job then Select mediumPower from
computePower for CPU!
if Select large from size for Job then Select maxPower from
computePower for CPU!
```

We can append the following context-sensitive rule to the above to state an exception to the default action:

```
if Select small from size for Job then Select mediumPower from
computePower for CPU under EeeFamily!
```

This combination has the effect, for a small job, of selecting miniPower from computePower except for the CPU under EeeFamily which is determined to be mediumPower. The following provides similar exceptions for other job sizes.

```
if Select medium from size for Job then Select miniPower from
computePower for CPU under HP!
if Select large from size for Job then Select mediumPower from
computePower for CPU under Apple!
```

An example of a pruning script is:

```
Select large from size for Job!
Select Apple from brand for Computer!
```

Here, pruning results in the selection of a large job and an Apple Computer. In this context, a context-sensitive rule determines that the computerPower is medium. If instead we have

```
Select EeeFamily from brand for Computer!
```

then the context-free rule applies and maxPower is selected for computePower.

Generally, a large job will be matched to a maxPower computer. However, due to the rule which falls within the Apple context, the result is selection of mediumPower.

Exercise

For the if-then rules just discussed, what selection is made for computePower for the following pruning script?

```
Select medium from size for Job!
Select Apple from brand for Computer!
```

8.2.3   The Unless or if-not Conditional Rule

So far we have had rules that check the truth of a condition and apply the associated action if it is true. However, the rule is mum on what to do if the condition turns out to be false. In this circumstance, the pruner will make a selection at random. However, we may not want to leave this decision to chance. This is where the utility of an if-not-then rule comes in. Consider the following SES:

```
From the system perspective, Monitor is made of Sensor and Patient!
From the monitor perspective, Sensor is made of MonitoringProgram and
SensorInterface!
MonitoringProgram can be lowSampling or highSampling in Rate!
Patient can be Exercising, Resting, Eating, or Sleeping in activity!
```

and the following if-then selection rule:

```
if select Exercising from activity for Patient then select
highSampling from Rate for MonitoringProgram!
```

Here, there is a definitive decision when the patient is exercising, namely to use a high rate of sampling for blood pressure, pulse, and other monitored variables. However, if the patient is not exercising, the pruner might select a high rate of sampling as well. Suppose that *unless* the patient is exercising a low sampling rate is preferred. Then, we can employ *the if-not-then* rule:

```
if not select Exercising from activity for Patient then select
lowSampling from Rate for MonitoringProgram!
```

The pruner handles this rule by transforming it into a set of if-then rules:

```
if select Resting from activity for Patient then select lowSampling
from Rate for MonitoringProgram!
if select Eating from activity for Patient then select lowSampling
from Rate for MonitoringProgram!
if select Sleeping from activity for Patient then select lowSampling
from Rate for MonitoringProgram!
```

We can see that each of the other activities is covered with the selection of a low sampling rate. Therefore, the effect of an if-not-then (also called an "unless") rule is to take the complement of the designated entity (e.g., exercising) in the set of entities of its specialization parent (namely resting, eating, sleeping) and create explicit rules to make the specified action for each. This spares you, the user, from having to do this operation manually to cover all the bases.

Exercise

Unless a power line carries very high current—in which case, it needs special high conductivity wiring—it only needs standard gauge wiring. Power lines can carry a range of currents that we can categorize as low, medium, high, and very high. Write an SES using if-not-then rules as appropriate to cover the various pruned entity structures that are allowable. Compare this SES with one that you write in which no if-not-then rules are used.

8.2.4 Example: Time-Critical Modeling and Simulation

Recall the SES for MSProcessSystem in Chap. 3 which has two aspects representing standard and fast versions of the modeling and simulation process. In a pruning script, the fast Process aspect can be selected with the statement:

```
select fastProcess from aspects for MSProcessSystem!
```

Now to link this selection to a characterization of the overall process, we can add the following specialization to the SES:

```
MSProcessSystem can be timeConstrained or timeUnconstrained in
constraint!
```

Exercise

Write an if-then rule of the form discussed above to force the selection of the fastProcess aspect when time Constrained is selected from the above specialization. How can the selection of the original process specialization be forced by the selection of time Unconstrained?

8.2.5   Random Selection from Choices Remaining

Random pruning makes selections remaining from those that have not been decided by applicable rules. For each entity occurrence that the pruning algorithm encounters, it first looks for rules in the script that apply to this occurrence. If such rules are found to apply to the occurrence under attention, the pruner makes a selection by following the conflict resolution method discussed previously (for rules that are applicable and have the same length the first in order is selected). However, if there are no applicable statements, then the pruner makes a random choice from the selection at hand. There may not be any applicable rules, because none have been placed in the *.ses file. However, this may also happen if the rules supplied do not completely cover all the occurrences of an entity. For example, in the example in Sect. 8.2, suppose the pruning script contains only the statement:

```
Select mediumPower from computePower for CPU under HP!
```

This determines the choice for the CPU under HP. However, because there is no longer the default to fall back on, this leaves open the choices to be made in the context of the other brands. This is where the pruner calls on a random number selection to make the open choice.

8.3   Executive Control of Experimentation

The kinds of complex models that we have seen above require effective simulation executives to control the experimentation such as running models with different starting conditions (including random number seeds), scanning through available alternatives as pruned from the SES and collecting data from multiple runs for analysis—either on the fly or offline. Although we can not provide a fixed algorithm for constructing such an executive, we can offer a methodology and supporting concepts that make this task more straightforward, reliable, and less time consuming. Moreover, the approach also lends itself to implementation on parallel and distributed platforms.

8.3.1   First Level Control of Simulation

We discuss three levels of control that increasingly rely on the SES and automated pruning to explore a family of models. At the lowest level, we employ the concepts of experimental frames to organize the experimental control.

The three types of components in an experimental frame, EF, are:

Generators—generate the input trajectories to the model,
Acceptors—check conditions for termination,
Transducers—collect data from the model while it is being executed.

Employing these components, we outline a pseudo-coded version of a generic execution control process. Then, we show how this pseudo-code can be implemented by modifying the autogenerated root execution method that it provides to execute a coupled model.

Executive control process (see Fig. 8.2)

1. Initialize the persistent data collection containers, dataStore
2. Set NumReps to desired number of repetitions
3. For each repetition in NumReps
4. Create new instance of ModelAndFrame, *mf*

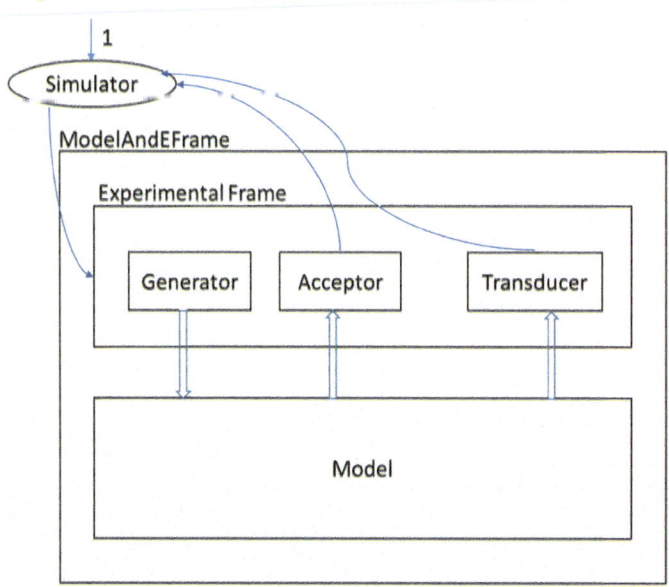

Fig. 8.2 Simulator in control of experimental frame coupled to model

5. Create a new Simulator instance, *sim* attached to *mf*
6. Access the Acceptor, and Transducer (*acc*, and *trans* resp.) components of *mf*
7. Tell *sim* to start (which starts the Generator)
8. Until iterations done{
9. For each iteration,
10. Tell *sim* to do one iteration,
11. Query *acc* for termination condition
12. If *acc* returns true {
13. Tell *sim* to stop
14. Query *trans* for data and store results in dataStore
15. }}

In MS4 Me, the program root execution method is the main routine for the class that contains the model. It is generated automatically for both coupled and atomic models and looks like this:

```
public static void main(String[] args){
        SimulationOptionsImpl options
                        = new SimulationOptionsImpl(args, true);
// Uncomment the following line to disable SimViewer for this
model
// options.setDisableViewer(true);
// Uncomment the following line to disable plotting for this
model
// options.setDisablePlotting(true);

        ModelAndFrame model = new ModelAndFrame ();
        model.options = options;
        if(options.isDisableViewer()){ // Command Line output
only
                Simulation sim = new
                SimulationImpl("ModelAndFrame
                Simulation",model,options);
                sim.startSimulation(0);
                sim.simulateIterations(Long.MAX_VALUE);
                }
                  else {
                  //Use SimViewer
                SimViewer viewer = new SimViewer();
                viewer.open(model,options);
        }
    }
```

Uncommenting to disable the viewer (and optionally the plotter), we focus on the code segment that relates to the pseudo-coded process described above. A template for modifying the given main routine together with correspondences to lines above is:

```
ModelAndFrame model = new ModelAndFrame ();
Simulation sim = new SimulationImpl("ModelAndFrame
Simulation",model,options);
        AtomicModel am =
            model.getComponentWithName("Acceptor");
            Acceptor acc = (Acceptor) am;
              am = model.getComponentWithName("Transducer");
              Transducer trans = (Transducer)am;
                sim.startSimulation(0);
                  for (int i = 0; i < NumIterations; i++) {
                    sim.simulateIterations(1);
                      if (acc.testIsTrue()){
                              sim.startSimulation();
                              trans.getResults();
break;
                    }
                  }
```

It may sometimes happen that the simulation fails to start—this can be tested with the method *isRunning()* as in:

```
If (sim.isRunning())

{ --do simulation iteration

sim.simulateIterations(1);

 --}

 else {--restart simulation

sim = new SimulationImpl("ModelAndFrame
Simulation",model,options);

sim.simulateIterations(1);

--}}

}
```

8.3.2   Second Level of Control with the SES

We add a next level of control of the simulation by generating models from a System Entity Structure (SES). This requires calling the SES functionality from the root execution program rather than from an interface that starts with the original SES development (as instantiated by the System Entity Structurer in MS4 Me.) Figure 8.3 shows how this can be done with the root execution method first (path 1) executing pruning and transformation of given SES and PES files and then (path 2) calling on the simulator to control simulation of the resulting model/frame pair.

Program Root Execution Method

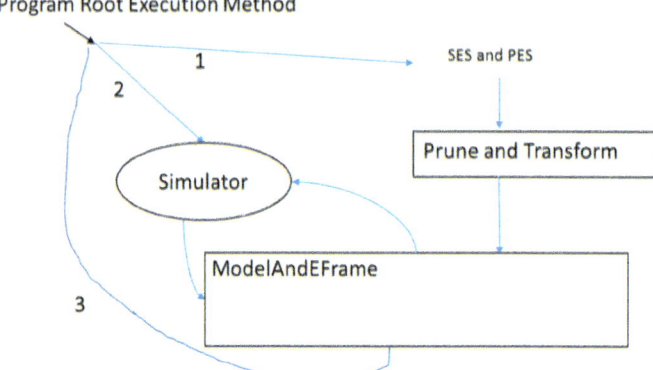

Fig. 8.3 SES control of model and experimental frame Simulation

In MS4Me, the main routine given above is extended with an initial part implementing the SES operations as illustrated below:

```
public static void main(String[] args){
String sesfile = "SESforModelAndFrame.ses";
String pesfile = "SESforModelAndFrame.pes";
 sesRelationExtend ses =
InternalUseSeS.getSesFromFileInstance(sesfile);
CoupledModelImpl model =

(CoupledModelImpl)InternalUseSeS.pruneNTransToGetModelInstance(se
s, pesfile);
//subsequently
Simulation sim = new SimulationImpl("ModelAndFrame
Simulation",model,options);

.........

}
```

Note that the class InternalUseSeS provides the pruning and transformation facilities required for interpreting the given ses and pes files.

8.3.3 Third Level of Control

Finally, we note that the code that generates and executes a model from an (ses, pes) pair can be wrapped within a loop of iterations (path 3) so that a sequence of model instances can be generated. The pes file can remain fixed throughout this sequence since the pruning process selects choices at random where the pes does not specify selections for alternatives. This generates samples of a subspace of the SES family of models specified by the selections actually made by the pes. The models so generated can be farmed out to processors or cores to be executed in parallel. Finally, including code for significance tests on statisticscollected in the loop within the loop can determine when it will terminate.

8.4   Summary

Recognizing that the exponentially growing combinatorial spaces that are set up by specialization and aspect selections can rapidly outstrip your capacity to do manual pruning, this chapter discussed automated pruning, an approach that allows the computer to make, some or all, pruning decisions. Enumerative pruning entirely eliminates manual pruning entirely but is restricted to small enough solution spaces. Random pruning samples from a large solution space to give a statistical picture of the space. Context-free and context-sensitive selection rules provide the ability to constrain the solution space to combinations that are more likely to meet your requirements. Where more than one rule applies to a selection, the pruner employs a conflict resolution method to resolve the decision. Random pruning starts from the choices remaining after the rules have been applied.

We presented a methodology and supporting concepts to create SES-based execution control of a family of models that lends itself to implementation on sequential computers as well as parallel and distributed platforms.

References

Zeigler, B. P., & Hammonds, P. (2007). *Modeling & simulation-based data engineering: introducing pragmatics into ontologies for net-centric information exchange*, Boston: Academic Press. 118 pages.
Zeigler, B. P., Kim, T. G., & Praehofer, H. (2000). *Theory of modeling and simulation: integrating discrete-event and continuous complex dynamic systems* (2nd ed.). Boston: Academic Press.

Part II
Advanced Concepts

DEVS Simulation Protocol

9

One of the hallmarks of DEVS modeling and simulation is its fundamental separation of models from the simulation engines that execute them. The alternative, which is more common in today's practice, is not to enforce such a clear separation and to indiscriminately mix constructs that relate to the model with those that relate to how it is being executed.

The separation between model and simulator leads to a layered architecture of services as illustrated in Fig. 9.1. Modeling services enable a modeler to specify a DEVS model, which is a description of a dynamic system. The simulation layer provides the ability to execute a model to get the results of simulation.

A DEVS modeler can write a DEVS model in any DEVS environment, say MS4 Me, and expect that it will be correctly simulated by a DEVS Simulator provided by that environment. Furthermore, in principle, the modeler can provide the model, as expressed in the DEVS formalism, to a friend who implements it in another environment, say ADEVS (Nutaro 2010). Now, if both environments implement the DEVS Abstract Simulator correctly, the friends are entitled to expect that the simulation results will be the same.

At this point, you have already become familiar with the Abstract DEVS Simulator, in the sense that you have worked with the methods in MS4 Me Java. As discussed in Chap. 4, these methods are in one-to-one correspondence with the DEVS characteristic functions of time advance, internal transition, external transition, confluent function, output function, and the associated sets of states, inputs, and outputs. To help grasp the concepts behind the Abstract DEVS Simulator, let's

© Springer International Publishing AG 2017
B.P. Zeigler and H.S. Sarjoughian, *Guide to Modeling and Simulation
of Systems of Systems*, Simulation Foundations, Methods and Applications,
DOI 10.1007/978-3-319-64134-8_9

consider an analogy with a calculation by a handheld calculator, or an equivalent application on your cell phone. The calculator program realizes an algorithm that specifies how it is to add, subtract, multiply, and divide—operations that are defined rigorously by arithmetic, the mathematical theory of numerical manipulations. There are many hand calculators in existence, and they are all assumed, indeed required, to correctly implement the mathematically specified operations. In the context of computing, these are abstractly specified because they don't refer to any program or computer. Nevertheless, because you were taught arithmetic, you know what to expect when you enter 2 + 2 into the calculator and would be disdainful of a device that gave 3 as an answer. In the same way that you enter an expression like 2 + 2 to a calculator and always expect 4 as the answer, you can provide a DEVS model to a DEVS simulation engine—and you should expect to get the same output no matter which engine you choose.

9.1 DEVS Simulation Protocol

As illustrated in Fig. 9.1, the tie that binds DEVS modeling and DEVS simulation services is the *DEVS Simulation Protocol* which is an extension of the DEVS Abstract Simulator in the context of networked environments. Figure 9.2 shows that the DEVS Protocol involves three types of objects, a coordinator, one or more simulators, each with an associated model (for simplicity, only one simulator and its model are shown). The coordinator has a coupled model associated with it. The DEVS Simulation Protocol specifies (1) *the interface that the model must present to the simulator* and (2) *the interface that the simulator must present to the coordinator to execute a valid DEVS simulation.*

The interface presented by the model to the simulator is determined by the Abstract DEVS Simulator.

Fig. 9.1 DEVS modeling and simulation layers

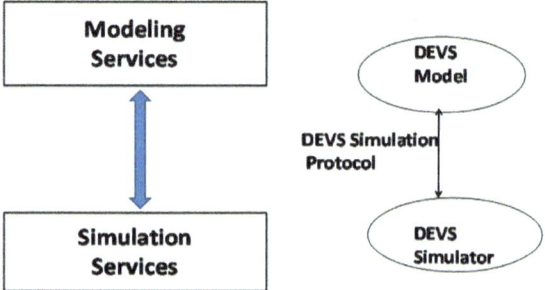

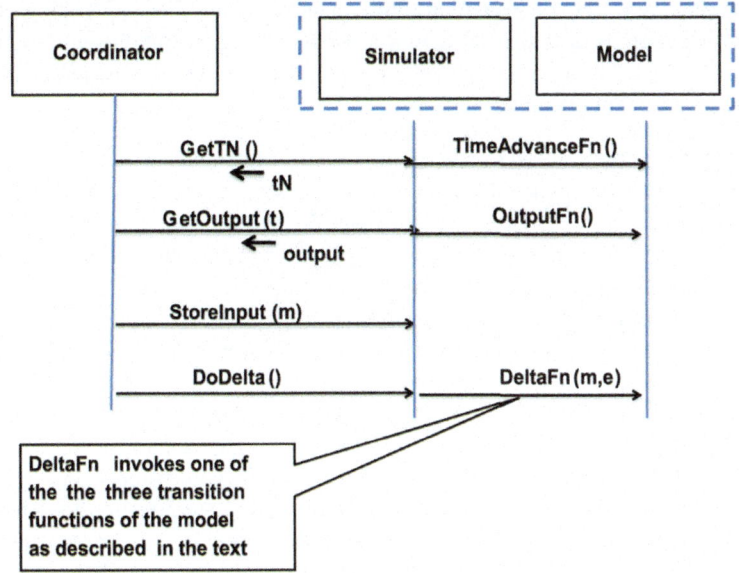

Fig. 9.2 DEVS Simulation Protocol

```
interface AbstractSimulator {
    public double TimeAdvanceFn();
    public message OutputFn();
    public void ExternalTransitionFn(message m,double
elapsedTime);
    public void InternalTransitionFn();
    public void ConfluentTransitionFn(message m,double
elapsedTime);
}
```

During an iterative cycle to be described, a simulator has to respond to opera-tions requested by a coordinator and specified in the following interface:

```
interface DevsProtocol {
    public double OperationGetTN();
    public message OperationGetOutput(double t);
    public void OperationStoreInput(message m);
    public void OperationDoDelta();
}
```

The iterative cycle is a repetition (until some condition dictates termination) of the following steps in which the coordinator issues the operation requests in the protocol and the simulator responds by interacting with its model using the Abstract DEVS Simulator:

Step (1)   OperationGetTN() requests the time of the simulator's next event—the simulator invokes its model's time advance function and adds the result to the time of last event to answer the coordinator's request.

Step (2)   OperationGetOutput(t) provides the current simulation time to the simulator and requests its output for that time, if any, in the form of a DEVS message—the simulator determines if the model is imminent (its time of next event equals the current time) and if so invokes the model's output function to get its output message.

Step (3)   OperationStoreInput(m) provides the input message, m, to the simulator, where m is a DEVS message which is a composite of messages sent to this simulator by other simulators. The coordinator gathered these messages in Step 2 and applied the coupling specification to determine which ones to package in this composite message.

Step (4)   OperationDoDelta() tells the simulator to cause its model's state transition—since the simulator knows the current time from step 2, as well as any input that it has received from step 3, it can determine whether the model is to undergo an internal, external, or confluent (both external and internal) transition. This is shown as DeltaFn(m, e) in Fig. 9.2, where m is the input message and e is the elapsed time which is the difference between the current time and the model's time of last event.

It is important to note that there are many ways in which this basic protocol can be implemented. Particularly, we do not require the strict adherence to the sequential control and message exchanges that the above rendering may appear to require—so long as the resulting behavior is what the protocol specifies. We discuss some important cases later.

9.2   MS4 Me Exposition of the DEVS Simulation Protocol

The DEVS formalism has an associated well-defined concept of simulation engine to execute models and generate their behavior. A coupled model in DEVS consists of component models and a coupling specification that tells how outputs of components are routed as inputs to other components.

The basic simulation paradigm is illustrated in Fig. 9.3. It consists of a coordinator that has access to the coupled model specification as well as simulators for each of the model components, only one of which is shown for illustration.

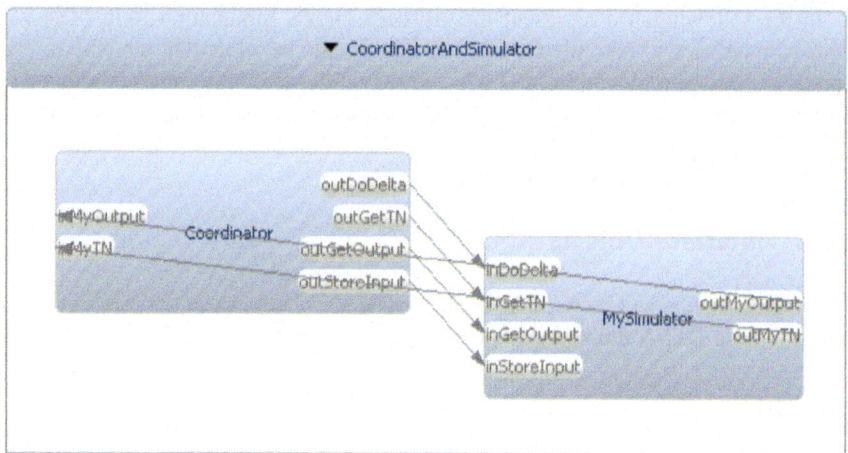

Fig. 9.3 MS4 Me simulation view of coordinator and simulator

We will use MS4 Me itself to explain the DEVS Simulation Protocol and the how the protocol works to correctly simulate DEVS models. The SES that gives rise to Fig. 9.3 is:

```
From the protocol perspective, CoordinatorAndSimulator is
made of Simulator and Coordinator!
From the protocol perspective, Coordinator sends GetTN to
Simulator!
From the protocol perspective, Coordinator sends GetOutput
to Simulator!
From the protocol perspective, Coordinator sends StoreInput
to Simulator!
From the protocol perspective, Coordinator sends DoDelta to
Simulator!
From the protocol perspective, Simulator sends MyTN to
Coordinator!
From the protocol perspective, Simulator sends MyOutput to
Coordinator!
```

Note that the interface between Coordinator and Simulator follows that given by the DEVSProtocol interface above. The coordinator performs time management and controls the message exchange among simulators in accordance with the coupled model specification. The simulators respond to commands and queries from the coordinator by referencing the specifications of their assigned models. The simulation protocol works for any model expressed in the DEVS formalism. It is an algorithm that has different realizations that allow models to be executed on a single host and on networked computers where the coordinator and component simulators are distributed among hosts.

In the following, we represent the Abstract DEVS Simulator within MS4 Me with its interfaces to both the Coordinator and its model. Note that the classes that appear are those employed in MS4 Me and may differ from the names employed in the general discussion above, e.g., MS4 Me employs MessageBag to represent the general concept of DEVS message.

9.2.1   Interface Objects

The objects exchanged between coordinator and simulators carry the relevant event times and the DEVS messages to be exchanged among them. They are defined as follows:

```
A DoubleEnt has value!
The range of DoubleEnt's value is double!
A NamedMessage has myName and myMessage!
The range of NamedMessage's myName is String!
The range of NamedMessage's myMessage is MessageBag!
```

9.2.2   Input and Output Ports

These objects are placed on the input and output ports by the operations invoked by the DEVS Simulation Protocol. In other words, the ports and types are defined to correspond to the operations in the interface of the DEVS Protocol.

For the Simulator, the port definitions are:

```
accepts input on GetTN!
accepts input on GetOutput with type DoubleEnt!
accepts input on StoreInput with type MessageBag!
accepts input on DoDelta!
generates output on MyTN with type DoubleEnt!
generates output on MyOutput with type NamedMessage!
```

These input and output ports are shown in Fig. 9.4.
For the Coordinator, the port definitions are:

```
accepts input on MyTN with type DoubleEnt!
accepts input on MyOutput with type NamedMessage!
generates output on GetTN!
generates output on GetOutput with type DoubleEnt!
generates output on StoreInput with type MessageBag!
generates output on DoDelta!
```

These input and output ports are shown in Fig. 9.5.
Note that the input and output ports of the simulator and coordinator match each other so that they can exchange data in a manner consistent with Fig. 9.3.

Fig. 9.4 Input and output
ports of simulator

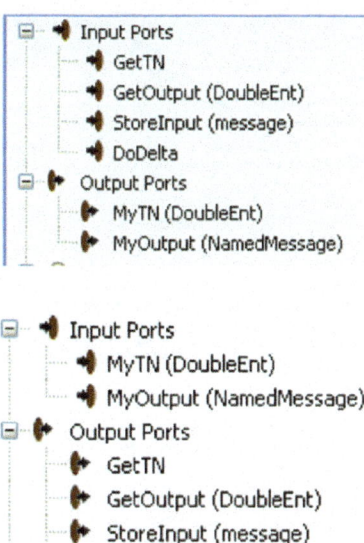

Fig. 9.5 Input and output
ports of coordinator

9.2.3 FDDEVS Specifications

The interaction between coordinator and simulator that carries out the iterative
cycle described earlier can be outlined in the FDDEVS natural language in the
following texts:

For the Coordinator, the FDDEVS specification is:

```
to start hold in sendGetTN for time 0!
after sendGetTN output GetTN!
output event for sendGetTN

from sendGetTN go to waitForAllTN!

passivate in waitForAllTN!

when in waitForAllTN and receive MyTN go to sendGetOutput!

hold in sendGetOutput for time 0!
after sendGetOutput output GetOutput!

from sendGetOutput go to waitForAllOutput!

passivate in waitForAllOutput!
when in waitForAllOutput and receive MyOutput go to
sendStoreInput!

hold in sendStoreInput for time 1!
after sendStoreInput output StoreInput!

from sendStoreInput go to sendDoDelta!

hold in sendDoDelta for time 1!
after sendDoDelta output DoDelta!
from sendDoDelta go to sendGetTN!
```

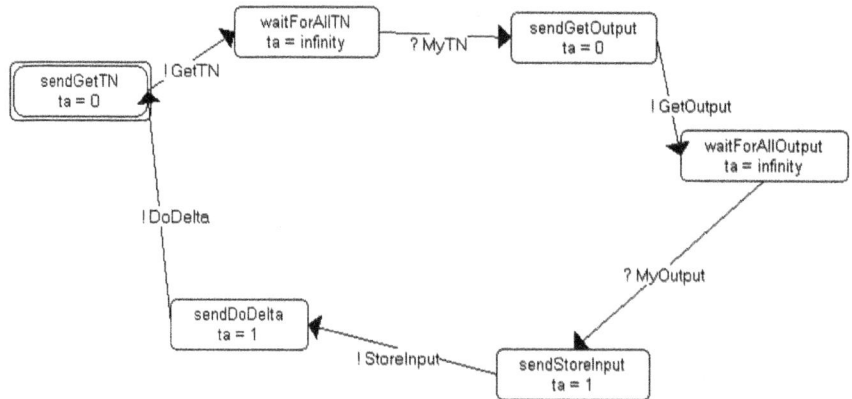

Fig. 9.6 Coordinator's state diagram

The state diagram generated from this text is shown in Fig. 9.6.

For the Simulator, the FDDEVS specification is:

to start passivate in waitForGetTN!
when in waitForGetTN **and receive**
GetTN **go to** sendMyTN!

hold in sendMyTN **for time** 0!
after sendMyTN **output** MyTN!
from sendMyTN **go to** waitForGetOutput!

passivate in waitForGetOutput!
when in waitForGetOutput **and receive** GetOutput **go to**
sendMyOutput!

hold in sendMyOutput **for time** 0!
after sendMyOutput **output** MyOutput!
from sendMyOutput **go to** waitForStoreInput!

passivate in waitForStoreInput!
when in waitForStoreInput **and receive** StoreInput **go to**
waitForMyDoDelta!

passivate in waitForMyDoDelta!
when in waitForMyDoDelta **and receive** DoDelta **go to**
waitForGetTN!

The state diagram generated from this text is shown in Fig. 9.7.

To create the simulation models, these specifications are filled in with tagged
blocks as illustrated in Appendices A and B.

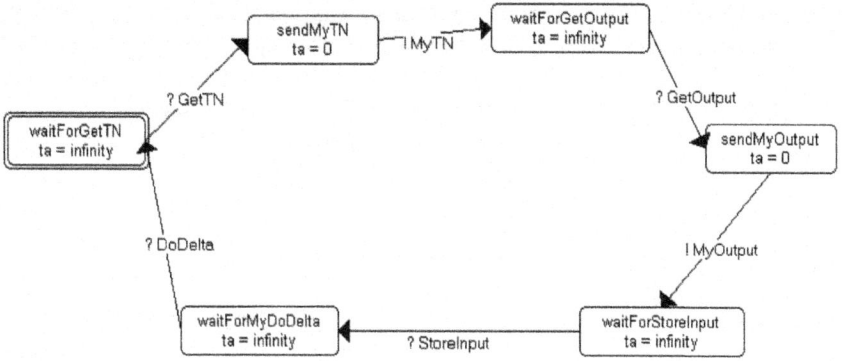

Fig. 9.7 Simulator's state diagram

Use the sequence design interface tool to develop a sequence diagram that describes the DEVS Simulation Protocol and generates SES and FDDEVS descriptions similar to those shown above.

9.3   Distributed Simulation Implementations of the DEVS Protocol

The DEVS Simulation Protocol is an abstract specification of how a distributed simulation should proceed to correctly generate the behavior of a DEVS coupled model. As emphasized before, this means that there can be many different implementations of the same specification. In the following discussion, we discuss three such implementations and illustrate them with formulations using MS4 Me. As before, in each implementation, the components of the coupled model are assigned to simulators in one-to-one fashion and the coupled model is assigned to the coordinator. However, the implementations differ in the degree to which the coordinator is involved in the routing of messages and management of time.

The implementations considered are:

1. **Standard DEVS Protocol**—the basic formulation in which the coordinator uses the coupling information supplied by its coupled model to distribute messages to the simulators.
2. **Peer Message Exchanging Implementation**—modifies the basic formulation by partitioning the coupled model coupling information according to its components and distributing these segments to the respective simulators. This allows the simulators to each exchange DEVS messages without intervention of the coordinator. There is an extensive literature on parallel and distributed simulation that extends this basic implementation (see, e.g., Zeigler et al. 2000 and Nutaro 2010.)

3. **Real-Time Message Exchanging Implementation**—takes the peer message
   exchanging implementation one step further by letting the simulators decide on
   when to execute their next events. This can work when the simulation proceeds
   in real time. This obviates the further coordination that is required when executed in logical time (see Gholami and Sarjoughian 2012 for an in-depth discussion of DEVS real-time simulation).

9.3.1 Standard DEVS Protocol

As expected, the coordinator and simulator definitions in Sect. 9.2 are employed in
the standard formulation. Furthermore, we capture the centrality of the coordinator
in controlling the simulators by plugging the coordinator and simulator into a larger
SES using a suitable multi-aspect as follows:

```
From the protocol perspective, DEVSDistributedSim is made
of Coordinator and Simulators!
From the multiSim perspective, Simulators are made of more
than one Simulator!
Simulator can be id in index!
From the protocol perspective, Coordinator sends GetTN to
all Simulator!
From the protocol perspective, Coordinator sends GetOutput
to all Simulator!
From the protocol perspective, Coordinator sends StoreInput
to all Simulator!
From the protocol perspective, Coordinator sends DoDelta to
all Simulator!

From the protocol perspective, all Simulator sends MyTN to
Coordinator!
From the protocol perspective, all Simulator sends MyOutput
to Coordinator!
```

Note the use of all-to-one and one-to-all coupling specification as discussed in
Chap. 6. Such coupling is illustrated in Fig. 9.8.

Fig. 9.8 Standard DEVS Protocol with multi-aspect coupling

9.3.2 Peer Message Exchanging Implementation

As described above, the Peer Message Exchanging DEVS Protocol modifies the basic formulation by distributing relevant segments of coupled model coupling to the respective simulators. The following FDDEVS specifications of the CoordinatorPeer and SimulatorPeer models illustrate how this allows the simulators to exchange DEVS messages without intervention of the coordinator.

CoordinatorPeer

```
to start hold in sendGetTN for time 0!
after sendGetTN output GetTN!
from sendGetTN go to waitForAllTN!

passivate in waitForAllTN!
when in waitForAllTN and receive MyTN go to sendSendOutput!

hold in sendSendOutput for time 0!
after sendSendOutput output SendOutput!
from sendSendOutput go to waitForAllDone!

passivate in waitForAllDone!
when in waitForAllDone and receive MyDone go to
sendDoDelta!

hold in sendDoDelta for time 1!
after sendDoDelta output DoDelta!
from sendDoDelta go to sendGetTN!
```

SimulatorPeer

```
to start passivate in waitForGetTN!
when in waitForGetTN and receive GetTN go to sendMyTN!

hold in sendMyTN for time 0!
after sendMyTN output MyTN!
from sendMyTN go to waitForGetSendOutput!

passivate in waitForGetSendOutput!
when in waitForGetSendOutput and receive SendOutput go to
sendMyOutput!

hold in sendMyOutput for time 0!
after sendMyOutput output MyOutput!
from sendMyOutput go to waitForStoreInput!

passivate in waitForStoreInput!
when in waitForStoreInput and receive StoreInput go to
sendMyDone!

hold in sendMyDone for time 0!
after sendMyDone output MyDone!
from sendMyDone go to waitForMyDoDelta!

passivate in waitForMyDoDelta!
when in waitForMyDoDelta and receive DoDelta go to
waitForGetTN!
```

A multi-aspect SES to couple the coordinator with simulators is and given by:

```
From the protocolPeer perspective, DEVSPeerDistributedSim
is made of CoordinatorPeer and SimulatorPeers!
From the sims perspective, SimulatorPeers are made of more
than one SimulatorPeer!
SimulatorPeer can be id in index!

From the protocolPeer perspective, CoordinatorPeer sends
GetTN to all SimulatorPeer!
From the protocolPeer perspective, CoordinatorPeer sends
SendOutput to all SimulatorPeer!

From the protocolPeer perspective, CoordinatorPeer sends
DoDelta to all SimulatorPeer!
From the protocolPeer perspective, all SimulatorPeer sends
MyTN to CoordinatorPeer!
From the protocolPeer perspective, all SimulatorPeer sends
MyDone to CoordinatorPeer!

From the protocolPeer perspective, all SimulatorPeer sends
outMyOutput to all SimulatorPeer as inStoreInput!
```

A pruning for three Simulators is illustrated in Fig. 9.7.

Note that in Fig. 9.9 the simulators exchange DEVS messages with each other directly without going through the coordinator.

Exercise

Prune the SES to select each of the alternative decompositions representing example implementations of the DEVS Protocol. Run the resulting models in the Simulation Viewer.

Fig. 9.9 Peer message exchanging implementation with multi-aspect coupling

Exercise

Use the sequence design interface tool to develop a sequence diagram that describes the Peer Message Exchange implementation of DEVS Simulation Protocol and generates SES and FDDEVS descriptions similar to those shown above.

Exercise

Provide tagged blocks for the SimulatorPeer and CoordinatorPeer FDDEVS specifications to implement the Peer Message Exchanging Implementation of the DEVS Simulation Protocol.

9.3.3   Real-Time Message Exchanging Implementation

As described earlier, the Real-Time Message Exchanging Implementation takes the peer message exchanging implementation one step further by letting the simulators decide on when to execute their next events to occur in real time. The following FDDEVS specifications of the CoordinatorRTPeer and SimulatorRTPeer models illustrate how this allows the simulators to determine their own time of next event in addition to exchanging DEVS messages without intervention of the coordinator.

CoordinatorRTPeer

```
to start hold in sendStart for time 0!

after sendStart output StartUp!
from sendStart go to sendStop!

hold in sendStop for time 100!
after sendStop output Stop!
from sendStop go to passive!
passivate in passive!
```

SimulatorRTPeer

```
to start passivate in waitForStart!
when in waitForStart and receive StartUp go to
sendMyOutput!
hold in sendMyOutput for time "modelTimeAdvance"!
after sendMyOutput output MyOutput!
from sendMyOutput to to sendMyOutput!
when in sendMyOutput and receive Stop go to waitForStart!
when in sendMyOutput and receive StoreInput go to
sendMyOutput!
```

A multi-aspect SES to couple the coordinator with simulators is given by:

```
From the realTimePeer perspective, DEVSDistributedSim is
made of CoordinatorRTPeer and SimulatorRTPeers!

From the rtsims perspective, SimulatorRTPeers are made of
more than one SimulatorRTPeer!

SimulatorRTPeer can be id in index!

From the realTimePeer perspective, CoordinatorRTPeer sends
Start to all SimulatorRTPeer!

From the realTimePeer perspective, CoordinatorRTPeer sends
Stop to all SimulatorRTPeer!
From the realTimePeer perspective, all SimulatorRTPeer
sends outMyOutput to all SimulatorRTPeer as inStoreInput!
```

Pruning for three Simulators is illustrated in Fig. 9.10.

Note that in Fig. 9.10, the simulators schedule their own next outputs and exchange DEVS messages with each other directly without going through the coordinator. A simulator invokes its model's time advance function to set the time at which to output a message (which can be infinity) and does this immediately after an internal, external, or confluent event. The role of the coordinator is reduced to stopping and starting a simulation run.

Exercise

Use the sequence design interface tool to develop a sequence diagram that describes the Real-Time Peer Message Exchange Implementation of the DEVS Simulation Protocol and generates SES and FDDEVS descriptions similar to those shown above.

Fig. 9.10 Peer message exchanging implementation with multi-aspect coupling

Provide tagged blocks for the SimulatorPeer and CoordinatorPeer FDDEVS specifications to implement the Real-time Peer Message Exchanging Implementation of the DEVS Simulation Protocol.

9.4   DEVS Protocol as a Standard for Simulation Interoperability

This book focuses on the DEVS modeling environment more than on the relation of DEVS to the wider world of simulation. However, one important question is the extent to which DEVS plays together with other simulation approaches. In the following, we study a typical Event-Scheduling simulator to understand how DEVS and non-DEVS simulators can be federated within the same distributed simulation.

9.4.1   DEVS Protocol with Event-Scheduling Simulator

An Event-Scheduling simulator typically can be described as follows:

- It maintains an event list ordered by time of next event.
- It has an operation, GetTimeOfImminentEvent (), which returns the time of the event at the top of the list, i.e., the smallest of all times of next event (call it tN).
- It has an operation, GetNRemoveImminentEvent(t), which stores the time, t, as the current time; then, if the current time equals tN, it also executes the code of the event at the top of the list (the imminent event) and as an effect of this code it may generate output and new events, as well as canceling already scheduled events; the output is returned as a result of the operation, and the events are inserted into the right places in the event list (these times of next event cannot be earlier than the current time).
- It has an operation, AddEvent(m, t), which treats the message, m, as an external input arriving at current time whose code is executed and may result in new events inserted into the right places in the event list.

We are interested in how to interoperate such an Event-Scheduling simulator with other models (DEVS and non-DEVS). To do so, we assign a DEVS Simulator to the event simulator which interacts with it and a DEVS Coordinator as illustrated in Fig. 9.11. In the following, we assume that the Event-Scheduling simulator accepts input and produces output in the form of DEVS messages. If it doesn't do this, then the DEVS Simulator has to be enhanced to make this translation. We return to this issue later.

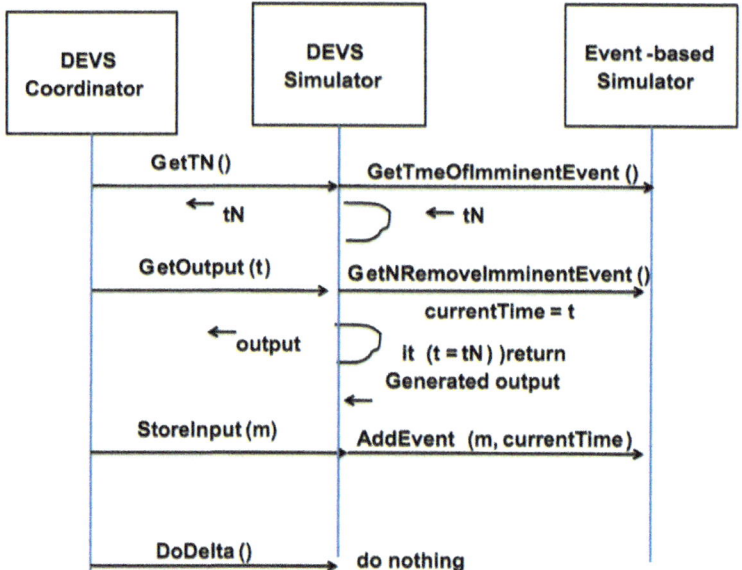

Fig. 9.11 DEVS Simulation Protocol applied to an event-based simulator

As shown in Fig. 9.11, the DEVS Simulator translates the DEVS Protocol operations sent to it by the DEVS Coordinator into operations that it invokes on the Event-Scheduling simulator. The operations GetTN, GetOutput, and StoreInput are translated into GetTimeOfImminentEvent, GetNRemoveImminentEvent, and AddEvent, respectively. The DoDelta operation is not passed on to the Event-Scheduling simulator since the latter has already executed its event code earlier.

Exercise

Develop a DEVS atomic model to implement an Event-Scheduling simulator. Use the approach of first developing an FDDEVS model and then enhance it using the process supported by MS4 Me. Hint: First define an event pair that pairs an event name with a time, e.g.,

```
An EventPair has myName and myTime!
The range of EventPair's myName is
String!
The range of EventPair's myTime is DoubleEnt!
```

Then, use a list to store and manage the event pairs appropriately. To represent how events cause outputs and schedule/cancel other events, define a method that interprets strings as instructions for generating outputs and manipulating the event list.

9.4.2 Lessons for Simulation Interoperability

From the operation of the Event-Scheduling simulator within the DEVS Protocol, we learn that there are two facets to interoperation of distributed simulators in general:

1. *Data exchange compatibility*—federates in a distributed simulation need to understand each other's messages. In the example, we assumed that the Event-Scheduling simulator understood DEVS messages and allowed that, more generally, the DEVS Simulator would have to translate between DEVS messages and a non-DEVS format. The general problem involves syntactic, semantic, and pragmatic agreements as explained in other publications (see Zeigler and Hammonds 2007; Himmelspach and Uhrmacher 2007; Kim et al. 2006; Seo and Zeigler 2012).
2. *Time management compatibility*—a correct simulation requires that all federates adhere to the same global time and their transitions and message exchanges are timed accordingly. One major feature of a DEVS-based approach is that the DEVS Simulation Protocol provides a means to enforce these timing requirements that is based on the DEVS framework, a sound theory of simulation (see Nutaro 2010 and Al-Zoubi and Wainer 2009 for a comparison with other approaches).

Developing models, simulations, and systems using MS4 Me enables you to work within a firm foundation of theory and concepts. DEVS's well-defined message and transition structures, with their well-defined semantics, give you assurance that your artifacts will stand their own ground when interfaced with non-DEVS artifacts. In subsequent chapters, we discuss how the DEVS Simulation Protocol is implemented in Data Distribution and Service-Oriented Computing middleware.

9.5 Summary

This chapter discussed the fundamental separation of models from the simulation engines that execute them intrinsic to the DEVS framework. This leads to a layered architecture of modeling and simulation services that provides the basis for simulating DEVS coupled models that are created in a DEVS modeling environment such as MS4 Me. We used MS4 Me itself to describe the operation of the DEVS Simulation Protocol in terms of its interface requirements. These require DEVS-based agreements between a component model and its simulator, and between the simulator and the coordinator that handles the time advance and message exchange within the coupled model. We showed how different implementations can satisfy the protocol using multi-aspects and uniform coupling patterns, which also illustrated the application of modeling concepts introduced earlier in the book. In addition, there was a discussion of how a typical event-based simulator can be simulated with the DEVS Protocol and casts light on the requirements for interoperability among DEVS and non-DEVS simulators.

A Extracts from Simulator.dnl

```
use tN with type double!
use tL with type double!
use t with type double!
use myInput with type MessageBag!
use myModel with type AtomicModelImpl!

a DoubleEnt has value!
the range of DoubleEnt's value is double!
a NamedMessage has myName and myMessage!
the range of NamedMessage's myName is String!
the range of NamedMessage's myMessage is MessageBag!

accepts input on GetTN!
accepts input on GetOutput with type DoubleEnt!
accepts input on StoreInput with type MessageBag!
accepts input on DoDelta!
generates output on MyTN with type DoubleEnt!
generates output on MyOutput with type NamedMessage!

Initialize variables
<%
myModel = new AtomicModelImpl("MyModel");
myModel.initialize();
tL = 0;
tN = tL + myModel.getTimeAdvance();
t = 0;
%> !
```

to start passivate in waitForGetTN!
when in waitForGetTN **and receive** GetTN **go to** sendMyTN!

external event for waitForGetTN **with** GetTN

```
<%
//no processing needed, just make the transition to send
the
time of next event, tN
%>!
```

hold in sendMyTN **for time** 0!
after sendMyTN **output** MyTN!
output event for sendMyTN

```
<%
//send tN out on port outMyTN
output.add(outMyTN,new DoubleEnt(tN));
%>!
```

from sendMyTN **go to** waitForGetOutput!
passivate in waitForGetOutput!
when in waitForGetOutput **and receive**
GetOutput **go to**
sendMyOutput!

external event for waitForGetOutput **with** GetOutput

```
<%
//get the value of the current time from the input port
GetOutput
$t = messageList.get(0).getData().getValue();$
%>!
```

hold in sendMyOutput **for time** 0!
after sendMyOutput **output** MyOutput!
output event for sendMyOutput

```
<%
//if myModel is imminent (has its tN equal to t), get
myModel's output and
//send it out on port MyOutput along with myName to
identify the source
NamedMessage sm = new
NamedMessage(getName(),computeOutput(t));
output.add(outMyOutput,sm);
%>!
```

from sendMyOutput **go to** waitForStoreInput!
passivate in waitForStoreInput!
when in waitForStoreInput **and receive** StoreInput **go to**
waitForMyDoDelta!

external event for waitForStoreInput **with** StoreInput

```
<%
//look through all messages in the incoming Bag
//if there is a message for me
//store the input message on port StoreInput in myInput
MessageBag bag = messageList.get(0).getData();
myInput = getMyMessage(bag);
%>!
```

passivate in waitForMyDoDelta!
when in waitForMyDoDelta **and receive** DoDelta **go to**
waitForGetTN!

external event for waitForMyDoDelta **with** DoDelta
```
<%
//execute myModel's transition: check whether this is a
confluent, internal, //or external event and apply the
designated transition function
doDelta();

%>!
```


B Extracts from Coordinator.dnl

use tN **with type** double!
use tL **with type** double!
//use t with type double!
use simulatorOutput **with type** HashSet!
use simulatorInput **with type** MessageBag!
use myModel **with type** CoupledModelImpl!

accepts input on MyTN **with type** DoubleEnt!
accepts input on MyOutput **with type** NamedMessage!
generates output on GetTN !
generates output on GetOutput **with type** DoubleEnt!
generates output on StoreInput **with type** MessageBag!
generates output on DoDelta!

Initialize variables
```
<%
myModel = new CoupledModelImpl("MyCoupledModel");
myModel.initialize();
tL = 0;
tN =0;
//t = 0;
%> !
```
to start hold in sendGetTN **for time** 0!
after sendGetTN **output** GetTN!
output event for sendGetTN
```
<%
//none needed
```

```
%>!
```

from sendGetTN **go to** waitForAllTN!

passivate in waitForAllTN!
when in waitForAllTN **and receive** MyTN **go to** sendGetOutput!

external event for waitForAllTN **with** MyTN

```
<%
tN = Double.MAX_VALUE;
    // get the time of next event from each Simulator
    // assume they all come in together

             // ensembleBag times =
x.valuesOnPort("inMyOutput");
         for (int i = 0;i<messageList.size();i++){
         double t =
         messageList.get(i).getData().getValue();
         // get their minimum
         if (t < tN)
         tN = t;
         }
%>!
```

hold in sendGetOutput **for time** 0!
after sendGetOutput **output** GetOutput!

output event for sendGetOutput

```
<%
//send the time of next event on port outGetOutput
//to enable simulator to check if it is imminent
//and respond with its output if it is
output.add(outGetOutput,new DoubleEnt(tN));
%>!
```

from sendGetOutput **go to** waitForAllOutput!
passivate in waitForAllOutput!
when in waitForAllOutput **and receive** MyOutput **go to**
sendStoreInput!

external event for waitForAllOutput **with** MyOutput

```
<%
//get the output from each Simulator
//assume they all come in together
  for (int i = 0;i<messageList.size();i++){
     NamedMessage simout = messageList.get(i).getData();
//store each message with the simulator
                   simulatorOutput.add(simout);
                   }
//then apply the coupling to get the messages to be sent to
each simulator
                   simulatorInput =
```

```
ApplyCoupling(simulatorOutput);
%>!
```

hold in sendStoreInput **for time** 1!
after sendStoreInput **output** StoreInput!

output event for sendStoreInput
```
<%
//send each simulator the collected inputs
output.add(outStoreInput, simulatorInput);
%>!
```
from sendStoreInput **go to** sendDoDelta!

hold in sendDoDelta **for time** 1!
after sendDoDelta **output** DoDelta!
from sendDoDelta **go to** sendGetTN!

References

Al-Zoubi, K., & Wainer, G. (2009). Performing distributed simulation with RESTful web-services approach. In *Proceedings of Winter Simulation Conference*, Austin, TX (pp. 1323–1334).

Gholami, S., & Sarjoughian, H. S. (2012). Real-time network-on-chip simulation modeling. In G. Riley, F. Quaglia, & J. Himmelspach (Eds.), *SIMUTOOLS, Fifth International Conference on Simulation Tools And Techniques*, 19th–23rd March 2012. Italy, Desenzano del Garda: ACM.

Himmelspach, J., & Uhrmacher, A. M. (2007). Plug'n simulate. In *Proceedings of the 40th Annual Simulation Symposium (ANSS'07)*, Norfolk, VA, March 2007 (pp. 137–143).

Kim, J.-H., Hong, S.-Y., & Kim, T. G. (2006). Design and implementation of simulators interoperation layer for DEVS simulator. In *Proceedings of M&S-MTSA'06*, Ottawa, July 2006 (pp. 195–199).

Nutaro, J. (2010). Building simulation software: Theory. In *Algorithms, and Applications*. New York: Wiley.

Seo, C., & Zeigler, B. P. (2012). Simulation model standardization through web services: Interoperation and federation on the DEVS/SOA platform. In *DEVS Integrative M&S Symposium Proceedings of the Spring Simulation Conference*, Orlando, FL, March 2012.

Zeigler, B. P., Kim, T. G., & Praehofer, H. (2000). *Theory of modeling and simulation: Integrating discrete-event and continuous complex dynamic systems* (2nd ed.). Boston: Academic Press.

Zeigler, B. P., & Hammonds, P. (2007). *Modeling & simulation-based data engineering: Introducing pragmatics into ontologies for net-centric information exchange*. Boston: Academic Press, 448 p.

Dynamic Structure: Agent Modeling and Publish/Subscribe

10

So far, the models we have considered were all static structure in the sense that while their states changed, their internal structure did not. In this chapter, you will learn more about dynamic structuring of models where you can specify how models can change their structure during run-time. We discuss agent modeling using dynamic structure capabilities. This capability then shows up in our consideration of mechanisms for implementing message exchanges in today's information technology. We will discuss in some detail one important mechanism, called Publish/Subscribe (P/S) that we describe using dynamic structuring. Then, we will go on to discuss a Data Distribution Service that provides middleware based on the P/S paradigm. Finally, we discuss how the DEVS Simulation Protocol for distributed simulation can be implemented in such middleware, and show how P/S can be employed to track mobile agents in a model.

10.1 Dynamic Structure and Agent Modeling

Recall the simple work flow of Chap. 4 in which jobs were sent around and processed. There, a job was an instance of class WordToDo whose state would be changed by the processing it was undergoing. Let's call a job object that can interact with a processor, a smart object, or an Actor. Also, let's define an Agent to be a processor that can interact with an Actor. Thus, an Agent is a processor that can receive an Actor (or smart object) as input and then interact with it through input/output ports. Agents in DEVS can have a wide range of cognitive abilities, particularly those that exploit the intrinsic temporal expressive power of DEVS. Although we cannot get into this in much depth, there is a growing literature on DEVS agent concepts to consult for further information (Duboz et al. 2006; Muzy et al. 2007; Uhrmacher and Kullick 2000; Douglass and Mittal 2012). Here, we focus on the dynamic structure of agents; let's see how this interaction can look. Consider this SES:

© Springer International Publishing AG 2017
B.P. Zeigler and H.S. Sarjoughian, *Guide to Modeling and Simulation of Systems of Systems*, Simulation Foundations, Methods and Applications, DOI 10.1007/978-3-319-64134-8_10

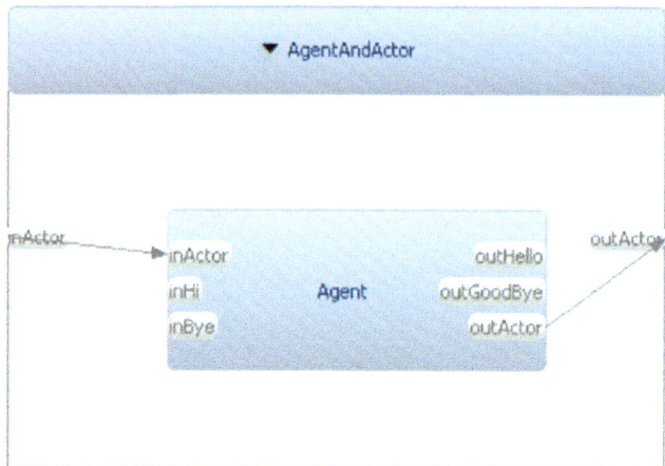

Fig. 10.1 Initial structure state of AgentAndActor model

From the dynamic **perspective,** AgentAndActor **is made of**
Agent!
From the dynamic **perspective,**AgentAndActor **sends** Actor **to**
Agent!
From the dynamic **perspective,**Agent **sends** Actor **to**
AgentAndActor!

After pruning, we have a coupled model with just an Agent component as shown in Fig. 10.1.

We start by injecting an input on port Actor that has a value that is an instance of Actor. In responding to this input, the Agent adds the incoming model (Actor) to the coupled model in which it is contained. The Agent also adds coupling required for it to communicate with the Actor instance which is now its peer component (Fig. 10.2). To add a model to the simulation, you use the dynamic structure method in a tagged code block:

```
addChildModel(model).
```

Here, *model* is either atomic or coupled, and the *addChildModel* method is invoked by an existing component of the parent coupled model. In this example, the model to be added is the Actor, the parent coupled model is AgentAndActor, and the existing component is Agent. To add coupling, you use a coupling statement:

```
addCoupling(source,srcport,destination,destport)
```

where each of the four arguments is a string with the source and destination are names of components in the parent coupled model. For example, in

```
addCoupling(this.getName(),"outHello","Actor","inHello");
```

the source is the name of the Agent while "Actor" is the name of the actor.

The Agent and Actor interact—converse—which will change the states of both. At the end of the conversation, the Actor sends itself (in its current state) to the Agent. The Agent then removes the Actor from the coupled model and sends the Actor instance to the output port outActor. The removal is done using the method

```
removeChildModel(model)
```

in similar manner to the invocation of the addChildModel method earlier. The end state of the AgentAndActor coupled model is the initial state in which the Agent is the only component.

Exercise

Create a coupled model that consists of two AgentAndActor models as components and coupled so that when an Actor is output from the first, the actor is input to the second. Hint: Start with the SES:

From the dynamic **perspective,** TwoAgentAndActor **are made of**
First_AgentAndActorPrune **and** Second_AgentAndActorPrune!
From the dynamic **perspective,** TwoAgentAndActor **sends** Actor
to First_AgentAndActorPrune!
From the dynamic **perspective,** First_AgentAndActorPrune **sends**
Actor **to** Second_AgentAndActorPrune!
From the dynamic **perspective,** Second_AgentAndActorPrune
sends Actor **to** TwoAgentAndActor!

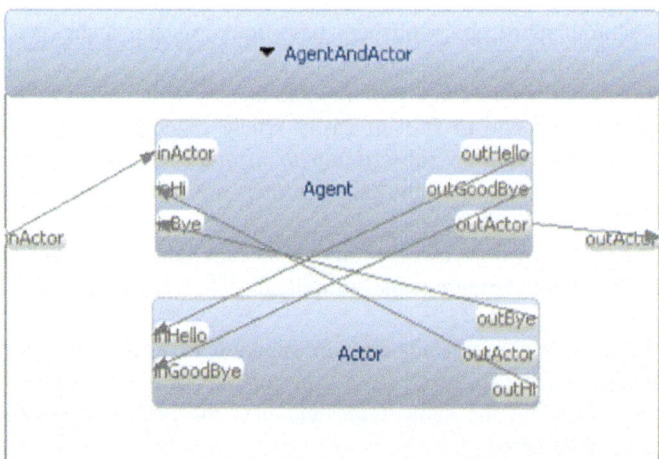

Fig. 10.2 Subsequent structure state of AgentAndActor model

Write an enhanced FDDEVS model that periodically generates actors that can be sent as inputs to interact with agents as in Fig. 10.1. Hint: Modify an agent to become a generator by going back to its initial state through an internal transition. Add your actor generator to the SES above to have it generate and start actors moving through locations of agent interaction.

10.2   Publish/Subscribe Data Distribution

We now discuss the mechanism for exchange of information called Publish/Subscribe (P/S) . Basically in the paradigm, a server in a network, here called a *PublishSubscribeRouter*, or Router for short, can be contacted by any client to either register as a *Subscriber* or a *Publisher* for a *topic*. A *topic* is roughly similar to a topic in ordinary language, such as the weather and the economy. However, in the P/S context, topics can be defined by the system administrator and do not necessarily have broader linguistic connotations. Indeed, topics behave as communication channels, and we shall implement them as ports in a DEVS coupled model. To do this, we use the dynamic structuring capability discussed in Sect. 10.1.

To register as a *publisher* for a topic, a client issues a request with its identity (in the simplest case, its name) and the topic name. After confirmation, the client can then "publish" on that topic which means to issue updates that contain data under that topic and that data will be routed to all clients that have subscribed to that topic. To *subscribe* to a topic, a client issues a subscription request bearing its name and topic similar to the publish request. The interesting thing about this approach, called *data-centric*, is that in order to exchange information clients only have to know which topics are available for publication or subscription. In contrast, in a connection-centric approach, publishers have to know the addresses and other information of particular computers on the network to send data to them. The data-centric concept makes for a very flexible and dynamic architecture in which connections can be made or broken easily where requests can be made to be removed from publication or subscription to a topic. Of course, this flexibility places performance demands on the central router as it becomes a bottleneck as all data exchanges go through it.

To explain the interactions involved in the P/S paradigm, let's follow an example scenario by stepping through some simplified FDDEVS models for the three participants.

Figure 10.3 displays a sequence diagram showing a scenario in which publisher issues a publish request followed by a topic update. A subscriber then issues a subscription request on the same topic and gets the update. Let's look at the participants in more detail.

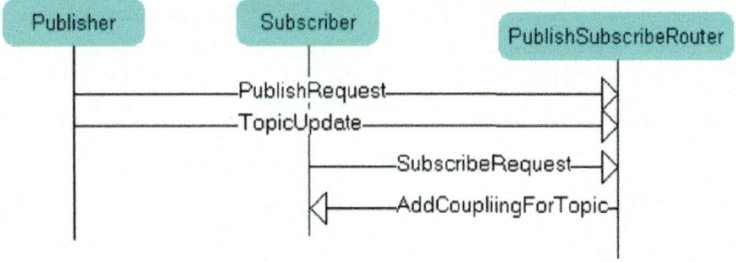

Fig. 10.3 Sequence diagram with simple scenario

10.2.1   Publisher

Below is the FDDEVS natural language for the Publisher and the corresponding state diagram (Fig. 10.4). The Publisher starts the sequence by issuing a request to publish.

```
to start hold in doPublishRequest for time 0.0!
after doPublishRequest output PublishRequest!
```

The publish request is a pair of strings bearing its name and the topic on which it seeks to publish.

```
from doPublishRequest go to sendTopicUpdate!
hold in sendTopicUpdate for time 10.0!
after sendTopicUpdate output TopicUpdate!
from sendTopicUpdate go to sendTopicUpdate!
```

As evident in the above text and in the self-loops of Figs. 10.4 and 10.5, after some time, the Publisher starts updating information about the topic. The data structure sent to the Router is a triple of strings, publisher name, topic name, and information on this topic.

Fig. 10.4 State diagram of publisher

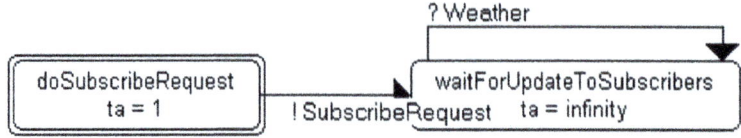

Fig. 10.5 State diagram of subscriber

10.2.2 Subscriber

Below is the FDDEVS model for the Subscriber and its state diagram (Fig. 10.3).

```
to start hold in doSubscribeRequest for time 1!
after doSubscribeRequest output SubscribeRequest!
```

Before it can receive updates on a topic, a subscriber must send a subscription request to the Router. Such a request is pair (subscriber name, topic name). The effect of this request is to add a coupling from the Router to the Subscriber for the topic, which becomes an input port with the same name.

Note that this is where dynamic structuring capability of MS4 Me is exploited. Figure 10.6 shows the Weather coupling from the Router to the Subscriber added dynamically by the Router in response to a subscription request to the Weather topic. A weather report is shown as a message update on Weather port. Now, when the Router puts a value on the output port for the topic, it will propagate to the Subscriber on this port. So as said earlier, in our DEVS representation of the P/S paradigm, topics are represented by ports.

Continuing with the FDDEVS text:

```
from doSubscribeRequest go to waitForUpdateToSubscribers!
passivate in waitForUpdateToSubscribers!
when in waitForUpdateToSubscribers and receive
UpdateToSubscribers go to waitForUpdateToSubscribers!
```

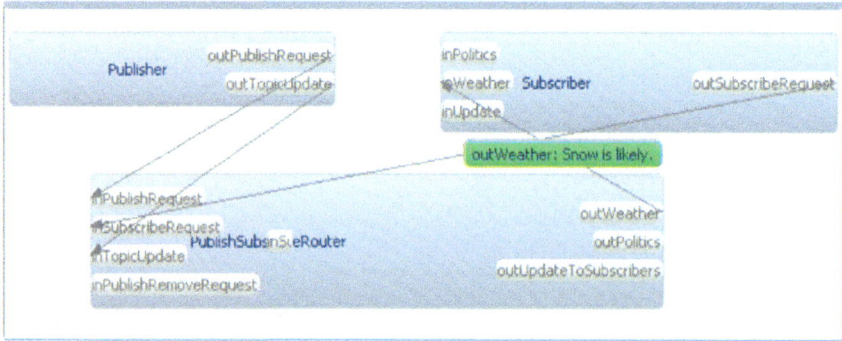

Fig. 10.6 Simulation Viewer of simple scenario showing added politics coupling

Now that the Subscriber has put in a subscription request for a topic; the Subscriber receives updates on that topic from the Router soon after the latter receives them from the Publisher.

10.2.3 PublishSubscribeRouter

As key component in this paradigm, the operation of the P/S Router is described through its FDDEVS model (Fig. 10.7) below and interspersed explanations. Excerpts from the enhanced MS4 Me Java model are given in Appendixes A and B.

```
to start passivate in waitForInput!
when in waitForInput and receive PublishRequest go to
handlePublishRequest!
```

The Router gets the (publisher, topic) pair in the incoming PublishRequest and stores it in a collection of such pairs, generally called a Relation, in this case, the PublisherTopic relation.

```
when in waitForInput and receive SubscribeRequest go to
handleSubscribeRequest!
```

The Router gets the (subscriber, topic) pair in the incoming SubscriberRequest, stores it in the SubscriberTopic relation, and adds a coupling to connect the topic output port of the Router to the topic input port of the subscriber.

```
when in waitForInput and receive TopicUpdate go to
sendUpdateToSubscribers!
```

The Router gets the (publisher, topic, TopicUpdate) triple in the incoming TopicUpdate message and then: (1) checks to see if the publisher and topic are in the PublisherTopic relation, and (2) if so, it places the TopicUpdate on the topic output port so that it is sent to all of the subscribers in the SubscriberTopic relation that have subscribed with the topic.

```
when in waitForInput and receive PublishRemoveRequest go to
handlePublishRemoveRequest!
```

The Router gets the (publisher, topic) pair in the incoming PublishRequest and removes it from the PublisherTopic relation. The rest of the description follows without comment:

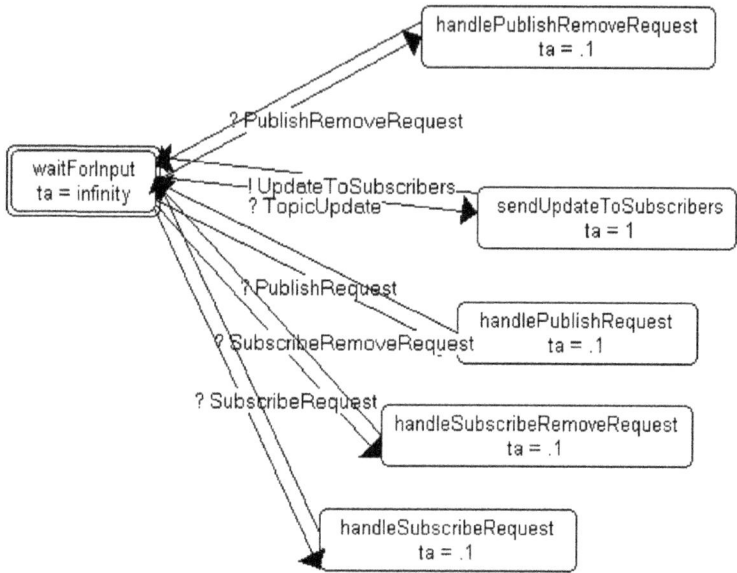

Fig. 10.7 State diagram of router

```
when in waitForInput and receive SubscribeRemoveRequest go
to handleSubscribeRemoveRequest!

hold in handlePublishRequest for time .1!
from handlePublishRequest go to waitForInput!

hold in handleSubscribeRequest for time .1!
from handleSubscribeRequest go to waitForInput!

hold in sendUpdateToSubscribers for time 1!

after sendUpdateToSubscribers output UpdateToSubscribers!
from sendUpdateToSubscribers go to waitForInput!

hold in handlePublishRemoveRequest for time .1!
from handlePublishRemoveRequest go to waitForInput!

hold in handleSubscribeRemoveRequest for time .1!
from handleSubscribeRemoveRequest go to waitForInput!
```

10.2.4 Publish Subscribe Operation

The behavior of the P/S Router implemented above can be tested under various
circumstances using an SES such as the sequence shown in Fig. 10.8.

Here, the first publisher requests to publish to a topic, e.g., Politics, while the
first subscriber requests to subscribe to the same topic. Likewise, the second
publisher and subscriber request to publish and subscribe, respectively, to another

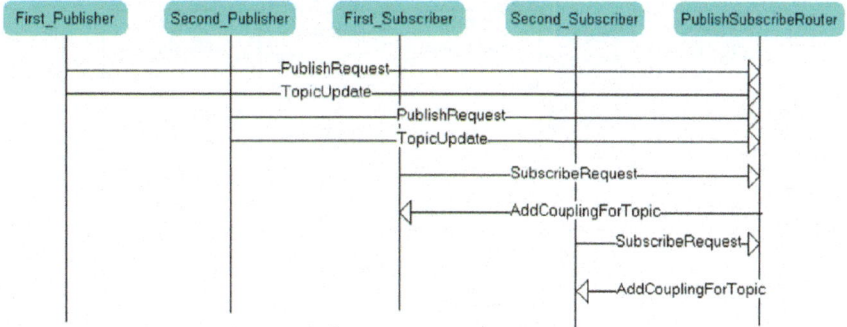

Fig. 10.8 Sequence diagram for test scenario

topic, e.g., Weather. Couplings from the Router to the subscribers were added as a result of the subscription requests by exploiting the dynamic structure capability of MS4 Me. Also note that updates from the first and second publishers are published to the correct subscribers due to the addition of the right couplings.

Exercise

Create a coupled model that implements the behavior of Fig. 10.8. Hint: Prune the SES just given and run the PES in the Simulation Viewer.

10.3   Data Distribution Service

Data Distribution Service (DDS) is a data-centric standard for real-time communication middleware that is based on the Publish/Subscribe paradigm discussed in Sect. 10.1. It automatically handles all aspects of message delivery (e.g., addressing, marshalling, delivery, flow control, and retries), allows the user to specify Quality of Service (QoS) parameters, and provides participants/nodes with automatic discovery mechanisms for dynamic plug and play and anonymous communication (OMG 2007; Kwon et al. 2011). The DDS standard defines several classes that together realize the P/S behavior. Among the basic ones are:

- Domain—a container for a set of applications that are to be federated through the service
- Topic—a class whose instances provide channels of communication with associated data types
- Publisher—a class for publishing data to one or more topics
- Data Writer—a class that supports publishing to topics and their associated data types by writing data in the required format (marshalling)
- Subscriber—a class for subscribing to one or more topics

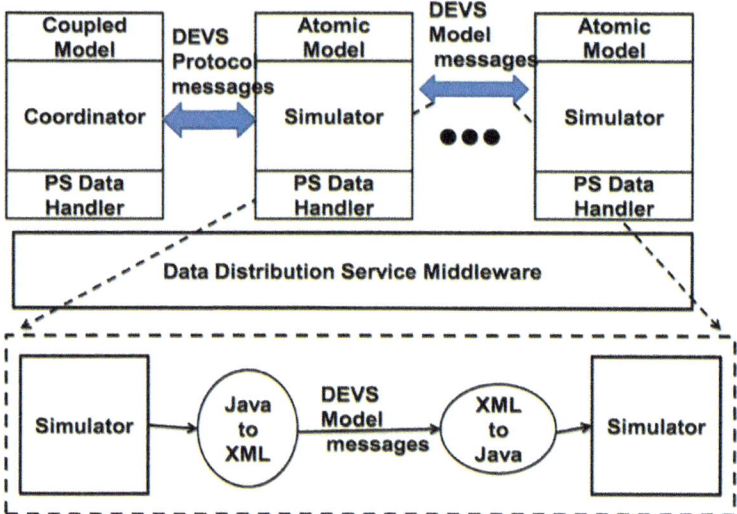

Fig. 10.9 DEVS/DDS distributed simulation architecture

- Data Reader—a class that supports subscribing to topics and their associated data types by unmarshalling the data from the incoming publication
- Participant—a container for publishers and subscribers in a particular domain
- Application—a program that contains participants.

In DDS terminology, a distributed simulation consists of participants (the Coordinator and Simulators) located on various nodes in a data network. To implement such a distributed simulation in DDS using a publish/subscribe mechanism, we utilize DDS topics (communication channels) to exchange information among such participants. These topics include DEVS Simulation Protocol control commands and the DEVS data messages. As shown in Fig. 10.9, DEVS/DDS simulation architecture has several components for DEVS models and simulators as well as DDS middleware. A DEVS participant contains a DEVS model and a simulator (or coordinator) which interfaces to data writers and readers that mediate the publication and subscription processes. The DDS middleware generates a domain for DEVS/DDS simulation and topics for sending and receiving data. A DEVS/DDS coordinator manages the DEVS Protocol with data written and read using a set of topics to be described. The coordinator disseminates DEVS messages using coupling information from its associated DEVS coupled model.

We note that a DEVS model in a simulator participant can be an atomic model or a coupled model. According to the closure on the coupling property of DEVS, a coupled model can be described as an equivalent atomic model. The DEVS/DDS simulation environment provides a converter class to translate behaviors of a coupled model to those of an atomic model. Therefore, any kind of DEVS models can be simulated on DEVS/DDS simulation environment.

10.3.1   DEVS Simulation Protocols in DDS

Table 10.1 defines the topics through which the DEVS Simulation Protocol control information and the DEVS data messages are exchanged between a coordinator and simulators. A single cycle of the baseline DEVS Simulation Protocol (Chap. 9) is given by:

1. The coordinator publishes to the topic GetTN which is received by each of the simulators as subscribers.
2. Each simulator publishes its next event time to topic MyTN.
3. The coordinator publishes to the topic GetOutput which is received by each of the simulators as subscribers. The global time of next event, obtaining as the minimum of the simulator times of next event, is provided as data within the GetOutput topic.
4. Each imminent simulator publishes its model's output to topic MyOutput, where the form of the publication is a pair (model name, model output) and the model's output is a DEVS message.
5. As subscriber to MyOutput, the coordinator collects all the simulators' publications.
6. The coordinator applies coupling to the simulators' publications and publishes the individual input for each model to a specific topic, StoreInputForModel. This assures that each model receives the input intended for it (and not some other model's input).
7. The coordinator publishes to the topic DoDelta which is received by each of the simulators as subscribers.

This is one cycle of a baseline DEVS Protocol implementation. The coordinator and the simulators repeat the DEVS cycle ad infinitum or until terminated by some means. The coordinator and the simulators are processes to implement a DEVS simulation. Therefore, we need to synchronize them to follow the DEVS simulation

Table 10.1 Topics and associated publishers and subscribers for the baseline DEVS Protocol

Topic	Role	Publisher	Subscribers
GetTN	Asks all the simulators for their next event tune	Coordinator	Simulators
MyTN	Provides the next event time of a simulator	Simulator	Coordinator
GetOutput	Asks all the simulators for their outputs	Coordinator	Simulators
MyOutput	Provides the output of a simulator	Simulator	Coordinator
For each Model, StoreInputForModel	Provides each Model's input to its assigned simulator	Coordinator	Simulator for Model
DoDelta	Tells all the simulators to apply their transition function	Coordinator	Simulators

protocol. We put a wait function to subscription parts. For example, the coordinator waits until receiving data from Topic GetTN. The processes of the coordinator and the simulators are blocked until the coordinator goes to the next step in the cycle.

Exercise

One way to_terminate simulation is when the minimum next event time reaches infinity. Add a terminate topic to Table 10.1 that allows the coordinator to tell the simulators to stop executing as soon as they receive data from this topic.

10.3.2   DEVS Messages

DEVS message exchange occurs in steps 5 and 6 of the DDS implementation of the baseline DEVS Simulation Protocol. Recall that a DEVS message is a collection of port-value pairs. To implement this concept in a middleware such as DDS, we need an implementation that can be understood in a platform-neutral manner. In other words, the participants (coordinator and simulators) must be able to read and write such messages in a neutral data transport language different from the programming language in which their underlying DEVS simulation engines are implemented. XML has become a standard for such neutral data exchange. In DDS, this means that the DataWriters for publishers encode DEVS messages from the platform code, say Java, to XML and conversely, DataReaders decode the XML into a subscriber's code, say C++. To illustrate how such marshalling and unmarshalling of data is implemented, suppose that a Job has the variables Jid and processingTime. Then, a particular instance of this class might have values 2 and 10.4, respectively, and when appearing on a port inJob would be represented in XML as:

```
<?xml version="1.0" encoding="UTF-8"?>
<MessageBag ID = "0">
  <Message>
     <Port>
         <inJob/>
     </Port>
     <Data>
         <Job Jid = "2" processingTime = "10.4">
            </Job>
     </Data>
  </Message>
</MessageBag >
```

Indeed, this might be a message received by a job processor representing a job to be done arriving at its input port, inJob. Furthermore, there may be several port-value pairs in a message. For example, if a completed job and a newly started job both appear at the same time at a transducer, its incoming message would take the form:

```xml
<?xml version="1.0" encoding="UTF-8"?>
<MessageBag ID = "0">
   <Message>
      <Port>
          <inAriv/>
      </Port>
      <Data>
          <Job Jid = "2" processingTime = "10.4">
             </Job>
      </Data>
   </Message>
    <Message>
      <Port>
         <inSolved/>
      </Port>
      <Data>
         <Job Jid = "3" processingTime = "2.5">
            </Job>
      </Data>
   </Message>
</MessageBag >
```

Here, there are two job instances, one associated with input port Ariv and the other with input port Solved of the transducer.

Seo and Zeigler (2012) give more details on a tool for automatically creating XML Schema from DEVS Messages and conversely creating such classes given XML Schema for data types. Such Schema is placed into a namespace that can be accessed by DEVS developers for use in their models.

10.3.3   Relating Ports and Topics

Let's return to examine step 6 of the DDS implementation of the baseline DEVS Simulation Protocol. Here, the coordinator publishes DEVS messages to topics specific to each model, i.e., StoreInputForModel. Such a highly specific topic (with one subscriber) is allowed within the P/S framework. However, it does violate the spirit of P/S in which topics are independent from publishers and subscribers. Dependency between topics and participants has the effect of reducing flexibility since new participants cannot be as easily added to the simulation. Moreover, such specific topics reduce the efficiency of messaging relative to more general topics provided that more general topics result in the right behavior. We can gain some insight into the specificity of topics from concept of "all" and "each" introduced for coupling in multi-aspects (Chap. 6). Consider an SES for the SimonSays game:

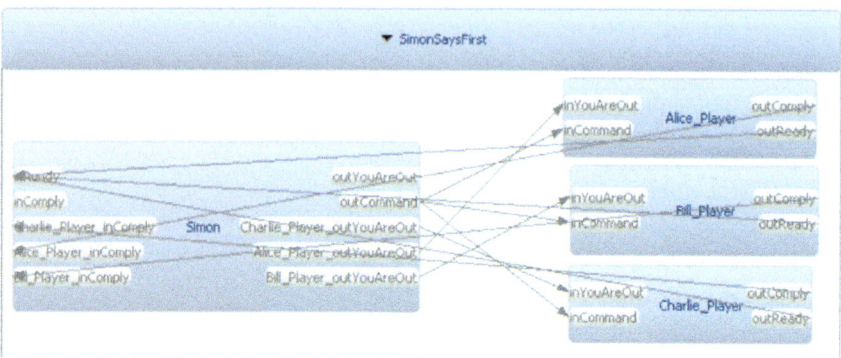

Fig. 10.10 Displaying the "all" and "each" coupling

From the game **perspective, the** Game **is made of** Simon **and**
Players!
From the player **perspective,** Players **are made of more than**
one Player!
Player **can be** Alice, Bill, **or** Charlie **in** identity!
From the game **perspective,** Simon **sends** Command **to all**
Player!
From the game **perspective,** Simon **sends** YouAreOut **to each**
Player!
From the game **perspective, all** Player **sends** Ready **to** Simon!
From the game **perspective, each** Player **sends** Comply **to**
Simon!

The effects of the "all" and "each" on the generated coupling are shown in
Fig. 10.10. This situation is portrayed in Table 10.2 which relates ports, the role
they play with respect to topics, and whether they need to be individualized to
models or not.

Consider the topic "Command." Since Simon sends the same command to all the
players, Simon can publish to the "Command" topic which can be a topic shared by
all subscribers. However, since YouAreOut only goes to non-compliant players, it
must be individualized to player as shown in the table. But, we can avoid such
specialization (i.e., use a single topic YouAreOut) if the data updated to this topic is
the set of non-compliant players. Then, when a player receives the content of this
topic, it can check to see if its name is in the set and act accordingly. "Comply"
must be individualized to players since each player's response may be different.
However, the general topic "Comply" will suffice if we have each player including
its name in its compliance message. Similarly, the topic "Ready" might have to
individualize to each player. However, Simon does not need to know which players
are ready to play—just that all of players are ready. So Simon can count the number
of updates to Ready and proceed when the number equals the number of players.

In conclusion, you can see that rather than requiring an indefinitely large set of topics (one for each player besides the one for Simon) the number of topics for the SimonSays model is actually reduced to 4 with the right approach. Therefore, it pays to examine the nature of the coupling for a DDS simulation of a coupled model so as to define a good set of topics.

Exercise

Write an algorithm that examines couplings of the "all" or "each" form and determines how model outputs have to be modified if necessary to avoid individualized topics.

Exercise

Consider DDS implementations of the peer-to-peer and real-time versions of the DEVS Simulation Protocol from Chap. 9. What parts of Table 10.2 change in each of these cases? How might assignment of topics be affected by such changes?

Exercise

Write and elaborate an FDDEVS model of Simon that is able to correctly respond to each of the external input events (Ready and Comply) and generate the output events (Command and YouAreOut) in Table 10.2. Consider only the case where a player includes its name in the messages it sends and can check if a received message is intended for it. Allow for the case that Ready and Comply inputs may not all arrive together (although subsets might), so you have to use the multiple input-handling techniques at the end of Chap. 4.

The coordination exhibited in this exercise is similar to that required for coordinators in executing the DEVS Simulation Protocol—with different implementations having somewhat different topic assignments.

Exercise

Tracking Actors with Publish/Subscribe Data Services

As illustrated in Fig. 10.11, a coordination center has a set of actors under its responsibility. With actor names (or other identification items) as topics, such

Table 10.2 Effects of "all" and "each" in coupling

Port	Role	Topic	Publishers	Subscribers
Command	Simon sends Command to all_Players	Command	Simon	Players
YouAreOut	Simon sends YouAreOut to each_Player	YouAreOut ForPlayer	Simon	Players
Ready	all_Player sends Ready to Simon	Ready	Players	Simon
Comply	each_Player sends Comply to Simon	ComplyByPlayer	Players	Simon

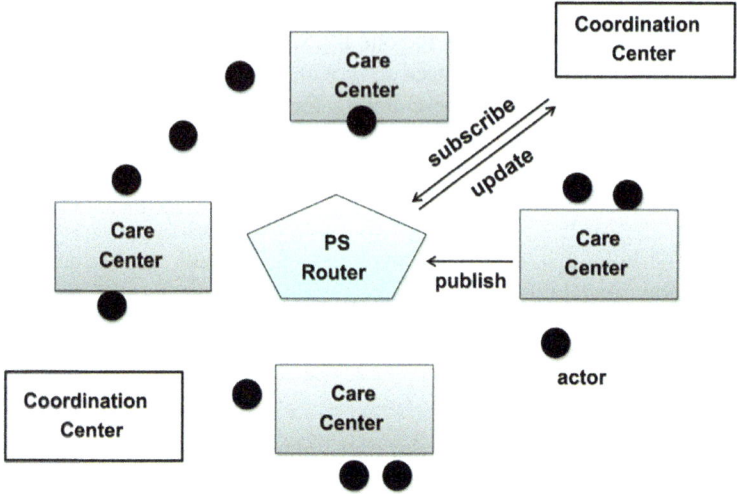

Fig. 10.11 P/S services for actor tracking

centers subscribe to the topics (actors) under their concern. When actors enter a care center, an agent publishes the actor's name to the PS router which then pushes this topic with associated data to the coordination center that is responsible for the actor. The associated data include the name of the care center and time instance when the actor arrived. Similarly, when the actor leaves the care center, an agent publishes an update to the actor's topic with the data concerning its departure.

Exercise

Develop an SES to organize the agent, actor, and PS Router models to represent the scenario of Fig. 10.10. For use in the care centers, extend the agent model to enable it to issue publication requests and publish updates to the PSRouter. Also, extend the Coordinator model to enable it to issue subscription requests to, and receive topic updates from, the PS Router.

10.3.4 Summary

This chapter opened with a brief description of dynamic structure and its application to agent modeling. The Publish/Subscribe data distribution paradigm was described using dynamic structuring together with a Data Distribution Service that provides middleware based on this paradigm. We showed how the DEVS Simulation Protocol for distributed simulation can be implemented in such middleware. We discussed how P/S topics support the exchange of DEVS Protocol commands and DEVS messages. We also discussed how topics that are individualized to components are not as desirable as those that can be subscribed to by all components. Insight into the choice of topics was gained by considering the all and each coupling of multi-aspects.

A Excerpts from PublishSubscribeRouter.dnl

```
PairOfString has Key and Value!
range of PairOfString's Key is String!
range of PairOfString's Value is String!

TripleOfString has Publisher, Topic, and Value!
range of TripleOfString's Publisher is String!
range of TripleOfString's Topic is String!
range of TripleOfString's Value is String!

use PublisherTopic with type Relation and default "new
Relation()"!
use TopicSubscriber with type Relation and default "new
Relation()"!
use TopicValue with type Relation and default "new
Relation()"
!

accepts input on PublishRequest with type PairOfString !
accepts input on SubscribeRequest with type PairOfString!
accepts input on TopicUpdate with type TripleOfString!
accepts input on PublishRemoveRequest with type
PairOfString!
accepts input on SubscribeRemoveRequest with type
PairOfString!

use PublishRequest with type PairOfString !
use SubscribeRequest with type PairOfString!
use TopicUpdate with type TripleOfString!
use PublishRemoveRequest with type PairOfString!
use SubscribeRemoveRequest with type PairOfString!

generates output on Weather with type String!
generates output on Politics with type String!

to start passivate in waitForInput!

when in waitForInput and receive PublishRequest go to
handlePublishRequest!

when in waitForInput and receive SubscribeRequest go to
handleSubscribeRequest!

when in waitForInput and receive TopicUpdate go to
sendUpdateToSubscribers!
```

when in waitForInput **and receive** PublishRemoveRequest **go to** handlePublishRemoveRequest!

when in waitForInput **and receive** SubscribeRemoveRequest **go to** handleSubscribeRemoveRequest!

hold in handlePublishRequest **for time** .1!
from handlePublishRequest **go to** waitForInput!

hold in handleSubscribeRequest **for time** .1!
from handleSubscribeRequest **go to** waitForInput!

hold in sendUpdateToSubscribers **for time** 1!

after sendUpdateToSubscribers **output** UpdateToSubscribers!
from sendUpdateToSubscribers **go to** waitForInput!

hold in handlePublishRemoveRequest **for time** .1!
from handlePublishRemoveRequest **go to** waitForInput!

hold in handleSubscribeRemoveRequest **for time** .1!
from handleSubscribeRemoveRequest **go to** waitForInput!

external event for waitForInput **with** PublishRequest
```
<%
for (int j = 0;j < messageList.size(); j++){
    PublishRequest = messageList.get(j).getData();
    String publisher = (String) PublishRequest.getKey();
    String topic = (String) PublishRequest.getValue();
    PublisherTopic.put(new PairOfString(publisher,
    topic));
}
%>!
```
external event for waitForInput **with** SubscribeRequest
```
<%
for (int j = 0;j < messageList.size(); j++){
SubscribeRequest = messageList.get(j).getData();
String subscriber = (String) SubscribeRequest.getKey();
String topic = (String) SubscribeRequest.getValue();
TopicSubscriber.put(new PairOfString(topic, subscriber));
CoupledModelImpl parent =
(CoupledModelImpl)this.getParent();
parent.addCoupling(this.getName(),"out"+topic,subscriber,"i
n"+topic);
}
%>!
```
external event for waitForInput **with** TopicUpdate
```
<%
for (int j = 0; j < messageList.size(); j++) {
            TopicUpdate = messageList.get(j).getData();
            String publisher = TopicUpdate.getPublisher();
            String topic = TopicUpdate.getTopic();
```

```
                    if (PublisherTopic.contains(publisher, topic)) {
                    String value = TopicUpdate.getValue();
                    TopicValue.put(new PairOfString(topic, value));
                    }
        }
%>!
```

output event for sendUpdateToSubscribers

```
Iterator ir = TopicValue.pairContainer.iterator();
while (ir.hasNext()) {
        PairOfString topicValue = (PairOfString) ir.next();
        String<%
g topic = topicValue.getKey();
        String value = topicValue.getValue();
        Port<String> port = (Port<String>)getOutputPort("out"
+ topic);
        a
%>!
```

add additional code

```
<%
class Relation {
        public HashSet pairContainer;
public Relation(){pairContainer = new HashSet();};
public void put(PairOfString p){};//adds a pair of strings
to pairContainer}
public HashSet getSet(String key){return new
HashSet();};//gets the values paired with key}
public boolean contains(String key, String value){return
true;};//true iff key,value pair is in its set}
public void remove(String key, String value){};//{removes
the key,value pair from its set}
}
%>!
```

B Excerpts from Agent.dnl

accepts input on Actor **with type** Actor !
accepts input on Hi !
accepts input on Bye **with type** Actor !
generates output on Hello !
generates output on GoodBye !
generates output on Actor **with type** Actor !

use count **with type** int **and default** "0"!
use storedActor **with type** Actor **and default** "new Actor()"!
use interactTime **with type** double **and default** "10"!

to start, passivate in waitForActor!
when in waitForActor and receive Actor then go to sendHello
!

```
hold in sendHello for time "interactTime" !
after sendHello output Hello !
from sendHello go to waitForHi !
passivate in waitForHi!
when in waitForHi and receive Hi then go to sendGoodBye !
hold in sendGoodBye for time 2!
after sendGoodBye output GoodBye!
from sendGoodBye go to waitForBye!
passivate in waitForBye!
when in waitForBye and receive Bye go to sendActor!
hold in sendActor for time 1!
after sendActor output Actor!
from sendActor go to waitForActor!
```

external event for waitForActor **with** Actor

```
<%
storedActor = messageList.get(0).getData();
CoupledModelImpl parent = (CoupledModelImpl)
this.getParent();
parent.addChildModel(storedActor);
parent.addCoupling(this.getName(),"outHello","Actor","inHel
lo"
);
parent.addCoupling("Actor","outHi",this.getName(),"inHi");
parent.addCoupling(this.getName(),"outGoodBye","Actor","inG
ood Bye");
parent.addCoupling("Actor","outBye",this.getName(),"inBye")
;
System.out.println("Received Actor with name "+
storedActor.getName());
holdIn("sendHello",interactTime);
%>!
```

external event for waitForBye **with** Bye
```
<%
storedActor = messageList.get(0).getData();
%>!
```

external event for waitForHi **with** Hi
```
<%
CoupledModelImpl parent =
(CoupledModelImpl)this.getParent();
parent.addCoupling("Actor","outActor",this.getParent().getN
ame (),"outActor");
%>!
```

output event for sendActor
```
<%
  output.add(outActor,storedActor);
```

```
%>!
    internal event for sendActor
<%
CoupledModelImpl parent =
(CoupledModelImpl)this.getParent();
parent.removeChildModel(storedActor);
System.out.println("Removed Actor with name "+
storedActor.getName());
%>!
```

References

Duboz, R., Versmisse, D., Quesnel, G., Muzzy, A., & Ramat, E. (2006). Specification of dynamic structure discrete-event multiagent systems. In *Agent-Directed Simulation (ADS 2006)*, Huntsville, AL, USA, April 2–6 2006.

Douglass, S., & Mittal, S. (2012). A framework for modeling and simulation of the artificial. In A. Tolk (Ed.), *Ontology, epistemology and teleology. Philosophical foundations for intelligent M&S*. New York: Springer.

Kwon, K.-J., Seo, C., & Zeigler, B. P. (2011). Automating DEVS over data distribution service for high performance and interoperability. In *MS-DEVS '11 Proceedings of the 2011 Symposium on Theory of Modeling & Simulation: DEVS Integrative M&S Symposium* (pp. 199–204).

Muzy, A., de Lara, J., & Guerra, E. (2007). Designing PRIMA: a precise visual language for modeling with agents, in a physical environment. In *International Conference on Modeling, Simulation & Visualization Methods* (pp. 231–238).

OMG (Object Management Group) Specification. (2007). Data distribution service for real-time systems, version 1.2, formal/2007-01-01. http://www.omg.org/spec/DDS/1.2/PDF/.

Seo, C., & Zeigler, B. P. (2012). Simulation model standardization through web services: interoperation and federation on the DEVS/SOA platform. In *DEVS Integrative M&S Symposium, Proceedings of the Spring Simulation Conference*, March 2012, Orlando, FL.

Uhrmacher, A. M., & Kullick, B. G. (2000). "Plug and test": Software agents in virtual environments. In *WSC '00: Proceedings of the 32nd Conference on Winter Simulation* (pp. 1722–1729), San Diego, CA, USA. Society for Computer Simulation International.

Interest-Based Information Exchange: Mappings and Models

11

To this point, we have discussed the generic user-oriented DEVS Modeling Environment which combines structural (SES) and behavioral modeling (DEVS) tools. We have seen how MS4 Me supports system design space exploration via automated SES-pruning-based model generation (Chap. 8). We have also seen how the publish/subscribe paradigm allows consumers to subscribe to topics and receive data of interest from publishers (Chap. 10). In this chapter, we consider the application of MS4 Me to data engineering for complex data and interest-based data distribution in which data is targeted to the consumer's interests. We will discuss mappings of Pruned Entity Structures, in the form of XML documents, based on underlying System Entity Structures. Then we will show how you can develop simulation models that implement such mappings and exchange XML documents in the manner of interest-based data distribution.

11.1 Background

We briefly summarize the relationship between the System Entity Structure (SES) with its pruned structures, (PES) and the implementation as an XML Schema with its documents. XML is the platform independent language that has become the standard for data exchange on the Internet (http://www.w3.org/XML/). As presented in Zeigler and Hammonds (2007), Fig. 11.1 shows that two levels of design are evident, *ontology* and *implementation*. As depicted in Fig. 11.1, at the ontology level, the modeler creates an SES describe states of the world generated by observations in a given application domain. The SES is expressed as an XML Schema at the implementation level. In this context, the family of pruned entity structures (PES) of an SES introduced in Chap. 5 represents a logically possible set of world state descriptions. Therefore, a family of XML document instances of a Schema is the concrete encoding of the family of pruned structures.

© Springer International Publishing AG 2017   169
B.P. Zeigler and H.S. Sarjoughian, *Guide to Modeling and Simulation of Systems of Systems*, Simulation Foundations, Methods and Applications,
DOI 10.1007/978-3-319-64134-8_11

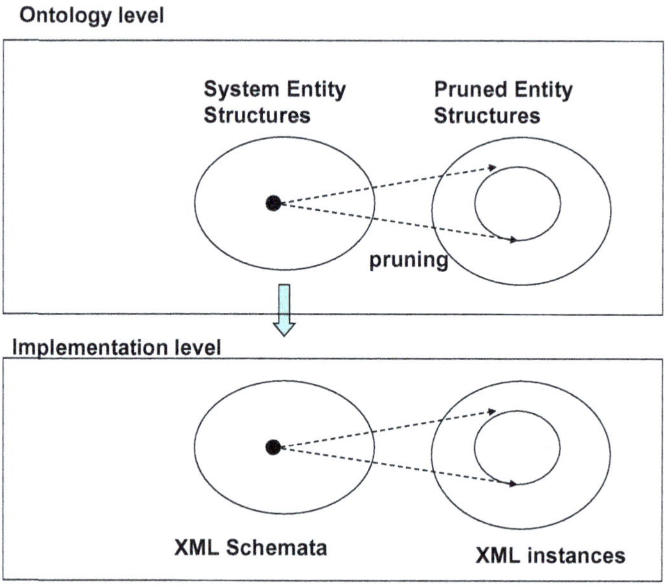

Ontology level

**System Entity   Pruned Entity
Structures   Structures**

pruning

Implementation level

XML Schemata   XML instances

Fig. 11.1 Relating SES and XML through ontology and implementations levels

Fig. 11.2 Restating the
information exchange
framework in the SES context

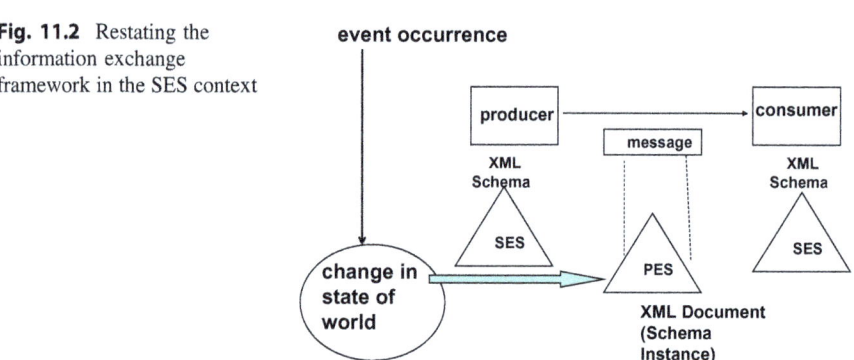

Figure 11.2 casts information exchange in the context of the SES ontology/XML implementation framework. An occurrence of an event that changes the world state is sensed by a sensor. The data acquired in this manner are sent as a PES in the form of an XML document in a message from producer to consumer. The consumer receives and interprets these messages using the same Schema which governed the XML in which they were sent.

11.1.1 Example: The Information Framework Applied to Car Purchases

In the information exchange framework, an event occurs when a customer buys a car. This event changes the world state because the car leaves the dealer's lot and it is now owned by the buyer. However, different parties can have different interests in the data emerging from the transaction. The Department of Motor Vehicles (DMV) wants to know about the identity of the purchaser and the specifics of the vehicle while the manufacturer's headquarters wants to know in aggregated form (say monthly) the number of cars purchased by model type to inform its inventory control policy. In this example, the producer is the same—the car dealer—but the consumers are different—DMV and manufacturer—and have different interests or *pragmatic frames*. In the first case, the dealer needs to provide specific information about the buyer. In the second case, the dealer needs to inform the manufacturer of how many cars of each make and model he sold during the month.

The following fragments illustrate the SES, its XML Schema representation, a pruning file, and a PES expressed as an XML instance of the Schema.

(1) *SES for Car Purchase*:

```
From the top perspective, CarPurchase is made of Vehicle and Buyer!
Vehicle can be Ford, GM, or Toyota in make!
Ford can be Fusion or Focus in model!
GM can be Buick, Cadillac, or Chevrolet in model!
Toyota can be Prius or Camry in model!
Vehicle has VIN and Weight!
The range of Vehicle's VIN is int!
The range of Vehicle's Weight is double!
Buyer has Name, SSN, and Address!
The range of Buyer's Name is string!
The range of Buyer's SSN is string!
The range of Buyer's Address is string!
```

(2) *Excerpt of XML Schema Generated from the SES*:

```
<?xml version='1.0' encoding='us-ascii'?>
<xs:schema xmlns:xs="http://www.w3.org/2001/XMLSchema"
elementFormDefault="qualified"
attributeFormDefault="unqualified">
   <xs:element name="Buyer">
  <xs:complexType mixed="true">
<xs:attribute name="Name" type = "xs:string" />
... .

</xs:complexType>
   </xs:element>
  <xs:element name = "Ford-modelSpec">
<xs:choice><xs:element name ="Fusion"/><xs:element name
="Focus"/>
  </xs:choice>
</xs:element>
   <xs:element name="Ford">
  <xs:complexType mixed="true">
  <xs:sequence>
  <xs:element ref = "Ford-modelSpec"/>
  </xs:sequence>
  </xs:complexType>
... .

<xs:element name = "Vehicle-makeSpec">
<xs:choice>
   <xs:element ref = "Ford"/>
   <xs:element ref = "Toyota"/>
   <xs:element ref = "GM"/>
</xs:choice>
  </xs:element>
   <xs:element name="Vehicle">
  <xs:complexType mixed="true">
  <xs:sequence>
  <xs:element ref = "Vehicle-makeSpec"/>
  </xs:sequence>
<xs:attribute  name="Weight"  type  =  "xs:double"  use  =
"optional" />
<xs:attribute name="VIN" type = "xs:int" use = "optional"
/>
  </xs:complexType>
   </xs:element>
... .

  <xs:element name = "CarPurchase-topDec">
  <xs:complexType>
<xs:sequence>
   <xs:element ref = "Buyer"/>
   <xs:element ref = "Vehicle"/>
  </xs:sequence>
... .

   </xs:element>
   </xs:schema>
```

(3) *Pruning script to generate a sub-family of PESs based on Toyota Priuses*:

```
Select Toyota from make for Vehicle!
Select Prius from model for Toyota!
```

(4) *An XML instance of the Schema representing a PES*:

```
<?xml version="1.0" encoding="UTF-8"?>
<CarPurchase                        xmlns:xsi              =
"http://www.w3.org/2001/XMLSchemainstance"
xsi:noNamespaceSchemaLocation="CarPurchaseSchema.xsd">
<aspectsOfCarPurchase>
<CarPurchase-topDec coupling = "">
    <Buyer Address = "1 Main Street,
    OurTown" Name = "Joe Smith"
    SSN = "12345678">
    </Buyer>
    <Vehicle VIN = "123123123" Weight = "3000">
      <Vehicle-makeSpec>
        <Toyota>
          <Toyota-modelSpec>
          <Prius/>
          </Toyota-modelSpec>
          </Toyota>
      </Vehicle-makeSpec>
    </Vehicle>
</CarPurchase-topDec>
</aspectsOfCarPurchase>
</CarPurchase>
```

Exercise

Using MS4 Me, prune the SES for various makes and models. Also, develop an SES that has a multi-Aspect, Vehicles with multi-entity, and Vehicles that contain only make and model as attributes.

11.2 Application to Network Data Collection

Packet data collection in computer networks offers a telling example of how the data engineering approach just introduced can be applied to real-world problems. Although there are several network traffic analysis tools, such as tcpdump, Ethereal, and other applications, they have weaknesses stemming from the fact that they store voluminous amounts of data consisting of all of the packet information, such as internet protocol (IP) addresses, port numbers, and packet sizes. Data gathered by such tools over several days, not to say weeks or years, can easily reach terabytes in size and challenge disk storage capacities. To process such data as a whole requires huge working memory (RAM) and extensive computational power. With this as background, we will discuss an approach to efficiently and quickly analyze a large number of network behaviors based on the concepts discussed above (see Kim et al. 2010 for more details).

11.2.1   Network Traffic Data Representations

Our first step is to develop an SES that represents some essential items that are contained in the headers of packets that are routed from node to node in a packet switching network (http://en.wikipedia.org.wiki/Network_packet). These items include event time, a source IP address, a source MAC address, a source port number, a destination IP address, a destination MAC address, a destination port number, a protocol, and packet length. These elements are organized hierarchically in an SES, described in natural language.

From the top perspective, PacketInfo is made of SrcHost, DestHost, Protocol, and Payload!

```
From the top perspective, PacketInfo is made of SrcHost, DestHost, Protocol,
and Payload!
PacketInfo has ID and EventTime!
The range of PacketInfo's ID is int!
The range of PacketInfo's EventTime is long!
Protocol can be HTTP, UDP, TCP, or FTP in pType!
From the channel perspective, SrcHost is made of AddressSection and Ports!
From the multport perspective, Ports are made of more than one Port!
Port can be id in index!
AddressSection has IPAddress and MACAddress!
The range of AddressSection's IPAddress is string!
The range of AddressSection's MACAddress is string!
From the channel perspective, DestHost is made of
AddressSection and Ports!
Port has portNumber!
The range of Port's portNumber is int!
Payload has numberOfBits!
The range of Payload's numberOfBits is int!
```

This SES describes the fundamental packet data that are captured by tools that monitor network traffic. Although such traffic data can be collected from existing networks, we can also consider other sources such as virtual data obtained from simulation experimental results, or datasets such as the KDD Cup (1999). Note that the number of events is very large—even within a small subnet—thousands of packets can be transmitted during one second. Accumulated over periods such as

Fig. 11.3 Information
exchange framework for
performance analysis and
security testing

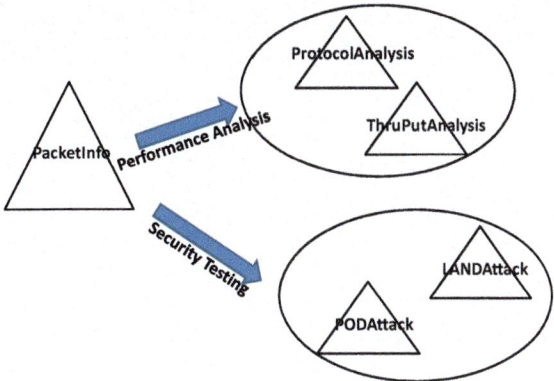

months or years, such data can require terabytes for mass storage. Fortunately, typical network behavior analyses require only certain slices or projections of such data to do their work. Therefore, our approach is to view the programs that carry out such analyses as consumers with specific data needs (pragmatic frames) that can receive, and operate upon, data directed to them by the network monitoring tool acting as producer.

This information exchange framework approach is illustrated in Fig. 11.3 where two major pragmatic frames are shown: performance analysis and security system testing. Within these major themes, some subdivisions are also shown. For example, protocol analysis and throughput analysis are two kinds of performance analyses. Security system testing employs subsets of network data that are relevant to various kinds of malicious attacks under consideration. Briefly stated, Intrusion Detection Systems (IDS) have become an essential component of computer network security. They monitor activities of computers and networks for attacks that inevitably occur despite security precautions. If attacks are discovered, such systems can alert administrators, defend against the attacks, or provide information that may help prevent future attack.

Two types of attacks, LAND and POD, are noted in Fig. 11.3. The LAND attack is a Denial of Service (DoS) attack that sends a special poison spoofed packet to a computer, causing it to lock up. The Ping of Death (POD) attack is another type of DoS attack in which the attacker sends a ping request to a server that is larger than the maximum size allowed by the TCP/IP protocol. This causes fragmentation into multiple smaller segments that overwhelm the server. Now consider trying to test intrusion detection systems for such attacks. One approach is to feed them all the packets, say, from the above-mentioned KDD dataset. This is prohibitive given the huge size of this data set. Instead, we can train an IDS using only relevant packets and test using a somewhat larger corpus consisting of training packets augmented with a baseline set of normal packets. This last approach, with the IDS developer as consumer, fits the information exchange framework to a tee!

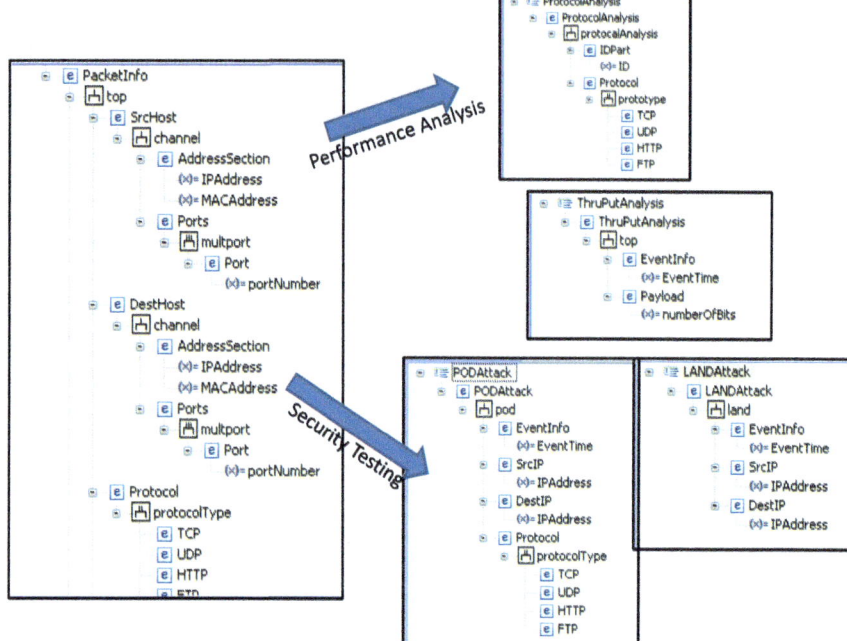

Fig. 11.4 Mapping of the master PacketInfo SES into the SESs characterizing consumers needs

To make this work, however, requires that we be able to filter out the subset of packets relevant to an attack. Figure 11.4 suggests that we can extract the right data by creating appropriate SESs and mappings from the master SES to such interest-based SESs.

To formulate the appropriate SES for an application, we must examine its workflow and the data items required for its processing chain. For protocol analysis, we are seeking to compute the distribution of events over protocol types. So an SES for this case specifies a way of identifying a packet and a specialization for types of protocols. For throughput analysis, we seek to compute the number of packets flowing through the network within a specified time interval. Accordingly, we need the event time of a packet to test whether it falls within the time interval. The LAND attack is recognizable because of its IP packets with identical IP address and destination. We may detect Ping of Death attacks with three items: a source host port number, a destination host port number, and a protocol. (See Kim et al. 2010 for details). The four outlines of SESs on the right of Fig. 11.5 reveal the packet items needed by the four types of consumers to do their processing work.

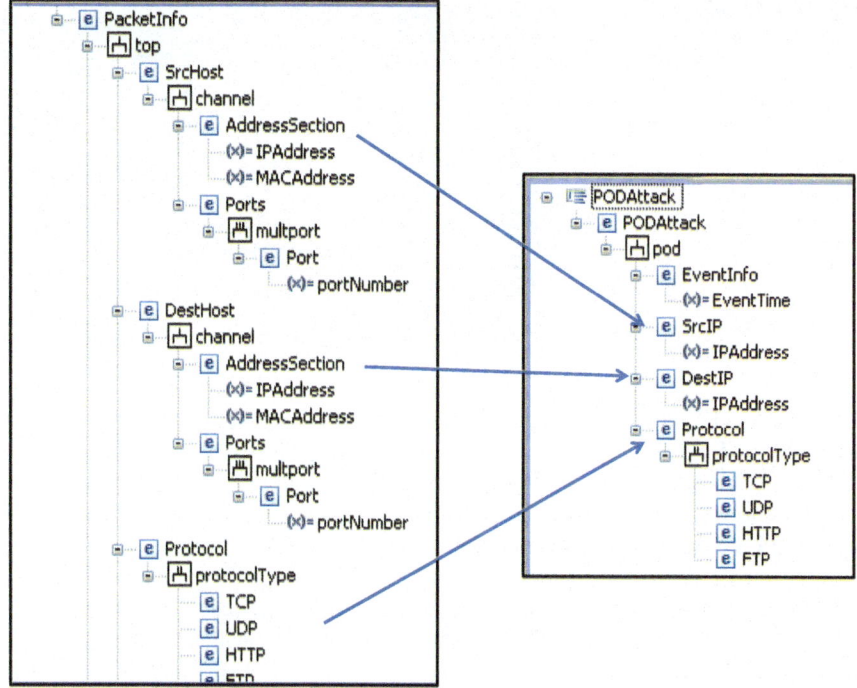

Fig. 11.5 Illustrating the mapping from the PacketInfo SES to the POD Attack SES

Use MS4 Me to develop the SES's for the four SES outlines shown on the right in Fig. 11.4. Compare with the specifications in the Appendix of this chapter.

11.3   Mapping Approach

Having SESs that characterize consumer's data needs, we are ready to set up the operations required to tailor the data collected by the producer to the form needed by a consumer. Such processing can be characterized as a mapping from a source XML instance to a target XML instance which can be specified by operations referring to the underlying Schemata. And since in the framework of Fig. 11.1, an SES underlies an XML Schema, the mapping from source to target instances should be specified by operations on the underlying SESs. For brevity of expression, we will refer to the mapping as going from one SES to a second SES even though the mapping actually provides a set of operations that will transform one PES to a second PES (each implemented as an XML document). Figure 11.5 illustrates such a "mapping" from the PacketInfo SES to the Protocol Analysis SES. In this

Fig. 11.6 Mapping from source SesPesPair object to target SesPesPair object

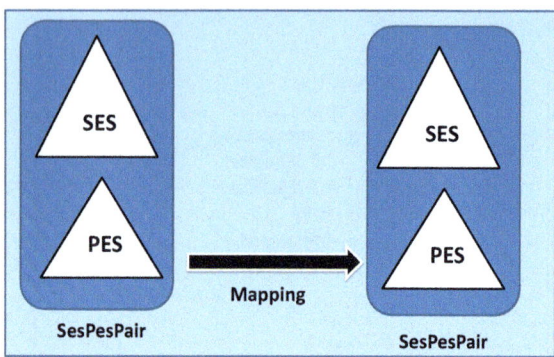

mapping, the IP addresses associated with Source and Destination hosts are mapped to corresponding addresses associated with SrcIP and DestIP elements of the POD Attack SES. Direct transfer of values illustrated in this mapping is a common operation to which we first turn our attention. Additional operations that are needed in general are discussed in Zeigler and Hammonds (2007).

It is convenient to package the information needed to implement a mapping into chunks that provide access to the information in an SES needed to operate on a PES of interest. Therefore, we define a class, *SesPesPair*, which encapsulates, as instance variables, an SES with a PES pruned from it. Constructors of the SesPesPair class can import existing SES and PES instances, as well as create new ones from natural language scripts. Additional methods can generate the XML Schema associated with the SES and the XML document associated with the PES.

Next, we define a second class, *MappingSesPesPairToSesPesPair* to encapsulate a source and target SesPesPair instances as depicted in Fig. 11.6. This class provides methods that can implement the operations needed to carry out the desired mapping from source to target.

Having the two classes, SesPesPair and MappingSesPesPairToSesPesPair, we are ready to consider the overall process for defining a mapping.

First, create a source SesPesPair, either from existing instances of SES and PES or newly created ones. Also create a target SesPesPair but with the following difference: the PES is generated as a generic (unpruned) structure (see Zeigler and Hammonds 2007). This allows the mapping to make its pruning operations without any constraint. After the operations have been completed, the pruning algorithm is executed to make any choices that have not been made.

Second, specify the operations to prune the target PES as needed. We consider only operations data from the first PES to the second as in the following:

• Transferring values from source element to target element:

```
transfer < source>'s < attribute > value to < target>'s
<attribute >
```

For example, mapping the PacketInfo SesPesPair to the EventInfo SesPesPair, we use:

```
transfer PacketInfo's EventTime value to EventInfo's
EventTime
```

- Transferring a specialization choice from source element to target element:

```
transfer < source>'s < specialization > choice to < target>'s
<specialization>
```

For example, mapping the PacketInfo SesPesPair to the ProtocolAnalysis SesPesPair, we use:

```
transfer Protocol's protocolType choice to Protocol's
protocolType
```

As a second example, mapping the PacketInfo SesPesPair to the LANDAttack SesPesPair, we use:

```
transfer AddressSection's IPAddress under DestHost to
DestIp's IPAddress
```

Note the first IPAddress above requires a context qualification (recall Chap. 8) because both SrcHost and DestHost have AddressSections with IP addresses.

As a third example, mapping the PacketInfo SesPesPair to the PODAttack SesPesPair, we use:

```
transfer Port.0's portNumber under Ports under SrcHost to
SrcPort's portNumber
```

Note the use of the dot notation as in Port.0, to identify which Port in the multiple entity Ports that we are referring to.

Exercise

Create instances of SesPesPair for each of the SESs that you created for the two types of consumers (Buyer and DMV) in the car purchase example.

11.3.1 Mapping Multi-aspects

Mapping from one multi-aspect to a second involves somewhat more work since multiple instances of the respective multi-entities are involved. After deciding on a pairing of multi-entities (in respective SESs), we must put their occurrences (in the respective PESs), into correspondence, recalling that there might not be the same number of each. As illustrated in Fig. 11.7 having such a correspondence, we can

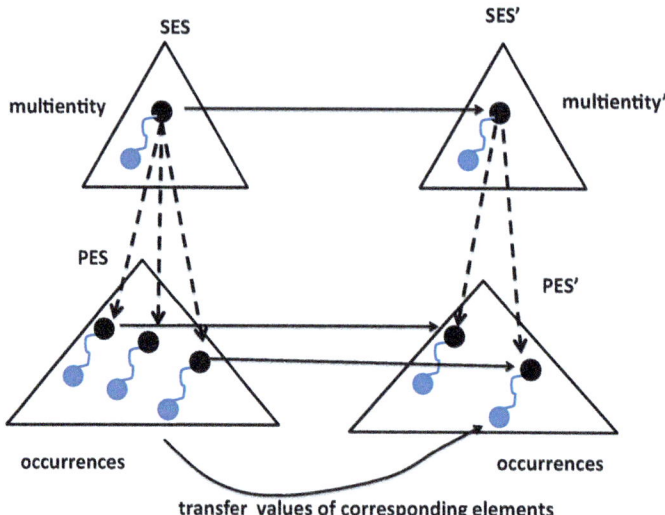

Fig. 11.7 Mapping between Multi-aspects

grab data values from the substructure of each source occurrence and pass them (possibly processed) to the desired slot of the corresponding target occurrence.

In outline, the mapping process takes the following form:

- Place the source's occurrences of entity into correspondence with those of the target's entity

```
pairUp < source>'s < entity > with < target>'s < entity>
```

- Use the correspondence so established to accept pairs that match

```
match < source>'s < element > with < target>'s < element>
```

- Transfer values from source elements to matched target elements:

```
transfer < source>'s < element > <attribute > value to
< target>'s < element >  < attribute >
```

The Satellite System architecture study in Chap. 13 offers an application of multi-aspect to multi-aspect mapping.

Exercise

Extend the PacketInfo SES and the various targets discussed so that they each have a multi-aspect for packets. Extend the mappings discussed to apply to the extended SESs.

- Create an instance of MappingSesPesPairToSesPesPair that maps from the overall car purchase SES to the department of motor vehicle's SES. Define the mapping using the transfer operations discussed in the text.
- Create an instance of MappingSesPesPairToSesPesPair that maps from the overall car purchase SES to the manufacturer's SES. Define the mapping using the transfer operations extended to indexed access to attributed values discussed in the text.

11.4 DEVS Models that Exchange XML

In the last sections, we showed how mappings of Pruned Entity Structures, in the form of XML documents could be based on underlying System Entity Structures. Now you will see how to develop simulation models that implement such mappings and exchange XML documents in the manner of interest-based data distribution.

11.4.1 Model for Generating XML Documents

We begin by illustrating how a model that generates XML instances of an XML Schema can be developed from a simple FDDEVS model as a starting point. The natural language specification has the following form:

```
to start, passivate in waitForStart!
when in waitForStart and receive StartUp go to sendOutput!
hold in sendOutput for time 2!
from sendOutput go to sendOutput!
after sendOutput output XML!
```

When saved as a GeneratorXML.dnl file and opened with the State Designer, the state diagram appears as shown in Fig. 11.8.

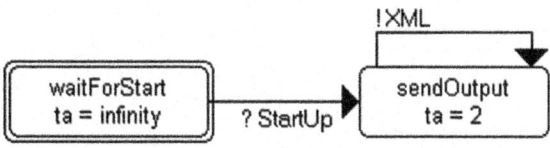

Fig. 11.8 State designer generated diagram for GeneratorXML

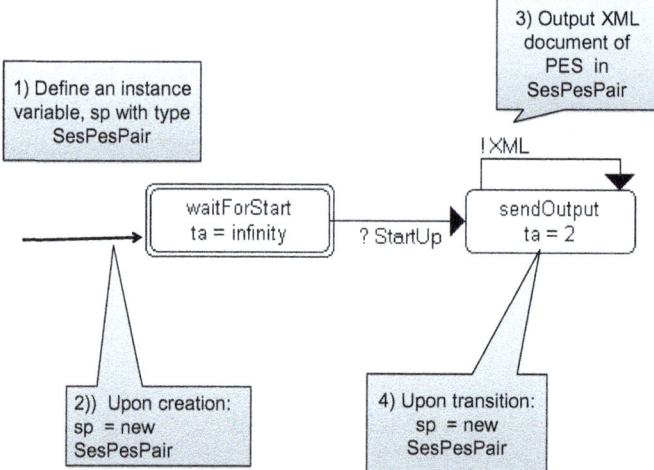

Fig. 11.9 Callouts on state diagram for GeneratorXML

The diagram shows that there is an input port, StartUp, and an output port, XML. There are two states, waitForStart and SendOutput where (1) waitForStart transitions to SendOutput as an external transition (when receiving the StartUp input) and (2) SendOutput transitions back to itself as an internal transition (after 2 units of time), outputting an XML document just before completing the transition. Therefore, an output is generated periodically with period 2. When you select the Run in the Simulation Viewer menu item, you automatically generate an atomic models class and an instance of it is displayed in the viewer. By injecting StartUp from the input menu of GenerateXML, and pressing the step button, you can verify that generated model displays the behavior you expect.

As discussed in Chap. 4, MS4 Me supports the ability to enhance the java code by adding additional definitions and java source code to the GeneratorXML.dnl file. Figure 11.9 shows a state diagram view of the DEVS model with the addition of callouts that suggest how to define the code fragments that are embedded in the FDDEVS source to implement the required XML generation.

To elaborate the GenerateXML model, we can define code for some of the code fragments which will then be copied and inserted into the GenerateXML class source file. The following text shows the augmented Generator.dnl file with captions that are keyed to the callouts in Fig. 11.9.

(1)   Declare State (instance) Variables

```
use count with type int!
use sp with type SesPesPair!
```

(2)   Instantiate the instance variables

```
Initialize variables
<%
count = 0;
sp = new SesPesPair();
sp.setProjectNm("DataHandling");
sp.setSesfile("PacketInfoSes.txt");
sp.setPesfile("PacketInfoPrune.txt");
sp.printXMLFile();
%> !
```

(3)   Generate output in the internal transition of SendOutput

```
output event for sendOutput
< output.add(outXML, sp.XMLPES);
%> !
```

(4)   Create a new PES and XML instance from the SES for PacketInfo

```
Internal event for sendOutput
<%
generatePrunings.setSeed(6879345 + count * 9);
//generate a new PES and XML
String XMLFile = util.ContentsWork.createNewXMLInst (
"DataHandling",
"PacketInfoSes.txt", "PacketInfoPrune.txt");
sp = new SesPesPair();
sp.setXMLFile(XMLFile);
sp.setProjectNm("DataHandling");
sp.setSesfile("PacketInfoSes.txt");
sp.setPesfile("PacketInfoPrune.txt");
sp.printXMLFile();
count ++;
%> !
```

11.4.2   DEVS Model for SES-Based XML Mapping

You now have a generator of XML instances of an XML Schema based on the system and pruned entity structures. Such a generator can send XML documents to a model that maps them into documents of a second SES. Taking the same approach as before, we write an FDDEVS to start the development for a model call MapXML:

```
to start, passivate in waitForInput!
when in waitForInput and receive XML go to sendOutput!
hold in sendOutput for time 2!
from sendOutput go to waitForInput!
after sendOutput output XML!
```

The corresponding state transition diagram with callouts for the transitions to implement a mapping is shown in Fig. 11.10.

Code fragments to implement a mapping from the PacketInfo SES to the ThruPutAnalize SES are:

(0)   **Declare an instance variable with type**

```
MappingSesToPesPairToSesToPesPair use mp with type
SesPesPair!
```

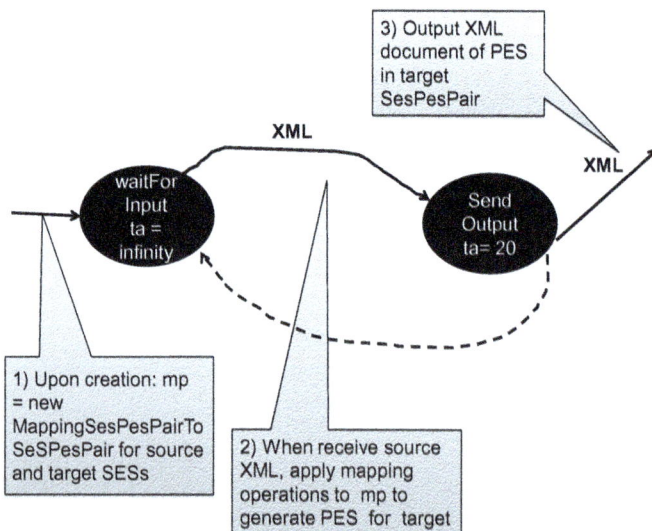

Fig. 11.10 Callouts on state diagram for MapXML

(1) **In the initialize method of the model, instantiate the instance variable**

```
MapSesPesPairToSesPesPair mp = new
MapSesPesPairToSesPesPair ();
```

(2) **When receive source XML, apply mapping operations to mp to generate the PES for target**

```
String XMLPES = messageList.get(0).getData();
mp.receiveSourceXML(XMLPES);mp.transferAttributeFromTo
("PacketInfo", "EventTime", "EventInfo", "EventTime");
mp.transferAttributeFromTo("Payload", "numberOfBits",
"Payload", "PacketSize");
mp.finishPruning();
mp.printXMLFile();
```

(3) **Output XML document of PES in target SesPesPair**

```
output.add(outXML,mp.toSp.XMLPES());
```

Exercise

Using the code fragments just given, follow the approach given for GenerateXML to complete the definition of the extended java source for MapXML. Test your model using the Simulation Viewer.

11.4.3 Models to Distribute Mappings of Master SES to Interest-Based SESs

Recall Fig. 11.4 which illustrated the mapping of the master PacketInfo SES into the SESs characterizing the needs of different consumers such as throughput analysis, and security analysis. To continue with this approach, we implement a coupled model in which the atomic model MapNDistribute implements the PacketInfo SES and generates a pruned entity structure of this SES at random. As illustrated in Fig. 11.11, MapNDistribute then maps this PES into several smaller PESs, one for each of the consumers in Fig. 11.4. It then sends the XMLs to atomic models representing consumers (Atomic models for ThruPutAnalysis, SecurityAnalysis and ProtocolAnalysis) that can process the XML they received based on the corresponding SESs. Note a variation in that while ThruPutAnalyse and ProtocolAnalyze receive their XMLs directly, SecurityAnalyze sends in a data request to get its XML.

The natural language *.dnl file for the MapNDistribute model and its image in the State Designer (Fig. 11.12) are given next:

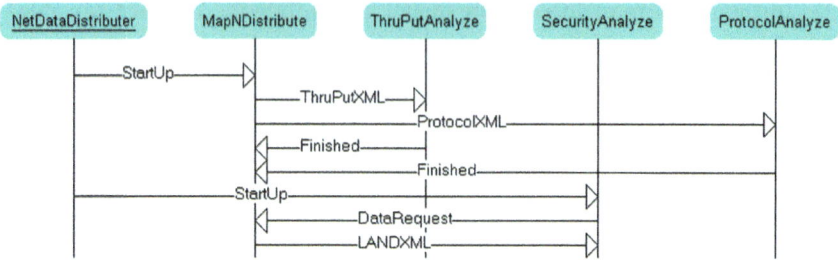

Fig. 11.11   Sequence diagram for NetDataDistributor

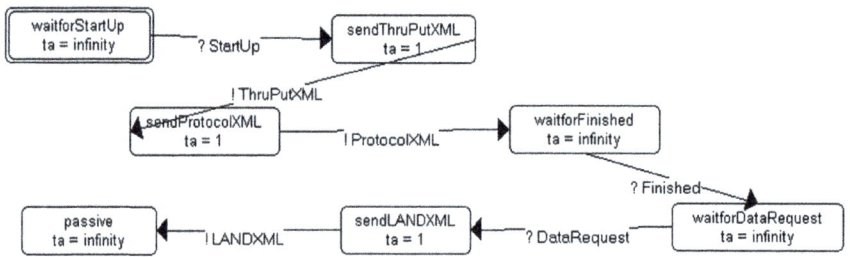

Fig. 11.12   State diagram for MapNDistributor

MapNDistribute
to start, **passivate in** waitforStartUp!
when in waitforStartUp **and receive** StartUp **go to**
sendThruPutXML!
hold in sendThruPutXML **for time** 1!
after sendThruPutXML **output** ThruPutXML!
from sendThruPutXML **go to** sendProtocolXML!
hold in sendProtocolXML **for time** 1!
after sendProtocolXML **output** ProtocolXML!
from sendProtocolXML **go to** waitforFinished!
passivate in waitforFinished !
when in waitforFinished **and receive** Finished **go to**
waitforDataRequest!
passivate in waitforDataRequest !
when in waitforDataRequest **and receive** DataRequest **go to**
sendLANDXML!
hold in sendLANDXML **for time** 1!
after sendLANDXML **output** LANDXML!
from sendLANDXML **go to** passive!
passivate in passive!

Exercise

Enhance MapNDistribute either from the dnl file directly by using the State Designer to implement the PacketInfo SES and generate a pruned entity structure of this SES at random. Also enable MapNDistribute to map this PES into several smaller PESs, one for each of the consumers in Fig. 11.4. Finally, enable it then to send the XMLs to the respective consumer atomic models.

Exercise

Construct another implementation of the mapping of Fig. 11.4 in which the original XML (as opposed to the mapped XML of the previous exercise) is sent to each of the targeted atomic models which do the mapping to their respective XML documents. Which implementation requires more data processing at MapNDistribute? Which may require less bandwidth and overall data storage volume?

11.4.4   Models that Exchange the Same XML

You have just worked with exchanges of XML documents in which a producer sends different XML documents to consumers depending on their interest in them. Another way that models can use XML is to exchange the same XML document but fill in different parts of the document as appropriate. An implementation of the SimonSays game introduced in Chap. 7 offers an example. Figure 11.13 illustrates how Simon and each player can be working off the same SesPesPair instance while Simon fills in a section for commands and players fill in their responses in another section.

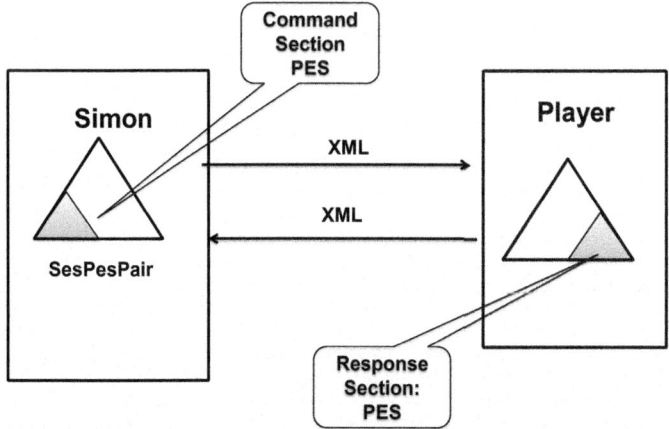

Fig. 11.13 XML exchange between models based on a shared SesPesPair

An SES for this information exchange example is given by:

From the top **perspective,** SimonSaysData **is made of**
CommandSection, ResponseSection, **and** YouAreOut!
From the command **perspective,** CommandSection **is made of**
SimonSays **and** Command!
Command **can be** Stand, Sit, HandsUp, **or** HandsDown **in**
commandType!
SimonSays **can be** Present **or** NotPresent **in** presence!
From the response **perspective,** ResponseSection **is made of**
Response **and** Comply!
Comply **can be** Present **or** NotPresent **in** compliance!
YouAreOut **can be** Present **or** NotPresent **in** evalType!

and illustrated in Fig. 11.14.

An example of pruning instructions to obtain Simon's part of the SES in a PES might be:

Fig. 11.14 SES outline for exchanged document in SimonSays

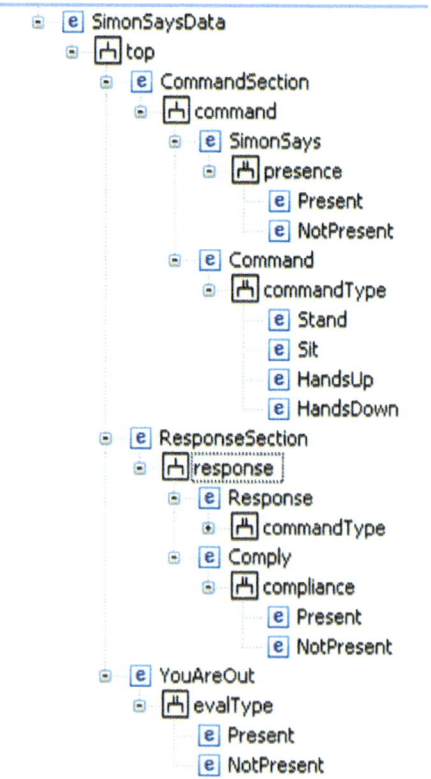

Command Section

select Present **from** presence **for** SimonSays !
select Stand **from** commandType **for** Command !

This would then appear within the XML document for the PES as:

```
<SimonSays>
<SimonSays-presenceSpec>
<Present/>
</SimonSays-presenceSpec>
</SimonSays>
<Command>
<Command-commandTypeSpec>
<Stand/>
</Command-commandTypeSpec>
</Command>
```

When the XML document is received, a player might prune the response section of the PES this way:

Response Section

```
select Sit from commandType for Response !
select Present from compliance for Comply !
```

to fill in the response section of the same XML document:

```
<Response>
 < Command-commandTypeSpec>
 < Sit/>
</Command-commandTypeSpec>
</Response>
 < Comply>
<Comply-complianceSpec>
 < Present/>
</Comply-complianceSpec>
</Comply>
```

Since the response is different from the command itself, and even though the player's intention was to comply, the player would be ordered out of the game:

select Present **from** evalType **for** YouAreOut !

filling in the last part of the document:

```
<YouAreOut>
<YouAreOut-evalTypeSpec>
<Present/>
</YouAreOut-evalTypeSpec>
</YouAreOut>
```

Exercise

Apply the approach of this chapter to implement the SimonSays game of Chap. 7 based on the SES just introduced. First, restrict your solution to a single player. Then extend the SES with a multi-aspect to represent any number of player responses and compliance evaluations.

To this point, we have discussed the generic user-oriented DEVS Modeling Environment which combines structural (SES) and behavioral modeling (DEVS) tools. We have seen how MS4 Me supports system design space exploration and optimization via automated SES-pruning-based model generation.

11.5   Summary

In this chapter, we considered the application of MS4 Me to data engineering for complex data and interest-based data distribution in which data is targeted to the consumer's interests. We discussed mappings of Pruned Entity Structures, in the form of XML documents, based on underlying System Entity Structures. Then we showed how you can develop simulation models that implement such mappings and exchange XML documents in the manner of interest-based data distribution. Distributed simulation implementations that employ the DEVS Protocol (Chap. 9) and data distribution services (Chap. 10) can deploy such models to provide the basis for information exchange based on the concepts of interest-based distribution.

Appendix: System Entity Structures for Examples

Throughput Analysis

```
From the top perspective, ThruPutAnalize is made of
EventInfo and Payload!
EventInfo has EventTime!
The range of EventInfo's EventTime is long!
Payload has PacketSize!
The range of Payload's PacketSize is int!
```

Protocol Analysis

From the top perspective, ProtocolAnalyze is made of IDPart
and Protocol!
IDPart has ID!
The range of IDPart's ID is string!
Protocol can be TCP, UDP, or FTP in protocolType!

LAND Attack

From the top perspective, LANDAttack is made of SrcIP and
DestIP!
LANDAttack has EventTime!
The range of LANDAttack's EventTime is long!
SrcIP has IPAddress !
The range of SrcIP's IPAddress is string!
DestIP has IPAddress !
The range of DestIP's IPAddress is string!

POD Attack

From the top perspective, PODAttack is made of EventInfo,
SrcPort, DestPort, and Protocol!
EventInfo has EventTime!
The range of EventInfo's EventTime is long!
SrcPort has portNumber !
The range of SrcPort's portNumber is string!
DestPort has portNumber !
The range of DestPort's portNumber is string!
Protocol can be TCP, UDP, HTTP, or FTP in protocolType!

References

KDD Cup. (1999). http://www.sigkdd.org/kddcup/index.php?section=1999&method=info/.
Kim, T., Seo, Ch., & Zeigler, B. P. (2010). Web-based distributed network analyzer using a system entity structure over a service-oriented architecture. *Simulation, 86*(3), 155–180.
Zeigler, B. P., & Hammonds, P. (2007). *Modeling & simulation-based data engineering: Introducing pragmatics into ontologies for net-centric information exchange.* New York: Academic Press.

Languages for Constructing DEVS Models

12

Now that you have experience with DEVS Modeling Environments in some depth, it is time to get a higher-level perspective on the approach it takes to computationally support constructing DEVS models for virtual build and test. We distinguish three major levels of such support: constrained natural languages, DEVS Specification Languages, and DEVS Simulators (Fig. 12.1).

Starting with the last mentioned, *DEVS Simulators* are the traditional simulation environments implemented in languages such as Java (e.g., MS4 Me Java) and C++ (e.g., ADEVS). These environments can exploit the full computational and representational power of object-oriented programming languages to provide complete and efficient implementations of the DEVS formalism.

Traditional simulation environments derive their strength from the fact that they mirror the DEVS formalism with its underlying mathematical constructs (e.g., set theory). Users skilled in DEVS constructs expressed in a traditional programming language are able to code complex behaviors in expert fashion. Unfortunately, these same constructs can put up barriers to programmers and modelers who are not familiar with the underlying mathematical concepts. Moreover, traditional DEVS simulators employ source code formats that mix pure DEVS constructs with those of the host language. This makes it difficult to provide specific assistance for DEVS model development since the native validation tools can only detect host language errors. Such impediments offer incentives to develop higher-level abstractions that are DEVS-specific and help to overcome the limitations of direct expression in traditional DEVS simulators.

DEVS Specification Languages provide linguistic constructs that are directly related to DEVS concepts. These constructs can be directly checked for correct syntax and semantics as well as consistency with other definitions. Moreover, assistance can be offered in context as the user develops the model. A validated specification then can be automatically transformed into a model that can be executed in a traditional DEVS Simulator. With this approach, it also becomes feasible to restrict the models specified to a subclass of all DEVS models. Restricting the structures allowed by a DEVS subclass can increase the tractability of checking

© Springer International Publishing AG 2017

B.P. Zeigler and H.S. Sarjoughian, *Guide to Modeling and Simulation of Systems of Systems*, Simulation Foundations, Methods and Applications, DOI 10.1007/978-3-319-64134-8_12

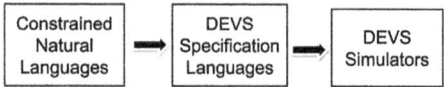

Fig. 12.1 Levels of support for virtual build and test

model behavioral properties by analyzing the structures. FDDEVS, as it appears in MS4 Me, is an example of a specification language that restricts the class of DEVS model to those with finite states and deterministic functions. This restriction enabled the development analysis tools that can check behavioral properties such as liveness and safety as demonstrated in the XSY software environment (Hwang 2011). The questions that arise for such languages are first, "how wide is the class of DEVS models that can be specified relative to the complete class of DEVS models" and second, whether its limitations can be overcome by an enhancement process.

Constrained natural languages employ familiar natural language forms to ease model description and are intended to hide computational complexities from the modeler's view. They are constrained in that only a small set of sentence forms are supported relative to what full scale natural language processing would allow. As with DEVS Specification Languages, the constraints on natural language forms enable model and consistency checking as well as content assistance. Then, the verified model maps to DEVS simulation model directly or via DEVS Specification Languages.

MS4 Me is built on the use of Extended Backus-Naur Form (EBNF, http://www.garshol.priv.no/download/text/bnf.html) grammars implemented by *xtext* in the Eclipse framework. EBNF is used to support the development of constrained natural languages and DEVS Specification Languages. We discuss their expressive power with respect to the full class of DEVS models. We show how System Entity Structures (SES) are supported within the EBNF approach and how it extends to expression of more advanced concepts such as Hardware Description Languages (e.g., VHDL) to provide a comprehensive tool set that goes all the way from natural language input to realization of DEVS models in hardware form.

12.1 Constrained Natural Language Specification of Atomic Models

We first discuss the path that goes from constrained natural language to FDDEVS to MS4 Me Java atomic models as illustrated in Fig. 12.2.

The GeneratorOfJobs (Chap. 4) offers an example of a constrained natural language statement entered in a *.dnl file:

Fig. 12.2 Illustrating the path from DEVS natural language to Java models

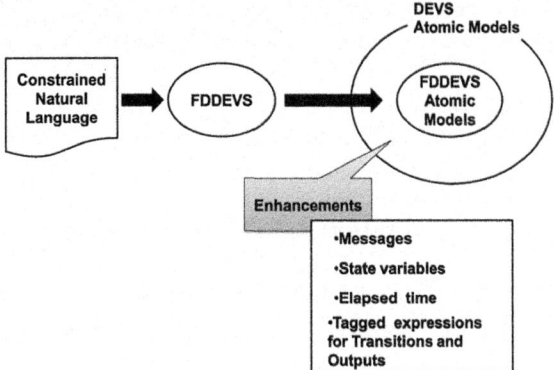

```
to start, passivate in waitForJob!
when in waitForJob and receive Job then go to sendJob!
hold in sendJob for time 50!
after sendJob output Job!
from sendJob go to waitForJob!
```

The EBNF that parses such strings and verifies their syntax is implemented in MS4 Me. Although you cannot see it explicitly, you can easily infer the grammar's rules by using the syntax assistance to step ahead for each symbol. See, for example, Fig. 2.4 of Chap. 2. The result of this interpretation is a model expressed in FDDEVS which has a formal definition given in the Appendix. The basic structure of an FDDEVS is given by a 7-tuple:

```
<IncomingMessageSet,
OutgoingMessageSet,
StateSet,
TimeAdvanceTable,
InternalTransitionTable,
ExternalTransitionTable,
OutputTable>,
```

where the constraints and semantics of the elements in the structure are given by the table in the Appendix. The particular structure of the FDDEVS model generated from a *.dnl file is not explicitly available, but you can view this information in the outline generated when saving the file.

When you save a file such as Example.dnl, MS4 Me generates a MS4 Mc Java atomic model with the file name, e.g.,

```
public class Example extends simView.ViewableAtomic {
//generated code
}
```

The generated artifact is truly a MS4 Me Java model in the sense that it is fully defined and expressed as a syntactically correct Java class which implements the AtomicModel interface. This model can be executed using the MS4 Me Java simulation methods, viewed and executed in the Simulation Viewer, and coupled with other models to compose MS4 Me Java coupled models.

12.1.1 Limitations of FDDEVS Models

The strength of an FDDEVS model lies in its simplicity and understandability, while nevertheless allowing you to express the underlying transition logic of the model you have in mind. However, an FDDEVS model in MS4 Me Java lacks many features that may be needed to express desired behavior. These features are:

- *DEVS Messages*—FDDEVS models have input and output ports, but they can only carry strings as values. Allowing ports to carry arbitrary values is needed to facilitate exchanging information among models. As we saw in Chap. 4, in MS4 Me, ports can be given types, including any user-defined subclasses of Object.
- *State Variables*—An FDDEVS model has a single state variable that controls its phase. The "state" of an FDDEVS model is actually implemented by a state variable called "phase" in its MS4 Me implementation. The phase can take on only a finite set of values consistent with the finite state nature of FDDEVS. On the other hand, MS4 Me atomic models can have an arbitrary number of instance variables which are not limited to finite ranges of values.
- *Elapsed Time*—Although FDDEVS models specify a time advance for each phase, they cannot make use of the elapsed time in a phase and cannot change the value of the time advance initially assigned to a state. On the other hand, an MS4 Me atomic model can access and use the time that has elapsed in its current state (this elapsed time is supplied to it by its simulator). The atomic model can (optionally) use this data to determine its next state as well as set the time advance of this next state.
- *Executable Code Transition and Output Functions*—FDDEVS model specifications have nowhere to provide instructions on how to produce "side effects" of external and internal transitions as well as to condition the values produced by the output function. On the other hand, MS4 Me atomic models can operate on their state and output variables as a result of executing their transition and output functions.

12.1.2 FDDEVS Enhancement Facility

The enhancement facility provided by MS4 Me augments the *.dnl file with declarations and slots to let you recapture the just-mentioned missing features while still retaining a tight connection with an originating FDDEVS specification. Let's review the enhancements that you have worked with in earlier chapters:

Declarations

The enhancement facility allows you to make the following declarations:

- *Extension of port declarations* with types that ports can accept or generate, e.g.,

```
accepts input on Job with type WorkToDo!
```

declares that there is an input port with name inJob and whose incoming values must be instances of Java class WorkToDo. A similar declaration holds for output ports. This extension allows the augmented FDDEVS models to generate and accept the full class of DEVS messages.

- *Declaration of State Variables.* For example:

```
use storedJob with type WorkToDo and default "new WorkToDo()"!
```

creates an instance variable of type WorkToDo and makes the indicated default assignment in the initialization statement.

- *Declaration of new classes.* For example:

```
WorkToDo has id, startTime, and processingTime!
```

creates a new Java class with the named instance variables. Other statements give types and default assignments to these variables. Instances of these classes can be used in DEVS messages as well as anywhere in a model or other models since the classes are global.

Tagged code blocks The enhancement facility allows you to add Java code to the generated atomic model in places determined by the following types of tagged blocks:

```
Initialization tag:
```
Initialize variables
```
<%
//assign values to variables when model is started
or restarted
%>!
```

```
Internal event tags:
```
Internal event for <phase>
```
<%
//assign values to variables when model is about to
transition to the//designated phase
%>!
```

```
External event tags:
```
external event for <phase> **with** <inport>
```
<%
```

```
//assign values to variables when model is in <phase> and receives input on//
<inport> - the incoming port-value pairs and the elapsed time are
available//for use
% >!
```

Output event tags:
```
output event for <phase>
<%
//fills in the entity slots for port-value pairs to create
DEVS messages
%>!
```

Other tags:
add test inputs
```
<%
//add test inputs to inject into model in the simulation
viewer
%>!
```
add library
```
<%
//add imports to use external libraries
%>!
```
add additional code
```
<%
//add java code to the model class source file
%>!
```

12.1.3 Development Advantages of the Enhancement Facility

Together, these declarations and tagged block features make it easy to enhance
FDDEVS models to become full-capability MS4 Me Java models. The enhancements enable you to define and work with:

- *DEVS Messages*—augmented FDDEVS models provide entity subclass types
  that allow fully-fledged DEVS messages.
- *State Variables*—augmented FDDEVS models can have state variables with
  types as needed.
- *Elapsed Time*—augmented FDDEVS models can make use of the elapsed time
  in external transition functions supplied by the simulator and can set the value of
  time advance for the next transition.
- Executable Code Transition and Output Functions—augmented FDDEVS
  models have tags to inject code into slots for external and internal transitions as
  well as output events.

Note that the executable code in the tagged locations provide the mechanism by which you manipulate the DEVS messages, state variable, and elapsed time features. Moreover, all this can be done in a very structured manner where the correspondence between the specifications in the *.dnl file, and the code in the associated MS4 Me Java source file is continually maintained. Java errors you make are reflected back into the *.dnl file so you can correct them there. This makes it easier to keep track of changes and speeds your development. All changes to your model should now be done in the *.dnl file and not in the corresponding Java file.

12.2   Constrained Natural Language Specifications of Hierarchical Coupled Models

Consider the process that transforms a natural language file to a System Entity Structure, in original and then pruned forms, to an MS4 Me Java hierarchical coupled model.

Let's follow the progression starting with constrained natural language entered in a *.ses file, for example, containing the text:

```
From the top perspective, SimpleWorkFlow is made of
GeneratorOfJobs, ProcessorOfJobs, and Transducer!
From the top perspective, GeneratorOfJobs sends Job to
ProcessorOfJobs!
From the top perspective, GeneratorOfJobs sends outJob to
Transducer as inAriv!
From the top perspective, ProcessorOfJobs sends outJob to
Transducer as inSolved!
From the top perspective, Transducer sends stop to
GeneratorOfJobs!
GeneratorOfJobs can be High or Low in Frequency!
ProcessorOfJobs can be Fast or Slow in ProcessingSpeed!
```

The result of your interaction with the MS4 Me pruner is a *.pes file with the selections made in the interaction (Chap. 5). For example, the file might contain:

```
Select High from Frequency for GeneratorOfJobs!
Select Fast from ProcessingSpeed for ProcessorOfJobs!
inherit from GeneratorOfJobs!
inherit from ProcessorOfJobs!
```

Such a *.pes file is transformed into a coupled model as illustrated in Fig. 12.3. There are two ways that this transformation occurs as illustrated in Fig. 12.4. The first, and main approach, transforms the pruned entity structure into a hierarchical coupled model sewing together components available for atomic model classes stored in the model repository. These atomic models may have been developed in the FDDEVS enhancement process just discussed. Alternatively, they may have

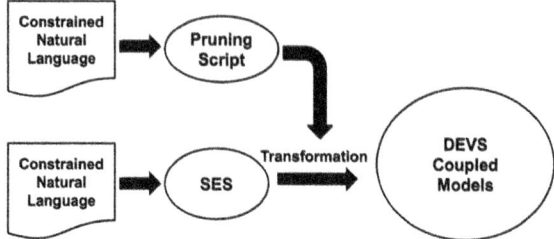

Fig. 12.3 Illustrating the path from natural language to SES to MS4 Me Java models

Fig. 12.4 Illustrating
convergence of FDDEVS and
SES generation paths

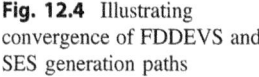

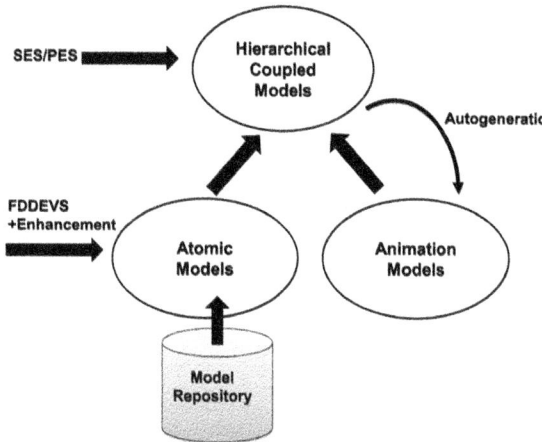

been developed in other ways—so long as they implement the AtomicModel interface. The second interpretation is to generate an animation that portrays the message exchanges among the components. Instead of drawing upon atomic models in the model repository, the animation process generates its own atomic models. These classes are derived from a base class that supplies the required input/output behavior when supplied the input and output ports derived from the SES (Chap. 3).

In the main approach, the transformation process searches for components in the model repository that match the names of the leaf entities in the SES. If such a name does not contain underscores, the name of the matching atomic model class must be equal to it. If the name contains underscores (so it represents a composite of parent and child classes, Chap. 7), then the base class specified in the pruning file (or by default) is the one sought for in the repository. Note that the SES can be used to access and compose models from repositories other than containing MS4 Java models so long as the subsequent composition process properly interprets the SES couplings in the target language.

12.3   DEVS, UML, and EMF

Unified Modeling Language (UML) has become a standard for software modeling (OMG 2005) so it is natural to consider its relation to the DEVS and SES modeling and simulation framework. Although UML is often viewed as a software development aid, it is much more attractive to take an inclusive perspective and view the DEVS/SES simulation and UML software modeling frameworks as complementing one another (Hong and Kim 2004; Huang and Sarjoughian 2004; Mittal 2007). As illustrated in Fig. 12.5, UML can serve as source framework to support DEVS specification as well as a target framework into which DEVS models can be mapped.

Let's consider mapping DEVS to UML which amounts to providing another form of DEVS simulator. In particular, DEVS models can be mapped to the UML component and statechart diagrams (Zinoviev 2005). From the distributed simulation perspective, DEVS atomic models can be mapped to XML statecharts (Risco-Martin et al. 2009). In another work, atomic models are expressed as statecharts (Mooney and Sarjoughian 2009). Users can develop DEVS-UML statecharts that are executable as DEVS models. This accounts for time in UML models through implementing the DEVS Protocol as a system-wide protocol of events without relying on the timing in the statechart simulator. Equivalency between statecharts and DEVS was employed in modeling embedded systems (Schulz et al. 2000).

An attractive aspect of UML is availability of tools to develop models that can be automatically transformed to code snippets for target programming languages (Mellor and Balcer 2002). Tools such as Eclipse integrate modeling tools and with powerful IDEs to develop the code snippets created from class specifications and statecharts that can execute in target DEVS simulators (e.g., MS4 Me, DEVS-Suite, and VLE). In this view, class, statechart, and sequence models fill the gap from abstract DEVS mathematical specifications to their implementation in target programming languages.

Fig. 12.5 UML in relation to DEVS specification languages

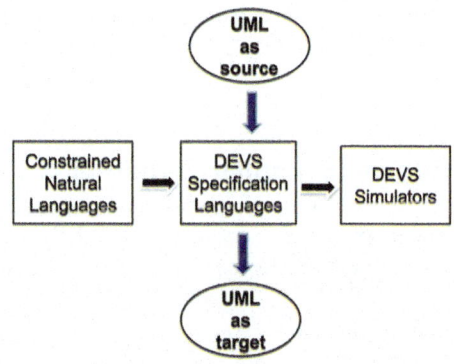

For application (domain-specific) DEVS model development, UML is also useful. Software design patterns with their UML models can be used to define domain knowledge atop DEVS domain-neutral model abstractions (Ferayorni and Sarjoughian 2007). Due to the abstract nature of DEVS formalism, UML models are particularly useful for developing simulation models that have complex system structures and behaviors. This approach is exemplified in the model development approach in Chaps. 14 through 16. Tool support also has been developed for translating general UML models to DEVS (Shaikh and Vangheluwe 2011). Non-UML domain specific languages mapping into DEVS (Mittal and Douglass 2011) can also augment the general mapping approach shown in Fig. 12.1.

DEVS simulation model development can also be defined using meta-modeling. The Eclipse Modeling Framework (EMF) is a meta-level modeling environment (Steinberg et al. 2008). It is used to introduce EMF-DEVS approach (Sarjoughian and Markid 2012). EMF-DEVS modeling environment supports meta-level atomic and coupled DEVS model specifications defined in terms of the Parallel DEVS formalism. It can be used to develop domain-specific models. A key advantage of the EMF-DEVS is adding constraints for user-defined models atop pre-defined ones for the generic atomic and coupled EMF-DEVS models. These constraints can help automate validation of structural properties of atomic and coupled model before generation of concrete simulation models for a target tool such as the DEVS-Suite simulator.

12.4 Summary

This chapter first provided a higher-level perspective on the approach that MS4 Me takes to computational support for constructing DEVS models for virtual build and test. After describing this approach, we expanded our view to include the possibility that UML can provide a more expressive framework for DEVS specification. For completeness, we also looked at how UML can serve as a target for implementation DEVS models. In the next part of the book, we will discuss implications and applications of the capabilities provided by DEVS Modeling Environments including MS4 Me, DEVS-Suite, and VLE.

Appendix: Formal Definition of FDDEVS

We employ the definition of XFD-DEVS presented at http://duniptechnologies. com/research/xfddevs/

```
XFD-DEVS = <
incomingMessageSet,
outgoingMessageSet,
```

```
StateSet,
TimeAdvanceTable,
InternalTransitionTable,
ExternalTransitionTable,
OutputTable>
```

where

incomingMessageSet, outgoingMessageSet, StateSet are finite sets,

TimeAdvanceTable: StateSet $\rightarrow$ R_0, ∞_+ (the positive reals with zero and infinity)

InternalTransitionTable: StateSet $\rightarrow$ StateSet

ExternalTransitionTable: StateSet $\times$ incomingMessageSet $\rightarrow$ StateSet, and

OutputTable: StateSet $\rightarrow$ 2outgoingMsgSet (= the set of subsets of outgoingMsgSet)

The mapping from an XFD-DEVS to a DEVS model is given in the following table:

XFD-DEVS parameter	DEVS specifications	Comment
incomingMessageSet	x = {(inMsg, Msg): Msg $\in$ incomingMessageSet}	for each incoming message, Msg, we construct an input port inMsg and allow Msg as the only value on it
outgoingMsgSet	Y = {(outMsg,Msg): Msg $\in$ outgoingMessageSet}[b]	For each outgoing message, Msg, we construct an output port outMsg and allow Msg as the only value on it. Bags of such message output are allowed. They can be constructed by providing rows in the internal transition table having different output paths for the same transition
StateSet	S = {(phase,sigma): phase $\in$ StateSet and sigma $\in$ $R_{0,\infty}^+$}	States in XFD-DEVS become phases in DEVS and have an associated time advance value, sigma
TimeAdvanceTable: StateSet $\rightarrow R_{0,\infty}^+$	ta: $S \rightarrow R_{0,\infty}^+$, where ta(phase, sigma) = sigma	The TimeAdvanceTable in XFD-DEVS is used to assign initial sigma values in DEVS as is seen below
InternalTransitionTable: StateSet $\rightarrow$ StateSet	δ_{int}: S $\rightarrow$ S, where δ_{int} (phase,sigma) = (phase', TimeAdvanceTable(phase')). where phase' = Internal-TransitionTable(phase)	The InternalTransitionTable in XFD-DEVS determines the phase of the next phase in DEVS, while the TimeAdvanceTable determines the initial value of sigma in this phase
ExternalTransitionTable: StateSet $\times$ incomingMessageSet $\rightarrow$ StateSet	δ_{ext}: Q $\times$ X $\rightarrow$ S, where δ_{ext} (phase,sigma,e,(inMsg, Msg)) = (phase', TimeAdvanceTable(phase')). where phase' = External-TransitionTable(phase,Msg) provided that	When it is defined, the ExternalTransitionTable in XFD-DEVS determines the phase of the next state in DEVS, while the TimeAdvanceTable determines the initial value of sigma in this state. We say that the

(continued)

(continued)

XFD-DEVS parameter	DEVS specifications	Comment
	ExternalTransitionTable (phase,Msg) is defined. otherwise, δ_{ext} (phase,sigma,(inMsg, Msg)) = (phase, sigma − e)	ExternalTransitionTable is defined for a state and incoming message when there is an entry in the table for that pair. Thus, when you don't provide a next state for a particular combination of states and inputs in XFD-DEVS, it is interpreted in the DEVS model as an order to ignore the input and continue in the state to the original transition time
	δ_{con}: Q × X → S is not specified by XFD-DEVS	The confluent function must be specified by the modeler in the DEVS model constructed from XFD-DEVS
OutputTable: StateSet → $2^{outgoingMsgSet}$	$\hat{y}$:S → Y^b where $\hat{y}$(phase,sigma) = {(outMsg, Msg): Msg ∈ OutputTable (phase)}	The output in the DEVS model is obtained by applying the XFD-DEVS output table to the phase component of the DEVS model state. The resulting value could be the empty set, in which case no output is emitted, a single value or multiple values, in which case, a bag of values is constructed

Note XFD-DEVS does not specify a unique DEVS since the confluent transition function is not specified

Note While the output of an XFD-DEVS can be a bag, the input is always a single element of the incomingMsgSet, not a bag

It is sometimes useful to retain the same time of next event even when a phase change is specified. To do this, an input may be distinguished as schedule preserving with the following effect on its DEVS.

Schedule preserving incoming message, Msg	δ_{ext}: Q × X → S, where δ_{ext} (phase,sigma,e,(inMsg, Msg)) = (phase', sigma − e) where phase ' = ExternalTransitionTable (phase,Msg) provided that ExternalTransitionTable(phase, Msg) is defined. otherwise, δ_{ext} (phase,sigma,(inMsg, Msg)) = (phase, sigma − e)	When it is defined for a schedule preserving input, theExternalTransitionTable in XFD-DEVS determines an immediate transition to the phase of the next state in DEVS with the next transition scheduled at the original transition time. Otherwise, it is interpreted in the DEVS model as an order to ignore the input and continue in the state to the original transition time

References

Ferayorni, A., & Sarjoughian, H. S. (2007). Domain driven modeling for simulation of software architectures. In *Summer Computer Simulation Conference*, San Diego, CA, USA (pp. 1–8).

Hong, S.-Y., & Kim, T. G. (2004). Embedding UML subset into object-oriented DEVS modeling process. In *Summer Computer Simulation Conference*, San Jose, CA, USA (pp. 1–6).

Huang, D., & Sarjoughian, H. S. (2004). Software and simulation modeling for real-time software-intensive systems. In *IEEE International Symposium on Distributed Simulation and Real-Time Applications*, Washington DC, USA (pp. 196–203).

Hwang, M. (2011). XSY: DEVS simulation and verification tool. http://code.google.com/p/x-s-y/.

Mellor, S. J., & Balcer, M. J. (2002). *Executable UML—A foundation for model-driven architecture*. Reading: Addison-Wesley.

Mittal, S. (2007). *DEVS unified process for integrated development and testing of service oriented architectures*. Ph.D. thesis, University of Arizona.

Mittal, S., & Douglass, S. (2011). From domain specific languages to DEVS components: Application to cognitive M&S. In *Proceedings of the 2011 Symposium on Theory of Modeling & Simulation: DEVS Integrative M&S Symposium* (pp. 256–265). Society for Computer Simulation International.

Mooney, J., & Sarjoughian, H. S. (2009). A framework for executable UML models. In *SpringSim Multi-conference*, San Diego, CA, USA (pp. 1–8).

OMG. (2005). UML 2.0 superstructure specification. http://www.omg.org/.

Risco-Martin, J. L., Mittal, S., Zeigler, B. P., & de la Cruz, J. (2009). eUDEVS: Executable UML with DEVS theory of modeling and simulation. *Simulation: Transaction of the Society for Modeling and Simulation, 85*(11–12), 750–777.

Sarjoughian, H. S., & Markid, A. M. (2012). EMF-DEVS modeling, symposium on theory of modeling and simulation—DEVS integrative M&S symposium. In *SpringSim Multi-conference*, April, Orlando, FL.

Schulz, S., Ewing, T. C., & Rozenblit, J. W. (2000). Discrete-event system specification (DEVS) and StateMate StateCharts equivalence for embedded systems modeling. In *IEEE International Conference and Workshop on the Engineering of Computer Based Systems*, Edinburgh (pp. 308–316).

Shaikh, R., & Vangheluwe, H. (2011). Transforming UML2.0 class diagrams and statecharts to atomic DEVS. In *Symposium on Theory of Modeling & Simulation*, Boston, MA, USA (pp. 203–212).

Steinberg, D., Budinsky, F., Paternostro, M., & Merks, E. (2008). *EMF eclipse modeling framework*. Reading: Addison-Wesely.

Zinoviev, D. (2005). Mapping DEVS models onto UML models. In *DEVS Integrative M&S Symposium*, San Diego, CA, USA (pp. 750–777).

Part III
Applications

Flexible Modeling Support Environments

13

The introduction laid out the theme of this book—it is about modeling and simulation to support "virtual build and test" of Systems of Systems (SoS). Constructing a computer model and testing the design of a configuration of components before implementing it in reality is increasingly the only workable approach to creating a SoS. The focus of Parts I and II was to elucidate the concepts underlying the approach to "virtual build and test" based on DEVS methodology in the context of the MS4 Modeling Environment. As we begin Part III, we now take a broader look at DEVS methodology and support environments from a number of different perspectives.

In this chapter, we discuss a design environment that supports the implementation of a novel architecture for systems of fractionated satellites—these are satellites that are composed from modular components. Although framed as applying to fractionated satellites, the considerations equally apply to many other types of SoS. The environment includes a comprehensive user input interface intended to elicit stakeholder objectives, values, and service requirements and a Modeling and Simulation Support Environment (MSE). As a core component of this environment, the MSE should be capable of providing simulations that evaluate spacecraft system architectures in response to the requirements of diverse stakeholders such as satellite designers, communications specialists, and space experimenters.

13.1 Supporting Multiple Paths Through Development Process

The goal of responding to the requirements of diverse stakeholders is contrasted with typical modeling and simulation (M&S) workflows conceptualized in Fig. 13.1. The workflow in Fig. 13.1a is that of a sequential waterfall process like that discussed in Chap. 3. It has phases such as conceptualization, design,

© Springer International Publishing AG 2017
B.P. Zeigler and H.S. Sarjoughian, *Guide to Modeling and Simulation of Systems of Systems*, Simulation Foundations, Methods and Applications, DOI 10.1007/978-3-319-64134-8_13

implementation, and testing together with the possibility of iterations that return the flow through earlier phases of the process. In contrast, the concept illustrated in Fig. 13.1b envisions a flexible system architecture that supports a wide variety of stakeholders who may be taking different paths through the environment. Depending on diverse interests, objectives, and values, different modeling, simulation, and analysis services as well as different pipelines of services may be appropriate. This expanded approach conforms better to a theory-based methodology for developing simulation models of complex systems (Aumann 2007). The key to achieving this flexibility is to provide an appropriate classification of stakeholders that places users with similar paths in the same equivalence class.

In the following, we evolve from a structured workflow such as in Fig. 13.1a to flexible environment such as Fig. 13.1b in a series of steps that show the advantages and utility of the latter concept as well as the requirements for control of activities and flow of information that need to be met to make it work.

Figure 13.2 depicts an example workflow process that starts with a formulation of requirements for a training system that a simulator is to support, e.g., flying a newly developed jet airplane, controlling a nuclear power plant, or a team collaboration in a war game (Kim et al. 2011). Such requirements state the kinds of behaviors that the training system should display and the kinds of interactions that users (trainees) can have with it. Analysis of these requirements then results in the kinds of objects that should be included, their attributes and behaviors, and the types of measurements that can be made of trainee performance. Next, a DEVS model is constructed that contains the objects and attributes as well as realizing the specified behaviors and measurement indexes. The model is implemented in a DEVS simulator which typically will be a distributed platform with multiple simulation nodes. Execution of the simulator by trainees (possibly training as a group in a distributed simulation) completes the process.

Fig. 13.1 Accommodating diverse stakeholders in a flexible MSE

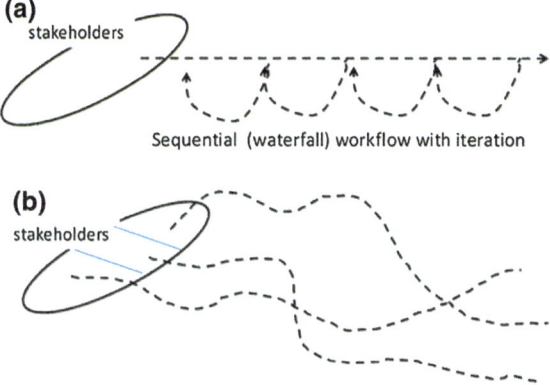

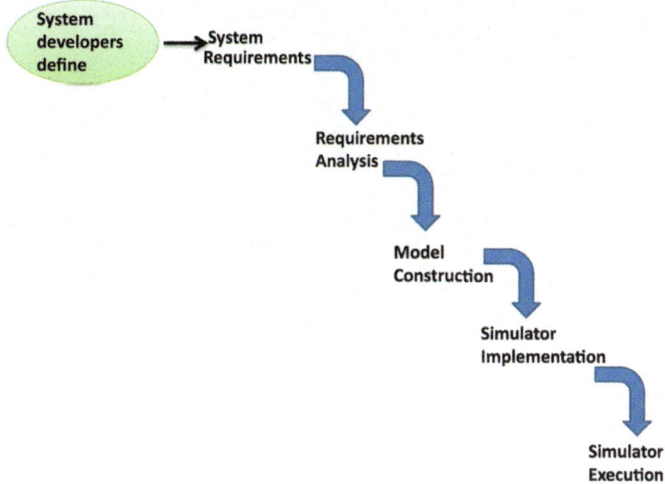

Fig. 13.2 Another formulation relating to developing training simulators

Sequential step-by-step depictions such as those in Fig. 13.2 are good at showing a normal workflow or idealized progress through M&S development processes.

A workflow depiction is a good starting point but fails to provide a sufficient basis for understanding how tools and services can support such processes.

- One defect is that the idealized nature of the waterfall sequence fails to portray how activities in real-world development processes proceed where departures from this pattern are more common than not.
- A second defect is the fact that the arrows signify flow of control without explicitly showing the information artifacts produced and consumed at each step.

Figure 13.3 addresses the first defect by showing one pattern in which the process can return to earlier steps in an iterative manner. We will refer to software applications or concepts that help you check your work at each step and enable you to return to this or earlier steps as *verification and validation* (V&V) tools. These tools can be contrasted to those that enable you to advance from one step to the next in the workflow, which we will call *progress* tools.

Figure 13.4 addresses the second defect by showing process steps as information processing modules with input and output data objects. In this diagram, the information flow follows along the lines of the sequence of processing steps so that whenever a step (or module) completes its work, the products are shown as outputs that are sent to the next module as inputs. This kind of information flow diagram can be enhanced to show data objects being sent forward to modules in the chain beyond the immediate next step, as well as in the reverse direction.

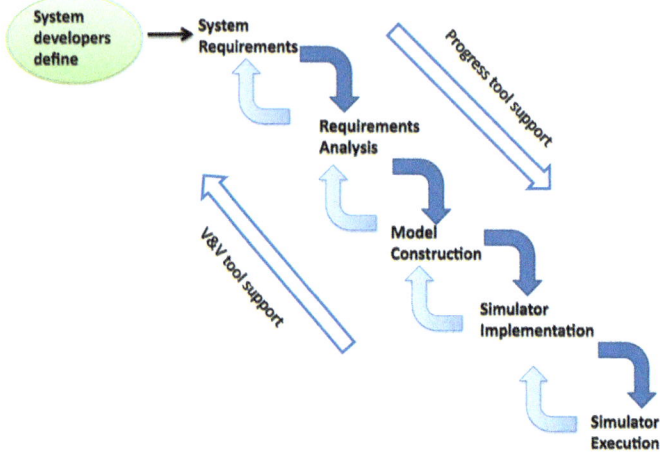

Fig. 13.3 Simulator development process with reverse verification steps

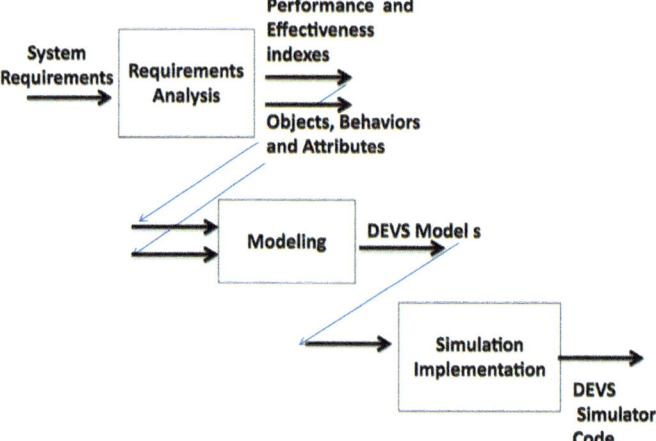

Fig. 13.4 Simulator development process showing information flow

However, we can get some better insight by taking another perspective, which focuses on the data and model objects produced and consumed by the progress and V&V tools. Following the approach of Kim et al. (2011), for M&S simulator development, we display in Fig. 13.5 some of the tools they developed. These tools include progress tools such as the concept of employing M&S Objectives to derive measures of performance and effectiveness from the given system requirements in the requirements analysis phase (step). Also included is the Object-Attribute-Index Matrix, which is a relation among objects, attributes, and performance indexes. This can be viewed as a relational database in which you can enter the performance or effectiveness indexes that were identified as needed during requirements analysis and get suggested objects and attributes to support work in the following model development phase. Requirements analysis also identifies behaviors of objects needed to realize the M&S Objectives. These behaviors are then expressed in UML sequence diagrams that capture the interaction of objects over time in various use cases that are also products of the requirements analysis. The V&V tools can do things like generate correct execution sequences that the implemented simulator must display. Any departures from such sequences signal that you should regress to the model development phase to redefine some of the DEVS models that may be the source of the errors. Not shown are also a host of progress and V&V tools that relate to the implementation of the simulator in a distributed simulation environment. See Kim et al. (2010) for details.

You can see that the more tools that are available *and* the more that they are effective and easy to use, the faster progress will be in achieving your objectives and requirements. A good part of the effectiveness of tools depends on their getting the right data produced by other tools. The workflow approach in Fig. 13.4 offers one way to do this by having tools send their outputs directly to tools that need their products as inputs. However, it is a rigid approach that can overly constrain development work as we shall see later. Figure 13.5 suggests a more flexible approach in which tools can deposit their output products in a persistent form and draw upon the products of others as needed from the common data store. This approach is not as straightforward to implement and brings up a number of interesting issues that we will address.

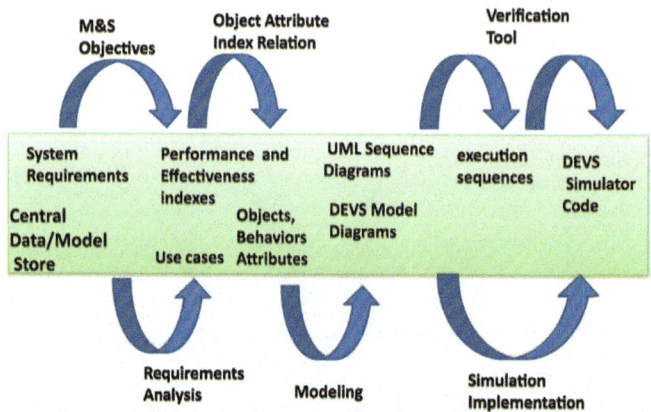

Fig. 13.5 Simulation development supported by tools interacting with a central store

13.2   M&S Tools as Services in a Service-Oriented Architecture

So far we have talked about formulating the activities of M&S in terms of processes and carrying out the phases of these processes with the help of tools. A sequential process such as in Fig. 13.1 provides a "baseline" to formulate the succession of activities that must be undertaken for a successful result. Real M&S activities depart from this baseline, but it still serves as way to support the M&S process with what we have called progress and V&V tools (Fig. 13.3). In such an extended process, the information exchange in which tools produce and consume data objects can be supported by peer-to-peer message flow (Fig. 13.4) or by reference to a common data store (Fig. 13.5). With this as background, we can make the leap to a service oriented architecture (SOA) environment as a framework for supporting M&S activities. Tools are encapsulated into Web services that are hosted on Web servers. Some instances of such services are shown in Fig. 13.6. The operations of Web services need the right interface descriptions to properly share data, whether directly or as mediated by the common model and data store. Moreover, service operations must be orchestrated, i.e., invoked in the proper order to execute the baseline M&S process or extended versions of it. Such interfacing and orchestration will be discussed later.

A SOA environment provides a number of important benefits:

- flexibility to support a diversity of users taking a multitude of different varia- tions from the baseline process,
- discoverability of the data and models developed and stored in the common data repository,
- reusability of discovered data and models in new compositions,
- learning over time based on mining the data in the common repository.

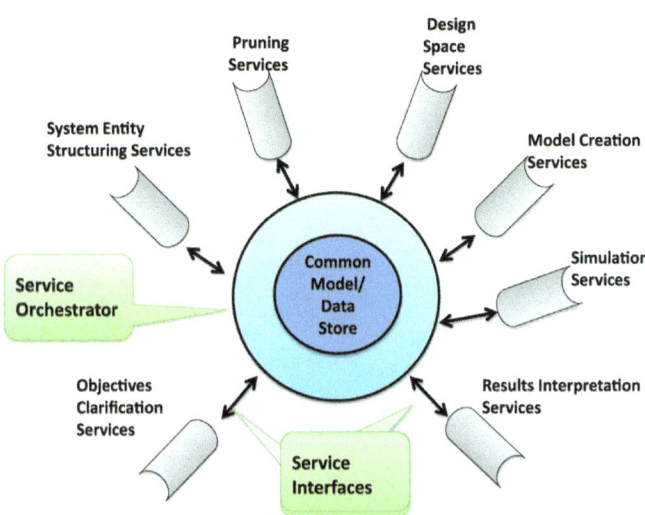

Fig. 13.6 Tools as services to support M&S in a SOA

13.3 Case Study: Fractionated Satellite Systems

The Frontier design environment is a research product of the DARPA System F6 Program (Future, Fast, Flexible, Fractionated, Free-Flying Spacecraft United by Information Exchange). This program envisions the evolution of spacecraft architectures from the point of view of the future with its potential for radically new satellite design and launch technologies that can support large numbers of smaller, modular, satellites organized by networks of communication and control. A central feature in the design of the Frontier MSE is to address the focus of the F6 program, which is to assess whether there can be fractionated architectures that can outperform current monolithic satellite systems. The following text is based on the article published by Zeigler et al. (2012). Phrased more broadly this question asks whether a proposed system of system can outperform the current system in operation.

We acknowledge that the term "outperform" will depend on the interests and objectives of stakeholders—there may not be a one-size-fits-all solution acceptable to everyone. Accordingly, we created a characterization of stakeholder interests that encapsulates the diversity of such interests within a space spanned by Strategic/Tactical and Supply/Demand dimensions. The Strategic/Tactical axis refers to the horizon (long versus short) and level (high versus low) of planning. The Supply/Demand axis refers to the characterization of stakeholders' requirements for services provided by the network of satellites (Demand) versus spacecraft assets and resources available to provide those services (Supply).

We briefly present this characterization and discuss its suitability to the problem. The interests of stakeholders for evaluations of potential fractionated spacecraft architectures available in the future are characterized in the Strategic/Tactical axis as either:

- *Strategic:* This reflects an interest in evaluations of how well architectures do overextended time spans (e.g., 20 years), assessing system architectures for their *ability to adapt, evolve, and survive* in the face of changing patterns of demand for services supplied by such architectures. This particularly emphasizes long-term market-oriented financial comparison of monolithic and fractionated cluster architectures.

or

- *Tactical:* This typically evaluates proposed architectures over relatively short time spans (e.g., 1 year) with a focus on system behavior and physical constraints (e.g., imposed by orbital mechanics) to address engineering and technological issues at the system level.

Refining this bipolar axis, we further break down stakeholder's interests into the four main categories:

- *Strategic/Supply* focuses on system developers, enabling them to explore the long-term financial performance of their proposed architectures or technologies.
- *Strategic/Demand* focuses on system user communities, enabling them to explore the long-term financial viability of their proposed profiles of demands, e.g., the range of experiments of interest to a NASA space exploration community.
- *Tactical/Supply* focuses on system developers, enabling them to explore the technical performance of their proposed architectures or technologies (e.g., the effect of spacing of satellites within a cluster on its ability to meet demands for services). This category includes engineers and scientists working on the technical aspects of the F6 program.
- *Tactical/Demand* focuses on individual system users, enabling them to explore the technical feasibility of their proposed profiles of demands (e.g., a set of experiments of interest to a particular mission developer).

Stakeholders are not limited to a single characterization; the same user may adopt different characterizations to gain insights available from different perspectives—e.g., switching between Strategic and Tactical to understand both economic prospects and technical feasibility of a potential solution.

The MSE is built upon a configurable framework that adapts to each of the four stakeholder types spanned by the above dimensions. Given such a stakeholder type, the MSE configures a simulation that outputs a set of architectures that are evaluated and ranked according to their ability to meet the user's requirements. The simulation is based on various levels of abstraction that are designed to support the stakeholder's questions and objectives. This allows a given set of architectures to be evaluated, on traditional attributes (cost, weight, etc.) as well as engineering: "iities" (adaptability, reliability, etc.).

13.3.1 How the MSE Adapts to Types of Stakeholders

The MSE is built on a set of harmonized components implemented as Web services that can be orchestrated to fit the stakeholder's requirements. The services are briefly enumerated and outlined:

- *Pre-Simulation Service (PSS):* interprets user inputs in the form of documents that specify demand and evaluation metrics (for experimental frames) and architectures (for models) needed by the downstream simulation.
- *Development and Pruning of Alternatives Service (DPAS):* is the core component that applies input pruning scripts to master characterization architectures to generate a subset of potential satellite cluster architectures to be explored.

- *Simulation Service:* includes both the Strategic and Tactical Simulation Services and simulates the architectures in response to the generated demands and supplies results for evaluation and ranking. The simulation is configured to either Strategic or Tactical forms depending on stakeholder interest. The Simulator Service module takes on two fundamental simulator configurations. The simulator configurations are based on models that embody abstractions of the investigated system architecture and its environment. These abstractions are tuned to the stakeholder types: Strategic (Supply or Demand) and Tactical (Supply or Demand). The simulators also tune the breadth and depth of the solution space and fidelity of the simulations (low and high) so support the user type.

  - *The Market Model Simulator (Strategic Level):* encapsulates an experimental frame (see Chap. 18) (generating demand inputs and collecting cluster outputs) that interacts with a Market Model to perform financial evaluation over a long time span composed of successive Simulation Analysis Intervals (e.g., quarterly).
  - *The Physical Model Simulator (Tactical Level):* encapsulates an experimental frame that interacts with a simulation model of the proposed architecture over a specified interval to evaluate system performance at the physical behavior level.

- *Results Analysis Service (RAS)*: transforms data generated by the simulation runs into information that can be presented to the user. The input to the RAS comes from the MSE and the PSS. The input from the MSE is the data from individual simulation runs for all value metrics aggregated by Simulation Analysis Interval (SAI). Among other items, the RAS generates an overall performance score for each cluster configuration instance from a weighted average of all value metrics and an overall operational risk score for each cluster configuration. These out puts provide the basis for ranking cluster configurations instances by performance score.
- *Evaluation Service (ES)*: provides the user with an interactive tool to perform decision analysis at increasing levels of detail and sophistication using the data compiled by the RAS. The functions performed by the ES include aggregating information from the RAS and generating evaluation scores to support advanced decision-making features, providing information to the user in form of decision analysis tools to support advanced interaction and analysis by the user, and collecting refined user criteria from the GUI to reassess the ranking order and current results, as well as to support sensitivity analysis of those results.

The MSE, as composed of harmonized Web services, is intended to meet a multitude of stakeholder requirements by configuring itself to enable each user to pursue multiple paths through the system. It is convenient, however, to begin with a more constrained view of user interaction with the system in which there are two main paths corresponding to the Strategic and Tactical user classification. Such paths can be viewed as the normal workflows visualized in Fig. 13.7. Both types of

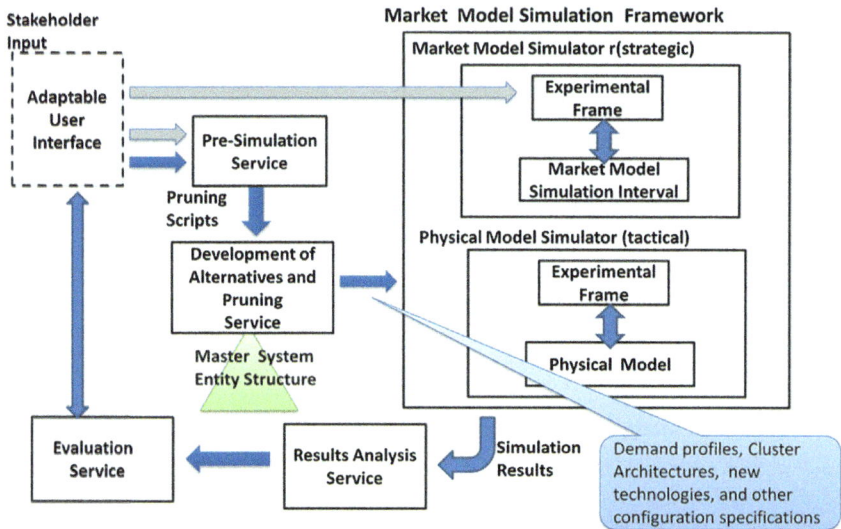

Fig. 13.7 MSE Workflow showing typical service sequencing (*purple*) and information flow (*gray*)

users start entering inputs at the Adaptable User Interface. Such elicited information is mapped into elements of experimental frames (EF) for later interaction with the models. After all available data have been entered, processing proceeds to the PSS and then the DPAS modules. At this point, the paths bifurcate according to the stakeholder characterization, where either the Market (Strategic) or Physical (Tactical) simulator service is invoked. Simulation results are then fed back to the user interface through the analysis and evaluation services.

This will typically initiate an iterative process in which the user's processing cycles several times through the corresponding work flow until arriving at a satisfactory outcome.

Although convenient as a first conception, such constrained workflows do not offer the flexibility we seek. Accordingly, we exploit the reconfigurability inherent in a Service Oriented Architecture with the orchestration of the offered services to provide much greater flexibility. Such flexibility allows users to flow through the processing steps at will bypassing intervening steps if appropriate. For example, users may iterate between the input GUI and the ES in order to try out different weights on their value attributes. Or a user may alternate between the Strategic and Tactical stances to gain the perspectives of both views on the feasibility of his/her technology proposal. In another case, especially after the system has accumulated simulation experience, the user may bypass simulation and employ estimates of cluster worth offered up the built-in learning mechanisms. Moreover, such flexibility allows users to interact intermittently with the system over time, building up individual profiles of work that provide a basis for starting from accumulated experience rather than from a clean slate at any time.

13.3.2 System Entity Structure (SES): Key Support for MSE Flexibility

The core component of the MSE necessary for its user-adaptive flexibility is the Development and Pruning of Alternative Service (DPAS). As indicated earlier, the DPAS generates instances of clusters that can potentially meet the user's requirements. The key enabler of such generation is a Master System Entity Structure (SES) (Chap. 3, Hagendorf and Pawletta 2010) which is the overall specification of all possible components and their relationships. In previous chapters, we have discussed tools to support specification of SESs in constrained natural language format, to prune SES so as to result in well-defined model specifications, and to transform such pruned entity structures (PES) to executable simulation models. Further, a constrained natural language approach to pruning not only allows easy manual pruning but also enables automated specification through input pruning scripts. This capability provides a key element in achieving the flexibility to adapt to user requirements. In the standard workflow of Fig. 13.7, the PSS outputs a pruning script to the DPAS which prunes the Master SES to constrain the model's structure (viz., the cluster architectures) to be evaluated via simulation. The family of PESs generated by the DPAS from a single pruning script constitutes the solution space. These PESs are encoded in XML and with the help of an XMLToOWL converter stored in the common data service (OWL-S 2004). In this form, they are available on demand to the simulators, whether Strategic or Tactical, as well as to other Frontier services (such as the RAS).

13.3.3 MSE Implementation: Service-Oriented Architecture

Figure 13.8 illustrates the implementation of the MSE as a set of Web service components that can be configured to adapt to stakeholder requirements. In the initial phase of the Frontier project, we implemented the constrained workflow of Fig. 13.2, and all information exchanges between services are mediated by the common data service supported by the Web Data Server. This is envisioned within a Web Services Environment that supports a "Semantic Bus" to be described shortly.

In the constrained workflow, an ad hoc function serves as orchestrator to move the processing steps along the paths illustrated in Fig. 13.9. However, a more flexible orchestration is required to implement automatic invocation of modeling services in such a way as to maximize value for the stakeholder. Depending on interests, objectives, and values, the stakeholder is categorized into one of the four basic categories discussed earlier, and different modeling services and different pipelines of services may be appropriate. Eventually, an intelligent learning system can make such decisions. However, initially, the orchestrator must be seeded with some criteria for selecting services and invoking them in a particular order, with outputs from some services passed as input to others.

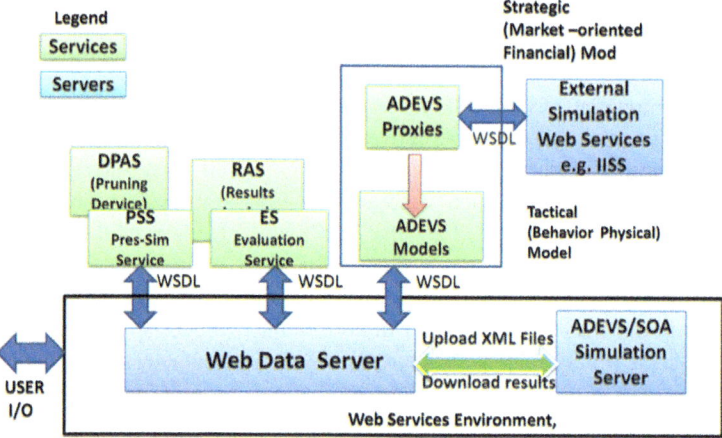

Fig. 13.8 Overall implementation of MSE

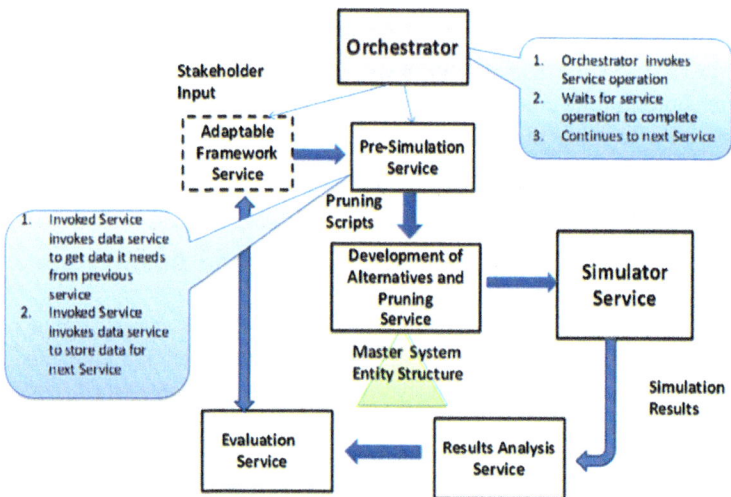

Fig. 13.9 Constrained orchestration of the MSE workflow

There are two overall methods for seeding such information.

- Hard coded representation in the orchestrator source code
- Representation in a process (service orchestration) specification.

We want to avoid hard coding such knowledge because it will be difficult to change as the experience with the system accumulates. There are well-established precedents for representing service orchestration in high-level specification languages, e.g., the Business Process Execution Language (2012), which is XML-based, and OWL-S (2004) in the semantic technology world. Because Frontier is a semantics-based system, an OWL-based representation is most appropriate. This representation will reside in the common data service and implemented in TripleStore (2012), thus providing support for orchestrating services.

The next level up in flexibility from a static OWL representation is to provide intelligence to perform simple matching between the declared capabilities of the basic MSE services (outlined in Fig. 13.8) and the declared needs (including values) of the user. We have argued above that the categorization into four types of users (along Strategic/Tactical and Supply/Demand dimensions) provides a good initial basis for such matching, particularly with respect to the choice of model abstraction for simulation.

Eventually, an intelligent learning system can make better matches, i.e., those that maximize the value for the stakeholder. The easiest and most simple-minded form of matching will look for explicit matches, i.e., equal values, between corresponding attributes (OWL properties) of the Frontier services and the user requiring the services. Such matching will, at first, be crude, but it will be more than syntactic signature matching because the properties represent semantic information about both the demand and supply side. More advanced matching will involve dynamic orchestration decisions, such as examining the results from one service and inferring—at that point—whether they should be passed to another service, or whether perhaps the previous inputs should be passed to another service, etc. Whether such learned rules and/or choices can themselves be represented in OWL or must be kept in a sub-symbolic neural representation is not yet clear, but in either case, the goal is to provide the ability to adapt services to stakeholder needs and different notions of stakeholder value. We can envision that the orchestrator will maintain models for the users which represent their beliefs, goals, and intentions in relation to using the tools and executing the steps toward getting the results they expect. The concept of agents, as represented in DEVS, discussed in Chap. 10, is appropriate here.

13.3.4 MSE Simulation Service

The simulation service constitutes another key component in the realization of the overall objective of the Frontier design environment. Recall that its task is to provide an environment that caters to the interests of a wide variety of stakeholders in the construction of a novel architecture of fractionated satellites. Indeed, the MSE relies on the simulation service to provide simulations that evaluate spacecraft system architectures in response to diverse stakeholders' requirements. The simulation service includes both the Strategic and Tactical Simulation Services and simulates architectural models in response to the generated demands and supplies results for evaluation and ranking. The simulation is configured to either Strategic or Tactical forms depending on stakeholder interest. The Tactical Simulation Service encapsulates a DEVS coupled model containing an experimental frame (EF) (see Chap. 18) that interacts with the Physical Model Simulator (PMS) as seen in Fig. 13.10. The EF generates space system service requests over a simulation time interval to the PMS. The parameters of the service request stream are derived from the demand profile elicited through interactions with the stakeholder. The PMS simulates the processing of these requests based on a cluster configuration that has been developed for it by the DPAS. A cluster consists of a networked group of satellites evaluated in the simulation. The cluster may be made up of specific satellites, or satellites may rotate in and out of the cluster due to the line of sight considerations or module hardware/software failures. The total time encompassed by each simulation is the same for all instantiations, and each run of a specific cluster instantiation results in a single series of time-ordered events that describe in specific changes in the cluster as the simulation progresses. During the simulation, outputs of the PMS are continually sent to the EF as events occur. At the end of the simulation interval, the EF provides the values for performance measures that it has developed by summarization and statistical operations performed on the received data. The performance metrics originate from the input elicited through interaction with the stakeholder.

The Market Model Simulator (Strategic Level) consists of an experimental frame that interacts with a Market Model (MM) to perform financial evaluation over a long time span composed of successive Simulation Analysis Intervals (e.g., quarterly). The goal of the simulation is to generate time series data that can be used in the market analysis in the RAS. As for the tactical case, the simulations use instantiations of clusters generated by the DPAS and are designed to output data that will support the evaluation of the values, goals, and metrics derived from the stakeholder input by the elicitation process. As shown in Fig. 13.11, the MMSF

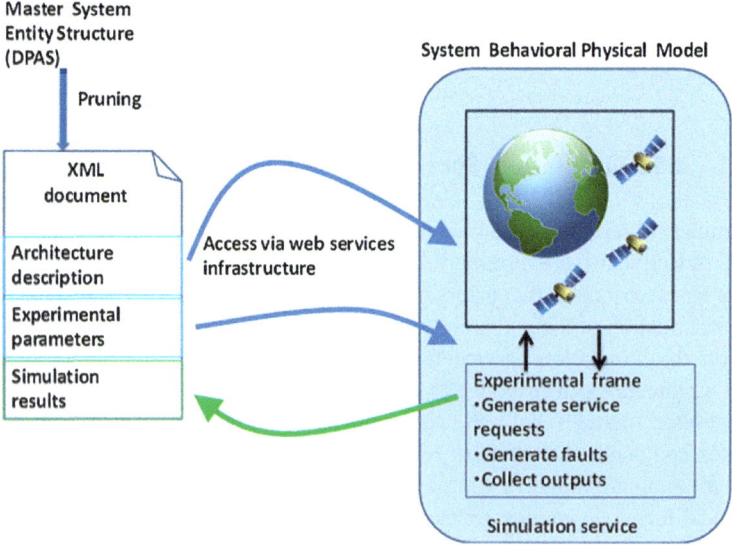

Fig. 13.10 Simulation service with encapsulated experimental frame and PMS

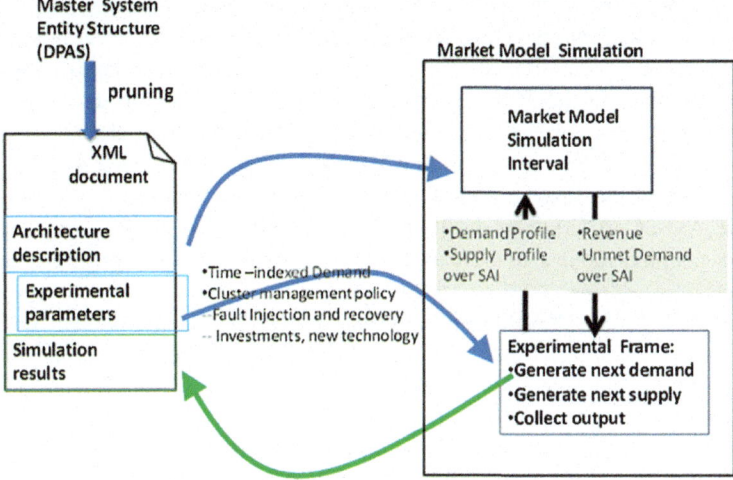

Fig. 13.11 Interaction of the experimental frame

contains an experimental frame that interacts with the MM. Similarly to the interaction with the PMS, the EF receives input (via the common data service) from the DPAS in an XML format. The total time encompassed by each simulation run remains constant for all simulations of all instantiation for a given cluster. Each simulation run of a specific cluster instantiation will result in a single series of time-ordered events that describe in specific changes in the cluster as the simulation progresses.

In contrast to the PMS, in the interaction with the MM, this series of changes is divided into time periods during which the cluster configuration and atomic services do not change. These periods of stable cluster configuration are referred to as Simulation Time Periods (STPs) and consist of a varying number of Simulation Analysis Intervals (SAIs). Each STP and the cluster configuration associated with it defines the data that are output to the common data service and stored in TripleStore for market evaluation. Because a single series of events generated by s single simulation run cannot be considered an adequate description of the entire range of possible event strings, multiple simulation runs are conducted with the same cluster and environment. The data gathered from all the simulations runs are aggregated to generate probability distributions on the parameters of interest. These distributions describe the range of possible outcomes for the parameters of interest and provide the basis for the risk analysis component of the RAS.

13.3.5 Simulation Using Web Services

As illustrated in Fig. 13.8, the implementation of Frontier Simulation Services is based on the extension of the open-source ADEVS (2012) environment to support simulation using Web services. This work was comprised of three major steps: (1) enabling models expressed in ADEVS to be provisioned on server hosts and to be simulated in a federation employing Web technologies, (2) adapting the simulation coordinator in the Main Service to execute in C++ and to exchange simulation control messages with the simulators, and (3) adapting the simulators to exchange DEVS payload messages in XML format. These steps were accomplished with the help of the Apache Axis2C and Staff tools for Web service development (Apache Axis2C 2012). The resulting environment, called ADEVS/SOA, allows ADEVS coupled models to be executed on an open-source Tomcat-based SOA platform.

In contrast to the DEVS/SOA (Seo and Zeigler 2012) environment based on DEVSJava (Sarjoughian and Zeigler 1998), there are limitations to the ADEVS/SOA environment that should be noted:

- ADEVS/SOA (C++) does not support dynamic instantiation of ADEVS models.
- ADEVS/SOA (C++) does not support reflection functions for object classes' variables.
- ADEVS/SOA does not support dynamic creation of XML DEVS messages from ADEVS messages.
- ADEVS/SOA does not create ADEVS Simulator Services with uploaded ADEVS models.

These limitations, stemming from the C++ language, imply that work must be done in individually tailored, rather than automated, fashion to integrate an ADEVS model to execute on ADEVS/SOA. In particular, simulation servers must be individually provisioned with simulator services with preassigned atomic models. In contrast to the DEVS/SOA environment, atomic models can be downloaded to generic simulation servers and locally compiled. An ADEVS/SOA Simulation Client takes a folder containing pruned entity structure (PES) XML files and sends the selected XML file to an ADEVSMainService hosting simulation services. Such a client operates in the following sequential manner:

1. The client selects the PES XML file from a resident folder at its machine.
2. The selected XML file is uploaded to the ADEVSMainService.
3. The client invokes the start simulation service of the ADEVSMainService to coordinate ADEVS Simulator Services.

Once the simulation is over, the aggregated simulation logs from various servers are forwarded to the client's machine.

Also as shown in Fig. 13.8, ADEVS/SOA can reach out to external Web service simulations through ADEVS proxy models that can participate in ADEVS coupled models while invoking remote Web services. Due the limitations of C++ libraries for dynamic invocation of Web services, the creation of ADEVS proxies is not as convenient as in the ingestion process developed for DEVS/Java. However, ADEVS proxies can be generated with a Java-based program using a similar process in DevsJava because Staff tools provide libraries for dynamic invocation and XML handling functions. We conclude that despite its execution performance advantages, a C++-based environment is not as suitable as a Java-based counterpart for flexibility and extensibility such as envisioned for the Frontier environment.

13.4   MSE in Operation: An Example Thread

We follow an end-to-end workflow thread in which cluster architecture is compared against a monolithic satellite for the same input service demand profile. A master cluster architecture containing satellites that can have different types of sensors and different communication capabilities is illustrated in the SES partially displayed:

```
From the sys perspective, GeneralClusterArch is made of
ExperimentalFrame and SatelliteModules!
From the mult perspective, SatelliteModules are made of
more than one SatelliteModule!
SatelliteModule can be id in index!
From the activity perspective, SatelliteModule is made of
Energizing, Propulsing, Communicating, Navigating,
Controlling, and Sensing!
From the subSensSys perspective, Sensing is made of Sensor!
From the subCommSys perspective, Communicating is made of
Communication!
From the subCDHSys perspective, Controlling is made of
CommNDataHandling!
Sensor can be Present or NotPresent in presence!
Sensor can be Visual, InfraRed, Radar, or MultiCapability in
EMType!
...
```

Note the use of the multi-aspect concept for SatelliteModule to allow any number of modules to be used to make a satellite system. The top level of satellite decomposition, called activity aspect, includes functions that any satellite optionally has. These functions are further broken down at the next level into decompositions with components that can implement the functions and/relevant specializations. Two such functions, Communications and Sensing, are broken out in the Fig. 13.12.

The Master SES can be pruned to generate different cluster configurations, or instantiations, which are points in the solution space. Of course, the user's requirements will dictate which points count as solutions for him/her. Cluster instantiations include dimensions such as:

Fig. 13.12 Master SES provides a characterization of service demands and potential architectures to be explored

- Cluster size (number of satellites in the cluster),
- Satellite configuration (e.g., which satellites have which types of sensors),
- Atomic Services (modules) to be included in the cluster,
- Functional dependencies,
- Communications capabilities (e.g., intersatellite or down to ground),
- Module-specific parameters
- Mean times to failure,
- Sensor, and communication footprints
- Susceptibility to external influences.

The PSS generates scripts that condition the SES to generate a more focused solution space. Some of the operations available for use are illustrated by the following:

- A pruning operation (e.g., *select Radar from EMType for Sensor!*) selects Radar from the EMType specialization for every Sensor—a context specification can be added to restrict the selection to only those Sensors in the context.
- An SES restructuring operation (e.g., *don't select Radar under Sensor!*) eliminates the selection of Radar from specializations that occur under Sensor everywhere Sensor occurs.
- Statements that check resulting PESs and accept only those that satisfy specified conditions:

- set count bounds for Visual_Sensor as [0,2]!
- set count bounds for CommUpNDownLink as [1,2]!

The distinction between general clusters and a monolithic baseline is embodied in different count bounds for the general cluster case (e.g., ***set count bounds for SatelliteModule as [3,6] !***) and for the monolithic case (e.g., ***set count bounds for SatelliteModule as [1,1] !***).

A particular specialization, *presence*, has a specific connotation (e.g., ***select Present from presence for CommInterSatelliteLink!***) results in the presence of CommInterSatelliteLink in the PES vice (***select NotPresent from presence for CommInterSatelliteLink!***) in which CommInterSatelliteLink is eliminated from the PES. The first selection applies to the general clusters case, while the second is appropriate to the monolithic case.

The output of the DPAS is a collection of PESs expressed as XML documents. In principle, such a PES can be interpreted by any suitable model. However, in practice, models are tuned to the objectives they are built to serve. Reflecting this circumstance, an SES for Physical Model is less inclusive in scope and more detailed in physics than the Master SES. The SES for Physical Model is partially displayed:

```
From the topSys perspective, FrontierPMS is made of
ExpFrame and SatelliteModules!
From the multiSatellite perspective, SatelliteModules are
made of more than one SatelliteModule!
SatelliteModule can be id in index!
SatelliteModule has ID!
The range of SatelliteModule's ID is int!
SatelliteModule can be ImageSat or RelaySat in moduleType!
From the image perspective, ImageSat is made of
SensorModule, CommModule, and Orbit!
SensorModule has fov, viewRange, and imageBits!
...
```

As with the GeneralClusterArch SES, the use of the multi-aspect concept for SatelliteModule allows any number of modules to be used to make a satellite system. However, in this case, SatelliteModule has a specialization in ImageSat or RelaySat so that there can be any number of image and relay satellites, respectively, as illustrated in Fig. 13.13 (also see Chap. 6).

A mapping from GeneralClusterArch (Master) SES to Physical SES relates the two abstractions as illustrated in Fig. 13.14.

One main difference between the GeneralClusterArch SES and the Physical Model SES is that the latter distinguishes satellites as either imaging or relay, while the former treats all satellites uniformly with the distinction arising from the selection of alternatives in the pruning phase. Thus, as discussed in Chap. 11, the mapping actually is at the pruned level so that a pruned GeneralClusterArch SES is mapped to a pruned Physical Model SES. Indeed, the mapping expressed at the

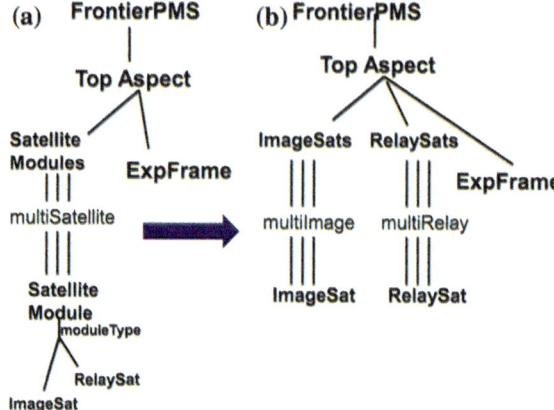

Fig. 13.13 Illustrating the restructuring of SatelliteModules into ImageSats and RelaySats

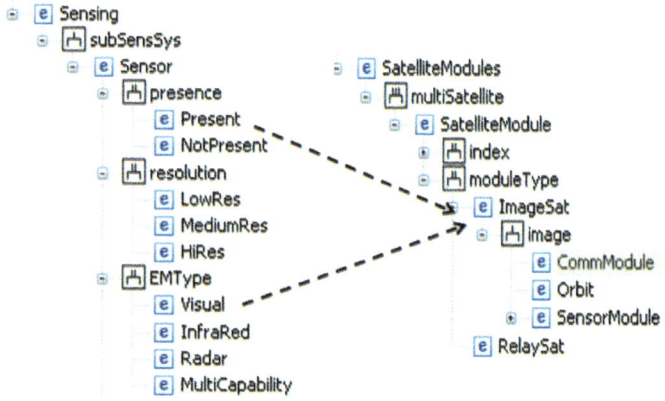

Fig. 13.14 Mapping from Master SES to SES for Physical Model

XML level constructs an XML document configuring a Physical Model from an XML document representing configured cluster architecture. To illustrate the mapping, consider the following illustrated in Fig. 13.14:

```
For each SatelliteModule in the cluster,
if
    both an inter-satellite communication link (or any type)
 and a Sensor (of any type) are present in the
 substructure under the SatelliteModule,
then
 add an imageSat to the Physical Model cluster.
```

A similar rule to create relay satellites requires the presence of intersatellite communications and Up/Down Links to Earth as well as the absence of a Sensor. This kind of mapping has some very desirable attributes:

- It allows pruning of the Master SES to consistently configure multiple model abstractions—manual configuration of a single simulator model is difficult to let alone consistent settings across multiple models.
- It allows the simulator to fill in missing information that it knows best (e.g., the mapping need not determine all choices in the Physical Model SES, only those that guarantee a compatible structure).
- It provides constraint criteria for improving Master pruning yield (percentage of pruned SESs that are desired instantiations). This needs further explanation. The mapping from master cluster architecture PESs to Physical Model PESs is actually not defined on the full domain of pruned entity structures, i.e., many master PESs do not yield a valid Physical Model configuration. For example, a SatelliteModule with no intersatellite communications does not correspond to either imaging or relay assignment. To increase the probability of generating a meaningful Physical Model configuration, we should require that an inter-satellite communication link be present in every satellite. This can be done by an appropriate pruning illustrated above. Thus, the yield of the pruning operation can be identified as the size of the range set of the mapping. This can be increased by properly constraining the domain of the mapping, i.e., judiciously applied conditioning pruning rules.
- The mapping supports criteria for validation of the source SES. Assuming that the mapping is correct, any violation must be laid at the foot of the master SES itself.

Mapped clusters are simulated in the PMS and evaluated according to metrics of interest to the user. When invoked, the simulator service gets the given cluster instantiation and experimental frame data from the common store and starts execution. Since the latter data is the same for all candidate clusters, the performance evaluation of candidate clusters produced by the simulation allows them to be compared on equal footing. A ranking of instantiations may contain several monolithic architectures mixed in with truly fractionated clusters. If under a wide variety of conditions, the fractionated clusters dominate the monolithic cluster, the case for fractionation would be established.

13.5 Summary

In this chapter, we have discussed the Frontier Modeling Support Environment whose goal is to provide the flexibility to adapt its workflows, tools, and models, to diverse stakeholders in the DARPA F6 program. We outlined the unique features of the MSE that support its use by a wide spectrum of potential users and developers of a system of fractionated spacecraft. These features include:

- identification of user types to enable routing the user through relevant processing stages,
- automated generation of model artifacts adapted to selected pathways,
- conditioning of the solutions space to increase the opportunities to find suitable fractionated architectures,
- flexible simulation services,
- consistent configuration across multiple abstraction models, and
- semantics-based orchestration of service-oriented architecture.

Joint MEASURE (Zeigler et al. 1999) is a simulation system that evolved to measure the utility of intelligence collection assets and strategies. The MSE was developed to abstract and re-implement Joint MEASURE's features on the SES and DEVS/SOA platform. Although the MSE is in its initial capability phase of development, the major features just stated have been demonstrated in a prototype. Much remains to be done including design and implementation of the semantics-based orchestration and an automated approach to mappings of the Master SES to incorporated abstractions. We also need to go beyond to the current pair of models (physical and market) to populating the environment with services and models to address a full range of stakeholder's objectives. As discussed above, the ingestion process for external Web services is a key to such extensibility and may require the adoption of Java-based, rather C++-based, proxies. Beyond the ability to exchange messages and invoke services enabled by such proxies, the perennial problem of harmonizing the data formats and operations protocols of external tools must be tackled. An ontologies-based approach is under development consistent with the development of the semantics-based data store discussed above. The advance of Semantic Web technology and the development of pragmatics-based data engineering (Zeigler and Hammonds 2007) provide some hope that significant progress can be made, particularly within a restricted domain such as spacecraft architectures.

As is readily apparent, the approach taken in the design and development of the Frontier MSE is based on fundamental principles that have application much beyond spacecraft fractionated systems. This generic quality of the MSE concept suggests the applicability of basic design to virtual build and test of today's system of systems.

Acknowledgements This research was supported in part by the DARPA F6 Program. Technical area 1: Design Tools for Adaptable Systems.

Appendix 1: GeneralClusterArchSeS.txt

From the sys perspective, GeneralClusterArch is made of
ExperimentalFrame and SatelliteModules!
From the mult perspective, SatelliteModules are made of more
than one SatelliteModule!
SatelliteModule can be id in index!
From the activity perspective, SatelliteModule is made of
Energizing, Propulsing, Communicating, Navigating,
Controlling, and Sensing !
From the subSensSys perspective, Sensing is made of Sensor!
From the subCommSys perspective, Communicating is made of
Communication!
From the subCDHSys perspective, Controlling is made of
CommNDataHandling!
Sensor can be Present or NotPresent in presence!
Sensor can be Visual, InfraRed, Radar, or MultiCapability in
EMType!
Sensor can be SingleBand or MultiBand in band!
Sensor can be LowRes, MediumRes, or HiRes in resolution!
Sensor can be LowTolerant or HighTolerant in
faultTolerance! Sensor can be Stereoscopic or Monoscopic in stereo!
Sensor can be StabalizedPointing or NonPointing in
pointingCapability!
Sensor can be DataIntensive or NotDataIntensive in
dataHandling!
From the SensoryFunctionA perspective, Sensor is made of
EarthObservation, and RemoteSensing!
EarthObservation can be Present, or NotPresent in presence!
RemoteSensing can be Present, or NotPresent in presence!
From the SensoryFunctionB perspective, Sensor is made of
SpaceObservation, and DataCollecting!
SpaceObservation can be Present, or NotPresent in presence!
DataCollecting can be Present, or NotPresent in presence!
Communication can be Present in presence!
From the Subsystem perspective, Communication is made of
CommUpNDownlink, CommInterSatelliteLink, and
ProcessingPayload!

From the commSys perspective, CommUpNDownlink is made of
CommUplink and CommDownlink!
From the Component perspective, CommUplink is made of
ULAntenna, and Receiver!
CommUpNDownlink can be Present, or NotPresent in presence!
CommInterSatelliteLink can be Present, or NotPresent in
presence!
From the Component perspective, CommDownlink is made of
DLAntenna, and Transmitter!
CommInterSatelliteLink can be HighBandwidthLink, or
LowBandwithLink in Option!
HighBandwidthLink can be LaserLink in HBLink!
LowBandwithLink can be RadioLink in LBLink!
From the Component perspective, ProcessingPayload is made of
OnBoardProcessor, SpaceQualifiedRouter, Diplexer,
Coupler, Transciever, Amplifier, Modulator, Filter, Mixer,
Frequency_ClockGenerator, and Multiplexer!
ProcessingPayload can be Present, or NotPresent in presence!
CommNDataHandling can be Present or NotPresent in presence!
From the SubSystem perspective, CommNDataHandling is made of
CDHUplink, CDHDownlink, and TelemetryTracking!
From the component perspective, CDHUplink is made of
ReceiverAntenna, and ReceiverSystem!
From the component perspective, CDHDownlink is made of
TransmitterAntenna, and TransmitterSystem!
From the Subsystem perspective, TelemetryTracking is made
of OnBoardComputer, Processor, and IntersatelliteLink!
Sensor has weight,volume, and cost!
The range of Sensor's weight is double !
The range of Sensor's volume is double !
The range of Sensor's cost is double !
Sensor has fov, viewRange, and imageBits!
if select Present from presence for CommUpNDownlink then
select Present from presence for Communication!
if select Present from presence for CommInterSatelliteLink
then select Present from presence for Communication!

Appendix 2: Outline of GeneralCusterSeS

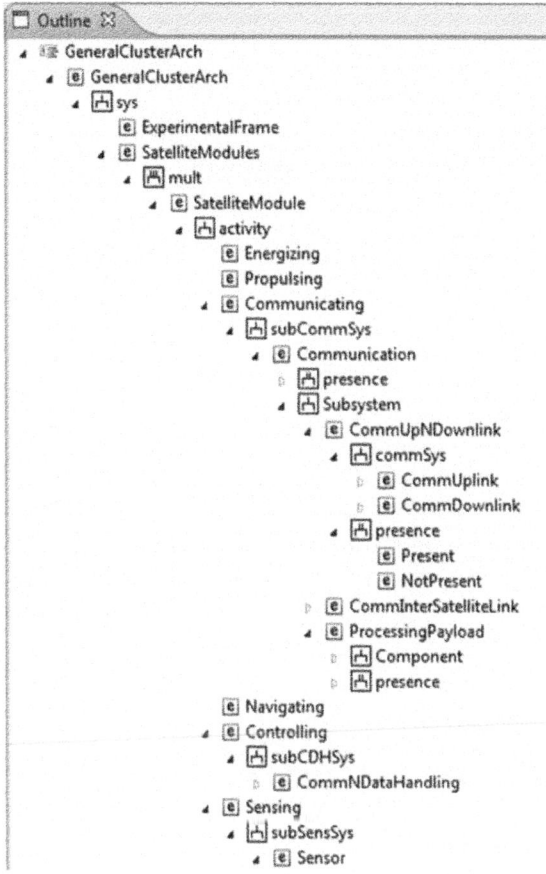

Appendix 3: GeneralClusterArchBasicPrune.pes

```
don't select Radar under Sendor !
don't select MultiCapabilty under Sendor!
don't select LowRes under Sensor !
don't select Stereoscopic under Sensor !
don't select MultiBand from band under Sensor !
don't select StabilizedPointing under Sensor !
don't select DataIntensive under Sensor !
restructure multiaspects using index !
set multiplicity of index as [6] for SatelliteModule !
set count bounds for SatelliteModule as [3,6] !
```

```
select Present from presence for CommInterSatelliteLink !
set count bounds for Visual as [1,2] !
set count bounds for Infrared as [1,2] !
set count bounds for CommUnNDownLink as [1,2] !
set count bounds for ProcessingPayload as [1,2] !
set count bounds for LowTolerant_Visual_Sensor as [0,2] !
set count bounds for HighTolerant_InfraRed_Sensor as [0,1] !
set count bounds for Visual as [0,1] per SatelliteModule !
set count bounds for Infrared as [0,1] per SatelliteModule !
set count bounds for CommInterSatelliteLink as [1,2] per
SatelliteModule!
set count bounds for CommUnNDownLink as [0,1] per
SatelliteModule !
set count bounds for ProcessingPayload as [0,1] per
SatelliteModule !
```

Appendix 4: GeneralClusterArchMonolithicPrune.pes

```
don't select Radar under Sensor !
don't select MultiCapabilty under Sensor !
don't select LowRes under Sensor !
don't select Stereoscopic under Sensor !
don't select MultiBand from band under Sensor !
don't select StabilizedPointing under Sensor !
don't select DataIntensive under Sensor !
restructure multiaspects using index !
set multiplicity of index as [6] for SatelliteModule !
set count bounds for SatelliteModule as [1,1] !
select NotPresent from presence for CommInterSatelliteLink !
set count bounds for Visual as [1,2] !
set count bounds for Infrared as [1,2] !
set count bounds for CommUnNDownLink as [1,2] !
set count bounds for ProcessingPayload as [1,2] !
set count bounds for LowTolerant_Visual_Sensor as [0,2] !
set count bounds for HighTolerant_InfraRed_Sensor as [0,1] !
```

References

ADEVS. (2012). An open source C++ DEVS simulation engine. http://www.ornl.gov/~1qn/adevs/index.html.

Apache Axis2C. (2012). http://axis.apache.org/axis2/c/core/.

Aumann, G. A. (2007). A methodology for developing simulation models of complex systems. *Ecological Modelling, 202*, 385–396.

Business Process Execution Language. (2012). http://en.wikipedia.org/wiki/Business_Process_Execution_Language.

Hagendorf, O., & Pawletta, T. (2010). Framework for simulation-based structure and parameter optimization of discrete-event systems. In G. A. Wainer & P. J. Mosterman (Eds.), *Discrete-event modeling and simulation: Theory and applications*. Boca Raton: CRC Press.

Kim, T. G., et al. (2010). DEVSim++ toolset for defense modeling and simulation and interoperation. *Journal of Defense Modeling and Simulation, 8*(3), 129–142.

Kim, T. G., Sung, C. H., Hong, S.-Y., Hong, J. H., Choi, C. B., Kim, J. H., et al. (2011). DEVSim++ toolset for defense modeling and simulation and interoperation. *The Journal of Defense Modeling and Simulation: Applications, Methodology, Technology, 8*(3), 129–142.

OWL-S. (2004). http://www.w3.org/Submission/OWL-S/.

Sarjoughian, H. S., & Zeigler, B. P. (1998). DEVSJAVA: Basis for a DEVS-based collaborative M&S environment. In *Proceedings of the SCS International Conference on Web-Based Modeling and Simulation*, San Diego (Vol. 5, pp. 29–36).

Seo, C., & Zeigler, B. P. (2012). Simulation model standardization through web services: interoperation and federation on the DEVS/SOA platform. In *DEVS Intergrative M&S Symposium, Proceedings of the Spring Simulation Conference*, Orlando, FL, March 2012.

TripleStore. (2012). http://en.wikipedia.org/wiki/Triplestore.

Zeigler, B. P., & Hammonds, P. (2007). *Modeling & simulation-based data engineering: Introducing pragmatics into ontologies for net-centric information exchange*. New York: Academic Press.

Zeigler, B. P., Hall, S. B., & Sarjoughian, H. (1999). Exploiting HLA and DEVS to promote interoperability and reuse in Lockheed's corporate environment. *Simulation Journal, 73*(4), 288–295.

Zeigler, B. P., Nutaro, J., Seo, C., Hall, S., Clark, P., Rilee, M., Bailin, S., Speller, T., & Powell, W. (2012). Frontier modeling support environment: Flexibility to adapt to diverse stakeholders. In *Symposium on Theory of Modeling & Simulation—DEVS Integrative M&S Symposium*. Orlando: SpringSim.

Service-Based Software Systems

14

Service-Oriented Computing (SOC) systems are examples of Systems of Systems (SoS) within the realm of information technology. This chapter continues the theme of modeling and simulation (M&S) to support "virtual build and test" of SoS, in this case, focusing on services as components of software systems. We have already encountered Service-Oriented Architecture (SOA) concepts in Chap. 12. Here, we will show how DEVS-based M&S offers one-of-a-kind capabilities for under-standing SOC systems, also referred to as *Service-Based Software Systems* (SBS) . "Virtual build and test" of such systems must support two goals: (1) complying with Service-Oriented Architecture (SOA) standards and (2) satisfying multiple, competing Qualities of Service (QoS) requirements. Toward these two goals, a set of generic SOA-based models is developed based on the Discrete-Event System Specification (DEVS) framework. We describe the ideas and specifications for the SOA-Compliant models and extend the publish/subscribe concepts introduced earlier (Chap. 10) to the publisher, subscriber, and broker models common to service-based software systems. These model elements are then extended to support service-based software systems which can dynamically add and delete publishers and subscribers in order to adapt to changing conditions that may be needed due to changes in service quality requirements. In contrast to earlier chapters, our dis-cussion uses DEVS-Suite (Kim et al. 2009; DEVS-Suite 2017), an extension of the DEVSJAVA simulator, to present the resulting SOA-based DEVS (SOAD) models. However, since they are based on DEVS and can be simulated using the DEVS Protocol (Chap. 9), equivalent models can be developed using MS4 Me.

14.1 Introduction

Simulation is considered useful and increasingly indispensable across all phases of system development life cycle (i.e., conceptualization, design, implementation, deployment, and operation). This observation applies strongly to service-based

B.P. Zeigler and H.S. Sarjoughian, *Guide to Modeling and Simulation of Systems of Systems*, Simulation Foundations, Methods and Applications, DOI 10.1007/978-3-319-64134-8_14

systems as there is a recognition that these systems are inherently more challenging to develop and deploy.

The DEVS component-based modeling framework is well positioned to create model abstractions for service-based systems. The systems of systems requirements including service autonomy, composability, and reusability with message-based interactions can be modeled rigorously using the DEVS modeling formalism (Sarjoughian et al. 2008; Kim 2008; Muqsith et al. 2011; Yau et al. 2009). DEVS modularity and hierarchy combined with model scalability and simulation efficiency is a strong match for building SOC simulators. This is because the dynamics of a typical SBS system can be characterized in terms of time-based simulation model components. They can process input events (messages) and generate output events (messages) as is common for service-based software systems. Furthermore, DEVS formalism provides basic abstractions for describing concurrent processing and the event-driven nature of arbitrary system modeling. Parallel atomic/coupled DEVS models can be executed in distributed settings (including grid services) and therefore is a suitable modeling framework to characterize complex, large-scale service-based systems as in SOA-Compliant DEVS (SOAD) modeling and simulation environment (Sarjoughian et al. 2008).

14.2 Service-Based Software Systems

The concept of Service-Oriented Computing (SOC) paradigm has received much attention as the next generation of distributed computing platforms (Papazoglou 2003). The Service-Oriented Architecture (SOA) provide the basis for building software systems from services (Erl 2006). This computing paradigm is based on the concept of "software as a service" where services are well-defined, self-contained software modules providing functionality to interested subscribers. To achieve this goal, the Adaptable service-based software system is developed (Yau et al. 2009). Such adaptable service-based software systems can be conceptualized as shown in Fig. 14.1 where Monitoring and Adaptation sub-systems should support choosing services given expected QoS in the presence of uncontrollable, but predictable changes. A fundamental consideration in developing SOA-based software systems is supporting multiple quality of service (QoS) attributes. Basic QoS are timeliness, throughput, and accuracy (see Table 14.1).

A set of real composite services is developed and used to validate their simulated counterparts (Yau et al. 2009). These simulated services lend themselves for realization of the ASBS concept: in particular, enable design, implementation, and testing of the Monitoring and Adaptation sub-systems. With simulated services, the Monitoring and Adaptation sub-systems are actual services. Simulated services directly account for time, thus, allow studying trade-offs among time-based quality of service attributes.

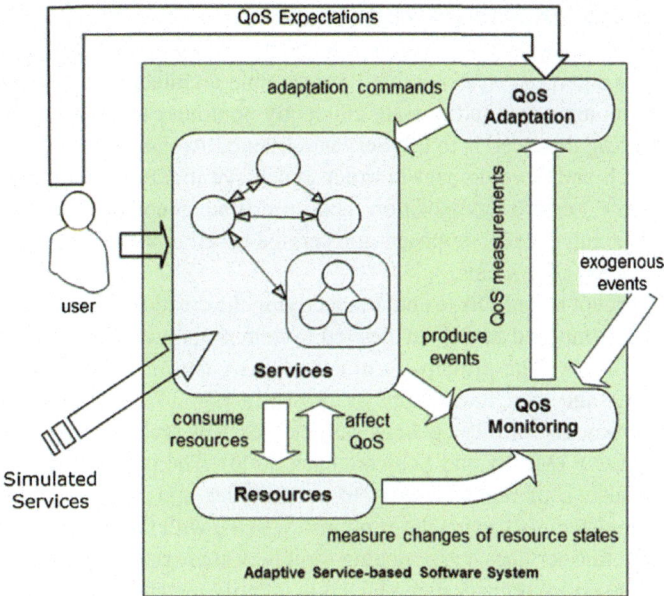

Fig. 14.1 A conceptualization of adaptive service-based software system

Table 14.1 Quality of service metrics for service-based software systems

QoS attributes	Metrics	Experimental data
Accuracy	Loss rate	Number of bits lost between two nodes
	Error rate	Frequency of erroneous bits between two nodes
Timeliness	Response time	Difference between the time of submitting a service request and the time of receiving the service confirmation
	Service delay	Difference between the time of submitting a service request and the time of receiving the service result
	Jitter	Variation of delay generated during transmission
Throughput	Data rate	Rate at which data is transmitted
	Bandwidth	Data transfer rate measured in bits per second

Simulations should capture the inherent properties of SOA-compliant software systems (Sarjoughian et al. 2008). The simulation framework must have a set of SOA elements (i.e., publisher, subscriber, broker services, and messages) and relationships (e.g., subscriber can discover published services only via a service broker) that comply with the SOA principles. The resulting SOA-compliant simulation framework can support creating different user-specific simulation models that are built on the top of verifiably correct SOA model components.

14.3   Service-Oriented Architecture

The desire for enterprise systems that have flexible architectures, detailed designs, implementation agnostic, and operate efficiently continues to grow. A major effort toward satisfying this need is to use Service-Oriented Architecture. Moreover, there is new research and development in order to achieve more demanding capabilities (e.g., workflow service composition with run-time adaptation to change QoS attributes) that have been proposed for service-based systems, especially in the context of system of systems.

A basic concept is for SOA to enable specifying the creation of services that can be automatically composed to deliver desired system dynamics while satisfying multiple QoS attributes. The principal artifacts of SOA are publisher, subscriber, and broker services and their interactions as shown in Fig. 14.2 (Erl 2006). The communication protocols for these general-purpose services are supported with WSDL, UDDI, and SOAP (Møller and Schwartzbach 2006). The publisher and subscriber services are also sometimes referred to as provider and requester, respectively. A publisher registers its service descriptions (WSDL) with the broker service, and a subscriber can find services it is searching for if they are registered with a broker. The broker uses its service registry using UDDI to identify matched service descriptions. Then, a subscriber can invoke a publisher and obtain the requested service. The message interactions among the services are supported by the SOAP mechanism.

A fundamental SOA capability is to support flexible composition of independent services. This basic concept is crucial since it separates details of how a service is created and how it may be used. This kind of modularity is defined based on the

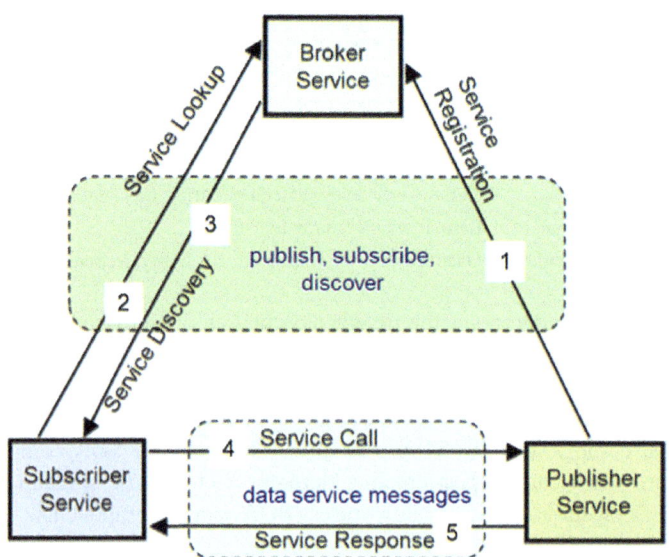

Fig. 14.2 Services and messaging patterns in service-oriented computing

concept of brokers and its realization as the broker service. The SOA conceptual framework lends itself to the separation of concerns ranging from application domains (e.g., business logic) to IT infrastructure to the choices of programming languages and computational platforms. The interoperability at the level of services means loose coupling of reusable services.

The description of the SOA principals does not account for the operational dynamics of services and especially with respect to time-based requirements (Sarjoughian et al. 2008). Therefore, understanding the dynamics of a service-based system using simulation is important. Simulation can also support specific kinds of service-based software systems that are targeted for business processes with specialized domain knowledge. For example, the steps in creating services (e.g., defining service capabilities, selecting services, specifying service flows, and deploying services) can be captured as simulation models. A simulation framework capable of modeling SOA-compliant software systems offers a basis that can be extended to conceptualize and evaluate interesting aspects of higher levels of services (e.g., automated service composition) for different application domains.

14.4   SOA-DEVS Simulation Modeling

The SOA model elements are developed using DEVS and SOA (Sarjoughian et al. 2008). They can be divided into two groups. First, services, service description, and messages represent the *static* part of SOA. Second, communication agreement, messaging framework, and service registry and discovery represent the *dynamic* part of the SOA. As a generic SOA-complaint simulator, we have defined a set of DEVS elements that represent the static and dynamic aspects of the SOA SOAD Simulator (see Table 14.2). The DEVS atomic models have a one to one correspondence with the basic elements of the SOA architecture.

The service provider, service client, and service broker are mapped to DEVS atomic models. Similarly, composite service is mapped to a DEVS coupled model. In addition, the messages and their exchanges in the DEVS can be extended to represent service description and messages. DEVS model communications via messages, ports, and coupling are used to represent the SOA publish/subscribe concept.

Table 14.2 Correspondences between the DEVS and SOA elements

SOA model elements	SOAD model elements
Services: provider, client, broker	Atomic models: provider, client, broker
Service description	Entity: service-information
Messages	Entity: service-lookup and service-call
Messaging framework	Ports and couplings
Service registry and discovery	Executive model
Composition of services	Coupled model: service provider

The publisher, subscriber, and broker services are the basic elements for service-oriented software systems. They can be synthesized to form primitive and composite service composition. A simple model of a network is used to complement the software aspect of SOA. The network is conceptualized as a link with finite capacity, transportation delay, and FIFO message queue. This component is not a service—it models the medium (hardware) through which services send and receive messages.

14.4.1   Primitive Models

The primitive service composition using DEVS atomic models (publisher, subscriber, and broker) is shown in Fig. 14.3. Messages produced by a service and consumed by another are shown as envelops. A message may contain a service description or other content consistent with a chosen messaging framework. For example, the message from the Broker to the Subscriber is a service description which contains an abstract definition (an interface for the operation names and their

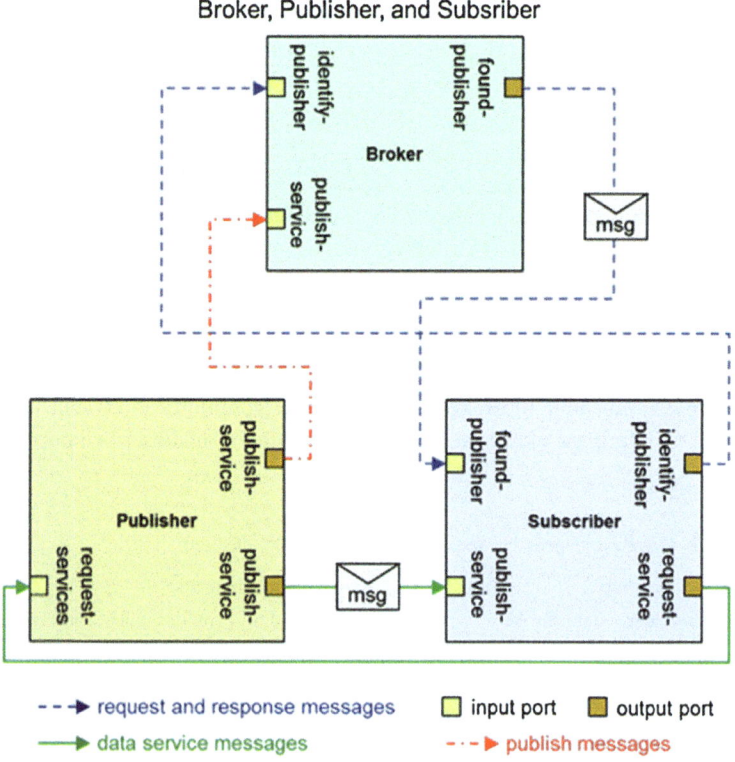

Fig. 14.3 SOA-Compliant DEVS primitive service composition

input and output messages) and a concrete definition (consisting of the binding to physical transport protocol, address or endpoint, and service). Another message could be from the Publisher to the Subscriber where the result of the requested service is a returned message from the Publisher. The implementation of these messages can be based on SOAP. In the basic SOA framework, the internal operations of atomic services and their interactions are deferred to specific standards and technologies (e.g., . NET Lenz and Moeller 2003).

14.4.2   Composite Models

An essential capability for simulating service-based software systems is to support modeling of composite service composition. As shown in Fig. 14.4, a composite service composition has publisher or subscriber service, which is not a primitive service. Since broker service is required for both primitive and composite service composition, two cases can be considered—i.e., either a single broker service or multiple broker services are used. Both cases can be supported. Use of a single broker service is shown in Fig. 14.4. To avoid cluttering, the brokers shown inside the composite Subscriber and Publisher services are the ones used for these services. The three kinds of couplings provided in coupled DEVS models support use of a single broker for the primitive service compositions (i.e., Subscriber and Publisher) and their composite (hierarchical) service composition. For example,

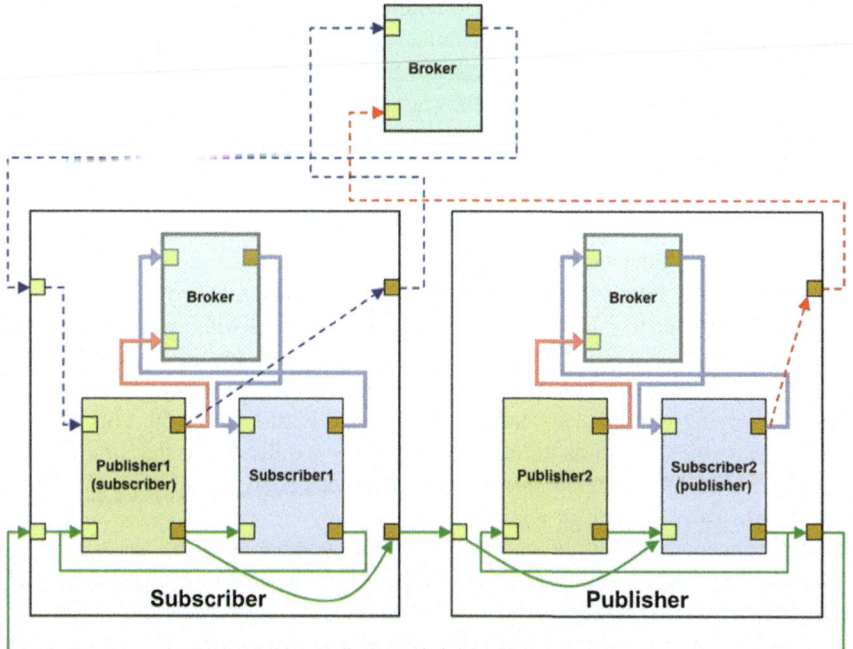

Fig. 14.4 SOA-Compliant composite service composition

Publisher1 has the role of a subscriber with respect to the Subscriber2 which has the role of a publisher. The common concept of DEVS and SOA modularity allows creating composite service compositions without restrictions.

14.5   SOA-DEVS Model Components

An important consideration in choosing a modeling and simulation framework is its direct support for message-based communication among independent model components. This is obviously important since the concept of SOA is grounded in autonomous services that can only influence each other via messages. The combination of publisher and subscriber interaction via messages matches well the strict modularity of the DEVS framework (Zeigler et al. 2000).

The basic idea for the SOAD framework is to enable modeling and simulating of primitive and composite services as if they were actual services. The concept of simulated services is distinct from that of simulated objects. The DEVS and object-orientation concepts, compared to DEVS and SOA, are closely related. The SOA is defined in terms of principles that are intended to guide architecture, design, implementation, testing, and operation of service-based systems. These principles may be used to develop details of SOA which can result in different realizations both for the SOA itself and user applications. The DEVS formalism, on the other hand, is a mathematical specification intended for developing time-based models that can be simulated. We also note that while atomic and coupled models require abstract atomic and coupled simulators in order to be executed, the services (publisher, subscriber, and broker) contain their own execution logics.

Given the disparities between DEVS and SOA frameworks, our aim is to develop a framework for SOAD. Two basic approaches can be taken. One is to infuse the concept and capabilities of DEVS concepts and capabilities into the SOA framework. The other is to extend the DEVS framework such that it can account for the SOA concept and capabilities. In this work, we chose the latter approach.

Before we consider the SOA and DEVS frameworks together, it is important to recall that one is intended to build real services and the other to build simulated services. In this section, DEVS framework refers to DEVS with Dynamic Structure capability. Also, it is useful to appreciate that while a primitive (subscriber or publisher) service and atomic model can be considered as components (or objects), their underlying concepts are inherently distinct. Furthermore, the concept of a composite service (either as publisher or subscriber) differs from that of a coupled model. Further details on similarities and differences between the SOA and DEVS frameworks can be found in Kim (2008).

The concepts of loosely coupled and discoverable services are similar to dynamic structure DEVS, where the structure of a model can change during simulation execution—i.e., capability is provided for adding and removing atomic and coupled models. The concept of executive in a dynamic structure resembles that of a broker service, but it is not the same as described above. As noted earlier, the fundamental difference between DEVS and SOA is the "broker" concept. The message-based interactions between the publisher and subscriber services can only be established by the broker service. The concept of broker is not defined in the DEVS formalism, and thus, the DEVS atomic or coupled components are not *service-enabled*—i.e., the generic syntax and semantics of the atomic and coupled components are insufficient for describing service-based software systems. Furthermore, the SOA is not the same as dynamic structure DEVS even though the structure of a coupled model can be modified during simulation.

14.5.1   Generic Messages

As shown in Fig. 14.2, there are three principal message usages—i.e., publishing, lookup, and subscribing of message between services in the SOA. These three different usages require three types of messages due to varying data requirements in each message. They are derived from the entity class as shown in Fig. 14.5.

14.5.1.1   Service Info and Service Lookup Messages
The WSDL is used in the real environment between services and service brokers. In the simulation environment, among the three message types, *ServiceInfo* and *ServiceLookup* capture characteristics of the WSDL (see Table 14.3).

These messages are needed for publishing services and their discovery. The *ServiceInfo* message type is used to publish the service to the service broker. It contains the service definition given a service name, description, service type (atomic or composite), endpoints, and binding information as shown in Fig. 14.6. The endpoint consists of two parts: exposed method name and argument type for

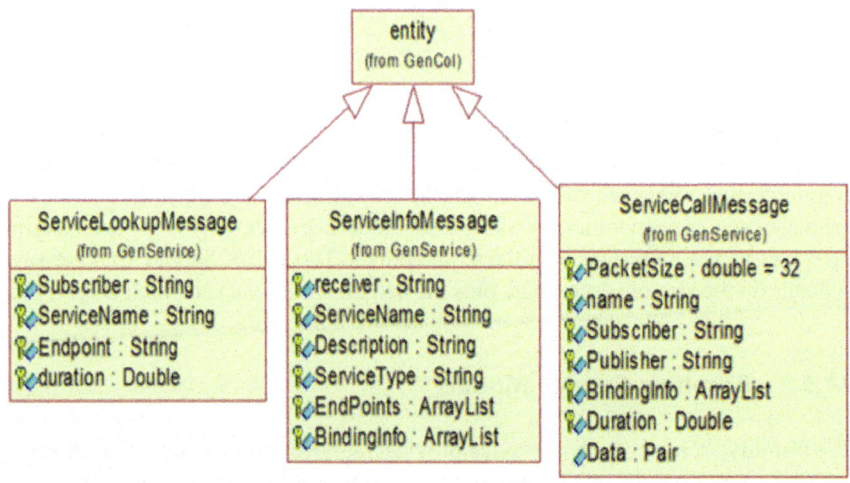

Fig. 14.5 Messages in the SOAD

Table 14.3 WSDL and
ServiceInfo and
ServiceLookup messages

WSDL	Service information	Service lookup
Interface	Service name, endpoints	Service name, endpoint
Message	n/a	Data
Service	n/a (ports and couplings)	n/a (ports and couplings)
Binding	Binding info	n/a

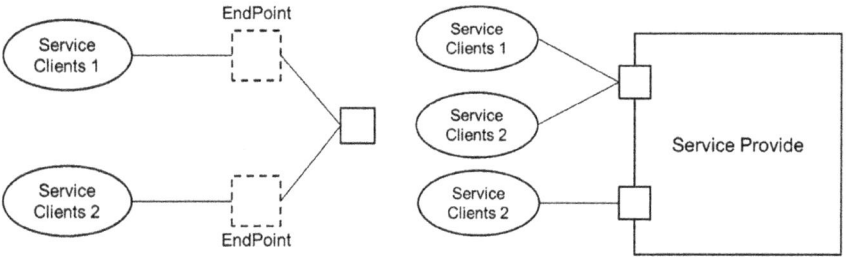

Fig. 14.6 Connection between service clients and an endpoint

the method. The method accepts one argument to perform its functionality. Binding information contains the list of services with endpoints. Logically the order of services in the list represents the order of service in the composition.

ServiceLookup message type contains the subscription information, the name of the service provider, the endpoint to service client, the data type to be sent, and the time frame to subscribe service. The name of the service provider and an endpoint in that service provider are used as key value to find the desired service information in the Service Broker. The service client can use a service description or a specific combination of service information to lookup the broker to locate a service. However, this capability is limited to use of service name with an endpoint for the simulation.

14.5.1.2   Service Call Message

The SOAP, XML-based communication protocol, is used over HTTP in the communication between services. In the simulation environment, ServiceCall message type corresponding to the SOAP properties is employed for exchanging messages between services with the required data. The size of Service Call message depends on the size of service data plus the default size of packet which is 32 Bytes.

14.5.2   Primitive Service Models

The primitive services such as service provider, service client, and service broker as a DEVS atomic model are proposed as shown in the Fig. 14.7. These simulation services have a one-to-one correspondence with the SOA service. Services in the

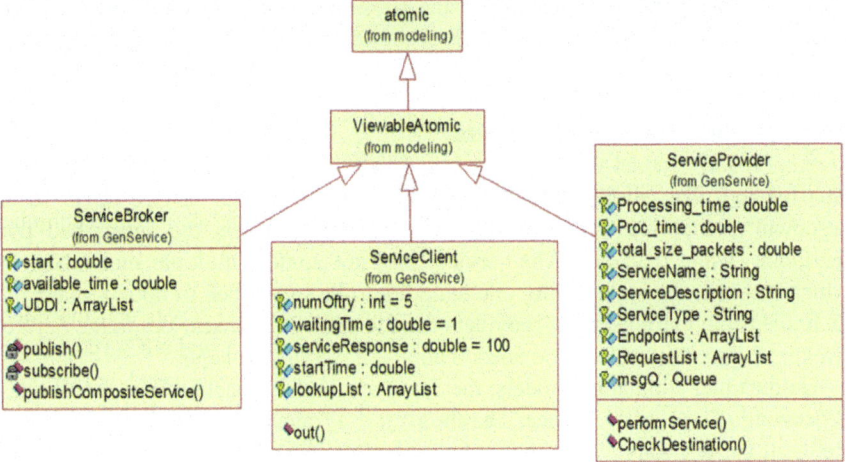

Fig. 14.7 Primitive services in the SOAD

SOA can be considered as components in the component-based system. Unlike a component, a service is fully self-contained and loosely coupled.

ServiceBroker model. *ServiceBroker* model has a container (UDDI) to store *ServiceInfo* messages as a service description. The desired service can be discovered by looking up an endpoint from the *ServiceClient* as a key. Figure 14.7 shows two important methods as characteristics of SOA,

- Publish: Store the published service information as a *ServiceInfo* message into the UDDI.
- Subscribe: Return the index of the matched service in the list. An endpoint from the service client is used to lookup the services. If no service is found, then a negative value is returned. Service Broker sends the matched service information (*ServiceInfo*) or "No Found" message to the client.

14.5.2.1   Service Client Model

ServiceClient model defines a service client in the SOA. A service client can be defined with the list of service that the service client wants to subscribe sequentially. At the beginning, a client with a given start time begins to look up the service broker to search whether the desired service is currently available or not. If the endpoint is not available or even if the service broker itself is not available yet, the service client attempts to lookup the service broker again after a set amount of time units until the specified number of attempts, as shown in Fig. 14.8. If the endpoint is found and gets the service information, then the service client sends a message with a required data for the endpoint and then waits for the response from the service for the given response time. After completion of a service subscription, if there are more services remaining in the subscription list, then the service client looks up the broker again and subscribes the service until no more services are in the list.

14.5.2.2 Service Provider Model

ServiceProvider model defines behavior of its specific service with a *performService* method. The *performService* receives a data from the service client as an argument and performs its specified service depending on the subscribed port (endpoint) using that data. The service does not contain multiple methods in it, which means a service has only one endpoint to be subscribed to upon request. As an initial behavior, all service providers need to publish their services to the Service Broker. Figure 14.8 shows the specifications of *ServiceProvider*.

Unlike other simulation models, the *ServiceProvider* model has two time logics, Processing Time and Service Duration, for a queue and a list, msgQ and RequestList, respectively, as shown below.

Processing Time is the required time for a request to be processed before servicing. In other words, a request needs to wait in the msgQ for the Processing Time. For example, if the Processing Time is 5 time units, then R4 has waited for 5 simulation time units before it is stored into the RequestList to be served for the requested Service Duration. All service requests, R1 to R4, in the RequestList are handled by the *performService* method for each request at a time.

The functionality of the RequestList is to handle multiple user requests for the same endpoint or service simultaneously. Multiple service clients can subscribe to the same endpoint at a time (see Fig. 14.6). At the programming level, endpoint objects from the same endpoint are created for and assigned to each request. Therefore, it looks like only a service client subscribes this endpoint at a time. This capability is implemented by the RequestList. Multiple requests are stored in the RequestList, and they are serviced simultaneously by iterating the entire list at one time. Then the simulation time is advanced.

The internal event function as a DEVS atomic model loops itself by changing three states, "processing," "looping," and "servicing" sequentially until msgQ and RequestList become empty. At the first "processing" state, if the Processing Time

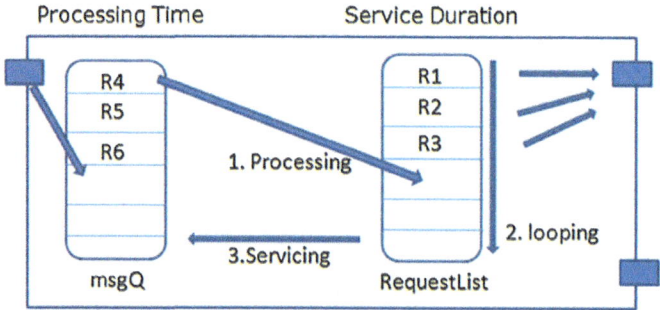

Fig. 14.8 Internal event function in the ServiceProvider

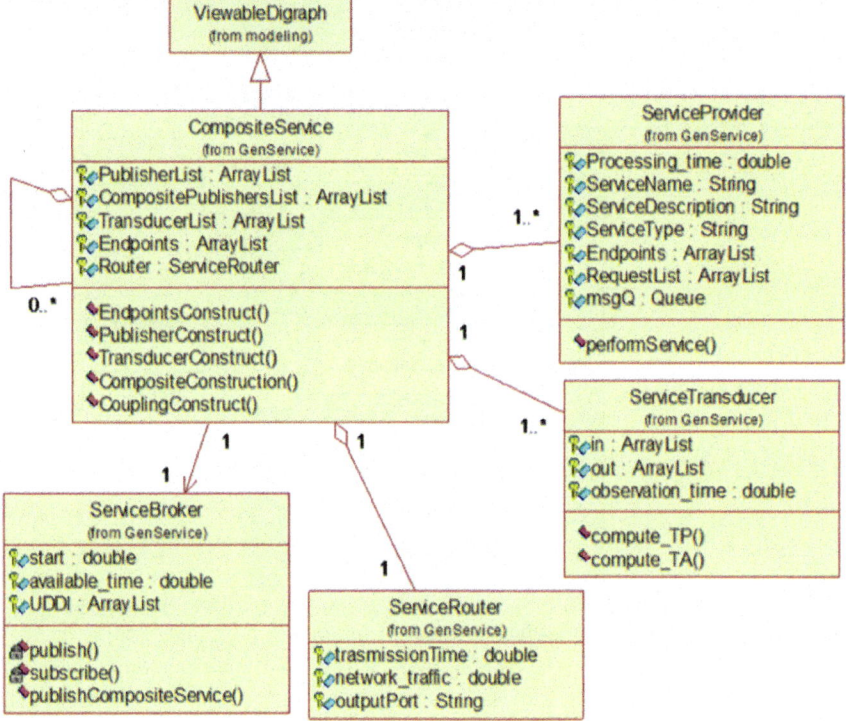

Fig. 14.9 Composite service model

becomes zero, then the top request is pulled out from the msgQ and added into the RequestList. In the "looping" state, the service provider loops the RequestList to serve each request if the requested Service Duration for the request is not equal to zero and then sends output messages to each corresponding service client by changing the state to "servicing." If Service Duration for a request is zero, then it skips to the next request. At the "servicing" state, after all requests in the RequestList are handled, it then removes requests which have zero Service Duration from the RequestList. Finally, the state is changed to "processing" again for another loop.

14.5.3 Composite Service Model

The composite service model contains at least two service providers (either primitive or composite service) models to represent a composite service (see Fig. 14.9). The flow of service invocations needs to be specified at the service model design stage. Figure 14.10 shows how the real services are composed using BPEL. This is a basic capability for hierarchical service provider composition which has to be extended to support different kinds of workflow patterns (Russell et al. 2006).

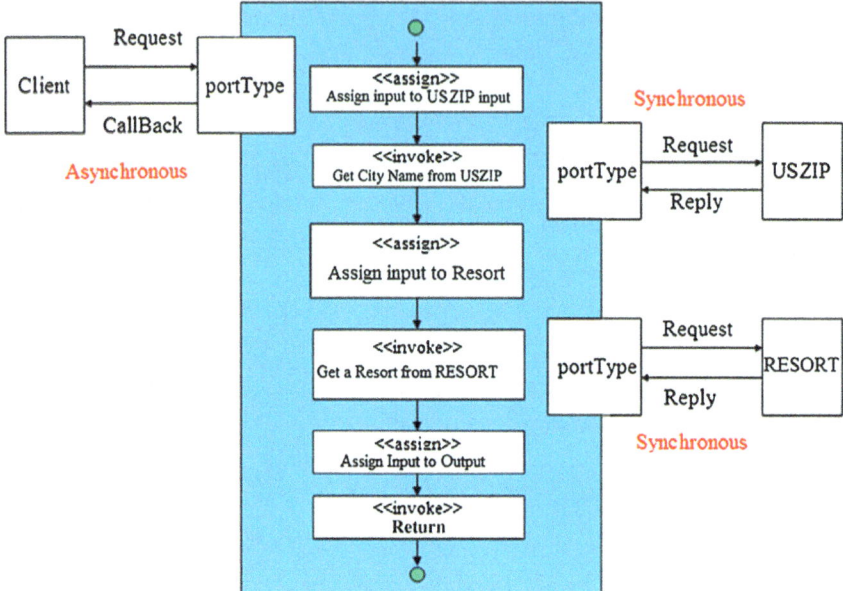

Fig. 14.10 Business process execution language

14.6 Exemplar Simulation Model

Models for the primitive and composite service compositions are developed in the
DEVS-Suite simulator which supports SOAD. The model shown in Fig. 14.11 has
4 software components (one subscriber (Travel Agent), two publishers (USZip and

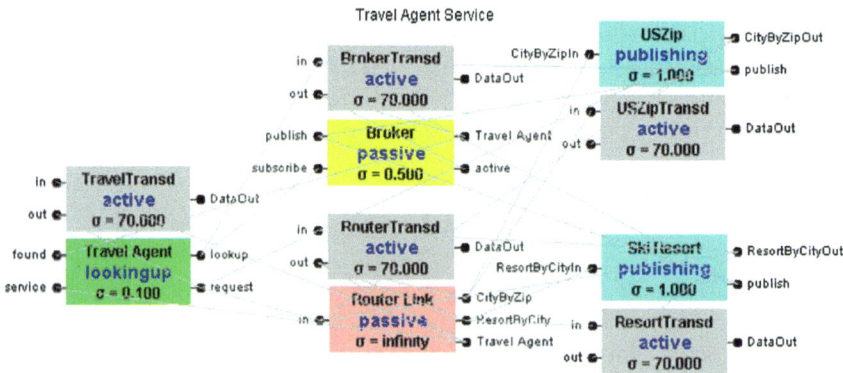

Fig. 14.11 Travel agent service model

Ski Resort), and one broker (Broker)) and one simple hardware component (Router Link) (Kim 2008). The model also includes five transducers for each of the software and hardware components. Another simulation model is for a real Voice Communication Service (Yau et al. 2009) which is used to validate the design and implementation of the SOAD simulator. The Travel Agent Service and Voice Communication Service are used to show the primitive and composite service compositions.

The simple Travel Agent Service is used to show modeling of services and their dynamics in terms of basic throughput, timeliness, and accuracy QoS for SOA-compliant software-based systems. For example, the dynamics of the Travel Agent subscriber can be observed in terms of the events it generates and consumes. The output events are defined for the service lookup, the service lookup retry, and the publisher service request. The output events times relative to time instances at which they can be generated are defined to be 0.5, 0.0, and 1.0 s, respectively. The scheduling of these events is defined in state transition functions. The first event is scheduled by the internal transition function. The second and third events are due to the external transition function—i.e., processing of input events from the Broker. There is also another external transition function for processing the input event received from a publisher (either USZip or Ski Resort). The time allocated for δ_{ext} is 1.0 s. The dynamics of the USZip and Ski Resort are the same. Each takes 1.0 s to process a received request from the Router Link and produce an output event. The Router Link takes 0.5 s to deliver a publisher's output event as an input event to a subscriber. The Router Link also takes 0.5 s to deliver a subscriber's output event as an input event to a publisher. The Broker takes 0.0 s to respond to the Travel Agent subscriber (whether it finds a requested service or not). For simplicity, in this example, the subscriber sends its requests to the publishers sequentially, but simultaneous requests are straightforward to model. Table 14.4 shows sample quality of service measurements for the Travel Agent Service operating for a period of 71.5 s. The generic SOA DEVS models can have stochastic timings. Deterministic timings are used to verify the logical correctness of the model. Hierarchical models such as the Voice Communication model that uses the USZIP can also be developed as depicted in Fig. 14.12. Code snippets for primitive USZIP and Resort services, as well, as the composite ResortByZip service are shown in Fig. 14.13.

Table 14.4 Selected metrics for the Travel Agent Service model

Component	Quality of service measurements
Travel agent	Average turnaround time (s): 2.0
	Total size of data received (Kbytes): 640.0
	Number of subscribed publishers: 2
USZip	Publisher throughput (msgs/sec): 0.156
	Amount of data received (Kbytes): 320.0
	Number of subscribers: 1
Ski Resort	Publisher throughput (msgs/sec): 0.156
	Amount of data received (Kbytes): 320.0
	Number of subscribers: 1
Router	Average transmission Time (s): 0.5
	Total size of message received (Kbytes): 1280.0
	Utilization for a period of time (%): 1.7073

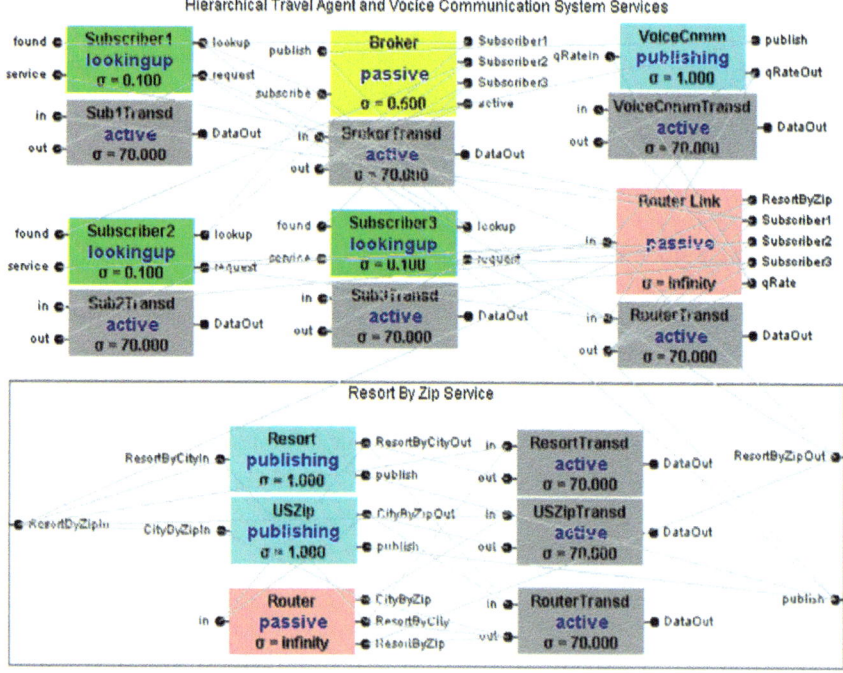

Fig. 14.12 Hierarchical US ZIP service with voice communication

```
public Pair performService(Pair data){
  double sizeOfmsgs = 32;
  Double doubleVal;
  Pair returnVal = new Pair();

  doubleVal = Double.parseDouble(data.value.toString());

  //if the zip code is 85281, then return Tempe
  if(doubleVal == 85281){
          returnVal.key = "String";
          returnVal.value = "Tempe";
  }
  else{
          returnVal.key = "String";
          returnVal.value = "No Found";
  }
  ServiceReturn.setSize(sizeOfmsgs);
  return returnVal;

  }


public Pair performService(Pair data){
  double sizeOfmsgs = 32;
  Pair returnVal = new Pair();

  //if argument is Tempe, then return Phoenix Resort
  if(data.value.toString().equals("Tempe")){
          returnVal.key = "String";
          returnVal.value = "Pheonix Resort";
  }
  else{
          returnVal.key = "String";
          returnVal.value = "No Found";
  }

  ServiceReturn.setSize(sizeOfmsgs);
  return returnVal;

  }


public void CompositeConstruct(){

  ArrayList <Pair> Endpoints = new ArrayList <Pair> ();
  Endpoints.add(new Pair("ResortByZip", "Double"));
  ResortByZipServices Service2 = new ResortByZipServices();
          CoupledPublishersList.add(Service2);
  ServiceInfo CompositeService = new ServiceInfo("ResortByZip",
          "Find a resort by zip", "composite", Endpoints);
```

Fig. 14.13 Primitive USZIP and resort services with composite ResortByZip service

```
    //Set Binding Info (Service, endpoint)
    CompositeService.setBindingInfo(new Pair("ResortByZip",
    "ResortByZip"));
    CompositeService.setBindingInfo(new Pair("USZip",
    "CityByZip"));
    CompositeService.setBindingInfo(new Pair("Resort",
    "ResortByCity"));

    Broker.publishCompositeService(CompositeService);

}


public class ResortByZipServices extends
    ServiceCoupledPublishers{

    public final static double observation = 70;

    public ResortByZipServices(){super("Resort By Zip Service");}

    public void EndpointsConstruct(){
          Endpoints.add(new Pair("ResortByZip", "Double"));
    }

    public void PublisherConstruct(){

          ArrayList <Pair> Endpoints = new ArrayList <Pair> ();

          Endpoints.add(new Pair("CityByZip", "Double"));
    USZipService Service1 = new USZipService("USZip", "City by Zip
    Service", "Atomic", Endpoints, 1);

    Service1.setBackgroundColor(Color.CYAN);
          //Construct the publisher list
          PublisherList.add(Service1);

          Endpoints = new ArrayList <Pair> ();
          Endpoints.add(new Pair("ResortByCity", "String"));
    ResortService Service2 = new ResortService("Resort",
    "Resort by City Service", "Atomic", Endpoints, 1);
          Service2.setBackgroundColor(Color.CYAN);
          PublisherList.add(Service2);

}
```

Fig. 14.13 (continued)

14.7 Dynamic Structure SOAD

Service-based software systems developed in SOAD can adapt to controllable demands Dynamic Structure SOAD (DSOAD) (DEVS-Suite 2017; Muqsith et al. 2011), which uses Dynamic Structure DEVS modeling approach (Barros 1997; Hu et al. 2005). Services can be added or removed using an executive model. This variant of an atomic DEVS model has an element representing the network structure and a function that defines rules for adding and removing services with their couplings dynamically (i.e., during simulation execution). This executive model which conforms to the Dynamic Structure Discrete-Event Network specification is implemented in DEVSJAVA. The executive model has the knowledge of a network model structure at any time instance. It is not coupled to the any primitive or composite service.

In accordance with DS-DEVS, any service model developed in DS-DEVS contains the executive model that enforces SOA-compliancy. In particular, if a subscriber is dynamically instantiated in DSOAD, the executive needs to ensure that it has couplings to the broker. The structural properties identified to make a configuration SOA compliant are defined below.

1. The subscriber(s) to publishers(s) communication must be discovered through the broker.
2. The publisher(s) can directly communicate to the broker.
3. The subscriber(s) can directly communicate to the broker.
4. The hierarchical composition of the publishers and subscribers cannot violate any of the above properties.

Enforcing correct message flow directions among the broker, publisher, and subscriber are also important. Although the concept of direction of message flow is not different from the concept already in SOAD (represented as incoming messages through input ports and outgoing messages through output ports), there is a need to account for this in DSOAD. SOAD component interactions through messages are pre-defined by the modeler, and the modeler takes the direction of message flow into account. However, couplings are configured at run-time in DSOAD. Hence, the executive must contain the knowledge of the direction of the message flow (and thus input versus output ports) so that SOA-compliant structural rules are enforced.

The executive model aids in enforcing SOA structural compliancy under dynamical settings. It facilitates the establishment of relations among publishers, subscribers, and the broker. The DS-DEVS executive model by itself does not account for SOA and, in particular, does not account for the concept of the broker. One possible approach to accommodate the executive model is to associate it with the SOAD broker model. In this context, it is important to develop the association between the DS-DEVS executive model and the SOAD broker. The complementary relation of the broker and the executive is as follows.

1. The broker mediates the publisher and subscriber relation. Similarly, the executive model can facilitate dynamic flat and hierarchical structural component relations.
2. The broker implicitly enforces the direction of message flow by responding (or not responding) to incoming messages.

The executive model can connect I/O ports of services to ensure the correct message flow direction. However, the following dissimilarities exist between the broker and executive.

1. The executive can only support composite structures or can generate structures using predefined rules. The broker concept is aimed at supporting any publisher —subscriber relation.
2. The executive model, unlike the broker, does not conceptually distinguish between subscriber and publisher.
3. The executive model has complete knowledge of the service components and the structure of their composition. The broker may track publishers and subscribers that have communicated with it.
4. The executive model can support service composition and execution. The broker does not support composition and execution.

Considering the association between the executive and the broker models, we account for both the broker and the executive such that together they form the broker-executive model. Since the functionality of the executive is to enforce constraints on the structural composition of the services, the broker-executive accounts for the following rules.

I. When a publisher is added to the system:

   1. connect the publisher output port publish service to the broker input port publish service.

II. When a subscriber is added to the system:

   1. connect the subscriber output port identify publisher to the broker input port identify publisher;
   2. connect the broker output port found publisher to the subscriber input port found publisher;
   3. connect the subscriber output port request service to the publisher input port request service;
   4. connect the publisher output port publish service to the subscriber input port publish service.

Rules I.1 and II.1 and II.2 establish the relations between the broker-executive, the subscriber and the publisher. Similarly, rules II.3 and II.4 establish the relation between the subscriber and publisher. In SOA, the subscriber-publisher relation is discoverable with the help of the broker and initiated by the subscriber. Interestingly, we need to account for the cases where publisher and subscribers can be dynamically added (and removed). In such cases, we need to resolve how and when the models and couplings should be reconfigured. Considering SOA's loosely coupled property, delayed coupling is appropriate. For simplicity, we include rules II.3 and II.4 as part of the broker-executive model. The rules for removal of the publisher and subscriber can be easily derived based on the rules that are defined for addition of services.

14.7.1 Broker-Executive Model Design

The Broker-Executive model in DSOAD is represented as a SOAD broker and a DS-DEVS executive (see Fig. 14.14). It is a single logical component which consists of the ServiceBroker and the Executive models.

The DSOAD uses the simple hardware model that is used in SOAD. The hardware model is defined as a component that orders messages it receives and

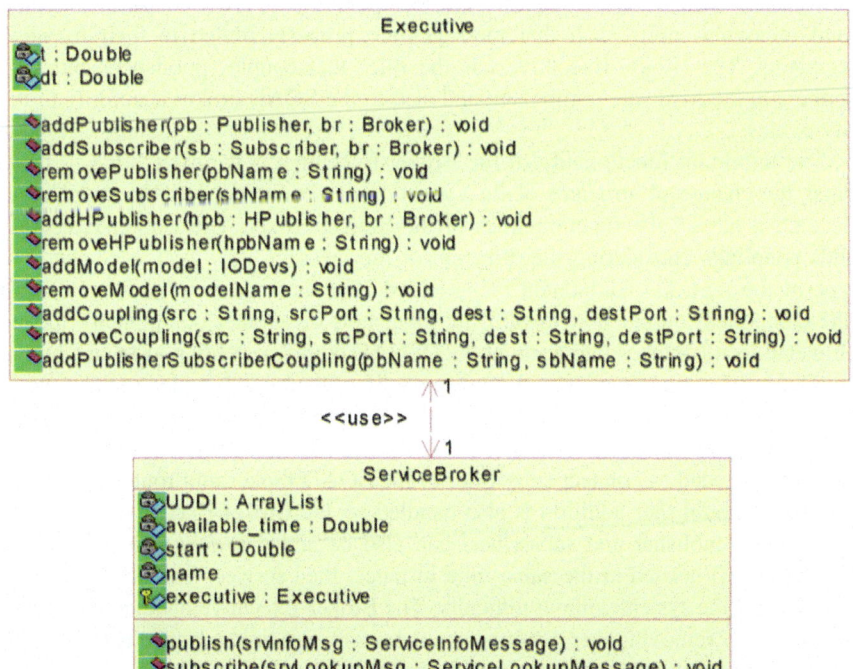

Fig. 14.14 Broker-executive class diagram model

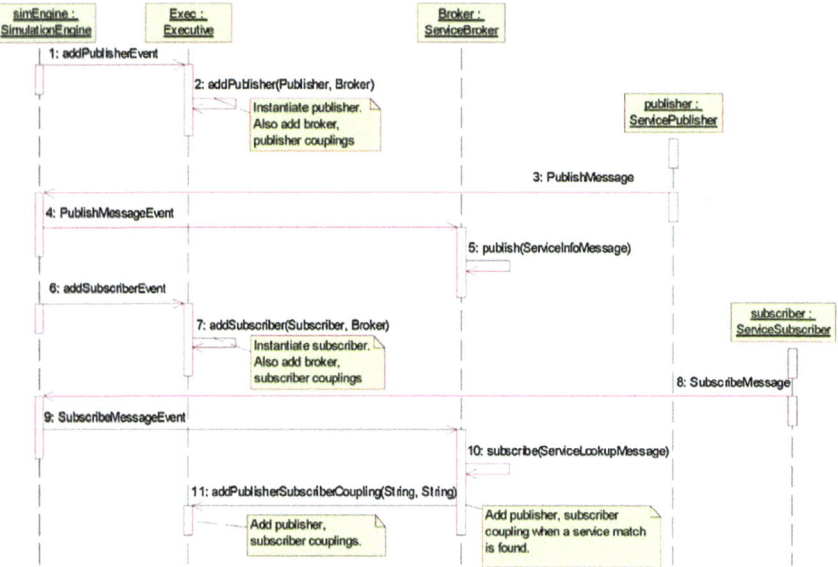

Fig. 14.15 Sequence diagram for the broker-executive model

routes them using FIFO discipline. The component supports dynamically adding (and removing) ports such that messages are properly routed to their intended recipients. The Broker-Executive has the rules that couples publishers and subscribers to the hardware component and also to the SOAD broker according to the SOA rules.

The important functionality of the Broker-Executive is twofolds. First, it facilitates the change of structure of the system while maintaining SOA-compliancy. Second, it has all the functionalities of the SOAD broker. The Broker-Executive adds couplings considering the direction of the message flow associated with the type of the DSOAD component being added. The message flow is directed from one component output port toward the input port of another component. So, the Broker-Executive takes into account the DSOAD component I/O port to ensure that couplings maintain compliancy. For example, if a subscriber is added to the system, the subscriber output port that sends message to SOAD broker to discover a publisher is coupled to the SOAD broker's input port that handles the messages. All the couplings needed to connect subscriber to the SOAD broker and router is created. Similarly, a publisher addition is also handled by the Broker-Executive.

Multiple publisher and subscribers can also be added in DSOAD. If addition (and removal) needed at the same time instance, then services can be added (and removed) to the system without difficulty. The Broker-Executive handles such cases by adding (or removing) services one at a time with zero time advance using default confluent function (internal transition followed by external transition).

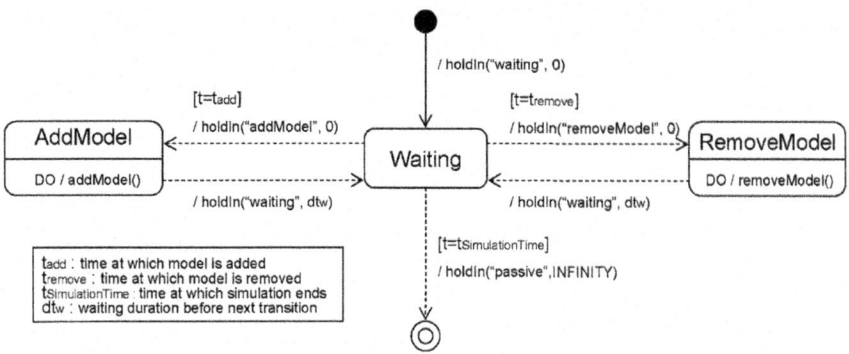

Fig. 14.16 Statechart diagram for the executive model

In the Broker-Executive model, the executive model has no DEVS-based I/O connection with the broker. However, the two models are related. The executive uses the broker model to create (or delete) structural connection with the model being added (or removed). The executive can add (and remove) SOA component models maintaining the SOA compliant structural relations. Once the structural compliancy is ensured, the logical relations among publisher and subscriber are maintained by the broker. This ensures SOA-compliancy. This is important to note as their interaction is not apparent as there are no couplings. The sequence diagram shows some of the main interactions between the executive and broker (see Figs. 14.16 and 14.17). The simulation engine refers to the simulator that executes models, facilitates DEVS message exchanges among models and schedules events. The underlying relation is captured in the UML model specifications. The modeler can specify time instances to add and remove SOA component models (i.e., t_{add}, t_{remove}). The addSubscriber and addPublisher methods provide the generic capability to ensure SOA compliancy in coupling the components. The time instances for adding or removing services can be arbitrarily scheduled (i.e., t_{add}, $t_{remove} \in t$, and the simulation clock t are updated by $dt \in R^{+}_{[0,\infty]}$). In addition, the states as presented in Figs. 14.16 and 14.17 are abstract representations of the complete states for the Executive and Broker models.

14.7.2 Flat and Hierarchical Model Compositions

Flat and hierarchical compositions correspond to their visibility to other interested services. Visibility of a service indicates whether the published service interface is available (or not) to the interested services. In flat composition, the services are visible to each other. In contrast, the visibility is set at levels of hierarchy in the hierarchical composition. The hierarchic composition can consist of publishers, subscribers, or their combinations thereof. In DSOAD, flat and hierarchical logical structures of services, unlike SOAD, are supported dynamically. Services may be

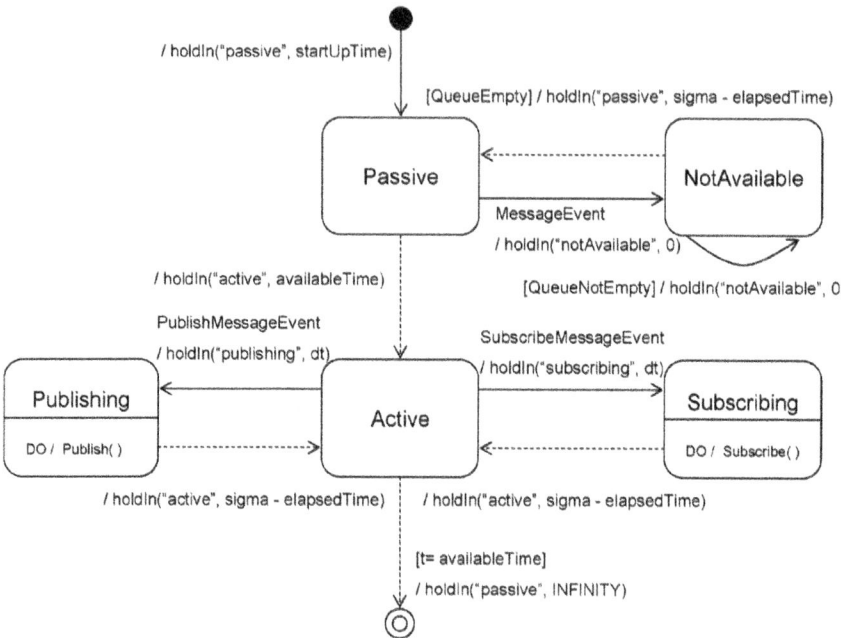

Fig. 14.17 Statechart diagram for the Broker model

published publicly or privately. Code snippets for adding publisher and subscriber are provided (see Fig. 14.18).

The deletion of publishers and subscribers requires removing their couplings followed by the models. The implementation also handles the creation and deletion of router ports. Based on the above formulation of DSOAD, the DEVS-Suite simulator is extended with the DS-DEVS API that is part of the DEVSJAVA simulator. This was attractive since the SOAD subscriber, publisher, broker, and router models as well as the DS-DEVS executive model are implemented in DEVS-Suite. The extended simulator supports the basic capabilities for dynamically creating SOA-compliant DEVS simulation models.

14.7.2.1   Dynamic Publisher Discovery Example

For dynamic discovery demonstration, we consider an example where at $t = 1.00$ subscriber S_1 is added with no publisher existing prior to adding P_1 at $t = 11.00$ (see Table 14.5). As a result, the lookup request to the broker from S_1 returns a "Not found" message prior to $t = 11.00$. Once P_1 is added and it publishes to the broker, the broker creates the couplings from P_1 and S_1 communication, returns a service information message on the lookup request, and then S_1 initiates communication with P_1.

```
public void addSubscriber(ServiceClient sb, Broker br,
ServiceRouter rt) {

    //add the subscriber model to viewcomponent
    addModel(sb);

    //subcscriber to broker
    addCoupling(br.getName(),sb.getName(),sb.getName(),"found");
    addOutport(br.getName(),sb.getName());
    addCoupling(sb.getName(),"lookup",br.getName(),"subscribe");

}


public void addPublisherSubscriberCoupling(ServiceProvider
pb,ServiceClient sb, ServiceRouter rt){

    //add port to the router for the publisher
    ArrayList <Pair> Endpoints = new ArrayList <Pair> ();
    Endpoints = pb.getEndpoints();
    String portName = Endpoints.get(0).key.toString();
    rt.addOutport(portName);

    //publisher to router
    //Commented to make it compatibe with DSOAD paper
    addCoupling(rt.getName(),portName,pb.getName(),portName+"In");
    addCoupling(pb.getName(),portName+"Out",rt.getName(),"in");

    // add port to the router for the subscriber
    addOutport(rt.getName(),sb.getName());

    //subcscriber to router
    addCoupling(sb.getName(),"request",rt.getName(),"in");
    addCoupling(rt.getName(),sb.getName(),sb.getName(),"service");
}


public void addPublisherSubscriberCoupling(String pbName, String
sbName, ServiceRouter rt, String endPointName) {

    //add port to the router for the publisher
    String portName = endPointName;
    String rtName = rt.getName();
    //init ports in router
    if(!rt.getOutportNames().contains(portName)){
    addOutport(rtName,portName);
    //publisher to router
    addCoupling(rtName,portName,pbName,portName+"In");
    addCoupling(pbName,portName+"Out",rtName,"in");
    }
```

Fig. 14.18 Code snippets for adding and removing publisher and subscriber

```
if(!rt.getOutportNames().contains(sbName)){
    addOutport(rtName,sbName);

    //subcscriber to router
    addCoupling(sbName,"request",rtName,"in");
    addCoupling(rtName,sbName,sbName,"service");
}

}
```

Fig. 14.18 (continued)

Table 14.5 Event times adding and removing publishers and subscribers

Example	Simulation time	Component	Operation	Sampling rate
1	11.00	S_2	Add	220.5
	11.00	S_3	Add	220.5
	11.00	S_4	Add	220.5
	41.00	S_2	Remove	–
	41.00	S_3	Remove	–
2	11.00	S_2	Add	220.5
	11.00	S_3	Add	220.5
	11.00	S_4	Add	220.5
	20.00	P_4	Add	–
	41.00	S_2	Remove	–
	41.00	S_2	Remove	–
3	1.00	S_1	Add	44.1
	11.00	P_1	Add	–
	30.00	S_3	Add	44.1
	30.00	S_4	Add	44.1
	41.00	S_2	Remove	–
	41.00	S_3	Remove	–

14.8   Summary

The goal of this chapter was to show the characteristics of service-based software systems and, in particular, how their simulation counterparts can be developed using DEVS modeling approach. One important aspect throughout this chapter was that systems of systems as exemplified with service-based software systems have their own unique requirements. Therefore, formulations of their structures and behaviors are necessary for developing useful simulation models. Another idea shown in this chapter is that standards such as Service-Oriented Architecture play key roles in developing simulation models that are better equipped to be inter-changed with their real counterparts. To this end, generic SOA-compliant DEVS model components as well as their extensions that can adapt (i.e., DSOAD) were developed. These generic model components closely represent their real counterparts. As such, they can be used to develop simulation instances of real service-based software systems. Users can prototype service-based software systems in simulated settings with capability to evaluate their quality of service attributes such as timeliness and accuracy in the developed SOA-compliant modeling and simulation framework systematically and efficiently.

14.9 Exercises

Exercise

Develop the sequence diagram shown in Fig. 14.15 using the MS4 Me. Discuss to what extent any UML sequence diagram can be developed in MS4 Me.

Exercise

Develop a Finite-Deterministic DEVS model in MS4 Me for the statechart diagram shown in Fig. 14.16.

Exercise

Develop the exemplar Travel Agent Service model in MS4 Me. Hint: the primitive service models can be developed first and thereafter extended with domain knowledge. The composite model shown in Fig. 14.11 can then be developed.

Exercise

Implement the model in the third exercise using DEVS-Suite simulator. Develop an experiment in which there are 5 travel agents making 10, 20,..., 50 requests per second. The model components have the same parameterization as those in Sect. 14.6. Plot the QoS measurements for the Travel Agent, USZip, Ski Resort services and the Router component.

Exercise

Consider the Travel Agent model described in Sect. 14.6. Assume this model has separate services for finding ski and beach resorts using zip code. The model has three subscribers: two serving beach resort requests and one serving ski resort

requests. Requests for both beach resort arrive at 1 s interval and the requests for
the ski resort arrive at 0.5 s interval. Simulate this model for a period of 2 min using
the DEVS-Suite simulator. Plot the QoS measurements listed in Table 14.4 for this
model.

Exercise

Extend the model from the fifth exercise such that the number of beach resort
subscribers doubles between time instances 0.5 and 1.5 min due to an additional
subscriber. Obtain throughput for the beach resort and utilization the router link.

References

Barros, F. (1997). Modeling formalisms for dynamic structure systems. *ACM Transactions on Modeling and Computer Simulation, 7*(4), 501–515.
DEVS-Suite Simulator (2009). Retrieved from http://devs-suitesim.sourceforge.net.
Erl, T. (2006). *Service-oriented architecture concepts, technology and design*. New York: Prentice Hall.
Hu, X., Zeigler, B. P., & Mittal, S. (2005). Variable structure in DEVS component-based modeling and simulation. *Simulation, 81*(2), 91–102.
Kim, S., Sarjoughian, H. S., & Elamvazuthi, V. (2009). DEVS-suite: A simulator for visual experimentation and behavior monitoring. In *High Performance Computing & Simulation Symposium, Proceedings of the Spring Simulation Conference*, 1–7 March, San Diego, CA.
Kim, S. (2008). Simulator for service-based software system: design and implementation with DEVS-suite. Master's Thesis, School of Computing, Information, and Decision Systems Engineering, Arizona State University, Tempe, AZ.
Lenz, G., & Moeller, T. (2003). *NET: A complete development cycle*. Reading: Addison-Wesley.
Møller, A., & Schwartzbach, M. I. (2006). *An introduction to XML and web technologies*. Reading: Addison-Wesley.
Muqsith, M. A., Sarjoughian, H. S., Huang, D., & Yau, S. S. (2011). Simulating adaptive service-oriented software systems. *Simulation, 87*(11), 915–931.
Papazoglou, M. P. (2003). Service-oriented computing: Concepts, characteristics and directions. In *WISE* (pp. 3–12).
Russell, N., Hofstede, A., Aalst, W., & Mulyar, N. (2006). *Workflow control-flow patterns: A revised view*. BPM Center Report BPM-06-22.
Sarjoughian, H. S., Kim, S., Ramaswamy, M., & Yau, S. S. (2008). A simulation framework for service-oriented computing systems. In *Proceedings of the Winter Simulation Conference*, Miami, FL, USA (pp. 845–853).
Yau, S. S., Ye, N., Sarjoughian, H. S., Huang, D., Roontiva, A., Baydogan, M., et al. (2009). Towards development of adaptive service-based software systems. *IEEE Transactions on Services Computing, 2*(3), 247–260.
Zeigler, B. P., Praehofer, H., & Kim, T. G. (2000). *Theory of modeling and simulation: Integrating discrete-event and continuous complex dynamic systems* (2nd ed.). San Diego: Academic Press.

Cloud System Simulation Modeling   15

15.1   Introduction

Hybrid software/hardware modeling has practical uses since services with desired Quality of Service (QoS) need to be simulated given not only in terms of operations of software services but also those of networked hardware. System architects and (software and hardware) engineers can develop early architectural designs and evaluate their expected functionality and quality of service performance.

Hardware resources such as available memory, CPU speed, and network bandwidth can constrain the operations of software services. Changes in execution platform (i.e., hardware resources) may have obvious as well as non-obvious impacts, especially resulting in complex interactions among services. In order to achieve desired service-level agreement, simulation must capture not only dynamics of software services, but also hardware parts. With this capability, critical system of systems architecture designs can be accounted if both software interactions are subjected to resource constraints. Basic conflicts that can arise from software and hardware interactions can be formulated and simulated at appropriate levels of abstraction. A set of software services and hardware parts synthesized together is defined to be a *cloud system*. The use of this term is inspired by the notion that software services may reside on networks that conform to the "cloud" characteristics. An example of a cloud system consisting of voice and motion detection services executing on assemblies of mobile devices to grid computers is illustrated in Fig. 15.1 (Hu 2007; Hu and Sarjoughian 2007). Unlike service-oriented computing systems, cloud systems are built from software service systems and networked hardware systems. A voice communication service-based software system is, therefore, a cloud system. The basic idea of co-design for cloud systems will be detailed in the remainder of this chapter.

© Springer International Publishing AG 2017
B.P. Zeigler and H.S. Sarjoughian, *Guide to Modeling and Simulation of Systems of Systems*, Simulation Foundations, Methods and Applications, DOI 10.1007/978-3-319-64134-8_15

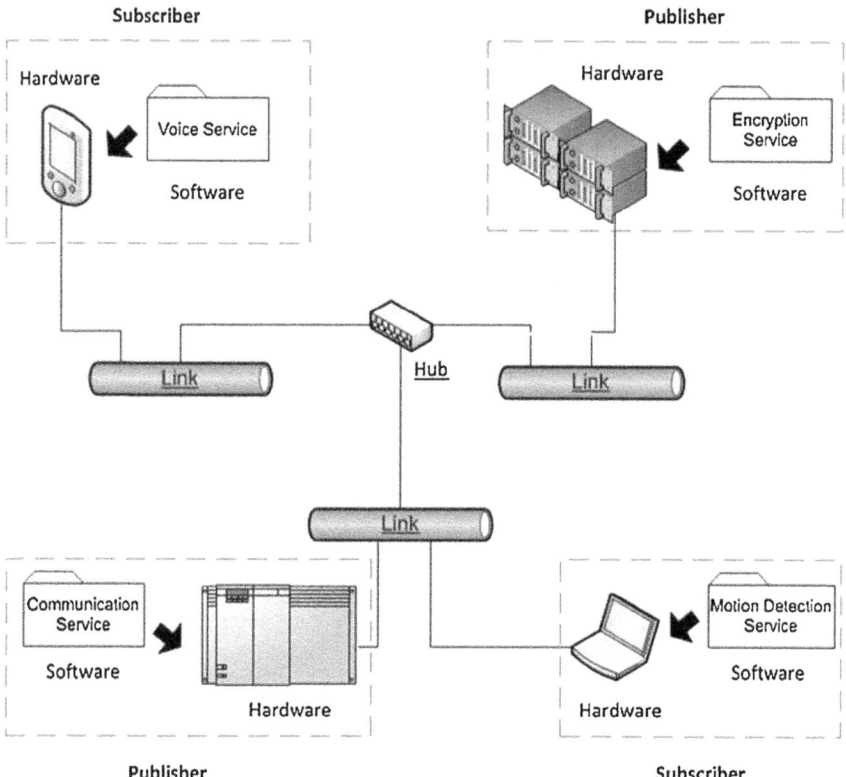

Fig. 15.1 Voice communication system exemplar

15.2 Software/Hardware Co-Design

The concept of co-design refers to partitioning a system under design in terms of software and hardware parts such that each can be developed separately and thereafter synthesized with the other (Butler 1995; Hild et al. 2001). The goal is to enable robust system designs with emphasis on improving hardware and software interaction. The SW/HW co-design concept has been successfully applied in embedded system simulation, design, and development (Wolf 1994; Edwards et al. 1997).

Since Service-based software systems depend on message-based interactions and computation resources, the emphasis on the "software only" design approach can leave out a critical part of the system, i.e., the underlying hardware. Cloud system design approaches focus on software with the role of hardware largely simplified (Sarjoughian et al. 2008).

Fig. 15.2 Elementary steps in system of system co-design process

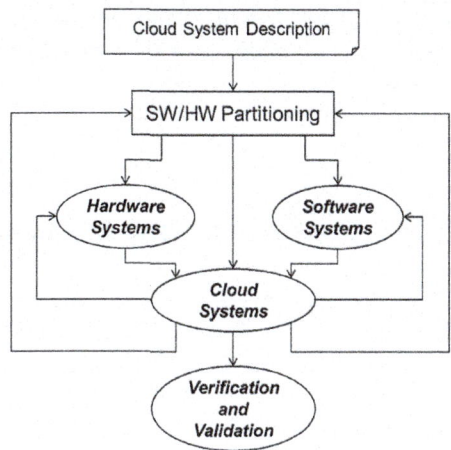

The key benefit of SW/HW co-design is that it affords system architects and system engineers three degrees of freedom. First, software system has a separate specification. Second, hardware system has a separate specification. Third, software and hardware systems are specified as a system of systems. Flexibility in independent software and hardware simulation-based designs provide an important capability to design for their integrated behavior. The main focus from modeling and simulation for software, hardware, and cloud system simulation modeling is depicted in Figs. 15.2 and 15.3.

There are critical differences between embedded systems, distributed software systems, and service-based software systems. Software services have district characteristics as described in the previous chapter. The goal is to enable flexible simulation-based system of systems designs under alternative composition of distributed software services and networked hardware resources. The software service system represents interacting software services. Similarly, the hardware system represents networked computing nodes and communication links. The interactions

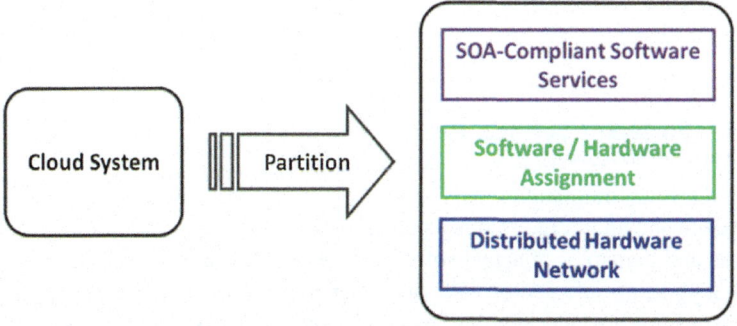

Fig. 15.3 Cloud system partitioning concept in terms of SW/HW parts and their integration

between these systems result in cloud system. Thus, the co-design concept is adapted for developing cloud system simulation. With SW/HW co-design, the concept of loosely coupled software services is extended to loosely, coupled hardware components and thus serving as a basis for cloud systems.

15.3 SOC-DEVS SW/HW Modeling

As SOA-compliant DEVS (SOAD), in SOC-DEVS simulation models adhere to the combined semantics of DEVS and SOA principles (Sarjoughian et al. 2008; Muqsith and Sarjoughian 2010; Muqsith 2011). The key concept introduced is characterization of the relationships between software service system and networked hardware system. The dynamics of services executing on hardware can be formulated as activities that simultaneously simulate hardware and software systems. Fundamental modeling and simulation co-design for cloud systems is summarized below.

- Separate specification for SOA-compliant software services and networked hardware components.
- Specification of individual software service to hardware component interaction.
- Specification of multiple software service interactions via single or network hardware components.

The simulation model components capture the basic functional and resource capabilities of the system. The software service performance depends on available hardware resources. Their interactions must be accounted for. A flexible mapping (assignment) specifies which software service is assigned for execution onto which hardware component(s). Co-design for networked software services are defined in terms of plurality of hard components. First, one or more software services are restricted to execute on a single hardware resource (CPU processing cycles and memory). Second, software services execute on a networked hardware resources (processing cycle and memory for two or more processors, as well as network communication bandwidth). These concepts, model abstractions, and their implementations are described next.

15.3.1 Software Service System Model

Software service simulation model service-oriented computing and service-oriented architecture shown in Fig. 15.4 is a generic, skeletal specification defining common structure and dynamics of actual software services. A software service is an atomic model supporting interaction with other software services and hardware components by receiving and sending messages and jobs. Basic operations such as

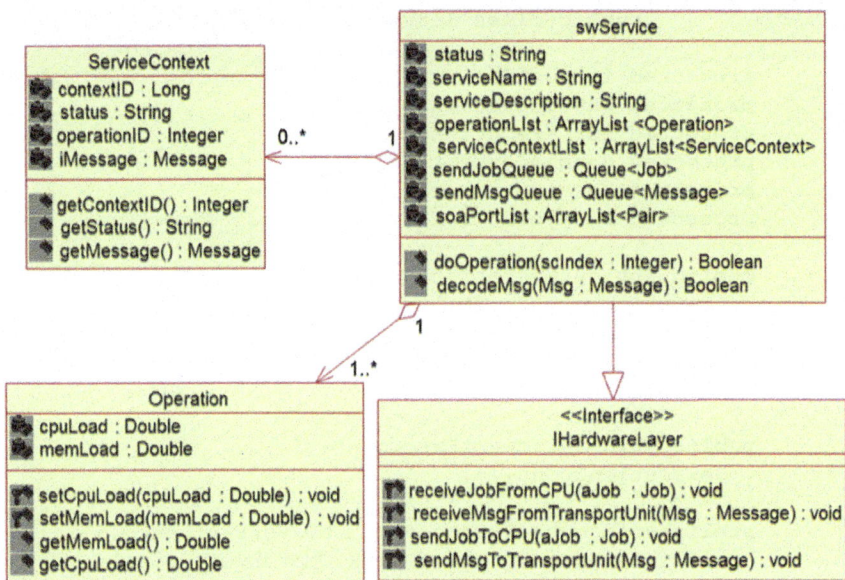

Fig. 15.4 Generic software service simulation model class diagram

message exchange and service invocation for software service (swService) are defined consistent with the SOA concept.

The interactions between any two software services occur in terms of *jobs* and *messages*. The former captures the concept of CPU resources (CPU cycles and memory) required for message executions. The latter is used for representing software service to software service interactions. The numbers of jobs and messages that can be executed are constrained given computing node and network system resources (e.g., CPU speed and network bandwidth). The combination of demanded software services and available hardware resources determine composite service execution.

The software service maintains a list of *operations* it can support (see Fig. 15.4). A message exchange interaction is defined as communication between software services. Every service decodes an incoming message and returns an associated message after executing its operation.

Software service *execution* is parameterized in terms of the CPU cycle and memory load of its designated processor. The cycle parameter (e.g., 2,400 cycles) is required to complete the operation and the load is the amount of memory (e.g., 4 Mbytes) consumed while the operation is being executed. Communication bandwidth between two CPUs also affects the time and priority of service execution. Thus, messages are parameterized with communication load in order to represent time-dependent behavior of service execution given dynamically changing hardware resources. The communication load is the amount of data (e.g., 1 Mbytes) that a software service sends as part of the executed operation semantics.

```
            public class ServiceContext{

    protected int getContextID;
    protected int operationID;
    protected int executionCount;
    protected double executionTime;
    protected Message iMessage;
    protected ArrayList<IOCardEvent> ioCardEventQ;

    public int getOperationId(){
        return operationID;}

    public Message getInvocationMsg(){
        return invocationMsg;}

    public void incrementExecCount(){
        executionCount++;}

    public void queueIOCardEvent(IOCardEvent ioce){
        if(ioCardEventQ.size()<maxIOCardEventQSize){
            ioCardEventQ.add(ioce);
        }
    }

    public IOCardEvent getIOCardEvent(){
        return ioCardEventQ.get(0);}

    public void addToExecutionTime(double dt){
        executionTime+=dt;}


    }
```

Listing 15.1 Service context code snippet

Every software service has a *service context* which maintains the state of the invoked operations and the messages that requested the operations (see Listing 15.1). Software service also creates a service context whenever an operation is requested. Any job initiated by a software service is associated with a service context and operations end when the completed jobs associated with the service context are received. Contexts and operation IDs are defined using getContextID and operationID. Timing associated with each service context is also defined as executionTime. Once an operation is completed, the associated service context is removed. The software service can support multiple operations (executionCount) with each requested operation specified in an incoming message. An invocation of an operation sends a job parameterized with CPU cycles and memory load to the hardware system. This can be seen, in part, as the queueIOCardEvent (IOCardEvent ioce) and adds new operations to be sent to the hardware for execution. A list of active service contexts that currently have jobs to be executed in the hardware is maintained. The service contexts support handling multiple invocation requests (iMessage) as well as simultaneous invocations of operations.

Obviously, network load, such as processing delay at routers and switches, directly impacts the time-dependent behavior of software services. The combination of CPU, memory, and communication load captures the dependency of distributed software service on available hardware resources.

As stated before, every job is associated with an operation and denotes the CPU cycle and memory requirement (Job < RequiredCPUCyles, RequiredMemory >). For a software service operation requiring 2,400 CPU cycles and 2 Kbytes of memory, a job is defined as job < 2400 cycles, 2048 bytes > . A message is defined as the unit of information that a service can exchange as part of the message-based service interactions. It contains the payload data that services may exchange and type of message denoting context of interaction. A message, therefore, is defined as Message < Type, PayloadSize >. The message < Generic, 1 MB > creates 1 MB of data to be sent to a recipient service.

The software service, named swService, is specified as a parallel DEVS atomic model. This model is the basis for developing other service models in SOC-DEVS. It is the template for modeling service functionality and I/O behavior with hardware components (i.e., processor, link, and switch (refer to Sect. 15.3.2). The input and output ports and their corresponding events are defined as {(inMsgs × iMessages), (inJobs × iJobs)} and {(outMsgs × oMessages), (outJobs × oJobs)}. For example, iMessage events arrive on inMsgs input port. The template model has an outgoing message queue (FIFO), an outgoing job queue (FIFO), and a list of active service contexts with standard state variables S = {phase × σ}. The values for phase are "passive" and "sending." The sigma can have any value ranging from 0 to infinity. Service context denotes the context in which invocation message is received and operation is requested.

Software service receives messages through its inMsgs port before they can be processed. Since multiple software services can be associated with the same port, the swService receiving the message checks whether the message is for itself or not using the isMsgForSelf(message) function. If it is, the decode(message) function decodes the incoming message and identifies the requested operation. Next, a new service context is created and a job associated with the operation is queued in the sendJobQ queue. After processing all the incoming messages, the swService enters phase "sending" for a small nonzero time period. Next, outputs (i.e., jobs) are created for "outJobs" port using sendJob(job). After the output is sent out, the swService transitions to phase "passive" for an indefinite amount of time using its internal transition function.

Similarly, when a completed job is received via inJobs port, it is examined by isMsgForSelf(job) function. If the message is intended for this swService, then the doOperation(job) function is executed. Otherwise, the received job is ignored and placed in the sendMsgQ queue to be sent out to another swService. Once all the incoming jobs are processed, the swService enters phase "sending" for a small nonzero time period. As before, the output function generates output(s) (i.e., messages) for the "outMsgs" port using sendMsg(message) function. The

1. `imsg` (e.g., request) is received at the `inMsgs` port
2. service context is created and added to `scList`, the service context list
3. `job` (e.g., computation load) associated with the service context is added to `outJobQ`
4. output function sends `job` through `outJobs` port
5. completed `job` is received at the `inJobs` port
6. service context associated with the completed `job` is removed from `scList`
7. `omsg` (e.g., response) is generated and sent to the `sendMsgQ`
8. output function sends omsg through `outMsgs` port

Listing 15.2 swService processing steps for handling jobs and messages

swService phase changes to "passive" and stays in this phase indefinitely using the internal transition function. As part of the internal transition function, the associated service context for the completed job is removed. Simultaneous I/O of messages and jobs (using $\sigma = 0$) are also allowed using the same semantics as two separate output queues for messages and jobs are maintained. The required time for job completion varies depending on hardware resource availability and the time it takes to complete service operation. The operations just described are enumerated in Listing 15.2.

The processing scheme is illustrated in Fig. 15.5. The basic sequential ordering starts with receiving a request message, creating an unprocessed job for the swService assigned processor, and creating and sending response messages. When requests are received simultaneously, they are processed in an arbitrary order which is facilitated by the two independent sendJobQ and `sendMsgQ` FIFO queues. In case there are multiple request messages, ordering becomes necessary which can be handled using external and internal transition functions along with confluent function.

A software service system can be easily defined as shown in Fig. 15.6 given the modularity of software services and the inherent modularity supported by DEVS. A software service system is independent of hardware upon which it can be assigned to. For example, the software services shown in Fig. 15.6 can be assigned to a single processor or multiple processors (see Sect. 15.3.3).

15.3.1.1 Broker, Publisher, and Subscriber

Generic Broker, Publisher, and Subscriber models are defined by extending the swService model described in the previous section. The class diagram specification in terms of swService and interfaces is shown in Fig. 15.7. These models differ in terms of their contexts—i.e., the message interaction each model supports and the resultant message exchanges. For example, in response to a subscriber's request message for a published service, a broker uses its lookup operation and returns the relevant information to the subscriber. Similarly, a publisher's responds to a sub-scriber's service request message by performing the service. According to the SOA standard, the subscriber's interaction with publisher is preceded by the subscriber to broker interaction. These SOA-compliant service interactions are supported in SOC-DEVS. Service invocation is initiated by a message exchange between a publisher and a subscriber. The service invocation message invokes a service

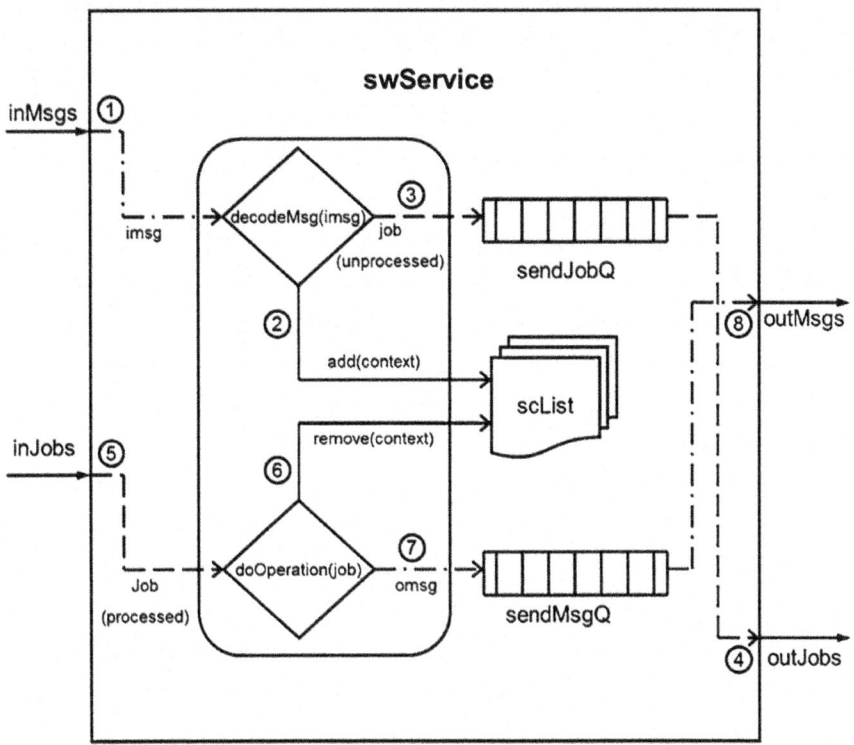

Fig. 15.5 swService flowchart for handling job and messages

Fig. 15.6 Software service system model

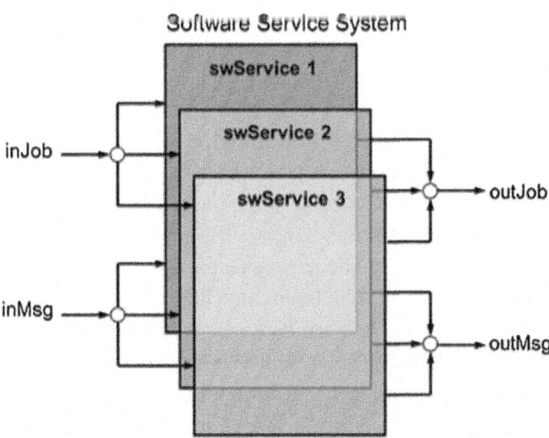

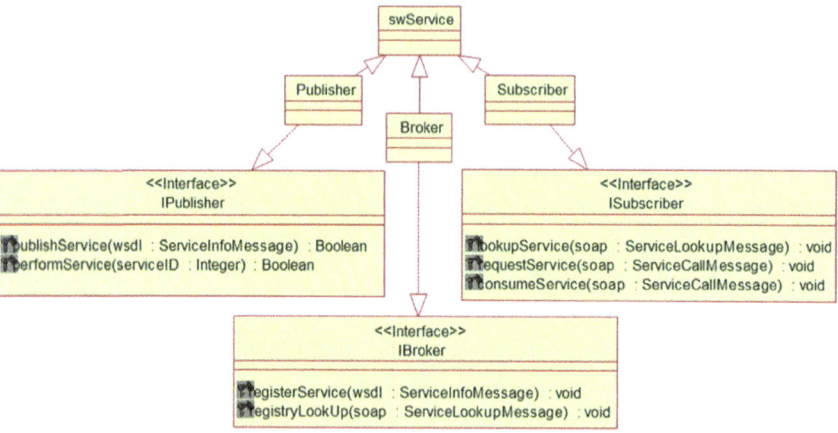

Fig. 15.7 Design specification for broker, publisher, and subscriber

operation associated with an endpoint in the publisher, the associated operation(s) may be executed multiple times based on requested duration, and return messages may be sent for each operation execution.

The operational semantics defined for swService are extended in the Broker, Publisher, and Subscriber models by differentiating response message and service operations required in each. For every service component, if a message is received through the inMsgs port, then the external transition function is invoked—i.e., the decodeMsg(message) operation is called, the service context and jobs are sent, and the service contexts are updated. Response messages and the type of operations are different for Broker, Publisher, and Subscriber services. In Broker, a service information message results in a service registration invocation (registerService) whereas a service lookup message results in a service discovery invocation (registryLookup) and sends the discovery result message to the service lookup requester. In Publisher, a service call message results in the requested service invocation and returning the service result to the requester. In Subscriber, a service result message invokes service consumption consumeService operation. Since all messages use the same message I/O ports, the logic of service interaction is incorporated into the decodeMsg(message) operation and doOperation (job) functions. The messages are extended to contain the relevant information as required to define such behaviors. The time required to execute any service operation is dependent on the hardware resources and specified in external and internal transition functions. The modular specification of publisher, subscriber, and broker models affords arbitrary accuracy in defining duration of operations. This benefit is due to both representing SOA-compliancy and timing afforded in DEVS models. If higher level abstraction is desired, these models can be extended to allow aggregate-level software behavior. For example, when a subscriber requesting a large number of service requests to a publisher, a probability can be assigned to multiple endpoints and one is chosen and executed at random.

Broker Model The Broker model responds to two types of messages, one called `ServiceInfoMessage` and the other `ServiceLookupMessage`. These message requests are handled by `decodeMsg(message)` function. Each job associated with a request is sent to sendJobQ. When the processed job is returned, the `doOperation(job)` function completes the returned process jobs as either service registration or service lookup. For the service lookup operation, a `ServiceInfoMessage` is sent to the sendMsgQ. For service registration operation, no message is sent. The input and output messages are `ServiceLookupMessage`, `ServiceInfoMessage`, and `ServiceInfoMessage`, respectively. The details for the `decodeMsg(msg)` and `doOperation(job)` function are defined in Listings 15.3 and 15.4.

Publisher Model The Publisher model responds to incoming `ServiceCallMessage` message type. Similar to the broker model, the `decodeMsg(message)` function given in the swService model is defined to evaluate the requested operation and send a job associated with the operation to sendJobQ. Once the job is returned, the `doOperation(job)` function completes it as either service publication or perform service operation. For service operation, a `ServiceCallMessage` is sent to the sendMsgQ. The input and output messages are `ServiceCallMessage` and `ServiceCallMessage`, `ServiceInfoMessage`, respectively. The `decodeMsg(msg)` and `doOperation(job)` functions are defined differently from those provided for the swService model (see Listings 15.5 and 15.6).

Subscriber Model Finally, the Subscriber model responds to incoming messages of type `ServiceInfoMessage` and `ServiceCallMessage`. As before, the requested operation is decoded and a job associated with the operation is sent to sendJobQ. Once the completed job is returned, then lookup service, request service, or consume service operation is called. For the first two cases, a `ServiceLookupMessage` or a `ServiceCallMessage` is sent to sendMsgQ,

```
      protected int decodeMsg(Message msg){
if(msg instanceof ServiceInfoMessage){
    int opID = this.getOperationID(REGISTERSERVICE);
    ServiceContext sc = new ServiceContext(REGISTERSERVICE,msg,
    opID);
    serviceContextList.add(sc);
    scID = serviceContextList.indexOf(sc);
}
else if (msg instanceof ServiceLookupMessage) {
    int opID = this.getOperationID(LOOKUPSERVICE);
    ServiceContext sc = new ServiceContext(LOOKUPSERVICE,msg,opID);
    serviceContextList.add(sc);
    scID = serviceContextList.indexOf(sc);
}
        }
```

Listing 15.3 Broker code snippet for message decoding

```
        protected boolean doOperation(int scIndex){
    int opID=serviceContextList.get(scIndex).getOperationId();

    if(OperationList.get(opID).getName().equalsIgnoreCase(
        REGISTERSERVICE)){
        ServiceInfoMessage si = (ServiceInfoMessage)
            serviceContextList.get(scIndex).getInvocationMsg();
        registerWithServiceDirectory(si);
    }
    else
    if(OperationList.get(opID).getName().equalsIgnoreCase(
        LOOKUPSERVICE)){
        ServiceLookupMessage sl = (ServiceLookupMessage)
            serviceContextList.get(scIndex).getInvocationMsg();

        ServiceInfoMessage si = new
        ServiceInfoMessage(selfAddress,sl.getSource(),new
            ServiceURL(selfAddress),'''',null,new
        ServiceRegistrationInfo());
        si.setType(Constants.MessageType.LOOKUPRESULTMSG);
        flag=legacyLookUp(sl,si);
    }
            }
```

Listing 15.4 Broker code snippet for message operation

```
        protected int decodeMsg(Message msg){
    if(msg instanceof ServiceCallMessage){
        activeInvocationRequests++;

        double pr=r.uniform(0,1);
        int opID = this.getOperationID(PERFORMSERVICE);
        ServiceContext sc= new ServiceContext(PERFORMSERVICE,msg,opID);

        sc.setAcceptIOCardEvent(useIOCard);
        sc.setAcceptTimerEvent(useSystemTimer);
        sc.setInstantiatedFlag(true);

        serviceContextList.add(sc);
        serviceInstanceInit(sc);
        scID = serviceContextList.indexOf(sc);
    }
            }
```

Listing 15.5 Publisher code snippet for message decoding

respectively. For the consume service operation, no message is sent. The input and output are ServiceCallMessage, ServiceInfoMessage and ServiceLookupMessage, ServiceCallMessage, respectively. Implementations for the decodeMsg(msg) and doOperation(job) functions are given in Listings 15.7 and 15.8.

```
      protected boolean doOperation(int scIndex){
ServiceContext sc = serviceContextList.get(scIndex);
int opID = sc.getOperationId();

if(OperationList.get(opID).getName().equalsIgnoreCase(
    PUBLISHSERVICE)){
    flag = publishService(sc);
}
else
if(OperationList.get(opID).getName().equalsIgnoreCase(
    PERFORMSERVICE)){

    if(!useIOCard){
        flag = performService(sc);
    }
}
        }
```

Listing 15.6 Broker code snippet for message operation

```
      protected int decodeMsg(Message msg){
if(msg.getType()==Constants.MessageType.LOOKUPRESULTMSG){
   int opID = this.getOperationID(REQUESTSERVICE);
   ServiceContext sc= new ServiceContext(REQUESTSERVICE,msg,opID);
   serviceContextList.add(sc);
   scID = serviceContextList.indexOf(sc);
}
else if(msg.getType()==Constants.MessageType.RESPONSEMSG){
   int opID = this.getOperationID(CONSUMESERVICE);
   ServiceContext sc = new ServiceContext(CONSUMESERVICE,msg,
   opID);
   serviceContextList.add(sc);
   scID = serviceContextList.indexOf(sc);
}
        }
```

Listing 15.7 Subscriber code snippet for message decoding

15.3.1.2 Voice Communication Publisher Model

The publisher, subscriber, and broker models described above provide the generic
capabilities to be extended to model specific applications of interest such as Voice
Communication System (VCS). As an example, Voice Communication Publisher
(VCPublisher) is specified consistent with the skeletal Publisher (see Fig. 15.7).
The generic states and state transitions in the base class Publisher.
Key-domain-specific application behavior for the performService function is
defined in the VCPublisher model. Common publisher's attributes such as the

```
        protected boolean doOperation(int scIndex){
    int opID = serviceContextList.get(scIndex).getOperationId();

    if(OperationList.get(opID).getName().equalsIgnoreCase(
        LOOKUPSERVICE)){
        ServiceLookupMessage(ServiceLookupMessage) sl =
            serviceContextList.get(scIndex).getInvocationMsg();
    }
    else
    if(OperationList.get(opID).getName().equalsIgnoreCase(
        REQUESTSERVICE)){

        ServiceInfoMessage sim = (ServiceInfoMessage)
            serviceContextList.get(scIndex).getInvocationMsg();
        requestSCM.setSource(selfAddress);
        requestSCM.setDestination(sim.getServiceURL().
        getServiceURLasP2PInfo());
        flag=requestService();
    }
    else
    if(OperationList.get(opID).getName().equalsIgnoreCase(
        CONSUMESERVICE)){
        ServiceCallMessage scm = (ServiceCallMessage)
            serviceContextList.get(scIndex).getInvocationMsg();
        consumeService(scm);
    }
        }
```

Listing 15.8 Subscriber code snippet for message operation

list of endpoints and self-description message, as well as CPU cycles and memory load, are declared. Application-specific attributes such as audio-base sampling rate, number of channels (mono or stereo), and buffer size are defined. In addition, parameters important for simulation experiments are also defined although not shown in Listing 15.9.

The performService method adds application-specific details such as subscriber's service request-related information (e.g., invocation message iMsg and request parameters sp) that are defined in its in ServiceContext. The Voice-Comm generates a response message scm which is then embedded in the audioData in each call to the performService method. The generated response messages are set up based on the subscriber's requested service parameters (e.g., sampling rate). The method determines whether or not the service has message (and job) to send to processor.

15.3.2   Hardware System Model

The hardware system is represented as either a single processor or a collection of interconnected processors. A processor can execute one or more services. Multiple services may also be executed on a distributed set of processors communicating to

```
        public boolean performService(ServiceContext sc) {
Message iMsg = sc.getInvocationMsg();
P2PInfo dst = iMsg.getSource();

VCServiceParameter sp = (VCServiceParameter)((ServiceCallMessage)
   iMsg).getServiceParameter();

ServiceCallMessage scm = new ServiceCallMessage(selfAddress,dst,
null);
scm.setType(Constants.MessageType.RESPONSEMSG);
scm.setName(sp.getSamplingRateInKHzAsString());

int Samplingrate = sp.getSamplingRate();
int BufferSize = sp.getBufferSize();
int channels = 2; int noBytesperSample=2;
int soundCardQSize = sc.getIOCardEventQSize();
IOCardEvent ioce = sc.getIOCardEvent();

for (int i=0;i<soundCardQSize && Math.ceil(dataSize)<BufferSize;
   i++){
   dataSize+=ioce.getInterval()*((Samplingrate*noBytesperSample*
   channels));
   noOfUsedEvents++;
}

scm.setSize(dataSize);
scm.setType(Constants.MessageType.RESPONSEMSG);
sc.incrementExecCount();

double baseCPULoad = (1e-6)*(2190E6);
if(sc.getExecTime()<= sp.getServiceDuration()){

   ComputationLoad jb = new ComputationLoad (cpuLoad,memLoad,sc);
   if(sc.getExecTime()>=sp.getServiceDuration()){
      jb.setUnloadFlag(true);
      sc.setAcceptIOCardEvent(false);
      sc.setAcceptTimerEvent(false);
   }
   if(sc.getExecCount()<=1){
      jb.setLoadFlag(true);
   }
   processHardwareDataDependentJob(sc,jb,noOfUsedEvents);
   sc.setPendingMsg(scm);
}
      }
```

Listing 15.9 Subscriber code snippet for voice communication publisher

one another via switches and links. These models are a variant of those developed for DEVS-Distributed Object Computing simulation (Hild et al. 2001). They differ in ways in which software services, as opposed to software objects, are connected to hardware components.

15.3.2.1 Processor

The processor consists of central processing unit (CPU), network interface card (NIC), transport unit (TransportUnit), and network card (IOCard) (see Fig. 15.8). The system timer (SystemTimer) and status collector (StatusCollector) support collecting data for the processor. The coupled model P_1 performs computational work for software services as well as enabling their interaction.

The CPU is specified with one input port and one output port along with CPU speed and memory size) (Hild et al. 2001). The input port accepts and executes requests (jobs) received from software service. The completed jobs are emitted via the output port. Available CPU speed and memory size parameters are used to restrict software service executions. The speed parameter determines how quickly data processing operations are executed and the memory size determines the number of jobs that can be loaded without using swap memory. If there is insufficient memory to handle a job, the job is placed in the waiting queue. Once memory becomes available, the job is placed into the active queue with a swap time penalty. Scheduling algorithm (FIFO) for operating system is supported. The FIFO discipline is supported in the CPU_FIFO atomic model. Other kinds of scheduling algorithms priority queue may be added and used without requiring changes to the software service.

The transport unit model (TransportUnit) supports input/output message transmission with segmentation to packets and their assembly. A message contains

Fig. 15.8 Components of the processor model (tree structure view from DEVS-Suite simulator)

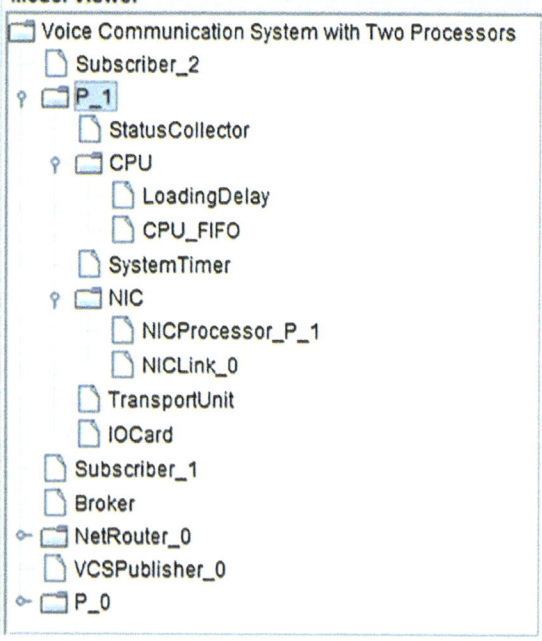

data abstractions for the software system and packets for the hardware system. Messages are transported to the software system or fragmented into packets to the network card based on the message to software system mapping. Outgoing messages for the network card must be divided into packets before sending. Incoming packets from the network card are queued for assembly into message and thereafter sent to the software system. The transport unit at a destination node receives and collects packets. When all packets for a message are received, the destination transport unit delivers the message to the destination software service. Transport capability supports basic packetizing (or depacketizing) overhead, and end-to-end communication with message to software system mapping. The network card provides network I/O for incoming and outgoing packets as well as buffering capability for packet loss prevention. Its addressing scheme with logical ports embedded in messages support identifying source and destination nodes.

15.3.2.2   Network Switch Model

Network switch routes packets between processors. It queues incoming packets and puts them in an outgoing queue after processing. The queue length and bandwidths for the outgoing links are two important parameters that can be used to configure various packet loss scenarios. The packet processing begins after obtaining input link to output link mapping (i.e., address lookup) from a routing table. Packet address information is used to make switching decisions to send a packet to a specific output link as necessary. Unlike real network switches where address mapping is obtained using a routing algorithm that automatically updates the routing table, the modeler needs to specify and initialize static address lookup tables in network switches.

15.3.2.3   Network Router Model

Network router is similar to the network switch. It uses neighbor connectivity to determine packets' destinations. The mapping is done using the routing algorithm that automatically updates the routing table. Based on the network connectivity and route discovery message propagation, the entire network route is discovered at initialization. The algorithm, however, does not support route rediscovery after initialization.

15.3.2.4   Link Model

Link is an abstraction for the physical medium that is used for connecting network nodes. Use of link is suitable when link layer behavior (e.g., propagation delay and frame collision) is desired. The link has input and output queues that can transmit packet fragments to/from network card (also network switch) at some specified speed (e.g., 100 Mbps). Additional details such as error coefficient (physical level noise) may be added to this model.

15.3.3   Service System Mapping

The Service System Mapping (SSM) assigns software services to processors and thus allows user-defined SW/HW configurations. From implementation perspective, it couples the `swService.outMsgs` port of a software service component to the `processor.inMsg` port of a processor. Similar couplings are defined for `swService.outJobs` to `processor.inJobs`. Remaining common couplings are shown in Fig. 15.9 (see also Fig. 15.6). For example, jobs from the publisher (`VCSPublisher_0`) are sent to the processor (`P_0`) and the completed jobs are returned. The messages are sent to the transport unit and disseminated to the destination processor. The incoming messages are delivered to the software services. The mapping from software to hardware layer is applicable for atomic services, as well, as composite services as the interface design is applicable for the generic software service interaction (see Figs. 15.10 and 15.11).

Exercise

Write an SES to describe Fig. 15.10, which has components swService1, swService2, and Processor1. The swServices send and receive jobs and messages to Processor1. Processor1 is decomposed further into NIC, TransportUnit, and CPU, and the external input coupling for this decomposition sends Jobs to the CPU and messages to the TransportUnit.

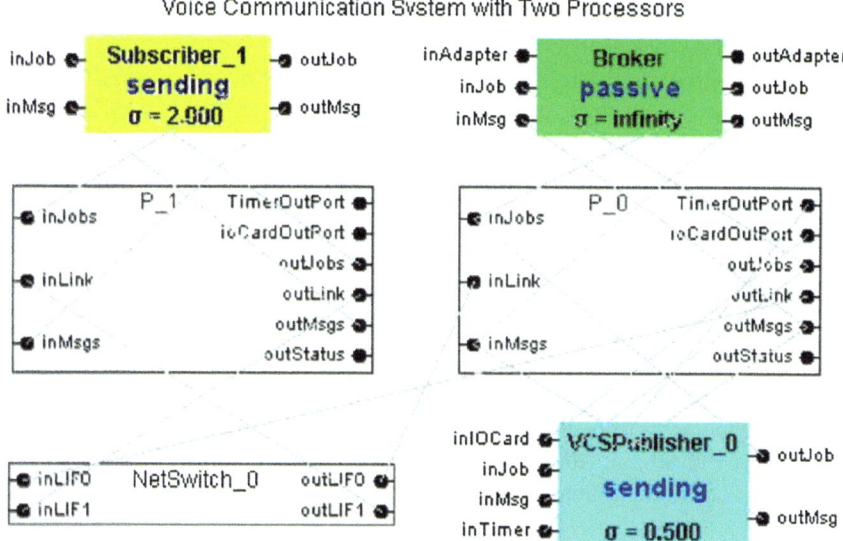

Fig. 15.9 I/O mappings among three software services, their respective processors, and a network switch

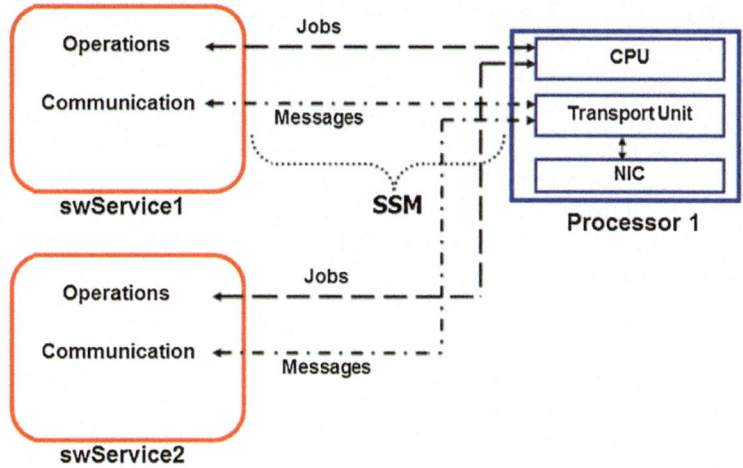

Fig. 15.10 Single processor supporting two software services

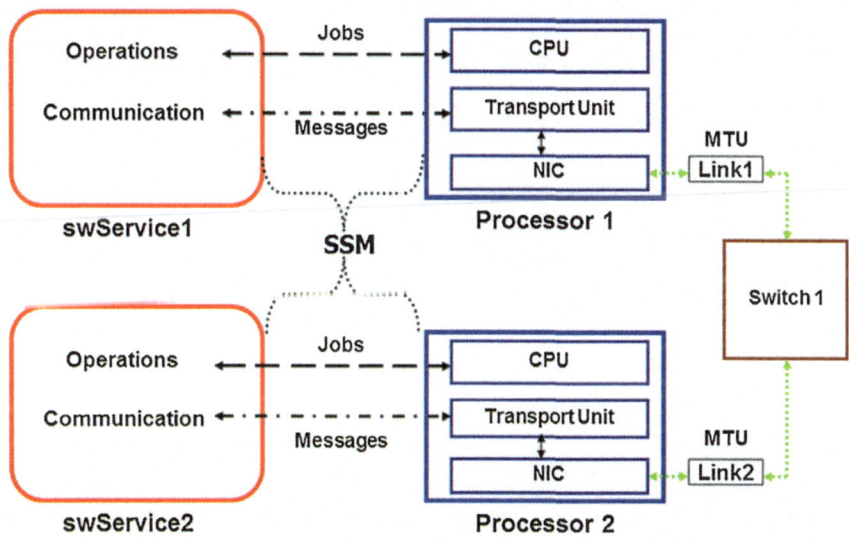

Fig. 15.11 Two software services interact using two processors connected via two links and a switch

Extend your SES for Fig. 15.10 to describe the configuration of Fig. 15.11. Add a switch and links to connect the processors through their network interface cards (NICs).

Exercise

Use multi-aspects to go from the particular instances of software/ hardware mappings, studied in Figs. 15.10 and 15.11, to a more general mapping concept. The approach to mapping considers the overall network to break into subnets each of which contains a router and a multi-entity called `ProcessorAndServices`. For the SES outline shown in Fig. 15.12, each `ProcessorAndService` component of a subnet is decomposed into a single processor and one or more `swServices`. After writing the SES for the subnet, express an overall network as a multi-aspect of subnets. Hint: See Chap. 6 examples of hierarchical multi-aspects.

As the software services compete for processor resources, their dynamics are driven by the performance of the processor, which in turn determines the performance of the software service to software service interaction. Furthermore, the performance of routers, switches, and links in a network can affect the publisher, broker, and subscriber quality of service. Thus, network topologies may be designed to achieve some desired quality of service for cloud systems.

The synthesis, therefore, is the mapping from the software service system to the hardware system is called Service System Mapping (SSM) . With such mappings, the hardware system acts as a constraining factor for the software system's maximum performance under dynamic conditions that may exist due to varying individual services, operations, and interactions.

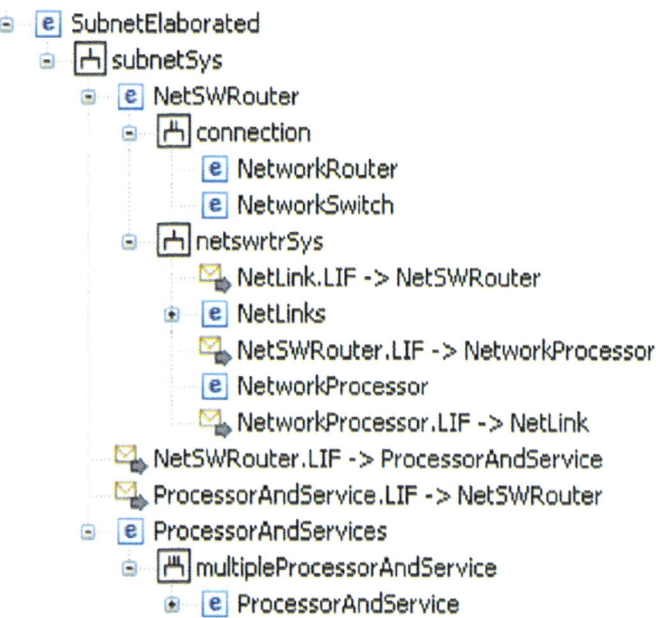

Fig. 15.12 SES for a subnet network

15.4   Service-Oriented Voice Communication System

An exemplar voice communication system (VCS) with data encryption capability is modeled based on the methodology described in earlier sections (Yau et al. 2009, 2011). It provides streaming audio based on user requested sampling rate. The system primarily consists of server(s) hosting streaming services. The servers are connected via routers, switches, and links to clients. Data packets are used to stream voice via the network. Streaming services can simultaneously stream voice for multiple clients. Sampling rate and streaming duration are two primary parameters the user selects. It impacts audio quality. Stream processing delay, network delay, and available network bandwidth along the routes from the server to the clients determine the resultant system quality of service.

VCS models are developed based on data collected from a prototype real system (Yau et al. 2009). Experiments are devised to study performance, timing, accuracy attributes of cloud systems, and their counterpart simulations. The sampling rate, key length, and encryption percentage attributes varied in the real and simulation experiments are given in Table 15.1. Larger sampling rates produce higher quality audio data as it contains more audio bits per sample. Larger key lengths lead to higher computation. Similarly, larger encryption percentages increase processing delays. Parameterization for hardware parts is shown in Table 15.2. The simulation results are used to validate the SOC-DEVS model abstractions as well as their realizations in DEVS-Suite simulator (DEVS-Suite 2017; Kim et al. 2009).

Exercise

Write an SES for the subnet shown in Fig. 15.13 so that the `Proces-sorAndService` entity contains a processor, a broker, and multi-aspects for

Table 15.1 Voice communication configuration

Software services	
Sampling rates	44.1, 88.2, 132.3, 176.4 220.5 kHz
Key length	64, 128, 256 bits
Encryption percentage	0 or 100%

Table 15.2 Hardware system configuration

	Real system	Simulation system
CPU	2.2 GHz	2.2 GHz
Memory	1024 MB	1024 MB
Network card	100 Mbps	100 Mbps
Network link bandwidth	100 Mbps	100 Mbps
Subscriber #	1–40	1–40, 100–1000
Data collection duration	60 s (wall clock)	60 s (logical lock)

Fig. 15.13 SES for
processors and services

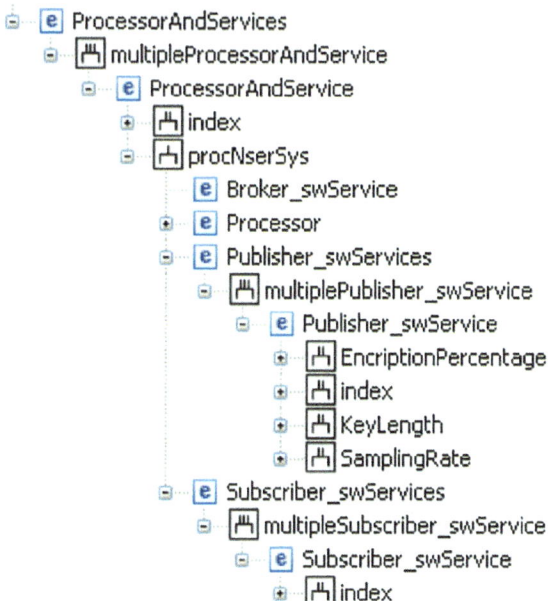

publishers and subscribers. Consistent with the class design of Fig. 15.7, use underscores to show that the broker, publisher, and subscriber are subclasses of swService (see Chap. 7). Add specializations to the publisher to capture the choices in Table 15.1.

Cloud systems may be divided into *communication-intensive*, *computation intensive*, and *mixed* types. Communication-intensive systems require high-degree of data communication and the latter requires high amount of data processing. The primary resource requirement in communication-intensive systems is network bandwidth. The dominant dynamics is software service communications and network hardware resources. Interactions among software services are affected by the load at the network routers, switches, and links. Hardware resource requirement is considered to be negligible from the perspective of user's QoS.

For computation-intensive systems, data processing, such as data encryption, or decryption has the dominant role and the communication is considered negligible. User requests data according to the user-specified encryption parameters. Data encryption processing is computation-intensive and the resource requirement depends on the encryption algorithm, key length, and amount of user data. Generally, longer key length increases encryption strength and has an inverse relation to computation delay for data processing (Yau et al. 2011). Mixed systems demand high resources for both communication and computation.

15.4.1   Basic Measurements

Metrics are defined to evaluate quality of service for VCS and, more generally, cloud systems. They capture key quantities for software services and hardware systems. These measurements are taken at the publishers (servers) and subscribers (clients), which take into account the hardware parts, such as processor, links, and routers. These following metrics support evaluating cloud system quality of service *timeliness*, *throughput*, and *accuracy* measurements.

Processor Utilization   It measures the ratio of the CPU cycles used in execution of a service with respect to the total CPU cycles available over an observation period. Given a processor P and an observation period T, the processor or CPU Utilization is defined as $100 \times (N_s/N_T)$, where N_s is the number of CPU cycles consumed for executing service, and N_T is the total number of CPU cycles generated by the processor.

Round Trip Delay   Round trip delay denoted as RT-Delay measures the time between sending of a client request and the receiving of the first data packet from the server (VoiceComm publisher) service. This metric is defined as RT-Delay $(C_i) = t_{receive,i} - t_{request,i}$ where C_i is ith client. This is a measurement for service response time that accounts for network delay and processing times at the client and server.

Average Data Throughput   It measures the amount of data bytes sent by the server (VoiceComm publisher) over a service period. All simultaneously active clients' aggregated data bytes sent by the server are used in calculating the average data throughput.

Sampled Data Throughput   It measures the amount of data bytes sent by the server between two consecutive data sampling events. In addition to the average throughput over the entire service period, this alternate sampled throughput is also observed over each data sampling period (e.g., 1 s). This metric is useful for calculating fine grain, transient system behavior.

Inter-Frame Time   It measures the time difference between two consecutive events at the server (VoiceComm publisher). This measurement excludes network delay; instead, its value depends on the processor and its elements (see Fig. 15.8).

Inter-Data Frame Delay   It measures the time difference between events of two consecutive sending events at the server (VoiceComm publisher). The measurement can also be for two arriving events at a client. Due to data processing and network communication, the time delay between two consecutive data frame arrivals can vary. At the server, the inter-frame delay is due to data processor delay and packet processing delay at the network card. At the client, the delay also includes delays due to links and network routers and switches which process packets.

Data Accuracy It measures the amount of data received by all simultaneously active clients (subscribers) as the percentage of all data sent by the server (VoiceComm service) in a given period of time. Network bandwidth, router packet capacity, and MAC layer collision can result in loss of data. Such data accuracy, for example, can be significantly higher for UDP protocol since packet (data) retransmission, as in TCP/IP, is not enforced.

Exercise

Add an experimental frame to your SES for a subnet that can support the basic measurements of Sect. 15.4.1.

15.4.2 Simulation Parameter Estimation

To develop useful simulation models, it is necessary not only for the models to be logically correct, but also parameterized accurately (Muqsith and Sarjoughian 2010; Muqsith 2011; Sarjoughian et al. 2012). Therefore, the formulation of a simulation model such as Voice Communication System needs to be augmented with data parameterization. Application domain knowledge is needed in capturing resource-dependent system dynamics. Basic processor (computational) and network (communication) data must be obtained for parameterizing software and hardware systems. To achieve this goal, one way is to build a small-scale real-world counterpart of the target cloud system. A real VCS supporting up to 40 services is developed using .Net technology. A counterpart VCS simulation model is developed and parameterized. The simulation models are configured using statistical techniques and analysis performed on data collected from the real VCS.

Experiments are conducted using three computers, one hosting VCS service and two machines emulating multiple clients using threads. The server and the client machines have identical CPU (2.2 GHz), memory (1 Gbytes), and NIC (100 Mbps). The machines are connected by a 100 Mbps router. The system is based on IIS server 5.0 running on Windows XP Service Pack 3, .NET version 3.5, and JDK version 1.6 (Sarjoughian et al. 2012). To collect run-time data, a measurement protocol has been developed with the help of Network Packet Monitoring tool.

As an example, a real VCS system which supports Data Encryption Standards (DES) is developed. Its simulated counterpart model, however, may exclude a complete, accurate abstraction of an encryption and decryption algorithm. Instead, it accounts for the algorithm by parameterizing CPU load as a function of sampling rate, which accounts for data encryption and decryption. Therefore, CPU load parameterization has a significant role in not only the processor dynamics, but also the overall system dynamics.

To capture the impact of DES algorithm, data generation rate is $G = S \times B \times C$ (bits/second) where S is the sampling rate (see Table 15.1), B is bits per sample, and C is the channel number (i.e., mono = 1, stereo = 2). The CPU load factor $LF = (V \times U)/E$, where V = CPU speed (MHz), U = CPU utilization (%), and E is the encryption rate. Under nominal load condition, the CPU utilization is primarily due to the encryption load and $LF = (V \times U)/G$. The average CPU load for encryption operation $L = LF \times S \times T$ where T is a time duration. Parameters for hardware parts are listed in Table 15.2. Aside from the parameters shown for hardware parts, each processor has a 0.1-s time penalty for memory swap. The swap penalty activates only when a processor's available memory is less than required to process a job.

15.4.3 Experimentation Setup and Execution

The SOC-DEVS simulation experiments are developed in DEVS-Suite simulation environment. The simulator is installed in a machine with an Intel Core 2 Duo CPU E8200 at 2.66 GHz, and 3.23 GB of memory and Intel 82566 DM Gigabit network card set at 100 Mbs. The OS is Microsoft Windows XP Professional with Service Pack 3 and JDK version 1.6. The network card is disabled while simulations are executed and only the DEVS-Suite is the active user-level application. For VCS model development in SOC-DEVS, Helios Eclipse IDE is used. For model development, the DEVS-Suite GUI is used. For experiments and data collection, only the console part of the simulator is used.

15.4.4 Example Simulation Model Results

A variety of VCS simulation models can be constructed using different software service configurations (e.g., a single voice communication service supporting many subscribers) mapped to different hardware topologies (e.g., two identical processors connected using a router). As noted above, the effect of background traffic on both communication and computation (e.g., encryption) can also be studied. The results shown in Figs. 15.14, 15.15, and 15.16 are for 10 simulation runs, each for a period of 60 s.

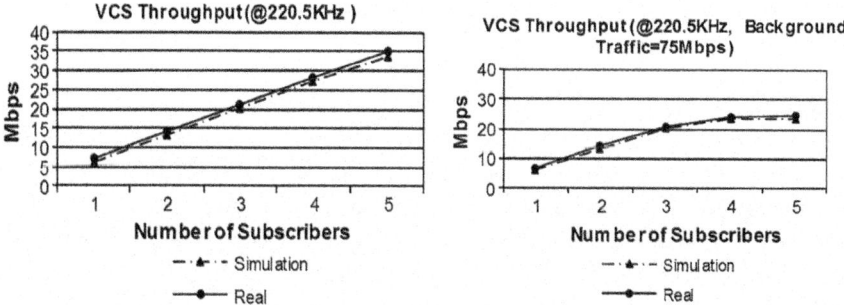

Fig. 15.14 Throughput measurements with and without background traffic

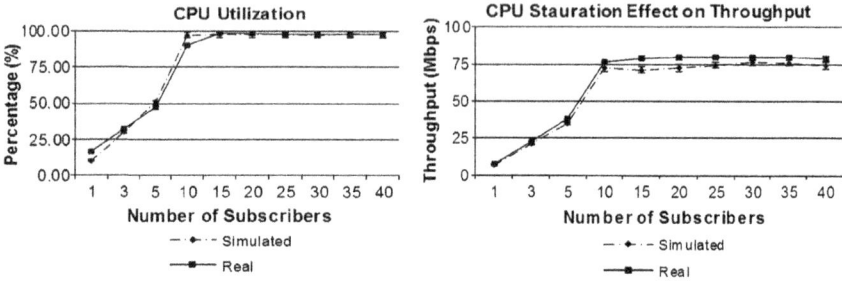

Fig. 15.15 Throughput measurements with and without background traffic

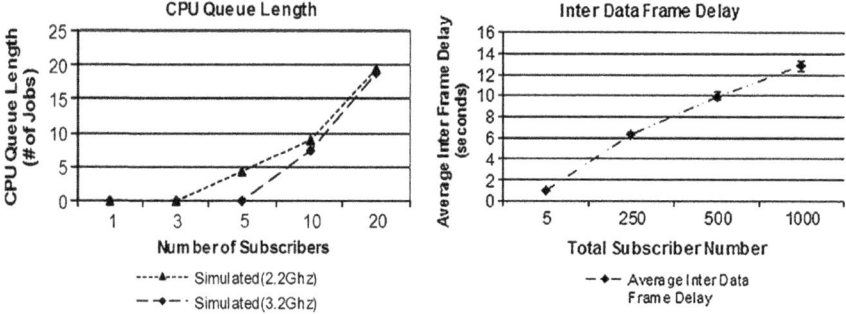

Fig. 15.16 Throughput measurements with and without background traffic

The impact of increasing the number of subscribers on CPU utilization can also be studied using the experimental setup used for VCS throughput. As depicted in Figs. 15.14 and 15.15, CPU utilization saturates as the number of subscribers reaches a threshold. Similarly, the effect of CPU saturation is shown on throughput as the number of subscribers increase.

Other measurements of interest include CPU queue length as a function of CPU speed and inter-data frame delay (see Fig. 15.16). Although such measurements may not be very accurate, they are useful in architectural design of cloud systems (Muqsith 2011; Sarjoughian et al. 2012).

Exercise

Show how you can write pruning scripts (*.pes files) that prune the SES you constructed above that will obtain simulation data for N subscribers, where N is an integer you can select. Hint: Use restructuring of multi-aspects and setting of multiplicity as in Chap. 6.

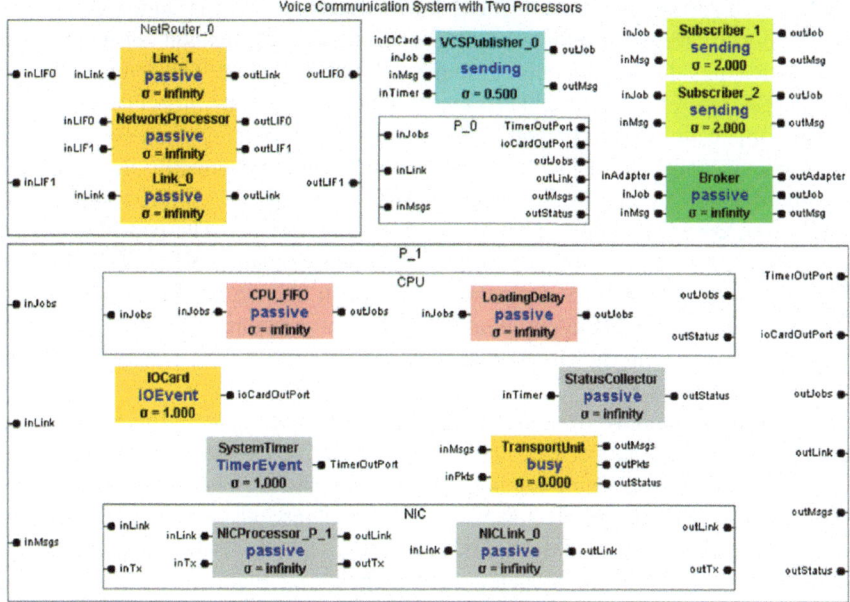

Fig. 15.17 Voice communication system with one publisher, two subscribers, one broker executing on two processors connected using a router

---

Calculate CPU load factor for 44.1 kHz sampling rate, 16 bits/sample, stereo channel, 2.2 GHz processor speed, and 5.7% utilization. Develop the simulation model shown in Fig. 15.17 and show the effect of CPU load factor for key length set at 128 bits with 50% of packets encrypted. The length of the experiment is 60 s with the network card and link bandwidth set at 100 Mbps and memory set at 1024 MB. Hint: See the `ComputationalLoad` and `CPU_FIFO` components in the `CORE.HWL.HardwareMod` and `Common.InteractionEntities` packages contained in the `SOC-DEVS` package [DEVS-Suite].

15.5   Summary

To develop simulation-based architecture designs for cloud systems, SOC-DEVS can be used to characterize the fundamental structure and dynamics of cloud systems. Details including service-to-service interactions within individual and networked hardware components are supported. The goal is not to support detailed designs that are required for building actual cloud systems. The software and hardware system of systems abstractions along with a system of system to synthesize them are developed. These models account for distributed co-design. These models were exemplified using a voice communication system which exhibits features that are common to numerous cloud systems. The formulations of software system of systems and hardware system of systems independent of any specific application are important since it supports developing simulation models for different domains of interest. This is achieved by directly incorporating SOA-compliancy into the simulation models. The SOC-DEVS simulation platform also can be used with actual services (e.g., security service). The software system may adapt itself during run-time (see Dynamic Structure DEVS (DSOAD) in Chap. 14). The SOC-DEVS simulation models can also be combined with actual cloud systems. This can support evaluating system structure scalability and operational efficiency using timeliness and accuracy attributes that are supported in the SOC-DEVS models.

This chapter employed exercises to show how the System Entity Structure introduced earlier in the book could be used to describe the architectures discussed here and how pruning could support the experiments performed on these architectures. However, the architectures were not developed and nor were the experiments performed using these tools. The next chapter will discuss CoSMo (Component-based System Modeler) (Sarjoughian and Elamvazuthi 2009) which introduces database capability to support construction of, and experimentation with, families of models akin to SES.

References

Butler, J. M. (1995). Quantum modeling of distributed object computing. *Simulation Digest, 24*(2), 20–39.
DEVS-Suite (2017). DEVS-suite simulator. Retrieved from http://devs-suitesim.sourceforge.net.
Edwards, S., Lavagno, L., Lee, E. A., & Sangiovanni-Vincentelli, A. (1997). Design of embedded systems: Formal models, validation, and synthesis. *Proceedings of the IEEE, 85*(3), 366–390.
Hild, D. R., Sarjoughian, H. S., & Zeigler, B. P. (2001). DEVS-DOC: A modeling and simulation environment enabling distributed codesign. *IEEE SMC Transactions-Part A, 32*(1), 78–92.
Hu, W. (2007). Visual and persistent co-design modeling for network systems. PhD Thesis, School of Computing, Information, and Decision Systems Engineering, Arizona State University, Tempe, AZ, USA.
Hu, W., & Sarjoughian, H. S. (2007). A co-design modeling approach for computer network systems. In *Winter Simulation Conference*, December, Washington DC, USA (pp. 685–693).
Kim, S., Sarjoughian, H. S., & Elamvazuthi, V. (2009). DEVS-suite: A simulator for visual experimentation and behavior monitoring. In *High Performance Computing & Simulation Symposium, Proceedings of the Spring Simulation Conference*, 1–7, March, San Diego, CA, USA.
Muqsith, M. (2011). Composing hybrid discrete-event system and cellular automata models. PhD Dissertation, Computer Science and Engineering, Arizona State University, Tempe, AZ.
Muqsith, M. A., & Sarjoughian, H. S. (2010). A simulator for service-based software system co-design. In *3rd International ICST Conference on Simulation Tools and Techniques, SIMUTools*, 1–9, March, Torremolinos, Malaga, Spain.

Sarjoughian, H. S., & Elamvazhuthi, V. (2009). CoSMoS: A visual environment for component-based modeling, experimental design, and simulation. In *2nd international ICST conference on simulation tools and techniques, SIMUTools*, 1–9 March, Rome, Italy.

Sarjoughian, H. S., Kim, S., Ramaswamy, M., & Yau, S. S. (2008). A simulation framework for service-oriented computing systems. In *Proceedings of the Winter Simulation Conference*, December, Miami, FL, USA (pp. 845–853).

Sarjoughian, H. S., Muqsith, M., Huang, D., & Yau, S. (2012). Validation of service oriented computing DEVS simulation models. In *Theory of Modeling and Simulation Symposium, SpringSim Multi-conference*, April, Orlando, FL.

Wolf, W. H. (1994). Hardware software co-design of embedded systems. *Proceedings of the IEEE, 82*(7), 969–989.

Yau, S. S., Ye, N., Sarjoughian, H. S., Huang, D., Roontiva, A., Baydogan, M., et al. (2009). Towards development of adaptive service-based software systems. *IEEE Transactions on Services Computing, 2*(3), 247–260.

Yau, S. S., Yin, Y., & An, H. G. (2011). An adaptive approach to optimizing trade-off between service performance and security in service-based systems. *International Journal of Web Service Research, 8*(2), 74–91.

Model Development and Execution Process with Repositories, Validation, and Verification

16

In earlier chapters, the FDDEVS constrained natural language and the System Entity Structure were used to develop families of simulation models in MS4 Me. In this chapter, we discuss another modeling and simulation environment that supports both development and storage of families of DEVS models for Systems of Systems. Component-based System Modeler (CoSMo) is grounded in a unified logical, persistence, and visual model development concept. Building on concepts introduced in Part 1 of the book, CoSMo empowers model management and visual component-based model development with structural complexity capability metrics. Entity Relation (ER) and XML data-centric concepts along with UML object-centric modeling concepts are used to enhance DEVS and SES concepts. An extension, Component-based System Modeler and Simulator (CoSMoS), incorporates the DEVS-Suite simulator with the aim of increasing support for collaborative modeling and simulation life cycle activities. We show how you can develop, store, retrieve, and instantiate DEVS SoS models such as those for service oriented and cloud systems (Chaps. 14 and 15).

Although simulation models are not generally amenable to formal verification and validation in all possible conditions, there are methods such as model checking to verify absence of some undesirable behaviors. We introduce a concept of Constrained DEVS to limit the range of dynamics atomic and coupled models can have that lends itself to model-checking. Such constrained DEVS models can be verified by the DEVS-Suite verification engine elaborating on the methodology of Chap. 8.

16.1 Introduction

It is important to develop families of models for Systems of Systems using a simple, yet systematic and scalable approach (Zeigler 1984; Sarjoughian 2005; Zeigler and Hammonds 2007). Visual modeling is desirable as it is more accessible to users

© Springer International Publishing AG 2017
B.P. Zeigler and H.S. Sarjoughian, *Guide to Modeling and Simulation of Systems of Systems*, Simulation Foundations, Methods and Applications, DOI 10.1007/978-3-319-64134-8_16

who may not want to specify mathematical models or develop code in programming languages. Furthermore, it is also desirable to represent models in database
repositories. Database repositories have the key advantage of supporting
large-scale, organized structuring of models, which in turn is attractive for modeling
and simulation life cycle activities including incremental and collaborative model
development and enforcing consistency among logical and visual model
specifications.

The above observation leads to the principal concept behind CoSMoS which is
scalable, multi-aspect/multi-resolution model development using a unified *logical*,
visual, and *persistent* model specification. Model persistence (database repository)
and hierarchical visual modeling concepts are introduced in combination with ER,
DEVS, SES, UML, and XML Schema in the *Component-based System Modeler*
(CoSMo), its predecessor, and its extensions (CoSMoS 2015; Elamvazhuthi 2008;
Fu 2002; Hu 2007; Hu and Sarjoughian 2007; Sarjoughian 2005; Sarjoughian and
Elamvazhuthi 2009; Sarjoughian et al. 2010, 2011). ER, SES and UML are used to
support developing families of DEVS and XML Schema models. Data-centric ER,
SES, and XML abstractions along with object-centric DEVS and UML abstractions
are empowered with model management capability. It is an environment with the
aim of supporting incremental and collaborative model development life cycle
activities for hierarchical Systems of Systems.

Component-based System Modeler and Simulator (CoSMoS) enables building
Parallel DEVS simulation models with direct support for model visualization and
model persistence that can be transformed to programming code (see Fig. 16.1)
(Sarjoughian and Elamvazhuthi 2009). System-theoretic simulation models
including DEVS models can be developed. Data models including XML Schema
(Chap. 11) may also be developed (Sarjoughian and Flasher 2007). CoSMoS
automatically generates partial code for the DEVS-suite simulator. Similar to the
approach described in Chap. 12, generated code has complete structural specifications for DEVS and XML Schema models. Behaviors for atomic DEVS models
(state transition, output, and time advance functions) need to be added to the
generated code before they, and coupled DEVS models in which they reside, can be
simulated.

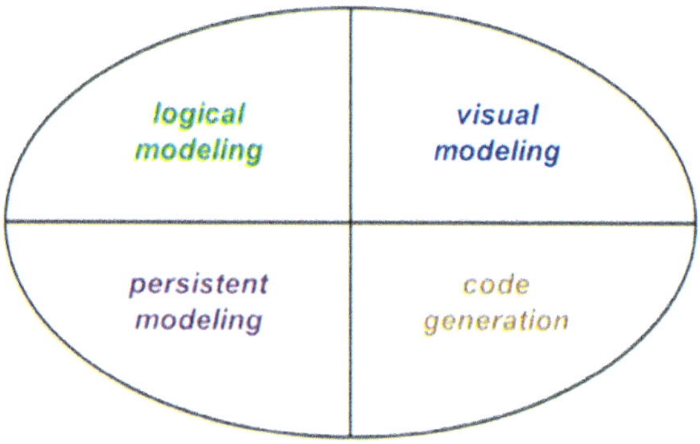

Fig. 16.1 Logical, visual,
and persistent modeling with
code generation

logical
modeling

visual
modeling

persistent
modeling

code
generation

The logical component-based models persist in relational databases and therefore simply lend themselves to be transformed into target-specific simulation and markup programming languages (Sarjoughian and Flasher 2007). The underlying system-theoretic modeling framework of CoSMoS lends itself for the well-known continuous, discrete-time, and discrete-event modeling approaches. Parallel DEVS-compliant modeling as stated above is supported with run-time animation, and viewing of time-based trajectories or alternatively the data for time-based trajectories is exported for post processing. CoSMoS offers a development process for systematic transitioning from visual modeling to code generation to selection and observation of simulation data. These capabilities help simplify simulation-based systems of systems model development and evaluation.

An important concept that is accounted for in CoSMoS is separating domain-neutral and domain-specific modeling. CoSMoS built-in models (see Sect. 16.2) are domain-neutral. They can be used to develop models for domains of interest. Furthermore, logical, visual, and persistent models offer a sound approach to hybrid (software/hardware) model specifications (Hu 2007; Hu and Sarjoughian 2007). The conceptual and realization of separation of logical, visual, and persistent model aids users in separately developing and managing software systems, hardware systems, and software/hardware systems of systems models (Chap. 15).

16.2   Unified Logical, Visual, and Persistent Modeling

A system may be described using *logical*, *visual*, and *persistent* model types (see Fig. 16.2). Each model type has its own syntax and semantics. Logical model specifications can be non-dynamical entities or dynamical components. A logical model can be defined according to the DEVS formalism or XML Schema. Visual models define graphical representations for logical models. Visual models have hierarchical, component-based graphical representations with ports and couplings. They have tree structures. Persistent model specifies the logical models according to the relational database concepts (i.e., representing structures as entities, tables, and relations with capability to modify them without scale constraint). The model entities and relationships comply with relational database syntax and semantics.

Supporting these three types of models together is important given their complementary benefits. Logical modeling enables defining model structures and behaviors in terms of their mathematical representations and properties. Visual modeling promotes rapid model development provided it has a logical specification counterpart. Persistent modeling supports storing all elements of models in databases which is well suited for very large-scale models. Compared to logical and persistent models, visual models are well suited for model development of systems especially as the complexity and scale of systems increase. Models can be used as persistent repositories and therefore be systematically reused for multiple purposes, maintained, and evolved over time.

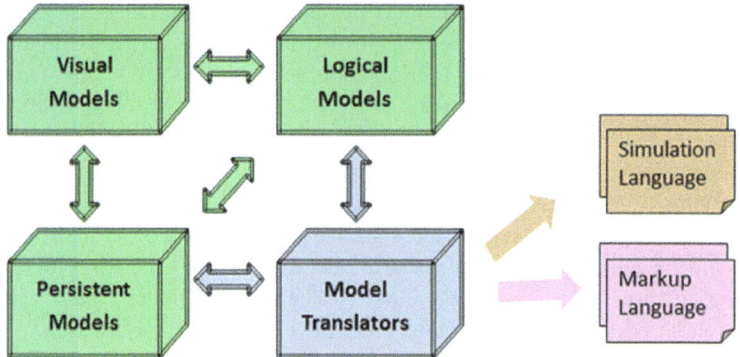

Fig. 16.2 Logical, visual, and persistent model types

Given the unique capabilities and advantages afforded by logical, visual, and persistence models, it is advantageous to have a modeling framework that supports their collective use in a consistent manner. That is to say, all visual model development activities must be sanctioned by the logical models, and all models that are stored in a database must be consistent with their logical specifications and thus their visual representations. This means in CoSMo the syntax and semantics for each model type is consistent with those of the others.

16.2.1   Simple Network Virus Model

Before proceeding further, a very simple exemplar for a model consisting of processors with virus detection is developed in DEVS-Suite (DEVS-Suite 2017; Kim et al. 2009) (see Fig. 16.3). It consists of routers that can detect some viruses. Some viruses are expected to be detected by the processors. This model has a generator (GenrMsg) for creating messages and two generators which create messages that are infected with viruses at slow and fast pace speeds. The generator that generates viruses at a high rate (GenrFasrVirus) is used in the experimental frame model. Later, using CoSMoS, these two virus generators will be used to create a small family of models.

16.2.2   Template, Instance Template, and Instance Model Types

Each of the logical, visual, and persistent model types are defined in terms of *Template* model, *Instance Template* model, and *Instance* model. The basic idea is to incrementally develop simulation models (see Fig. 16.4). These models collectively support representing alternative specifications of one or more hierarchical Systems of Systems. Every Instance Template model can exist only when it has a Template

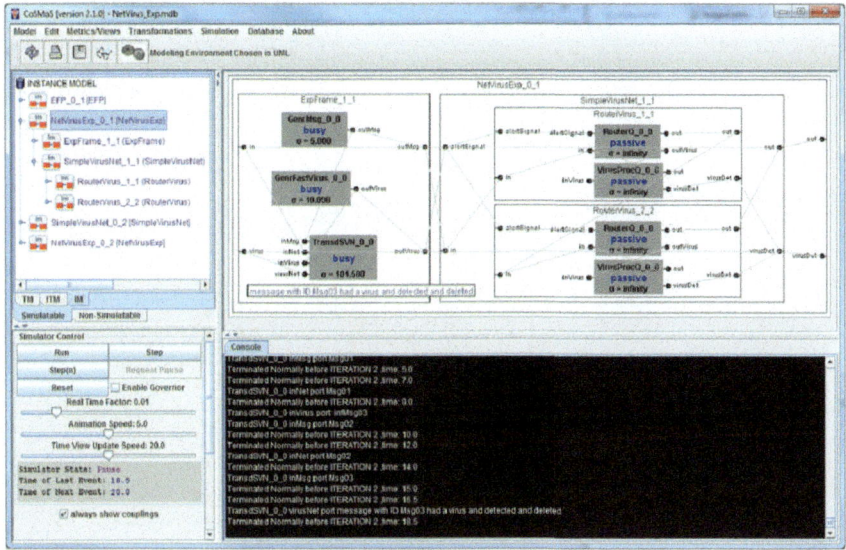

Fig. 16.3 A Virus Network model with support for detecting infected messages

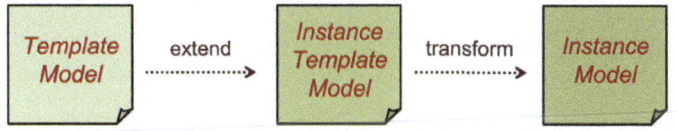

Fig. 16.4 Incremental model development process

model and every Instance model can exist only when it has an Instance Template model.

The *Template* model is defined to have composition and specialization relationships (Chaps. 3 and 5). Each Template model has at most hierarchy of length two. The composition and specialization relationships may be used together if there is self-composition. This is necessary for defining models as hierarchical tree structures. At the Template model abstraction level, separate models can be specified for systems that may or may not be related to one another using the composition and specialization relationships.

The *Instance Template* model, which extends the Template model, is defined to have any finite hierarchy. An Instance Template model represents an instance of the Template model since Template models may be combined using the composition and specialization hierarchies to specify alternative structures of a system. The use of the term instance is not in the sense of Object Theory where all instances of a class have an identical specification. Any two Instance Template models may share one or more Template models. Two Instance Template models may differ based on

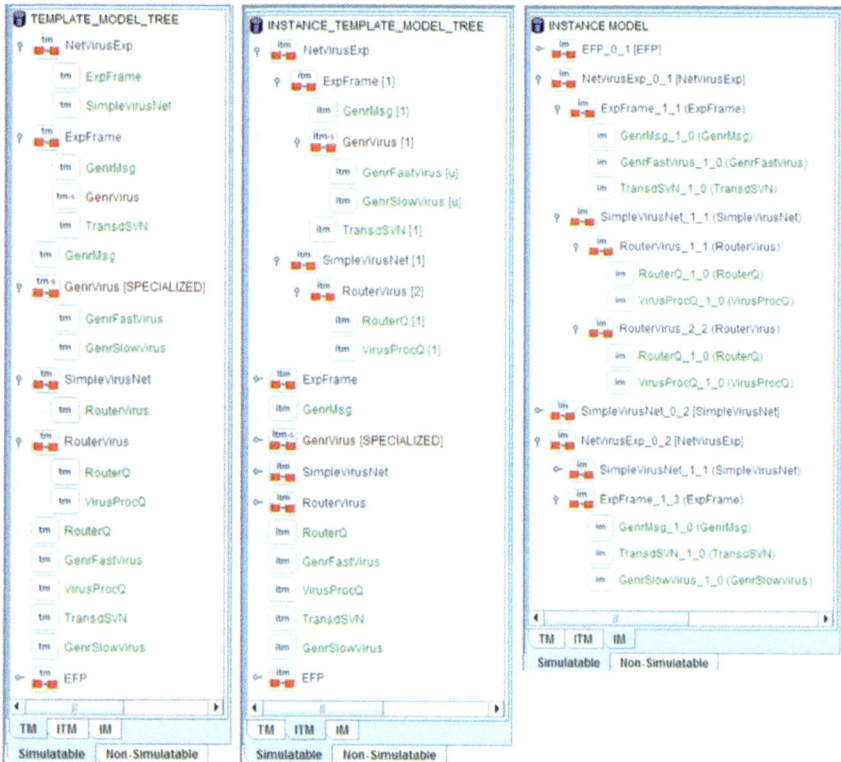

Fig. 16.5 Template, instance template, and instance models in their tree structure views for the exemplar Virus Network model

their specialization and composition choices. Composition at the Instance Template model abstraction, unlike Template model, specifies cardinality.

The *Instance* model is defined to represent models that have no specializations. It is instantiated by removing all specialization relationships that may be contained in an Instance Template model. Every Instance Model is a single model which may have a finite number of components (i.e., the system model can have a finite number of decomposition relationships).

The simple model shown in Fig. 16.3 is now specified in CoSMoS in Fig. 16.5. You can see that the Template model and Instance Template model separation offers complementary abstractions. The composite Template models are less complex than their Instance Template model counterparts. This is because the dependency among the Instance Template models is much higher since they have multiple levels of hierarchy. The *extend* relationship between Template model and Instance Template model supports defining alternative structures that are specified using hierarchical composition and specialization relationships. The *transform* relationship defines how Instance Template models are mapped to Instance models.

Complex structures can be modeled by combined use of composition and specialization relationships. Since there can be many alternative structures, it is important to keep these consistent with one another. A concept that is commonly used in specifying a model of a hierarchical system is uniformity that is defined for SES. A part of a system that is used in multiple places in a system's model hierarchy has a unique structure. When the structure of a model is restricted to be a tree instead of a graph, uniformity implies that for any sub-structure with a unique structure and name, all of its occurrences are identical. A consequence of enforcing this property is that changes made to the sub-structure are uniformly applied to the complete tree structure.

16.2.3   Simulatable and Non-simulatable Model Types

To represent models of a system, the concept of *Simulatable* models and *Non-simulatable* models is introduced (see Fig. 16.6). The Template, Instance Template, and Instance models are considered to be either *primitive* or *composite* simulatable models. Simulatable models have a Simulation Protocol that dictates their execution with respect to time. In contrast, non-simulatable models are not associated with any Simulation Protocol; instead, their behavioral logic is contained in the models themselves. To help distinguish non-simulatable models from primitive and composite simulatable model components, the terms *simple* and *complex* model components are introduced.

A simulatable model can have non-simulatable models. The simulatable models correspond to atomic and coupled DEVS models, and the non-simulatable models correspond to object-oriented models that are commonly used in developing object-oriented DEVS simulation models. For example, a state variable can have a complex type such as a list, and a port name can have a simple type such as a string.

The syntax and semantics of the composition and specialization relationships used for non-simulatable models is more general than those defined for the simulatable models. The composition relationship among non-simulatable UML classes allows a class to a have a composition relationship with itself. Or, a class can have a

Fig. 16.6 Logical model specifications

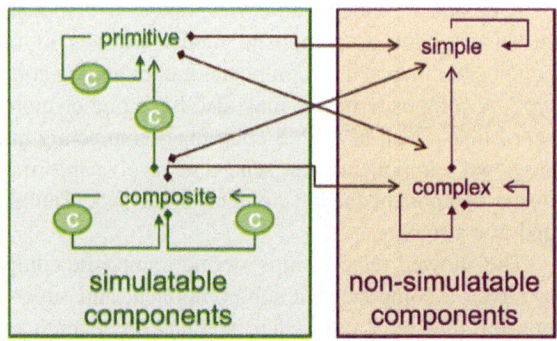

dependency or realization relationship to another class. Similarly, the inheritance (i.e., specialization) relationship among non-simulatable models allows a child component to extend or restrict its parent component. For simulatable models, the specialization relationship is restricted to a specialized component to replace its specializee component (see next section for more details).

Given the distinct roles the simulatable and non-simulatable models play in model development, the importance of differentiating them should be evident. The abstractions for the Template, Instance Template, and Instance model components are for specifying alternative architectural system models, whereas the simple and complex model components are intended for the specifications encapsulated within them. The simulatable model specifications can be transformed into simulation models that can be simulated. Non-simulatable may be developed using existing tools such as Astah.

16.2.4   Logical Models

Two basic elements that are used as foundational constituents in CoSMo are primitive and composite model abstractions. This classification serves as a unifying basis across logical, visual, and persistent model types. A primitive Template Model can have a finite number of state variables. Each state variable is defined to have a type and may be initialized. State variable types can be simple or complex classes. A primitive Template Model can also have inputs and outputs. Each input is defined to have a unique port name (i.e., string data type). Similarly, each output also must have a unique name. Input and output ports may be used to receive or send simple data types or complex objects.

A primitive Template model can be specialized using *is-a* relationship. The term *specializee* is used to refer to the component that has a specialization relation to a component called *specialized*. The input/output interface of every specialized component is defined to be the same as the interface of its specializee. The state variables of specialized components may be different. A pair of specializee and its specialized counterparts must be distinguishable based on their names. There are no specializee components for the Instance models. All primitive instant model components are distinguishable based on their names.

A composite model can correspond to a Template, an Instance Template, or an Instance model. A composite model consists of one to many primitive and/or composite models. The composite model and its components have the same model type. A composite model may also have one or more states, inputs, outputs, and a set of links (such as DEVS couplings) connecting the components that it contains. Any two components can send and receive information using links. Every composite component for a Template or Instance Template model has a unique name and tree structure.

The allowed relationships among composite components are *whole-part* and *is-a*. Given a component, a sub-component and super-component composition relationship may exist only when no sub-component can be the same as its sibling or super-component. The number of components of a composite model can be either specified or left unspecified. A composite component can also be specialized as in a primitive model. Composite components can be used in multiple composite Instance Template models. As stated earlier, the hierarchy depth of a composite component can be two or larger. All instances of a composite component (corresponding to the Instance model) are distinguishable from one another using their assigned (or given) names. The primitive and composite Instance models are instances of their respective Instance Template models. The whole-part and is-a relationships are constrained as described and comply with the uniformity property. These relationships are labeled with C in Fig. 16.6. The structure and semantics of the whole-part and is-a relationships between simple and complex classes are shown using UML visual notation. Other relationships might exist among the simple and complex classes (non-simulatable models).

Instance models can only be generated from their Instance Template models. An Instance model can be total or partial—i.e., a model hierarchy can be of any hierarchical depth depending on the model that is being transformed. For example, the `SimpleVirusNet` Instance Template model is instantiated as `SimpleVirusNet_1_1` and `SimpleVirusNet_0_2` Instance models. The cardinality of the `SimpleVirusNet_1_1` is defined in the `SimpleVirusNet` Instance Template model.

For every model component that is specialized, one of its specializations must be selected to replace its specializee. If the number of sub-components of a component is left unspecified, the number needs to be determined in the process of transforming an Instance Template Model into its Instance Model.

16.2.5   Visual Models

In CoSMo, simulatable models are shown as tree structures and block diagrams. In Fig. 16.7, Instance Template model for the experimental frame model in tree form is shown. The block diagram view with ports and couplings is also shown. Visual images (icons) in the tree structures contain tm (template model), itm (instance template model), or im (instance model) texts. Primitive (or atomic DEVS models) are shown as rounded rectangles. Composite (or coupled DEVS models) are shown as rectangles with two interconnected rectangles (filled boxes). The icons for the specialized primitive or composite Template and Instance Template model are appended with -s (e.g., itm-s).

Every composite block model can be navigated to its primitive parts using point-and-click user action. The `SimpleVirusNet` model and the decomposition of its `RouterVirus` are shown in Fig. 16.8. It is important to note that diagonal layout used for the block diagram view has the advantage of couplings to be simpler to read as compared with SimView at the expense of requiring more space. Nevertheless, since block diagram view can be easily navigated and there is the tree structure view, the diagonal layout is preferable. It should be noted that a composite

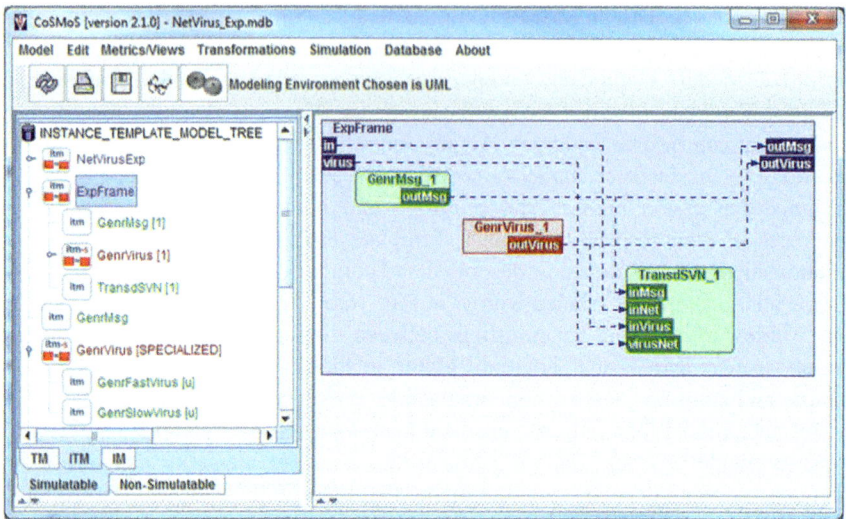

Fig. 16.7 CoSMoS UI depicting tree structure and block model views

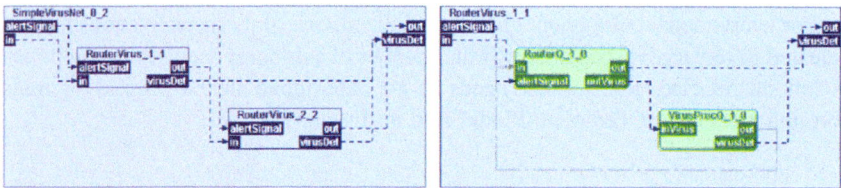

Fig. 16.8 Block diagrams for a composite instance template models containing other composite models and another composite model that contains primitive models

model may be divided into multiple levels should block diagram viewing become a concern.

The non-simulatable models can be viewed in composite in their tree structure form. They are not stored in the CoSMo's database. The models must already exist in the OS file system. No tool with support for developing UML models and, in particular, class diagram, is integrated with CoSMo.

During the simulation, the block model is replaced with SimView. The UI also provides two additional parts for the DEVS-Suite control panel and TimeView. Before simulating instance models, ports of every primitive or composite model component can be selected for observation. Data trajectories from selected ports (background color are changed to white) are viewable in TimeView or tabular form in the console or written to a CSV file.

16.2.6   Complexity Metrics

The structural and behavioral complexity metrics for the simulatable models can be easily obtained from the model database and viewed (see Fig. 16.9). Behavioral complexity metrics may also be viewed for primitive and composite model components.

16.2.7   Persistence Models

The Template, Instance Template, and Instance models are stored in relational databases and thus support large-scale model specifications. These persistent models are defined using the Entity-Relation approach (see Figs. 16.10 and 16.11). Tables defining the elements and relationships of each model type, as well as constraints that ensure consistency among model types, are specified using UML analysis and design techniques. The database tables collectively support specifying a family of models for system views of interest.

Using ER, the key relationships are between the Template Model (TM), the Instance Template Model (ITM), and the Instance Model (IM). The logical meta-model extend relationship is defined in terms of the ER specialization, componentOf, and TMtoITM relationships. The specialization and componentOf relationship represent specialization and decomposition of a Template Model. The TMtoITM relationship defines creating Instance Template Models from Template Models. The ITMtoIM and TMItoSIM relationships define the logical abstract-concrete transform relationship. The former transforms an Instance Template Model to Instance model and the latter represents which specialized model templates are instantiated. The componentOfI defines one or more Instance Model copies of an Instance Model with different multiplicities

Structural Metrics : NetVirusExp

Attribute	Value
Model Name	NetVirusExp
Model Type	COMPOSITE
Children	
Immediate	2
Total	11
Ports	
Input	0
Output	2
Total	2
Couplings	
Internal	4
External Input	0
External Output	2
Total	6

Behavioral Metrics : VirusProcQ

Attribute	Name	Type	Value
Model	VirusProcQ	PRIMITIVE	
Input variables			
At inVirus			
	virusMsg	GenCol.Pair	null
Output variables			
At out			
	outMsg	GenCol.entity	null
At virusDet			
	virusMsg	GenCol.Pair	null
State variables			
	virusQueue	GenCol.queue	null
NSM variables			

Fig. 16.9 Structural complexity metrics for the NetVirusExp model component and behavioral complexity metrics for the VirusProcQ model component

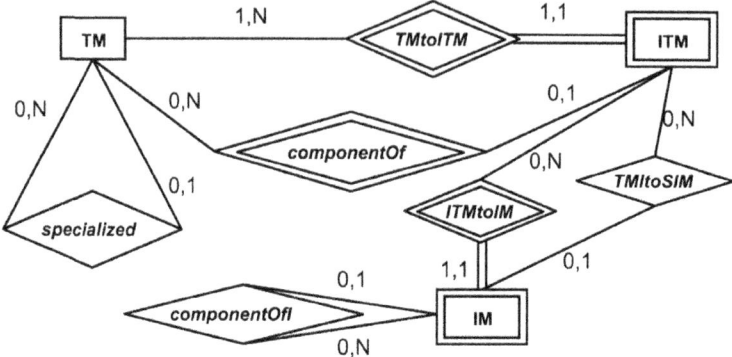

Fig. 16.10 Temple, instance template, and instance model entities with their relationships

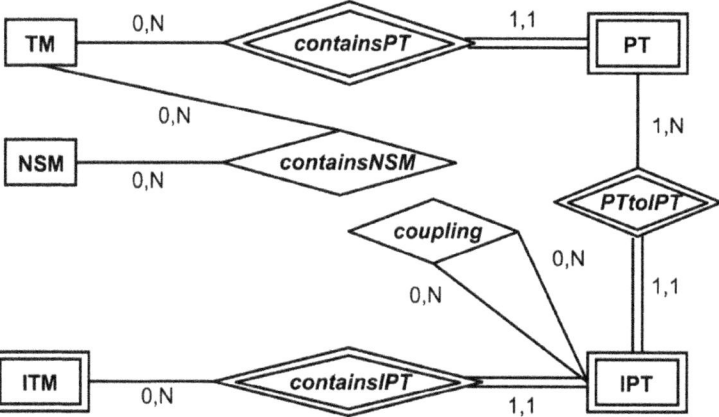

Fig. 16.11 Non-simulatable model and port with their relationships to temple and instance template models

16.2.8 Model Namespaces

An important activity in model development is managing models that are created, used, and possibly destroyed. These models can be categorized into databases and flat files as shown in Fig. 16.12. In the CoSMoS workspace, a root directory is defined within which any number of user-defined databases may exist. Each directory is unique w.r.t. the root directory. Each database directory has a *DataBase* directory called "MB_Models". In this directory, there can be any number of directories, each of which is given a name by modeler. Within every one of these directories called a *Model Base*, there are five directories (CoSMoS 2015). These are "Database", "Java Models", "NSM Models", "Statecharts Models", and "XML Models".

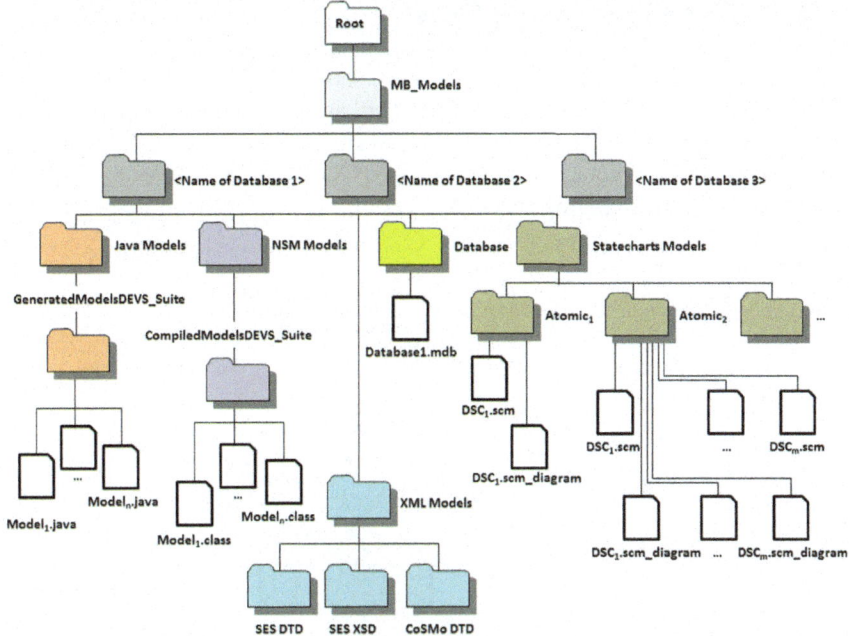

Fig. 16.12 CoSMoS directory workspace for storing databases and flat files

The logical models for the user-defined collection of models (e.g., see NetVirus_Exp in Fig. 16.7) are stored in a Microsoft Access relational database. The Java Models directory has a directory for generated source files (e.g., VirusProc_1_0.java) and another directory for compiled files (e.g., VirusProc0 1_0 class) (see Fig. 16.8). These directories have primitive and composite models which are atomic and coupled models for the DEVS-Suite simulator. As noted earlier, source code for the primitive models (e.g., atomic DEVS model) must be completed in order to be simulated. The separation of the directories, including the Generated and Compiled directories, is useful for creating models for different users and/or systems to be modeled and simulated.

The NSM Models directory has non-simulatable models. The Statecharts Models can have any number of directories for atomic DEVS models (Fard and Sarjoughian 2015). Each atomic model can have one or more DEVS Statecharts models. The logical specifications of these behavioral models (e.g., states, transitions, and actions) are stored in the relational database. Each DEVS Statecharts is also stored in two flat files as depicted in Fig. 16.12. Each pair is used for storing and retrieving the DEVS Statecharts Model (DSC) diagram specifying the layout for states, transitions, and actions. The XML Models directory is designated for storing XML models.

16.3 CoSMoS Process Life Cycle

The steps in the CoSMoS process life cycle are shown in Fig. 16.13 (Elamvazhuthi 2008; Sarjoughian and Elamvazhuthi 2009; Fard and Sarjoughian 2015). These are divided into three parts. The Model Development activities and the Experimentation Design and Configuration are supported by CoSMo. The model execution is supported by the DEVS-Suite simulator.

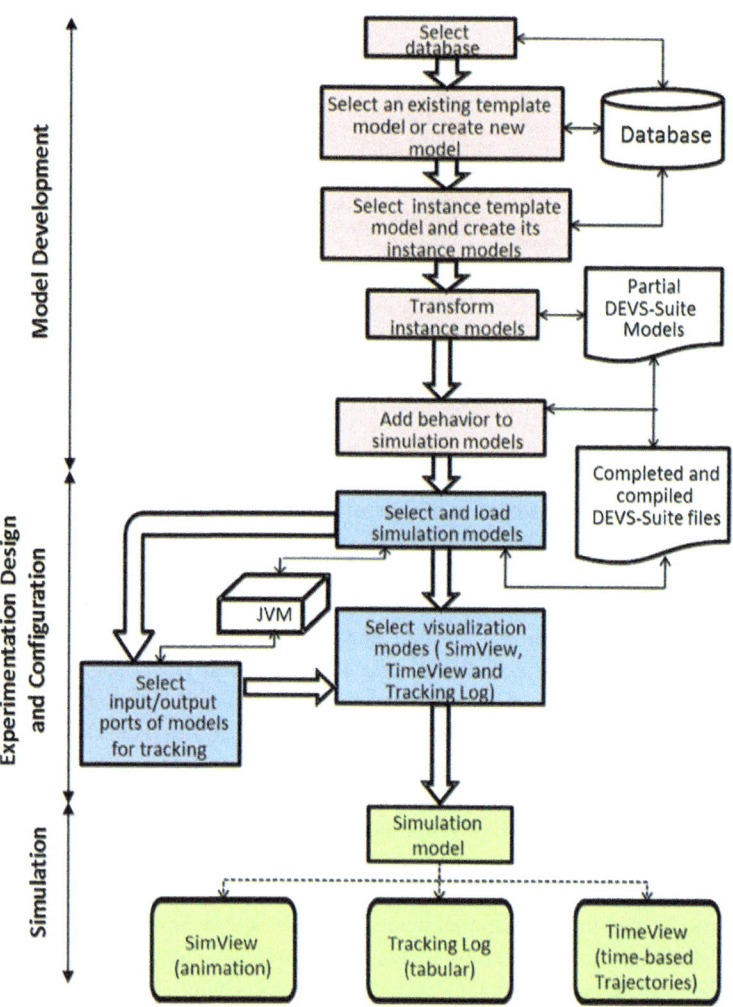

Fig. 16.13 CoSMoS life cycle process for developing models, configuring experiments, and executing simulations

A. Model Development

- **Select database**: User selects the database that serves as a repository for the logical models. This database has a predefined structure (ER Schema).
- **Select an existing model or create a new one**: User uses an existing set of (partial or complete) models or creates an empty template model. User develops a family of models. Users can also develop DEVS Statecharts models for any atomic DEVS models.
- **Select Instance Template model**: User selects one Instance Template model from those that are created in Step 2. Other instance models may be created.
- **Transform Instance models into source code**: User instantiates one of the instance template models. For every specializee model, the user must choose one specialized model. User may create a family of alternative instance models based on the specialized models that are chosen or alternative model composite models. Then, user can generate partial and complete source code for all instance models of the selected instance model.
- **Add behavior to the source code**: The primitive models can be completed using the NetBeans editor integrated into CoSMoS. Other IDEs may be used, but the user must ensure the source code remains consistent with its counterpart logical model. The behavior can be implemented based on the DEVS Statecharts models.

B. Experimentation Design and Configuration

- **Select and load simulation models**: User selects an instance model to be simulated. The source code for the instance model and all of its components are loaded in the DEVS-Suite. The loading is an iterative process between completing the source code and automated compiling within DEVS-Suite.
- **Select components and ports of models**: User selects models and their respective input and output ports. These selections are stored in the memory (JVM) in order to allow the user to select them for tracking (i.e., input/output trajectories, CSV export, and tabular form). The user may skip this step if no trajectories or tabulated data is to be viewed or no data is to be exported into a CSV file.
- **Select visualization modes**: The modeler is given the choice of viewing the models' simulation output data on different types of trajectory viewers. The animation includes the SimView and the tracking of the output is shown in Tracking Log and TimeView.

C. Simulation Execution

- **Execute model**: User starts simulation of the model. If any model component is selected for viewing (see Step B.2), the execution of the model is displayed as the animation of the model components, time-based trajectories, and tabulated form, as well as exported CSV files for post processing, depending on user's choice.

A family of models demonstrating CoSMo is shown below. These models, unlike those shown in Chap. 14, are organized and their relationships to one another are preserved in a database. Development of families of models, as can be seen below, is complex and the collection of logical, visual, and persistent models has an important role.

Exercise

Develop a virus network (`VirusNetwork`) model that may have two kinds of processors in CoSMoS. One of these can receive a trigger signal on port `trig-gerSignal` to activate or de-active virus detection. The variable name for trigger signal is trigger with string value of T or F. Determine the number of unique instance models that can be created in CoSMoS. Rank these models according to their structural complexity (i.e., total numbers of children, ports, and couplings for the `VirusNetwork` model). Assume the structure of any instance model is the same as the model (`NetVirusExp_1_1`) shown in Fig. 16.3.

Exercise

Consider the above `VirusNetwork` model. Extend this model to allow having a finite number of `RouterVirsus` parts instead of two. How many distinct VirusNetwork models can be specified such that their instance models are identical?

Exercise

Develop the above-extended `VirusNetwork` model (see Fig. 16.14) in MS4 Me. How many distinct VirusNetwork models can be specified such that their instance models are identical?

Exercise

The CoSMoS offers tree structure and block diagram modeling. Describe the advantages and disadvantages of each as the scale of a model increases. Also describe what role persistence models play as relates to other kinds of model representations. Hint: consider the whole-part and is-a relationships.

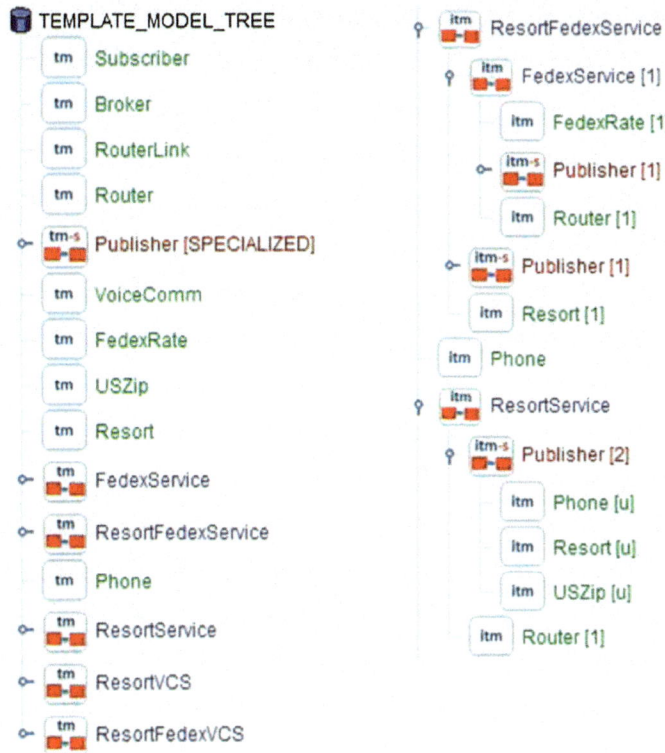

Fig. 16.14 Primitive and composite instance template models for example SOA services

---

Exercise

Discuss the use of CoSMoS for developing families of models. Compare the CoSMoS approach with that of the SES as illustrated in Fig. 15.12 of Chap. 15. Discuss possible ways to unify the two approaches.

16.4   Hybrid Software and Hardware Modeling in CoSMoS

To support independent model development for software systems, hardware systems, and their integration, additional logical, visual, and persistent model types are needed (CoSMoS 2015; Hu 2007; Hu and Sarjoughian 2007). New capabilities for tree and block diagram views and database are developed that span the Template, Instance Template, and Instance models in accordance to the DEVS-DOC (Hild et al. 2001). Additional tables (e.g., SMB$_{TM}$ corresponds to the Software System Model Base) and relationships are introduced to CoSMo according to the model classification shown in Table 16.1.

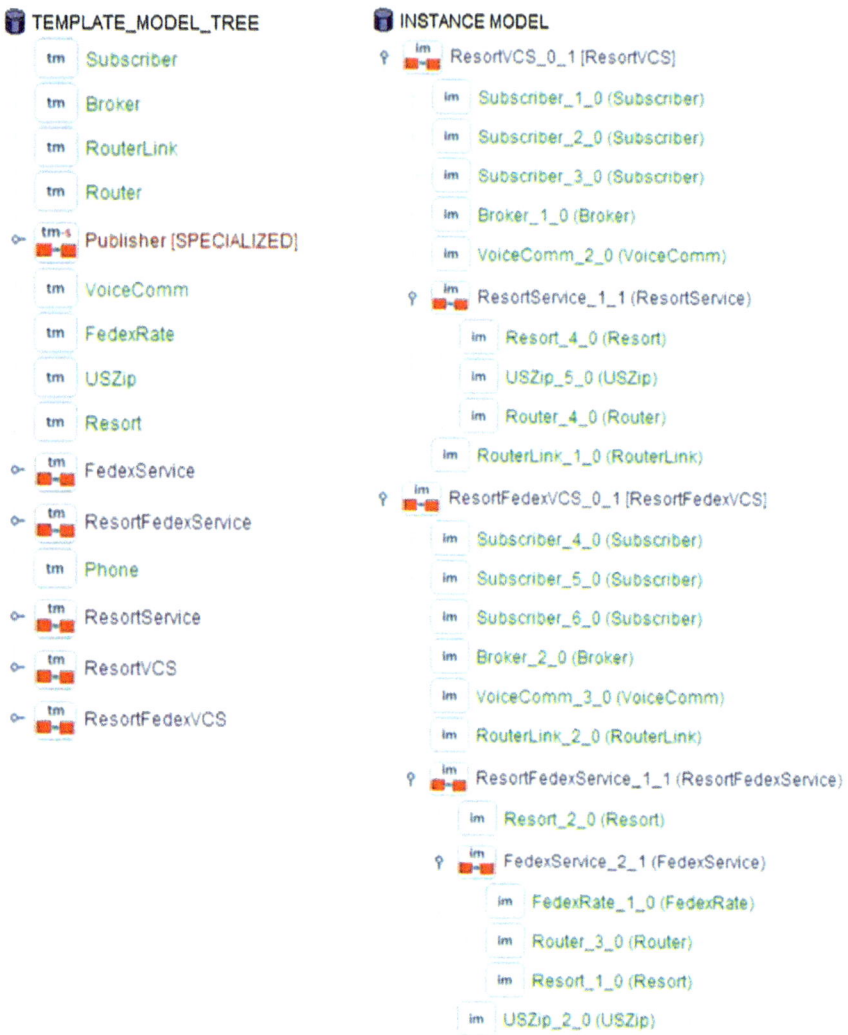

Fig. 16.15 Template and instance models for the instance template models shown in Fig. 16.14

Table 16.1 SW/HW co-design models

Model type	Software system	Hardware system	Service system mapping
Template	SMB_{TM}	HMB_{TM}	SMB_{TM}
Instance template	SMB_{ITM}	HMB_{ITM}	SMB_{ITM}
Instance	SMB_{IM}	HMB_{IM}	SMB_{IM}

The SW/HW co-design concepts described in DOC has important similarities to those of SOC DEVS. The basic similarities are the hardware system and software system mapping. The hardware component models in SOC-DEVS are devised to support software services which differ from software objects in how software services are mapped to hardware parts. Nevertheless, the basic concepts developed for DOC are applicable for SOC-DEVS. In the remainder, the key concepts that are important for supporting co-design model development in CoSMo are briefly described and the reader is referred to (Hu 2007) for details.

16.4.1 Hardware Models

The following hardware models are developed and supported. An important concept is grouping as in Processor Group Model (PGM). This is useful to help with visualizing and storing large-scale models in a hierarchical fashion. Another important point is that the couplings among hardware components are bi-directional. A particular hardware configuration styles such as H-Style is shown in Fig. 16.16. This helps avoid having large number of couplings specified and viewed.

1. Hardware System Model (HSM);
2. Processor (which includes CPU, Routing Unit, Transport Unit) Model (PM);
3. Network Interface Model (NIM);
4. Link Model (LM);
5. Router Model (RM);
6. Processor Group Model (PGM);
7. Network Interface Group Model (NIGM);

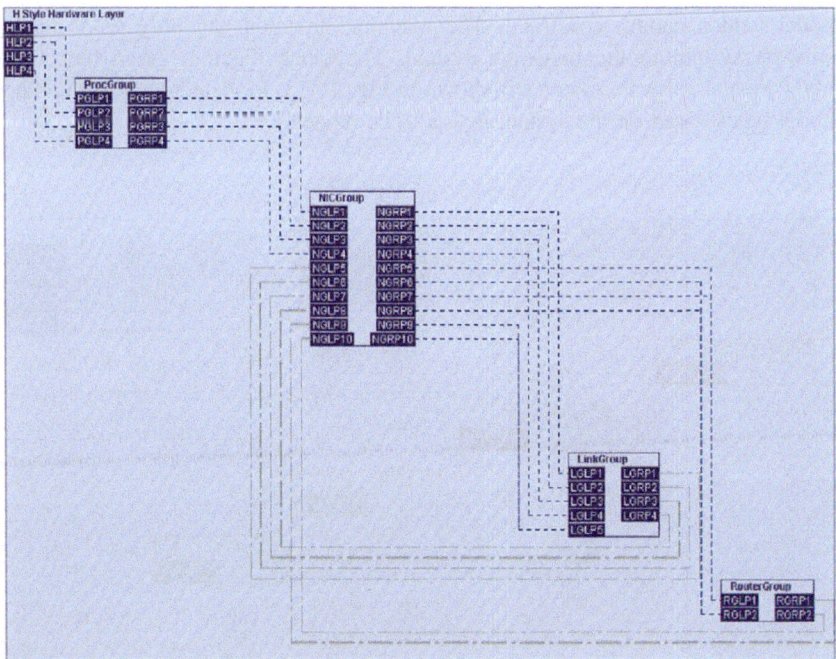

Fig. 16.16 H-Style hardware system model

8. Link Group Model (LGM);
9. Router Group Model (RGM);
10. Processor and Network Interface Model (PNM);
11. Processor and Network Interface Group Model (PNGM).

16.4.2 Software Models

Software system specification has two model types:

1. Software System Model (SSM);
2. Software Application Model (SAM).

SSM is a composite model composed from one or more SAMs. Each SAM is a primitive model that represents the abstraction of a software application which can run on an appropriate hardware component. Composite models may be also developed using the concepts described in Sect. 16.3. An example Software System model is shown in Fig. 16.17. As in the hardware system, the couplings are bi-directional.

16.4.3 Composite Software/Hardware Mapping Models

Unlike the software and hardware systems, the SW/HW system mapping represents mapping from the software system to the hardware system. It supports composite model with a certain constraint. The mapping direction can only go from the software system to the hardware system. The block diagram given the above hardware and software systems is shown in Fig. 16.18. Modelers may define other model types based on the system that is to be modeled.

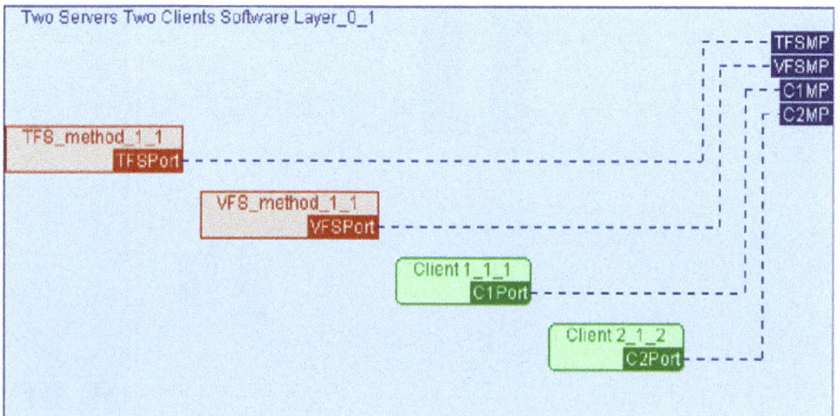

Fig. 16.17 Software system with two specialized template models

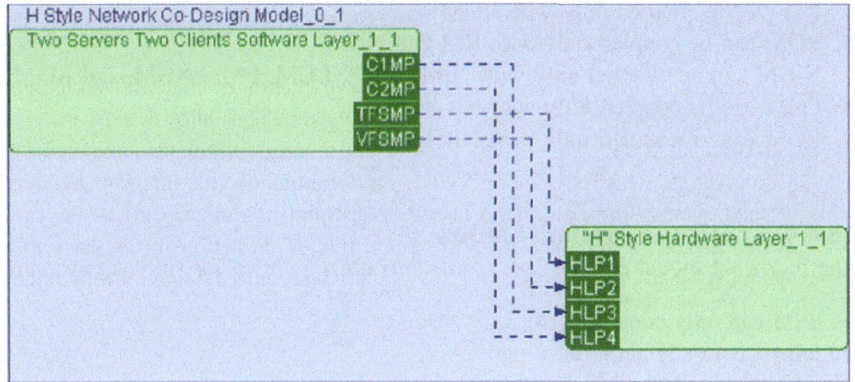

Fig. 16.18 Software system mapping model

16.4.4   Model Constraints

It is important for a modeling approach and its realization to define constraints on composite model specifications. As stated earlier, a model may contain only certain other models. CoSMo is extended to support the co-design concept described in Chap. 15. The model types in CoSMo entails three sets of model constraints. The first set is the composition relationship between two models. The second set is the coupling relationship between two models. The third set is the mapping relationship between software and hardware models.

16.4.4.1   Hardware System Models
The following composition constraints are supported.

1. HSM can contain only group models (PGM, NIGM, LGM, RGM);
2. PGM can contain only PM;
3. NIGM can contain only NIM;
4. LGM can contain only LM;
5. RGM can contain only RM;
6. PNGM can contain only PNM;
7. PNM can contain only one PM and one NIM;
8. RM, NIM, LM, RM are primitive models.

These model types and the connections between them will present different network topologies. The connection constraints between different model types are implemented by model coupling constraints as follows:

1. HSM can be coupled only with group models;
2. PM can be coupled only with PGM;
3. NIM can be coupled only with NIGM;
4. LM can be coupled only with LGM;

5. RM can be coupled only with RGM;
6. RGM can be coupled only with RM and NIGM;
7. NIGM can be coupled only with NIM, RGM, LGM, PM, PNGM, and RGM;
8. LGM can be coupled only with NIGM;
9. RGM can be coupled only with NIGM.

16.4.4.2 Software System Models

The following model *composition constraints* are supported for software systems:

1. SSM can only contain SAM;
2. SSM has to contain at least one SAM;
3. SAM is a primitive model.

The following model *coupling constraints* are supported in the software system:

1. SSM can only be coupled with SAM;
2. SAM can only be coupled with SSM.

16.4.4.3 Composite Software/Hardware Mapping Models

The composite constraint states that the system model contains only one SSM and one HSM. Modelers can define new models for computer network applications such as the search engine network. For example, in the above hardware models we have a processor model (PM) and a network interface card model (NIC). These two models can be composed as a `processorNIC` model. This assumes each processor has one network interface card to connect to the network. Accordingly, the hardware constraints need to be adapted to match the hardware system model types.

Exercise

Develop the Voice Communication System model shown in Fig. 15.9, Chap. 15 in CoSMoS, but without the use of software, hardware, and software system mapping formulation. Compare the two approaches with respect to various dimensions such as ease of development and scalability.

Exercise

Develop the Voice Communication System model shown in Fig. 15.9, Chap. 15 in CoSMoS by separately specifying software, hardware, and software system mapping models.

Exercise

Enumerate the types of SW/HW co-design model specifications that are different as compared to treating software, hardware, and system mappings the same.

16.5 Guided Model Validation and Constrained Model Verification

Two key roles of the CoSMoS framework are to enforce disciplined model validation and model verification. A variety of verification and validation (V&V) techniques (Sargent 2005; Whitner and Balci 1989), using software engineering concepts and methods, have been proposed. Model validation determines the degree to which a model of a system behaves as intended. Model verification determines whether the structure and behavior specifications of a system are correct. Validation considers only some dynamics of a model under certain experimental settings. Model's behavior is valid under certain initial conditions with finite input/output scenario, i.e., within an experimental frame. Verification aims to show all expected model dynamics are satisfied. This is because safety properties for some classes of systems are ideally guaranteed to hold for all possible functional and non-functional requirements. This means models of such systems must be verified to at least satisfy certain properties under some known (often finite) operational conditions. Therefore, guided model validation and constrained model verification are needed as generally neither can be exhaustively validated nor completely verified.

16.5.1 Model Validation

A close examination of the CoSMoS life cycle (see Fig. 16.13) reveals that its Experimentation Design and Configuration portion is well suited for guided specification of input/output scenarios. Such validation scenarios are easy to specify for any atomic and/or coupled DEVS Instance Models and therefore Instance Template Model and Instance Model. Rather than writing transducer models for collecting data from input, output and state variables, one simply selects any number of model components. For each component, any number of input and output ports and select state variables can be tracked during simulation. These time-based trajectories can be used to validate observed dynamics of any selected simulation model in complementary views and stored data via the DEVS-Suite simulator (see Fig. 16.13).

Validation experiments on a subject model may also be driven by outputs generated by some other models referred to as "Generators". More generally, every Instance Model derived from an Instance Template Model can be subjected to any number of experiments driven by generators, observed by transducers, and possibly controlled by acceptors (see Chap. 8). Therefore, any Instance Model can be considered to have three parts: the model under experimentation, the experiment itself, and their composition. An example is shown in Fig. 16.7 where the ExpFame Template Model has two generators (GenrMsg and GenrVirus) and one transducer (TransdSVN) Template Models. Instance Template models for these models can be GenerMad_1, GenrFastVirus_1, and TransdSVN_1. The Template Model SimpleVirusNet is the subject model. Its Instance Template model is SimpleVirusNet_1. An instance model for the composition of the ExpFrame_1_0 and SimpleVirusNet_1_0 is NetVirusExp_1_0. Instance Models GenrMsg_1_0, GenrFastVirus_1_0, TransdSVN_1_0 define a set of experiments for the Instance Model SimpleVirusNet_1_0. The input/output trajectories from the NetVirusExp_1_0 experiment can be used to validate or invalidate the observable dynamics of the SimpleVirusNet_1_0 model. The process shown in Fig. 13 with the DEVS-Suite simulator supports controlled experiments for the First and Second levels of experimentation design and execution described in Chap. 8 with the user in charge of guiding the auto-mated generation of models and completion of partially generated model code for the DEVS-Suite simulator. CoSMoS supports specifying a family of validation experiments through specifying families of subject models and experiments with their compositions. The combined model development and simulation execution is also positioned to support the Third level of control by iterating through some or all possible validation experiments using techniques such as control and termination rule-based logics.

16.5.2 Model Verification

Simulation models, in general, do not lend themselves to be proved to be free of undesirable behavior in all possible conditions (i.e., arbitrary experimental settings). The behaviors of these models are unbounded since no specific constraints placed on them aside from being state-based (i.e., state of a model can change due to its own state and possibly input). Nonetheless, there are methods such as model checking to verify absence of some undesirable behaviors. A prerequisite for coping with unboundedness of dynamic behavior is to restrict the range of possible input and state values and the number of state transitions to be finite and proportionate to some available computational resources. To achieve this, both the experiments and the model it can be subjected to must not allow unbounded dynamics. The Con-strained DEVS provides concepts and constructs to limit the range of dynamics atomic and coupled models can have (Gholami and Sarjoughian 2017). This variant of atomic DEVS model lends itself to model-checking. Such constrained DEVS models can be verified by the DEVS-Suite verification engine.

To achieve model verification, every atomic model's state space must be con-strained through configuration of its state and input variables as well as allowing for external inputs to arrive or be processed only at finite discrete-time instances. A model-checking protocol is needed for verification. In addition to these features, we discuss two additional features which are important for developing the verification protocol for the constrained DEVS-Suite model checking engine. One supports data exclusion, which further reduces the state space size and another relates to functional requirements of the system. An algorithm is needed to verify whether general model properties hold true or not. Specific properties such as unsafe states must be defined in models before they can be checked.

16.5.3   Constrained DEVS Model

A verification engine with guaranteed termination must know about the value sets for all state variables. To achieve this both primitive and compound state variables must be constrained. A primitive state variable can only be of certain types (e.g., Integer or Boolean variable in the Java programming language). Any compound state variable can be any combination of primitive and other compound state variables. These state variables can be defined as regular expressions (Gholami and Sarjoughian 2017). For example, a queue can hold 8 strings, each having size 4. A primitive state variable is Char that can be used to define compound state variables, e.g., $String(Char)^4$ and queue $(String)^8 \rightarrow ((Char)^4)^8$. A verifier can easily calculate the number of states for the queue state space and iterate through all of them.

All input and output ports for every atomic and coupled model must have defined types with value sets. Only external input ports must be constrained. The Constrained DEVS model is verified for all possible combinations of inputs that can be injected to it. The injected data comes from one or more generators (see Sect. 16.5.4). A verification engine explores state of a model through injecting external inputs to both atomic and coupled models to explore the entire state space of a model. The same idea just described for state configuration applies to port configuration. That is, value sets for these ports can also be specified via regular expressions. In the specification of input ports, an additional *NULL* (ø) value is required to allow internal state transition for atomic models (e.g., $(char)^4 \cup$). Couplings in any coupled model can support primitive and compound data types. Constraining external inputs is needed for reachability analysis (i.e., the verification engine applies a finite set of possible combinations of input events to all reachable combinations of state variables).

To bound a model's state space, every atomic must have its time advance function constrained to be finite (i.e., countable natural and rational numbers). This leads to restricting the invocations of both external and internal events to be finite. The receipt of external input events can only occur at finite time instances, thus limiting the number of state transitions. Similarly, allowing only a finite time instances prevents having infinitely many possible internal state transitions. If the Time Advance function of any atomic model is allowed to be the full set of real numbers, then this model and any other model that has it cannot be verified (see e.g., Hwang and Zeigler 2006).

The size of the state space of a model depends on data contained in it. To verify some classes of models, however, certain data sets are unnecessary to be stored and processed. This is useful since exclusion of data can directly lead to reduction in the model's state space size. An example is Network-on-Chip (NoC) model (Gholami and Sarjoughian 2017). In this kind of system, data (called flits) is communicated among processing nodes, links, and switches, but not processed. This kind of data can be excluded which results in lowering the state space size which is a key factor for model verification. For NoC model verification, source and destination nodes (i.e., processing elements and switches) are used to define state space. Inclusion of data can result in unbounded state space (i.e., models can be validated, but verified if appropriately constrained).

16.5.4 Verification Algorithm

To verify constrained atomic and coupled models, they are subjected to Algorithm 1 shown below. The verification engine is responsible for visiting all possible states through all possible input and state transitions relative to satisfying certain properties (e.g., identifying states that cannot be entered or exited). The model checking algorithm has variables for storing visited and unvisited states. The visited states V are those for which all possible transitions are explored. The unvisited states W are those that have at least one unexplored state transition.

For safety analysis, a state variable with values must be defined for states that are not safe states. Algorithm 1 verifies absence or existence of unsafe state of a constrained DEVS model (MOD). The generator (GEN) provides all possible combinations of inputs that can be injected to the constrained DEVS model. During state space exploration, the algorithm determines the model to be safe unless it identifies a state belonging to the safe state set U. In Steps 1 and 2, initial states and unsafe states are added to the to-be-visited states, W and the unsafe states, U respectively. The initial state(s) is the only state to be visited and added to W at initialization. A while loop checks through all reachable states (W). Steps 4 through 17 are repeated until W is nonempty. This while loop terminates given V, W, and U are finite sets. In Step 4 for each cycle of the loop one state is chosen and in Steps 5–16 all possible inputs are applied to it. Another while loop is responsible for applying all possible input values to the current state. This while loop also is guaranteed to terminate since the value set for input ports are finite and the input values can occur at a finite number of time instances. With the state of the model and giving the inputs to the GEN set in Steps 6 and 7, one cycle of the simulation is performed. In Steps 9–12, the resulting state is checked against the unsafe state set. If the resulting state belongs to U, the algorithm terminates with alert message identifying the source state and the input caused the unsafe state. Otherwise, in Steps 13–15, if the resulting unexplored safe state is added to W. In Step 17, after all possible inputs are applied to the current state, it is added to V and the next state is selected from W.

∅∅ ∈∉∧∉**Algorithm 1**: Model Checking Algorithm for Safety Analysis of Constrained DEVS Models

---

Input: MOD: *Verifiable*, GEN: *VerifierGen*

Output: invalidState: *StateVar*

Initialization: instantiate Q, V, and U; invalidState ← *null*

```
1:   add MOD.initialStates to Q
2:   add MOD.unsafeStates to U
3:   while Q ≠ ∅ do
4:       state-event ← Q.head ( )
5:       while state-event.inputSet ≠ ∅ do
6:           MOD.state ← state-event.state
7:           GEN.output ← state-event.inputSet.head ( )
8:           call simulate ( )
9:           if MOD.state ∈ U then
10:              invalidState ← MOD.state
11:              return invalidState
12:          end if
13:          if MOD.state ∉ Q ∧ MOD.state ∉ V then
14:              add MOD.state to Q
15:          end if
16:      end while
17:      add state-event to V
18: end while
19: return invalidState
```

Exercise

Compare the above model checking algorithm with the enumeration of pruned models and Fig. 8.3. In what ways are they similar and how are they different?

16.5.5 Dynamic Model Property Modeling

Modeling verification may include checking the presence or absence of certain dynamic properties such as satisfying performance requirements or exclusion of selected state transitions. To define such properties, you can incorporate experimentation and measurement features within your models. Specifically, Experimental Frame models (generators, transducers, and acceptors) become a part of the model to be verified. Therefore, experimentation and measurement become parts of the model and not separate concepts. Generators produce various combinations of inputs for the subject model. Likewise, transducers collect state and data from the subject model. Transducers in coordination with generators and acceptors can be used to determine satisfiability of actual versus desired properties of the subject model.

Dynamic properties of interest include performance measures such as end-to-end processing time, rate of task completion, and average latency. For the NoC model, the total delay of flits or the distribution of flit traffic are example properties that can be verified to be within some expected values. As we have seen, these properties can be modeled, measured, and verified using the DEVS-Suite simulator.

16.5.6   Model Development and Verification in CoSMoS

Again, examining the CoSMoS life cycle supports certain stages that are required for model verification. Specifically, families of Template Models, Instance Template Models, and Instance Models can be developed. Instance Models that are transformed to code for the DEVS-Suite must be suitably augmented to conform to Constrained DEVS. The verification engine of the DEVS-Suite can verify families of Constrained DEVS models for deadlock and livelock as well as user-defined safety properties as described above. Verifying dynamic properties is, in part, supported using transducer and acceptor models. The behaviors of these parallel DEVS models must be designed and implemented, for example using Statecharts and Activity modeling methods and tools (Fard and Sarjoughian 2015, Alshareef and Sarjoughian 2017). These specifications along with code templates developed in DEVS-Suite can serve toward implementing and verifying any number of instance models belonging to the families of models stored in the CoSMoS database.

16.5.7   Summary

It is challenging to develop families of models for systems. In earlier chapters, some of these challenges along with the features of SES as implemented in MS4 Me were described. In this chapter, a unified concept supporting logical, visual, and persistence modeling and simulation framework (CoSMoS) has been developed. It simplifies incremental model specifications and management. In particular, storing families of models in relational databases while providing multiple ways for visual development are supported. A benefit is the modeling and simulation life cycle which starts with model conceptualization and ends with partial code generation for target simulation engines and, in particular, the DEVS-Suite simulator. CoSMoS also lends itself for data (XML Schema) modeling and XML Schema code as well as cellular automata modeling (Sarjoughian et al. 2010).

The concept of SW/HW co-design for systems of systems fits seamlessly into the CoSMoS framework. This capability is useful for dividing up the modeling and simulation life cycle activities—i.e., supporting the basic co-design concepts that are shown to be important in simulation model development. With collaborative model development, greater support is available to modelers. The combination of such capabilities can help key modeling and simulation activities such as verification and validation. While being based on the same underlying concepts of DEVS model construction, the MS4 Me and CoSMoS environments offer somewhat different perspectives on support for such construction. In the next chapter, you will see how another DEVS Modeling Environment, the Virtual Laboratory Environment, serves as the basis for collaborative virtual build and test for an important segment of the agricultural community.

References

Alshareef, A., & Sarjoughian, H. S. (2017). DEVS specification for modeling and simulation of the UML activities. In *Spring Simulation Multi-Conference*, April. Virginia Beach, VA.

CoSMoS (2015). Component-based system modeler and simulator. Retrieved from http://sourceforge.net/projects/cosmosim/.

DEVS-Suite (2017). DEVS-Suite Simulator. Retrieved from http://devs-suitesim.sourceforge.net.

Elamvazhuthi, V. (2008). Visual component-based system modeling with automated simulation data collection and observation. School of Computing, Information, and Decision Systems Engineering, Arizona State University, Tempe, AZ, USA.

Fard, M., & Sarjoughian, H. S. (2015). *Visual and persistence behavior modeling for DEVS. In TMS/DEVS Symposium, Spring Simulation Multi-Conference, April.* DC: Wash.

Fu, T.-S. (2002). Hierarchical modeling of large-scale systems using relational databases. Master's Thesis, Department of Electrical and Computer Engineering, University of Arizona, AZ, USA.

Gholami S., & Sarjoughian, H. S. (2017). Modeling and verification of network-on-chip using constrained-DEVS. In *TMS/DEVS Symposium, Spring Simulation Multi-Conference*, April. Virginia Beach, VA.

Hild, D. R., Sarjoughian, H. S., & Zeigler, B. P. (2001). DEVS-DOC: a modeling and simulation environment enabling distributed codesign. *IEEE SMC Transactions-Part A, 32*(1), 78–92.

Hu, W. (2007). Visual and persistent co-design modeling for network systems. PhD Thesis, School of Computing, Information, and Decision Systems Engineering, Arizona State University, Tempe, AZ, USA.

Hu, W., & Sarjoughian, H. S. (2007). A co-design modeling approach for computer network systems. In *Winter Simulation Conference*, Washington DC, USA, December (pp. 685–693).

Hwang, M. H., & Zeigler, B. P. (2006). A modular verification framework using finite and deterministic DEVS. In *Proceedings of the DEVS Symposium, Spring Simulation Multi-Conference*, Huntsville, Alabama, USA (pp 57–65). Retrieved from https://acims.asu.edu/).

Kim, S., Sarjoughian, H. S., & Elamvazuthi, V. (2009). DEVS-suite: A simulator for visual experimentation and behavior monitoring. In *High performance computing & simulation symposium, proceedings of the spring simulation conference*, San Diego, CA, USA, 1–7 March.

Sargent, Robert G. (2005). "Verification and validation of simulation models." *Proceedings of the 37th WinterSimulation Conference*. 130–143.

Sarjoughian, H. S. (2005). A scaleable component-based modeling environment supporting model validation. In *Interservice/industry training, simulation, and education conference*, Orlando, FL, USA (pp. 1–11).

Sarjoughian, H. S., & Flasher, R. (2007). System modeling with mixed object and data models. In *DEVS Symposium, Spring Simulation Multi-conference*, Norfolk, VA, USA, April (pp. 199–206).

Sarjoughian, H. S., & Elamvazhuthi, V. (2009). CoSMoS: a visual environment for component-based modeling, experimental design, and simulation. In *2nd International ICST Conference on Simulation Tools and Techniques, SIMUTools*, Rome, Italy, 1–9 March.

Sarjoughian, H. S., Sarkar, S., & Mayer, G. R. (2010). A novel visual CA modeling approach and its realization in CoSMoS. In *Spring Simulation Conference*, Orlando, FL, USA (pp. 67–70).

Sarjoughian, H. S., Nutaro, J., & Joshi, G. (2011). Towards collaborative component-based modeling. *Journal of Simulation, 5*(2), 77–88.

Whitner, Richard B., and Osman Balci. (1989). "Guidelines for selecting and using simulation model verificationtechniques." *Proceedings of the 21st Winter Simulation Conference.* 559–568.

Zeigler, B. P. (1984). *Multifaceted modelling and discrete-event simulation.* San Diego: Academic Press.

Zeigler, B. P., & Hammonds, P. E. (2007). *Modeling & simulation-based data engineering: introducing pragmatics into ontologies for net-centric information exchange.* San Diego: Academic Press.

Modeling and Simulation of Living Systems as Systems of Systems

17

The beginning of the twenty-first century is marked by the awareness of several global crises. Our planet is under pressure because of climate change and variability (CCV), the rapid increase in human population, and associated problems such as overexploitation of natural resources, food crises, and the erosion of biodiversity. Humanity is facing many challenges related to these global issues, but surprisingly, these issues are not new. The first sentence of the preface of a 1973 book (Pattee 1973) says "We are well into a decade in which man can no longer evade the responsibility for his own survival. [...] It is a question of survival [...] in a society dominated by increasingly complex local constraints, but lacking stability and rational control." Thirty-nine years later, this assertion is still true, and its age emphasizes the urgency to act. Back then, the author envisioned a rational control of the dynamics of complex systems.

Today, this seems a doubtful proposition for living systems (biological, ecological, and sociological). Nevertheless, the spectacular progress of the Modeling and Simulation (M&S) field over the past decades enables a better understanding of complex phenomena and therefore better decision support tools to be designed. To begin to address the complexity of the questions raised by the different crises mentioned above, we will need to have more powerful and reliable decision support tools than we have today. These tools should help us to understand and control the dynamics of a reality that is vastly more complex than it was decades ago. In this context, M&S already plays a decisive role for the researchers who want to describe and to understand complex systems, and for the stakeholders who want to make better decisions. This chapter shows how to use DEVS to model living systems as systems of systems and to search through families of model architectures to find the best decisions to take within the virtual build and test paradigm.

Contributed by Raphaël Duboz and Jean-Christophe Soulié.

© Springer International Publishing AG 2017
B.P. Zeigler and H.S. Sarjoughian, *Guide to Modeling and Simulation of Systems of Systems*, Simulation Foundations, Methods and Applications, DOI 10.1007/978-3-319-64134-8_17

17.1   Challenges for Living System Modeling and Simulation

For living systems, as for any experimental field, researchers use real system observations to build simulation models that can reproduce observed system trajectories. For researchers, the objective is to understand and describe the real system. In one sense, they forecast the past to understand the present. In contrast, decision makers have another point of view. They want to use simulation models to help make decisions about which actions to take. As the famous Danish physicist Niels Bohr quoted, "Prediction is very difficult, especially if it's about the future." It is particularly true for living systems, for which we face four major practical and theoretical limitations:

- We do not know all the components or the associated processes. This myopic view of the system casts doubt on our ability to forecast.
- Living systems evolved. They grow, they continue to mutate, and their composition changes over time with births and deaths.
- The different organization levels of a living system (cells, organisms, populations, societies, etc.) are interdependent. In other words, scales matter, and we still do not have a good grasp of how to transfer knowledge from one scale to another.
- As for many physical systems, due to the sensitivity of models to the initial values of variables and parameters (initial conditions), chaos theory limits our prediction capabilities to some reduced horizons in space and time.

The above limitations cannot be eliminated by the huge computational power at our disposal today. Nevertheless, massive simulations can help to deal with these issues. By studying virtual experiments in a manner similar to real experiments, we can explore scenarios impossible to investigate on the real system because of practical, financial, or ethical issues. Indeed, computer simulations are achievable, cheaper, and safer than real experiments. Nevertheless, the relation between the virtual and the real system must be clear enough so we can use what we learned from the virtual experiments as an intelligence amplification (IA) tool. IA is designed to increase the information processing capabilities of the human mind. In that sense, virtual experimentation is a decision support system. Major difficulties of virtual experiments are related to model validation, model calibration, and sensitivity analysis. It requires particular statistical tools and computational power to explore the states space and to analyze the sensitivity of simulation results to the parameter values.

There is another difference between the researchers and the decision makers in addition to the fundamental difference in objectives. This difference is related to time. The former needs time to improve the theoretical and practical frameworks to address the limitations we mentioned before, and the latter does not have much time and want to make a decision right away. Therefore, if the decision makers want to use simulation models provided by researchers, they must have quick access to the most adequate models addressing the questions they have. To achieve that goal in the context of living systems, we need pragmatic and rigorous methodology and tools to build and use simulation models. These tools must facilitate the selection of the optimal simulation model regarding the available knowledge and the problems we are facing. Moreover, they must be supported by a software environment which enables execution and analysis of model behavior in the frame of experimentation sciences. This means that, in addition to model building, reuse, and modification, they must support good design of experimental plans and sensitivity analyzes. This is particularly relevant in the context of applied research where, by definition, researchers and decision makers must work together closely.

In this chapter, we illustrate how the DEVS and some of its extensions, and the Virtual Laboratory Environment (VLE) (Quesnel et al. 2009), a DEVS Modeling Environment, can be used to deal with the limitations mentioned above. We first explain why DEVS and VLE are well adapted to M&S of living systems. Thereafter, we give two practical examples of supporting virtual build and test of such systems of systems. The first is in the field of surveillance and control in animal epidemiology. This example illustrates how DEVS and VLE can be used for "virtual build and test" in the form of decision support systems for responding to epidemic outbreaks among livestock where testing such responses is not practical in real circumstances. The second example concerns modeling of plant growth. It illustrates how dynamic structure DEVS models can be used to faithfully capture the structures of plants as the growth process proceeds. Both examples illustrate how other important concepts such as scale transfer modeling and interoperation of different formalisms are supported in DEVS and VLE. We close this chapter with a discussion of model continuity and decision making for living systems.

17.2 Why DEVS and VLE for Living System Modeling and Simulation?

17.2.1 A Systemic Approach: Emergence and Scale Transfer

The DEVS formalism promotes a systemic point of view about reality. The modular and hierarchical properties of DEVS match the decomposition of a system into several interconnected components which are themselves recursively composed of interconnected components. This "Russian dolls" vision fits very well with the systemic approach adopted in the life sciences. From biology to ecology, living systems are considered to be composed of units (cells, organs, individuals, populations) exchanging matter, energy, and information (Chap. 18). The DEVS property of hierarchical composition facilitates the elaboration of morphism from a living system to an artificial one, the model simulator. Agent-based simulation (ABS), also called individual-based model (IBM), in the life sciences is very much used in M&S of living systems. Just as with the DEVS and hierarchical composition, ABS enables a quasi-direct analogy between real and artificial systems by reflecting agent behaviors (see Chap. 10). Nevertheless, ABS suffers from the lack of a common formalization, and the difficulty to communicate models without ambiguities, which is a fundamental issue in the scientific and engineering activities. Some works exist intended to formalize ABS using DEVS (Duboz et al. 2006). They show that the DEVS formalization of ABS is not unique—it depends on the definition we may have of an agent, its interactions with other agents and with the environment. This is not surprising considering the paradigmatic nature of ABS. Nevertheless, these works show that DEVS is a good candidate to overcome the communication issue in the field of ABS.

One very important notion ABS brought to the simulation domain is *emergence*. Indeed, emergence is very important in life sciences where emergent properties are central to understand living organisms' behaviors. The emerging properties "appear" when we simulate the model. They can be observed as the outputs of different types of simulators. When simulating ABS, DEVS simulators generate output trajectories for which emergence can be identified by the user. This should be viewed in relation to the scale issue mentioned in the introduction. Emergence and scale transfer are related since the latter is a model of the interdependence of one organization level upon one other (Duboz et al. 2003). Discrete-events formalisms can be used to specify, and then to simulate, fast and slow processes of the same system in the same model. This ability is critical for asynchronous system modeling. Nevertheless, the interactions between fast and slow processes are not easily modeled when timescales are very different. In this case, we have to compute emerging properties from the lower scale that become parameters in simulation models at the upper scale, and reciprocally, we compute the environmental constraints (initial conditions, global variables such as population size, temperature, etc.) from the upper scale to the lower scale (Duboz et al. 2003). The formalization of such a model of scale transfer is facilitated with DEVS.

17.2.2 Heterogeneous Formalisms and Living Systems Complexity

Ecological systems are complex systems. We need reliable tools and methodology to study them through simulations. The theory of modeling and simulation (Zeigler et al. 2000), with DEVS as its computational basis (see Appendix to Chap. 2), is very well situated to provide a foundation for the development of such a methodology. Aumann (2007) has shown how such concepts as model specification hierarchy, hierarchical coupled models, experimental frames, and morphisms provide a practical methodology for developing credible models of complex systems. Aumann introduces the notion of *focal* level to clarify the concept of level of interest in a developing model. For example, if the focal level is the individual level, as in an ABS, then models and frames at the immediate levels above and below this level must be considered and related to those at the focal level (Aumann

2007). Duboz et al. (2012) elaborated this methodology emphasizing the roles of experimental frames and model specifications.

Although work remains to provide a complete and fully usable methodology, recent initiatives such as the RECORD project (Bergez et al. 2012) in the domain of agro-ecosystems modeling illustrate the effectiveness of a DEVS-based approach to improve model reuse and collaboration between modelers. This success story is mainly based on two important DEVS characteristics: (1) model coupling and (2) integration of heterogeneous formalisms. The first characteristic comes from the modularity property of DEVS, the second one from the universality of DEVS (Chap. 2). DEVS can be extended to many existing formalisms as diverse as state charts, Petri nets, cellular automata, or differential equations (Zeigler et al. 2000). This multi-formalism ability fits well with the heterogeneous nature of living systems where chemical and physical processes cohabit with information processing (decision making). Furthermore, the Dynamic Structured DEVS extension (Barros 1997) allows the structure of the model to change over time (Chap. 10), which is a fundamental property of living systems. Therefore, multi-formalism and dynamical structure are the two main properties that make DEVS and DEVS-compliant simulation models well adapted to simulate living systems. Actually, differential equations and difference equations, continuous and discrete-time formalisms, respectively, are currently the two most used formalisms for living systems. Restricting model specification within these two formalisms impose constraints on the modeler who would like to increase the number of types of heterogeneous components in the simulation. As we said before, the tremendous diversity of components of living systems can only be expressed with a corresponding diversity of model formalisms.

Another very important issue for the modeling and simulation of living system is how to take spatial dimensionality into account. In many ecological or sociological systems, space plays an important role. DEVS can be seen as the specification of a network of models, i.e., the specification of a multi-graph where vertices are models and edges are the connections between them. In that sense, a DEVS coupled model instantiates a topology. Therefore, it is possible to build morphism between any kind of topology (lattice, small-world, scale-free, etc.), and a DEVS coupled model. It is then possible to model any type of space, surface or volume, by a connected neighborhood of space units (see Chap. 6). The realization of such a topology is greatly facilitated using the Dynamic Structured DEVS extension, especially when the number of space units is large, since the space need not be laid out all at once but can be unfolded in the neighborhood of active regions.

17.2.3   VLE and the Experimental Plans

As suggested by its acronym, VLE is a software environment to perform virtual experiments (Quesnel et al. 2009).[1] The VLE simulator is based on the DEVS

---
[1]See http://www.vle-project.org for last versions.

formalism and some of its extensions (Zeigler et al. 2000); therefore, as we said previously, we can couple heterogeneous models (discrete-event, discrete-time, and continuous model) to increase our ability to cope with the complexity of living systems. This feature is very important because, in addition with the DEVS property of modularity, we can choose the level of detail for the models without being limited by the expressiveness of a single formalism. It is not an answer to the first limitation mentioned in the introduction of the current chapter (myopic view on living systems), but this feature ensure we should be able to integrate new knowledge in our future models, and limit the impacts of changes on the current ones. The fourth limitation mentioned in the introduction (the chaos theory) obliges us to cope with experimental plan design and sensitivity analysis. This later is a fundamental activity in modeling and simulation that enable the modeler to draw valid and objective conclusions, improving the use of models in decision support systems (Saltelli et al. 2000). Here, it is more accurate to speak about virtual experiments' plan design. Indeed, we can control all of the model's parameters and variables, which is hardly the case for real experiment on living systems. The complete and efficient exploration of the space of parameters values is a difficult problem when the number of parameter is large. The difficulty increases if the model is stochastic. Furthermore, we can consider the structure of a coupled model as an initial state in a DS-DEVS for instance. Then, the structure can be part of the initial conditions and, therefore, can be part of the experimental plan. Some works exist dealing with these difficulties. For instance, it is possible to automate the selection of models by using criteria similar to the Akaike's information criterion (AIC) or the deviance information criterion (DIC). This was proposed by C. Piou et al. in 2009 for individual-based models, which are typical complex models of living systems (Piou et al. 2009). These open new possibilities for model selection based on evolutionary algorithms. Indeed, it is possible to set the unknown parameters values of stochastic IBMs using evolutionary algorithms (Duboz et al. 2010). This technique could be used for model selection based on information criteria.

Of course, there remains some work to achieve a complete formalization of the statistical methods for complex model selection and sensitivity analysis. Nevertheless, the tools to support such methods already exist, for instance R, a fully capable, free, and open-source statistical software (R Core Team 2012). In addition to classical statistics, R uses dedicated packages for experimental plan design, sensitivity analysis, and model selection. For this reason, the VLE community has chosen R to be coupled with the simulation engine (Quesnel et al. 2009). From the R scripting shell, we can set the parameters of models, run the simulations, and get the simulation results in R objects to perform the desired statistical post-analysis. VLE can also distribute the instances of the experimental plan on several CPUs. Doing so, it divides time to complete the experimental plan by the number of available core for the simulations. The experimental plan can also be executed by a simulation itself. This is an original feature of VLE. It provides the possibility to perform recursive simulations, i.e., simulations embedded in simulations (Zeigler 1990). This technique can be very useful for the modeling of anticipative agents (computational agents making decisions based on simulation results) or scale transfer between processes with very different characteristic timescales (Bonte et al. 2009). We present an example of recursive simulation in the next section.

VLE proposes other interesting features to enhance the collaboration between modelers of a particular application field. The French research institute in agronomy (INRA) has chosen VLE to integrate existing models of agro-ecosystems and to develop new ones. In a recent paper, the INRA team presents how to use VLE in concrete examples (Bergez et al. 2012). Another important French research institute, the International Center for Research in Agronomy for Development (CIRAD) uses VLE in different fields. In the following, we give two examples of applications developed in this institute, the first one in surveillance and control in animal epidemiology, and the second one in the field of plants growth.

17.3   Surveillance and Control in Animal Epidemiology

17.3.1   Motivations and Objectives

In this section, we consider the case of surveillance and control in animal epidemiology. It was originally developed to illustrate how we can evaluate models of systems that cannot be experimented with Bonté et al. (2012). This system illustrates the need for using multiple formalisms to model complex living systems considered as systems of systems. It also shows a decision-making process based on simulation technique mentioned above. As we said in the introduction, it is very difficult to forecast the consequences of decisions when we cause changes in the dynamics of natural systems. To test such decisions, decision makers should be able to simulate the consequences of their decisions so they can choose the most appropriate after considering different scenarios. We illustrate such a framework in the following.

Epidemiological surveillance can be defined as an observation method based on continuous recordings and analysis of epidemiological data. Epidemiological surveillance tracks the health status or the risk factors of a population to detect the emergence of a disease, to check an epizootic situation (the animal equivalent of epidemic in humans), or to monitor an endemic disease (i.e., one that has been present in the population for some noticeable time). The main objective of surveillance is to provide information to decision makers to help them decide whether to trigger control measures for the mitigation of the spread of a disease (Dufour and Hendrikx 2009). The control measures can be vaccination, quarantine, restriction of trading movements, or culling. The actors involved in surveillance and control are farmers, veterinarians, breeding technicians, biological analysis laboratories, policy makers, etc. Surveillance can be passive or active. Passive surveillance takes the form of spontaneous declaration of cases by the farmers, vets, or breeding technicians. In contrast, active surveillance includes intentional and planned activities preformed by official veterinarian services. Please refer to the

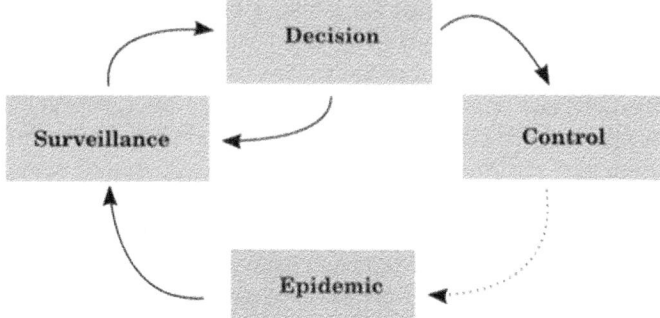

Fig. 17.1 General chart of surveillance and control in animal epidemiology. The *boxes* are the main processes. *Plain arrows* indicate information flows. The *dashed arrow* represents a physical action like vaccination, limitation of trading, or culling

book of Dufour and Hendrikx (2009) for a detailed presentation of epidemiological surveillance in animal health. In this section, we will consider a simplified version of the system by focusing on the main processes involved in surveillance and control. Fig. 17.1 provides a schematic representation of such a system.

The decision processes in epidemiological surveillance and control strongly depends on factors such as the social acceptability of control measures and the economical situation. Here, we simplify the system focusing on the use of a classical proxy in epidemiology to make the decision to control animal trading movements. Furthermore, we do not consider a particular disease. We present a generic model of a contagious animal disease spreading within a trading network. Such epidemics cause huge economic loses for countries that are affected, as was the case in England in 2001, with the foot-and-mouth disease, or in several countries of Southeast Asia facing the Highly Pathogen Avian Influenza H5N1 since 2003.

17.3.2   Model Description

Consider the four components of the systems of surveillance and control presented Fig. 17.1. The components are DEVS-based models; therefore, they can exchange information sending and receiving events on their output and input ports, respectively.

- The model of the *epidemic* is a network of coupled discrete-time atomic models. Each atomic model represents what we call an epidemiological unit. Here, they could be farms and markets. The links represent connected commercial routes between epidemiological units. The epidemic can start at any epidemiological unit in the network and spread through the links with a certain probability. The epidemiological units can be in two states, "S" for susceptible, meaning that they can get the disease and "I" for the infectious units. After a certain amount of time, the epidemiological units recover and become susceptible again, and this type of dynamic is called the Susceptible-Infectious-Susceptible (SIS) epidemiological model.

- The models of *surveillance* and *control* are pure DEVS models. The model of surveillance can receive samples from the epizootic model (passive surveillance). It can also request samples (active surveillance).
- The model of *control* apply the measure on the model of the epizootic by sending the intensity of the control (how many and which commercial routes to close or how many and which farms to vaccinate, etc.).

Figure 17.2 details the structure of the surveillance, decision, control and epizootic coupled model given Fig. 17.1.

The decision model is a particular DEVS model. It embeds a DEVS simulator in its state (actually an instance of the VLE engine). Then, it simulates a model with a different time base. The experimental process model first defines an experimental plan within an experimental frame; secondly, it performs the experiments and sends back the results to the decision model. This technique is useful here because it models the way that decision makers use simulations (scenarios) to forecast and to make their decisions. Fig. 17.2 illustrates how the decision model hosts an experimental frame to parameterize an ordinary differential equation (ODE) model. The ODE, solved with a quantized state space (QSS) integrator, is a mean field approximation of the SIS network model presented above (Bonte et al. 2009). At fixed dates, the decision model fits the results of the surveillance (the "observed" prevalence, i.e., the proportion of infected epidemiological units in the population) to a SIS model. Doing so, it computes a value useful to make its decision. This value is the initial reproductive number, or R_0. It corresponds to the number of secondary cases per primary case in a naive population (composed only with susceptible individuals) (Diekmann and Heesterbeek 2000). If the value of R_0 is greater than 1, then the epizootic will invade the population, otherwise the epizootic will quickly terminate. R_0 is related with the force of infection, reflecting the speed at which a disease can invade a population. This value is used as a proxy by the decision model to trigger the control measures. In our example, the control measures correspond to the restriction of animal displacement by cutting links of some of the detected infected epidemiological units.

17.3.3 Simulation Results

The model was implemented and executed using VLE. Fig. 17.3 shows the simulation results for a particular scenario where the control measures are able to stop the epizootic. We will not discuss here the results themselves. The objective of this section to illustrate the feasibility and usefulness of a multi-formalized approach when dealing with living systems considered as systems of systems.

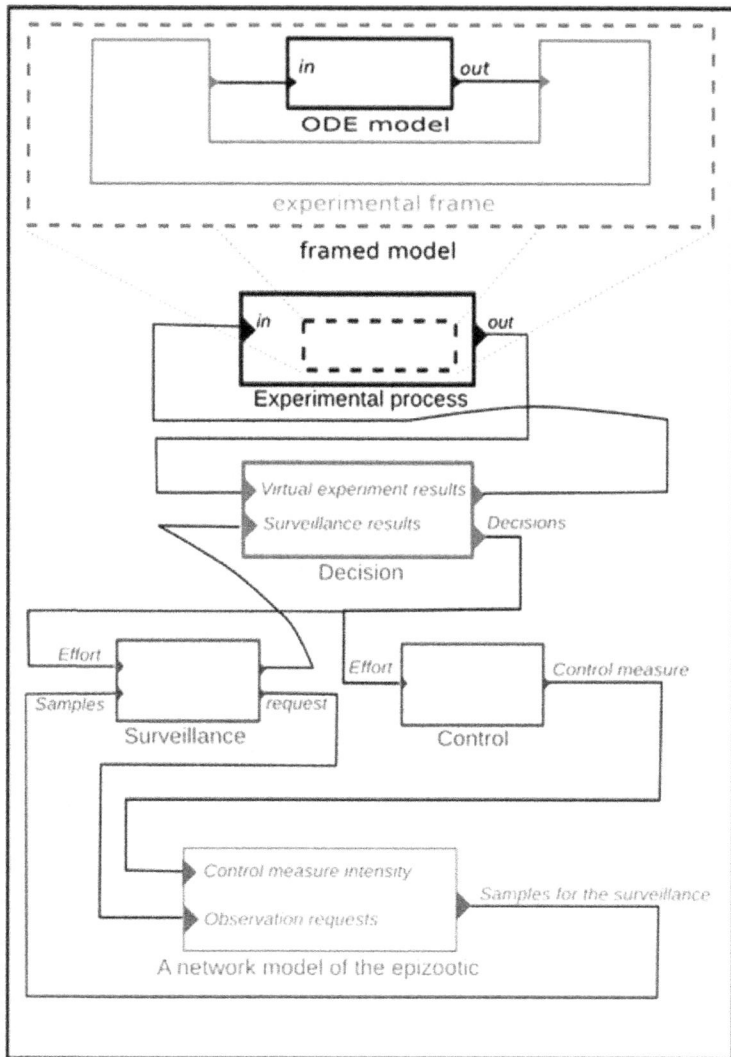

Fig. 17.2 Coupled model of surveillance, decision, control, and epizootic. Adapted from Bonté et al. (2012)

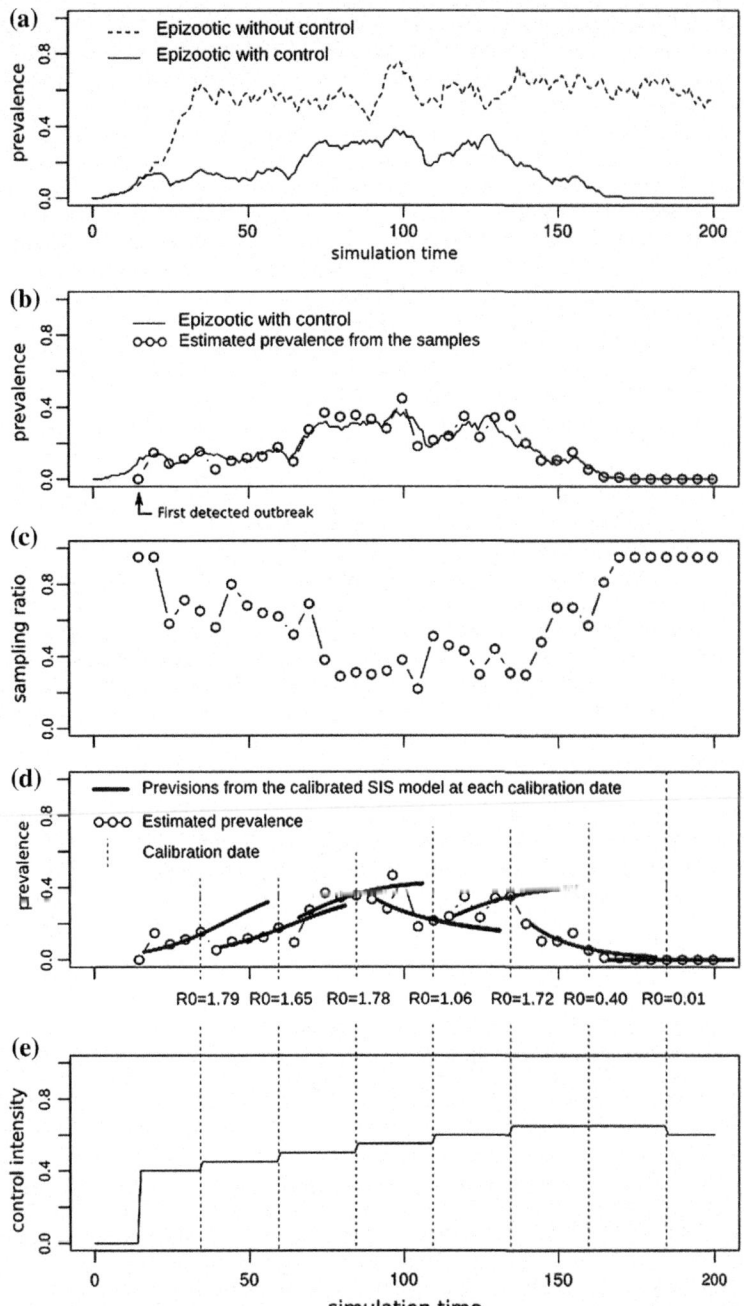

Fig. 17.3 **a** Trajectory of the epizootic with and without control. **b** Trajectory "observed" by the model of surveillance. **c** Trajectory of the sampling ratio. **d** Estimated trajectories by the experimental process model using the SIS model. **e** Trajectory of an indicator of the control intensity

Chart (a)	*Trajectory of the epizootic*. The plain curve corresponds to the evolution of the prevalence in the controlled epidemiological system. The dashed curve is the evolution of the prevalence for a simulation without control. Without control, the disease becomes enzootic (the prevalence is positive and approximately stationary)
Chart (b)	*Trajectory "observed" by the model of surveillance*. The dots correspond to the estimated prevalence computed by the model of surveillance. The true prevalence of the disease is the plain curve. We observe that the curves are very close from each other. The time between two dots corresponds to the sampling period
Chart (c)	*Trajectory of the sampling ratio*. The dots are the proportion of sampled epidemiological units (recall that the number of units to sample is computed by the surveillance model at each observation time step)
Chart (d)	*Estimated trajectories by the experimental process model using the SIS model*. Dots are the estimated prevalence by the surveillance model. Recall that calibrations performed by the experimentation process model are based on these data. The vertical dashed lines correspond to the dates at which calibrations occur. For each calibration, we have plotted the evolution of the simulated prevalence (plain short curves) from the date of the first observation used for this calibration (five observation before), to the prediction horizon (fixed to be the time interval between two calibrations). The value of the R_0 is computed for each calibration
Chart (e)	*Trajectory of an indicator of the control intensity*. The model of control is activated at the same time as the surveillance model (the control intensity is 0 before the first prevalence value is observed on charts (b), (c), and (d)). At each calibration date, the control intensity is revised. It increases if the estimated R_0 is greater than 1. It stays stable if R_0 is lower and close to 1, and decreases if R_0 is close to zero

What is interesting in this example is that it demonstrates simulations can be used to test control measures that cannot be tested on the real system. Fig. 17.3a illustrates the difference between an epizootic with and without control. We can then design different control scenarios and evaluate their effectiveness. The question of the validity of the epizootic model is important. As we said in the introduction, validation is very difficult for living systems. In the case of disease spread, it is only possible to validate an epizootic model a posteriori, which is too late if we want to use the model to forecast and to be able to enhance the control. Therefore, in addition to the study of control scenarios regarding one particular epizootic, we have to consider a family of disease spread models regarding one particular control scenario. The set of disease spread models to test obviously depends on the knowledge we have. In any case, using the experimental approach, we can greatly improve the effectiveness of the chosen control measures and help decision makers to make their decisions.

17.4 Plant Growth Modeling

17.4.1 Motivations and Objectives

Climate change and variability (CCV) are characterized by a steady trend leading to a global warming as well as an increasing frequency of extreme drought and thermal events (IPCC 2007). This exposes crops to considerable reductions in yield. With continued accumulation of greenhouse gases, this climatic pattern will keep intensifying. So there is a need to breed for varieties more adapted to current and future cropping conditions. This is particularly an emergency in developing countries where farmers have limited technical means to minimize the impact of climatic events on yield through modernized cultural practices (Giese et al. 2009). Cereal crops, particularly rice and sorghum, are of major concern in this regard because of their role in food, feed, and potentially, biofuel production.

To face CCV, genotypes are needed that combine potential for high yield, tolerance to warmer and drier conditions, and adaptive traits to face more extreme, unpredictable events. It is expected from this latter type of traits to provide the plant with the plasticity required for maintaining its performance and productivity under fluctuating conditions. This contrasts with the approach of the 90s when breeders attempted to design genotypes with reduced phenotypic plasticity as a way to "force" potential productivity. It is obvious today that this strategy is not adapted to current climatic issues, and there is a lot to gain from traits constituting phenotypic plasticity. This approach attempts to make the plant benefit from its inherent capacity to dynamically regulate its morphogenesis based on compensatory source-sink processes and to optimize thereby its productivity under fluctuating conditions (Dingkuhn et al. 2005; Nicotra et al. 2010). Crop performance involves many genes and is highly prone to interactions between genotype and environment (GxE). Regarding the challenge of combining high yield potential and adaptive capacities to face CCV, the necessity of combining constitutive and adaptive traits increases the complexity of GxE to deal with negative (physiological, genetic) feedbacks among traits. This can then increase the risk of a "counterproductive" plasticity (Nicotra et al. 2010). The challenge is getting even trickier when dealing with dual purpose crops such as sweet sorghum dedicated to grain and sugar production (Gutjahr et al. 2010).

In order to seek for the genetic bases and breed for such complex traits such as grain, biomass, or sugar yield, we have to identify the component traits having the strongest impact on the phenotypic expression of the whole plant in a given environment. Such traits are genetically and physiologically simpler, so they can be more easily analyzed and their GxE interactions unraveled (Dingkuhn et al. 2005; Hammer et al. 2005). For this purpose, modeling the plant system can be particularly useful in order to formalize in a dynamic manner the linkages among component traits and their combined impact on the whole-plant system. This behavior may strongly depend on the genotype (defined by parameter values) and its cropping environment (radiation, water, temperature within the plant population).

EcoMeristem (Luquet et al. 2006) was designed to address this challenging issue. This model aims at simulating plant morphogenesis and its regulation in the cropping environment, depending on genotypic sensitivity to resource availability.

17.4.2 The Ecomeristem Model

First, some standard terminologies used in studying plants (http://en.wikipedia.org/wiki/Botan):

- A **meristem** is the tissue in most plants consisting of undifferentiated cells, found in zones of the plant where growth can take place. The meristematic cells give rise to various organs of the plant and keep the plant growing. The shoot apical meristem (SAM) gives rise to organs like the leaves and flowers. The cells of the apical meristems—SAM and RAM (Root Apical Meristem)—divide rapidly and are considered to be indeterminate, in that they do not possess any defined end fate. In that sense, the meristematic cells are frequently compared to the stem cells in animals that have an analogous behavior and function.
- A **panicle** is a branched cluster of flowers in which the branches are *racemes*— flowers having short floral stalks along the axis or shoot, bearing the flowers. In a *raceme*, the oldest flowers are borne toward the base and new flowers are produced as the shoot grows.
- A **tiller** is a stem produced by grass plants and refers to all shoots that grow after the initial parent shoot grows from a seed. Tillers are segmented, each segment possessing its own two-part leaf. They are involved in vegetative propagation and, in some cases, also seed production.
- **Phytomers** are functional units of a plant continually produced by root and shoot *meristems* throughout a plant's vegetative life cycle. A typical phytomer consists of a node to which a leaf is attached, a subtending **internode**, and **axillary** bud at the base of the leaf.
- The **phyllochron** is the intervening period between the sequential emergence of leaves on the main stem of a plant.
- The **plastochron** index and the leaf plastochron index are ways of measuring the age of a plant dependent on morphological traits rather than on chronological age. Use of these indices removes differences caused by germination, developmental differences, and exponential growth.

The following System Entity Structure using multi-aspects (Chap. 6) describes the basic structure of a plant.

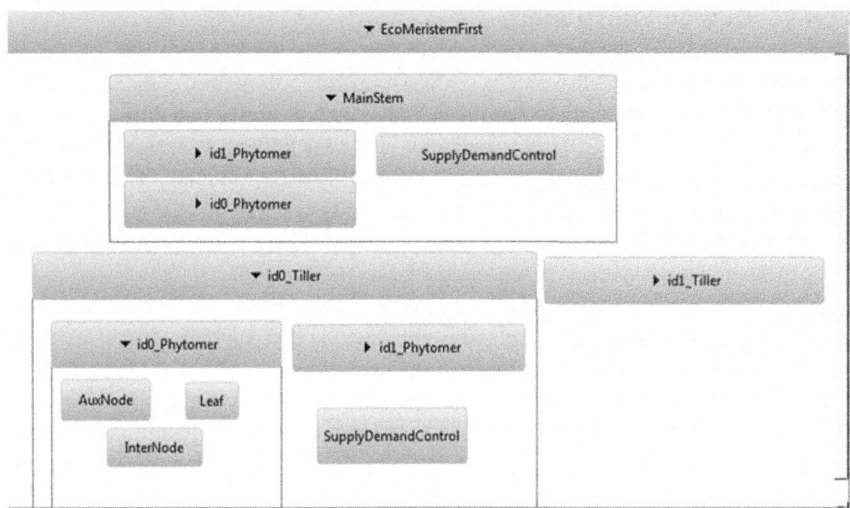

Fig. 17.4 MS4 Me view of Meristem model with 2 phytomers on the main stem and on 2 tillers

From the MeristemSys **perspective,** Meristem **is made of** MainStem **and** Tillers!

From the MainStemSys **perspective,** MainStem **is made of** SupplyDemandControl **and** Phytomers!

From the PhytomersSys **perspective,** Phytomers **is made of more than one** Phytomer!

Phytomer **can be** id **in** index!

From the PhytomerSys **perspective,** Phytomer **is made of** Leaf, InterNode, **and** AxNode!

From the TillersSys **perspective,** Tillers **is made of more than one** Tiller!

Tiller **can be** id **in** index!

From the MainStemSys **perspective,** Tiller **is like MainStem!**

This SES states that a Meristem consists of a main stem and tillers where the main stem is made of phytomers and a control for plant growth based on supply and demand of nutrients. There can be any number of phytomers, each of which made of a leaf, and internode, and an axillary node. There can be any number of tillers, each of which is constructed like the main stem. A pruned instance of this structure appears in Fig. 17.4.

Exercise

Using the above SES, write pruning scripts to generate a sequence of Meristems with increasing number of phytomers on the main stem. Similarly, generate a sequence with an increasing number of tillers.

17.4.3   Overall Functioning

EcoMeristem is a whole-plant, deterministic, dynamic, radiation and temperature-driven crop model within the category of Functional Structural Plant Modeling (Soulie et al. 2010). It includes also soil and plant water balance (to study, for instance, drought stress (Luquet et al. 2012)) modules. The main distinguishing mark of this model is its capability to simulate competition for assimilates (supply) among growing organs (demand). Fig. 17.5 from Luquet et al. (2006) illustrates the overall functioning of *EcoMeristem*.

Supply and demand are simulated at two different scales: Supply is simulated at the scale of the whole plant, while demand is simulated at the individual organ level and then aggregated to provide a whole-plant demand value. At each daily time step, the plant level supply and demand are compared and to simulate feedbacks of supply/demand imbalances on organ number (organogenesis), growth rate, and final size (morphogenesis). The supply/demand relationships are stored into a variable called IC (index of internal competition). Values of IC less than one trigger adaptive adjustments in plant organogenesis and morphogenesis, resulting in phenotypic plasticity.

If IC ≥ 1 (there is an excess of assimilates), the assimilates are reversibly stored as reserves, or, if the reserve compartment is saturated, there is feedback on photosynthesis (product inhibition). If IC < 1 (there is deficiency of assimilates), two types of adaptive responses occur: (i) the current assimilate shortfall for growth is buffered by reserve mobilization, organ senescence (followed by recycling) and

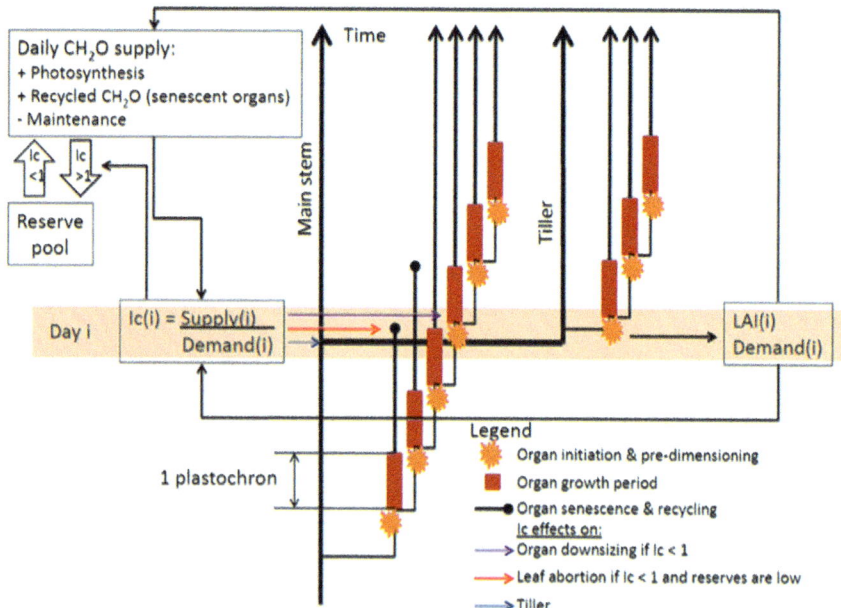

Fig. 17.5   Schematic diagram of EcoMeristem model

ultimately, delays in organogenetic cycles, in this order; and (ii) organs that are being initiated are down-sized, leading to smaller demand when they turn into active sinks. If IC < ICT (a genotypic parameter, ICT, threshold value for tillering), then new tillers are not created; otherwise, the potential number of tillers is created. This system of feedbacks stabilizes plant carbon balance by adjusting plant development to resources.

This model was initially developed and implemented within the MATLAB environment (http://www.mathworks.fr/products/matlab/). Due to computation time limitations, EcoMeristem was entirely rewritten into a dedicated platform called EcoPhen that is written under Delphi 6 (Pacheco 2001).

17.4.4 Topology

The topology of the plant consists of a principal axis or main stem, constituted by a sequence of phytomers (see Fig. 17.4). Each phytomer consists of a set a leaf (blade and sheath), a virtual axillary node, and an internode. An open-ended number of tillers can be created, depending on an evolving number of potential sites (one bud per phytomer on main stem and tillers). However, the actual number of sites depends on assimilate availability and genotypic sensitivity to it. Each tiller is defined by its time of initiation and the leaf on the main stem with which its first leaf will be synchronous, according to principle of cohorts. All subsequent leaves produced on the tiller, as well as internode elongation and panicle growth, are from then on synchronized with the main stem.

The expansion of a new leaf to its final size happens during a single phyllochron after initiation of the corresponding phytomer. On the main stem, potential leaf size increases from one phytomer to the next, a trend that is associated with an increase in the size of the apical meristem. In *EcoMeristem*, the apical meristem grows during each plastochron by a constant factor (parameter meristem growth rate, MGR) if assimilate supply is non-limiting. It grows less if IC < 1. The potential dry weight of a new leaf is assumed to be proportional to the meristem size at its appearance. Therefore, potential dry weight of leaf n on the main stem is equal to final, structural dry weight of leaf $n - 1$, multiplied by MGR. Final dry weight of leaf n is equal to its potential dry weight, or smaller if IC < 1. The down-sizing of the leaf when IC < 1 is non-linear (using IC^2 as factor, instead of IC) because a linear function was found to have unrealistic, disruptive effects on the simulation process. In summary, the final dry weight of a new leaf on the main stem depends on that of its predecessor, the genotypic value of MGR, and the resource situation (value of IC) at the time of its appearance.

Leaves produced by tillers are initially smaller than other leaves of the same cohort, but leaves appearing subsequently catch up in size with those on the main stem. In the model, we assume that the first leaf produced by a tiller has an intermediate (mean) size between the leaf simultaneously produced on the main stem (same cohort), and the very first leaf produced on the main stem. Subsequent leaves produced by the tiller are predimensioned at the time of their initiation as the mean weight of the previous leaf on the main stem and that on the concerned tiller, multiplied by MGR. Consequently, the weight of leaves appearing on tillers asymptotically converges toward that of leaves appearing on the main stem, and leaf size on older tillers (having several phytomers) is similar to that on the main stem.

The root system is not simulated with the same amount of detail as the shoot, although a detailed version is being developed. The present version of *EcoMeristem* considers the root system as a bulk compartment of the plant, with a daily carbon demand that is equal to the total plant carbon demand simulated on the previous day, multiplied with a genotypic parameter.

17.4.5 Implementation in DEVS

In order to implement *EcoMeristem* using DEVS and one of its implementation: Virtual Laboratory Environment (VLE) (Quesnel et al. 2009), we need to use a subset of VLE's extensions:

- **Difference equation**: This extension called *Difference Equation* allows to develop discrete-time model which calculates the value of a real variable at time t as a function of itself at earlier time steps, $t - 1, t - 2, \ldots$, as well as other real variables at these times.

This type of equation is used throughout the model. For instance, the computation of the thermal time is defined as follows, for a given time step:

$$DeltaT(t) = Ta(t) - Tb$$
$$TT(t) = TT(t - 1) + DeltaT(t)$$

where TT is the air temperature at t and Tb is the base temperature below which the plant does not have enough heat to grow (a parameter). Using the *DifferenceEquation* extension, the associated C++ code is (without header and class definition):

```
virtual double compute(const Time&)
{return Ta() - Tb;} //for the DeltaT computation
virtual double compute(const Time&)
{return  TT_(-1) + DeltaT();  }  //for  thermal  time
computation
```

- **Finite state automaton**: This extension called *FSA* allows us to define models as a graph of transitions between discrete states. In *EcoMeristem*, the plant can have different phases throughout the simulation: morphogenesis, no growth, elongation, panicle initiation, flowering, maturity. These phases correspond to the plant biological states. Fig. 17.6 illustrates the *EcoMeristem* FSA.

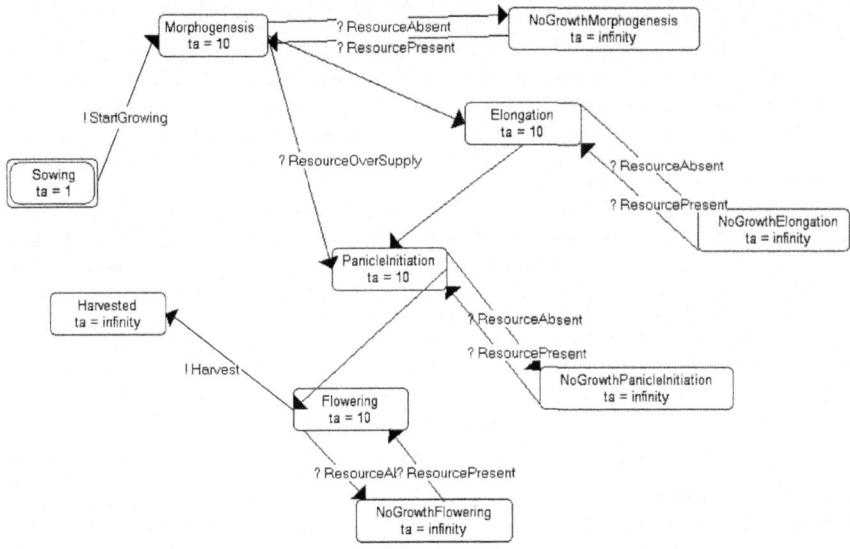

Fig. 17.6 Simplified finite state automaton for EcoMeristem

With the VLE's FSA extension, we can define the transition from the initial state to the morphogenesis state with the following C++ code:

```
states
(this) > > INITIAL < < MORPHOGENESIS < < NOGROWTH < < ...;
  transition (this, INITIAL, MORPHOGENESIS)
  ≪ guard(&Manager::c1)
  ≪ send(&Manager::output4);
  bool c1(const Time&)
  {return stock > 0 and phenoStage < nbleaf_pi}
  void output4(const Time&, ExternalEventList& output)
  const
  {output.addEvent(buildEventWithAnInteger("phase",
  "phase", MORPHOGENESIS));
```

The condition c1 means that *EcoMeristem* can move from the INITIAL state to the MORPHOGENESIS state if only and only if the plant stock is positive and the current phenological stage is lower than the leaf number required to allow reaching the panicle initiation state.

The output output4 will be sent to all connected models thanks to the connection graph in order to change their own states.

- *Dynamic model management*: The original structure of the coupled models (models and connections) was purely static. This means that the number of models, the number and nature of the connections did not change during of the simulation. Barros (1996, 1997) proposed an extension, the Dynamic Structure DEVS (DS-DEVS) to deal with structural changes (addition and deletion of models and connections at run-time). This extension, unlike the others, has implications for the synchronization core to ensure causality. The consequence is that structural changes are applied as a last place (after all the bags).

Within VLE, the DS-DEVS extension is used to change the structure during the simulation, and also to build the structure in the initial state. In the latter case, the idea is to offer to the modeler the possibility to build the model using an algorithm, the classic example being the cellular automaton. It is clearly easier to provide algorithmic rules to specify a cellular automaton (giving its dimension and neighborhood) then defining the connections "by hand" (see Chap. 6). VLE offers another mechanism: the notion of classes of models. An atomic or a coupled model can be defined as a class and be instantiated on the fly via the DS-DEVS Executive.

To design Ecomeristem, DS-DEVS is the key element and is accompanied by the notion of classes of models. Each entity is defined in the plant within a class of models: axis, phytomer, leaf, etc. As discussed earlier during simulation tillers, leaves are dynamically created, or destroyed, according to the thermal time and the index of internal competition, IC.

Using all of these extensions, the VLE version of EcoMeristem was created.

Exercise

Discuss the implications of the dynamic structure of Ecomeristem for pruning the SES that gave rise to Fig. 17.4. Is a concept of dynamic pruning required to enable capturing plant growth?

17.4.6   Validation

The original version of *EcoMeristem* has been validated in several studies. To cite one of them (Dingkuhn et al. 2006), the authors apply the model to an experimental

Stress   Without stress

Fig. 17.7 Plot of rice without and with stress shown for day 36 with stress beginning day 21

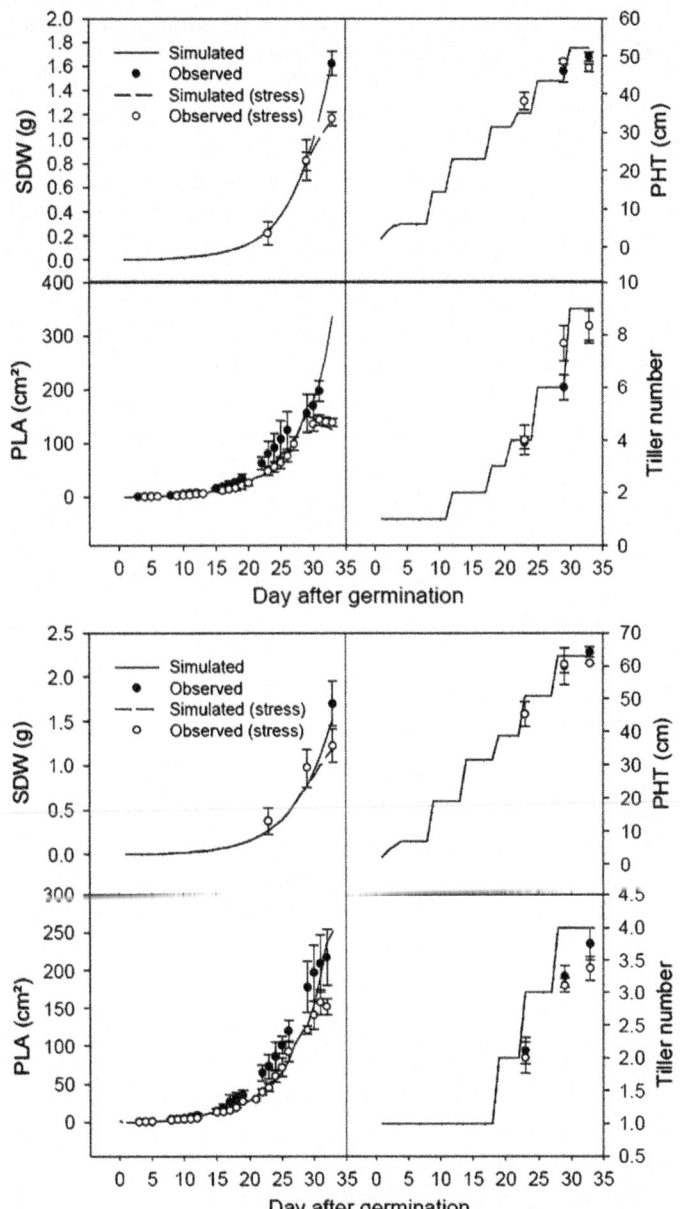

Fig. 17.8 Ecomeristem model validation for two genotypes: IR64 (*left*) and Azucena (*right*), SDW: shoot dry weight; PHT: plant height, PLA: plant leaf area

study on phosphorus deficiency effects on two morphologically contrasting rice cultivars, IR64 and Azucena, grown in controlled environments under hydroponics culture. Phosphorus deficiency caused severe biomass growth reductions in the shoot but not in the root, thus increasing the root/shoot weight ratio. It also inhibited tiller formation and leaf elongation, prolonged the phyllochron, and increased carbohydrate reserve pools in the plant. Analysis aided by the model identified inhibition of leaf extension and tillering as primary effects of the stress. Physiological feedback probably led to longer phyllochron, greater reserve accumulation, and root growth stimulation. The main effect of phosphorus deficiency appeared to be a reduction in demand for assimilates in the shoot, while photosynthetic radiation use efficiency remained nearly constant, resulting in spillover of excess assimilates into reserve compartments and root growth.

The validation of the DEVS VLE EcoMeristem version has been greatly facilitated by the fact that we already had the correct values of output with the previous version of EcoMeristem. Fig. 17.7 shows a 3D representation of a plot of rice (IR64) with and without water stress. Fig. 17.8 shows outputs for two genotypes grown in a phytotron in 2006 (CIRAD, Montpellier) in control and water stress conditions. Prior to validation of the new version, model calibration was performed for the two genotypes grown in a greenhouse experiment in 2008 with the same treatments.

17.4.7 Conclusion

By using simulation, sensitivity analysis, and parameter optimization, Ecomeristem builds a wide variety of virtual ideotypes that help ecophysiologists and breeders to gain a better understanding of plant functioning and its associated processes. As Ecomeristem is a GxE model, it allows studying the impact of fluctuating environments for a given set of genotypic parameters. Moreover, the model answers also the inverse question (by using parameters optimization): what are the genotypic parameters that would allow the plant to maintain, or improve its yield potentials for these various and heterogeneous environments? These environments represent the climate change variability that is challenging today's state-of-the-art agriculture and its food production crises.

17.5 Model Continuity for Living Systems

Model continuity refers to the ability to transition as much as possible a model specification through the stages of a system of systems development process (Hu and Zeigler 2005). Its usefulness is clear in engineering, where it supports consistent artifacts among the design stages, from modeling and simulation to a concrete implementation of the system in hardware. Ideally, the same DEVS models employed in the testing of the controls can be transferred to implementation with only a change in the simulation engine. Such consistency improves the design and reduces development costs by filling in the gap between the model and the implemented system. In a high new-to-existing component ratio, where components are manufactured from raw materials and assembled into new structures, knowledge about all the component systems is assumed to be sufficient for the implementation process (Chap. 1). On the other hand, living systems are characterized by the fact that the new components implementing the control or management policies constitute a relatively small part of the overall system and their interactions with the existing parts are less well understood. In this context, besides supporting using the earlier developed control models in implementation platforms, model continuity can be viewed as a back-and-forth dialog between the model and the real system. On the one hand, the modeler wants to learn about the system, on the other hand, the modeler wants to control or modify the system. In this case, "virtual build and test" involves a much higher proportion of developing reliable models of the existing component systems to support productive testing the policy or control components.

Despite the differences between artificial and living systems, DEVS is very well suited to enable model continuity for both. First, the clear separation between the design of the structure and the function (or behavior) facilitates the testing of hypothesis regarding how a natural systems works. We can easily figure out the channels for communication, matter, and energy transfer. Secondly, the internal processes in every functional unit can be embedded in modular atomic models which can be coupled to build complex networks of models. As we said in the introduction, DEVS adopts a systemic point of view which is closely related with the one in biology, ecology, and epidemiology. This compositional, "Russian dolls" aspect is so closely related with the natural hierarchies that DEVS seems ideal to provide a good mapping from models to the living systems. The decomposition property of DEVS is also very interesting since we often need to isolate living sub-components to study them in the laboratory, under artificial conditions. This reductionist approach is necessary, but can lead to mistakes since the environment of the sub-component often plays an important role in its dynamics. DEVS, together with the associated concept of experimental frame, can be used to model the isolation effect, which is a major concern for the study of living systems. Therefore, just as it has been shown that model continuity can be achieved for artificial systems (Hu and Zeigler 2005), it can be extended to the coupling of living and artificial systems, opening new ways to study advance living system applications, where real experiments are very problematic.

17.6 Summary

In this chapter, we have addressed some of the issues regarding modeling and simulation of living systems. We have seen that the systemic point of view of the DEVS formalism matches the systemic point of view adopted in the living sciences field. Two examples, one in animal epidemiology and the other in plant growth modeling, illustrated very different characteristics of DEVS and its extensions. The multi-formalistic abilities of DEVS increase the descriptive capacity of modelers when studying very complex systems. This capacity has not been used to its real potential in the field of living systems. Hopefully, its use will increase in the future since DEVS-based systems are very promising to help answer critical issues, as shown in this chapter, regarding natural risk management and poverty reduction. As we assume that DEVS can be used to specify a wide variety of living systems considered as a system of systems, it should be used for their specification. It is generic enough to work as a universal formalism for living dynamical systems modeling and simulation. Of course, using a software environment such as the VLE platform greatly facilitates the model design, its implementation, and its execution. DEVS is an abstract formalism and can be hard to manage when the modeling effort has to focus on the application domain. That is why projects like RECORD (Bergez et al. 2012) provides an environment where DEVS is used at the simulation level and where the modeling level is composed by a set of specialized modeling components, where components are represented by appropriate formalisms. Doing that, the modeler can design the model using the most suitable formalism, or coupling several ones, without any knowledge of DEVS. The mappings of the main formalisms that are used for living system modeling and simulation into DEVS already exist in VLE. The modeler can of course directly specify a model in DEVS as needed as well.

In this chapter, we have discussed model continuity in the context of living systems. It is a difficult question since living systems follow complex interaction rules and we are far from knowing all of them. Besides its usual function, model continuity can also apply here to help to the design of natural experiments based on virtual ones, saving time, and money. Such a very promising methodology to design experiments is still under construction.

If we want to use simulation models for decision making, we need reliable simulators based on rigorous and highly communicable formalisms to be able to share model specifications and compare simulation results. Pairs should be able to reproduce any published works to check the results. As model communication is a hard task, it is important to provide techniques to facilitate it. The morphism between DEVS models and DEVS abstract simulators is a property that provides confidence in the ability to reproduce simulation results with a given model. The DEVS version of the Ecomeristem model presented in this chapter was validated comparing its simulation results with a previous, already validated, non-DEVS version. Results perfectly matched. Verification by pairs is a fundamental practice in science. As simulation models are more and more popular in scientific activity, this practice must be insured—unfortunately it is not always the case. The necessary interdisciplinary works to tackle urgent issues such as the economical and ecological crises, diversity erosion, or poverty, will be based on creative compositions of shared representations. These shared models will embed heterogeneous knowledge elements at different scales, i.e., in heterogeneous formalisms. For these reasons, simulation models for living systems, viewed as systems of systems, should be formalized with DEVS and its extensions. While it is true that some work remains to standardize the DEVS simulators and specifications, we think that it is the most suitable formalism for heterogeneous model coupling. Such model coupling and cross-validation will play a critical role in the future of modeling and simulation in the field of living systems.

References

Aumann, G. A. (2007). A methodology for developing simulation models of complex systems. *Ecological Modelling, 202,* 385–396.

Barros, F. J. (1996). Dynamic structure discrete-event system specification: formalism, abstract simulators and applications. *Transaction of the Society for Computer Simulation International, 13*(1), 35–46.

Barros, F. J. (1997). Modeling formalisms for dynamic structure systems. *ACM Transactions on Modeling and Computer Simulation, 7,* 501–515.

Bergez, J.-E., Chabrier, P., Gary, C., Jeuffroy, M. H., Makowski, D., Quesnel, G., Ramat, E., Raynal, H., Rousse, N., Wallach, D., Debaeke, P., Durand, P., Duru, M., Dury, J., Faverdin, P., Gascuel-Odoux, C., & Garcia, F. (2012, in press). An open platform to build, evaluate and simulate integrated models of farming and agroecosystems. *Environmental Modelling & Software.*

Bonte, B., Duboz, R., Quesnel, G., & Müller, J. P. (2009). Recursive simulation and experimental frame for multiscale simulation. In *Proceedings of the summer computer simulation conference,* Istambul, Turkey (pp. 164–172).

Bonté, B., Duboz, R., & Muller, J. P. (2012). Modeling the Minsky triad: a framework to perform reflexive M&S studies. Accepted for publication in the proceedings of the Winter Simulation Conference (ACM/IEEE), Berlin, Germany, December 9–12.

Diekmann, O., & Heesterbeek, J. A. P. (2000). In S. Levin (Ed.), *Wiley series in mathematical and computational biology. Mathematical epidemiology of infectious diseases: model building, analysis and interpretation* (p. 303). Princeton: Princeton University Press.

Dingkuhn, M., Luquet, D., Quilot, B., & Reffye, P. D. (2005). Environmental and genetic control of morphogenesis in crops; towards models simulating phenotypic plasticity. *Australian Journal of Agricultural Research, 56,* 1–14.

Dingkuhn, M., Luquet, D., Kim Tambour, L., & Clément-Vidal, A. (2006). EcoMeristem, a model of morphogenesis and competition among sinks in rice: 2. Simulating genotype responses to phosphorus deficiency. *Functional Plant Biology, 33*(4), 325–337.

Duboz, R., Ramat, É., & Preux, P. (2003). Scale transfer modelling: using emergent computation for coupling an ordinary differential equation system with a reactive agent model. *Systems Analysis, Modelling, Simulation, 43*(6), 793–814.

Duboz, R., Versmisse, D., Quesnel, G., Muzzy, A., & Ramat, É. (2006). Specification of dynamic structure discrete-event multiagent systems. In *The conference proceedings of agent directed Simulation (spring simulation multiconference),* Huntsville, Alabama, USA, April 2–6.

Duboz, R., Versmisse, D., Travers, M., Ramat, E., & Shin, Y. J. (2010). Application of an evolutionary algorithm to the inverse parameter estimation of an individual-based model. *Ecological Modelling, 221*(5), 840–849.

Duboz, R., Bonté, B., & Quesnel, G. (2012). Vers une spécification des modèles de simulation de systèmes complexes. *Studia Informatica Universalis, 10,* 7–37.

Dufour, B., & Hendrikx, P. (2009). *Epidemiological surveillance in animal health* (2nd ed.). FAO, 386 p.

Giese, M., Brueck, H., Dingkuhn, M., Kiepe, P., & Asch, F. (2009). Developing rice and sorghum crop adaptation strategies for climate change in vulnerable environments in Africa RISOCAS. In *Proceedings of tropentag 2009,* Hamburg. University of Hamburg.

Gutjahr, S., Clément-Vidal, A., Trouche, G., Vaksmann, M., Thera, K., Sonderegger, N., Dingkuhn, M., & Luquet, D. (2010). Functional analysis of sugar accumulation in sorghum stems and its competition with grain filling among contrasted genotype. In *Proceedings of Agro2010*, Montpellier, France.

Hwang, M. XSY#: C# implementation of system theory. http://sourceforge.net/mailarchive/forum. php?forum_name=xsy-csharp-devssharp.

Hammer, G. L., Chapman, S., Van Oosterom, E., & Poldich, D. W. (2005). Trait physiology and crop modelling as a framework to link phenotypic complexity to underlying genetic systems. *Australian Journal of Agricultural Research, 56*, 947–960.

Summary for Policymakers. IPCC (2007). Cambridge, United Kingdom and New York, NY, USA.

Luquet, D., Dingkuhn, M., Kim Tambour, L., & Clément-Vidal, A. (2006). EcoMeristem, a model of morphogenesis and competition among sinks in rice: 1. Concept, validation and sensitivity analysis. *Functional Plant Biology, 33*(4), 309–323.

Luquet, D., Rebolledo, M.-C., & Soulié, J.-C. (2012). Functional-structural plant modeling to support complex trait phenotyping: case of rice early vigour and drought tolerance using Ecomeristem model. In M. Kang, Y. Dumont, & Y. Guo (Eds.), *Proceedings of the 4th international symposium on plant growth modeling, simulation, visualization and applications*, 31st Oct.–3rd 2012, Shangai, China (pp. 270–277). Los Alamitos: IEEE Computer Society Press.

Nicotra, A. B., Atkin, O. K., Bonser, S. P., Davidson, A. M., Finnegan, E. J., Mathesius, U., Poot, P., Purugganan, M. D., Richards, C. L., Valladares, F., & an Kleunen, M. (2010). Plant phenotypic plasticity in a changing. *Trends in Plant Science, 15*, 684–692.

Pacheco, X. (2001). Delphi 6 Developer's Guide. SAMS. 1200 p.

Pattee, H. H. (Ed.). (1973). *Hierarchy theory, the challenge of complex systems*. New York: Braziller.

Piou, C., Berger, U., & Grimm, V. (2009). Proposing an information criterion for individual-based models developed in a pattern-oriented modelling framework. *Ecological Modelling, 220*(17), 1957–1967.

Quesnel, G., Duboz, R., & Ramat, E. (2009). The virtual laboratory environment—an operational framework for multi-modelling, simulation and analysis of complex dynamical systems. *Simulation Modelling Practice and Theory, 17*, 641–653.

R Core Team (2012). R: a language and environment for statistical computing. R foundation for statistical computing. Vienna, Austria. ISBN 3-900051-07-0. URL http://www.R-project.org/.

Saltelli, A., Chan, K., & Scott, M. (2000). *Wiley series in probability and statistics. Sensitivity analysis*. New York: Wiley.

Soulie, J. C., Pradal, C., Fournier, C., & Luquet, D. (2010). Feedbacks between plant microclimate and morphogenesis in fluctuating environment: analysis for rice using Ecomeristem model coupled with 3D plant and energy balance computation tools in OpenAlea platform. In T. M. Dejong & D. Da Silva (Eds.), *Proceedings of the 6th international workshop on functional-structural plant models, September 12–17* (pp. 138–140). Davis: University of California.

Hu, X., & Zeigler, B. P. (2005). Model continuity in the design of dynamic distributed real-time systems. *IEEE Transactions on Systems, Man and Cybernetics. Part A. Systems and Humans, 35*(6), 867–878.

Zeigler, B. P. (1990). *Object oriented simulation with hierarchical, modular models: intelligent agents and endomorphic agents*. Orlando: Academic Press.

Zeigler, B. P., Kim, D., & Praehofer, H. (2000). *Theory of modeling and simulation: integrating discrete-event and continuous complex dynamic systems*. San Diego: Academic Press.

Activity-Based Implementations of Systems of Systems

18

A System of Systems (SoS) is a composition of component systems and is naturally modeled as a DEVS coupled model which is the computerized representation to support "virtual build, and test." However, given that SoS refers to something existing in the real world, there is also an implementation model, a model that reflects more about the characteristics of the environment in which the SoS will live. The implementation model is sometimes called the platform-specific model in contrast to the more abstract platform independent model (http://www.uml.org/). In this chapter, we are interested in the implementation model because it allows us to consider the energy consumption of the implemented system. You will see that by relating properties of the model to its energy consumption when implemented, DEVS and an associated concept, called "activity", make it possible to consider energy up front as part of the design. This can result in significant reductions of power consumption in hardware implementations of DEVS as we will show.

18.1 Energy and Activity

Energy is the general concept that represents the physical cost of action in the real world. *Information* is the general concept that models how systems decide on, manage, and control their actions. As in Fig. 18.1a, information and energy are two key concepts whose interaction is well understood in the following common sense manner: On the one hand, information processing takes energy. On the other hand, getting that energy requires information processing to find and consume energy-bearing resources. The information processing that a system can do is limited by the energy available to it. However, to increase the amount of energy available to it, a system must use its information processes—but these use some of that energy. A SoS is *sustainable* in the environment if the energy expended by the SoS to meet behavioral requirements is matched by the energy accruing to it by satisfying the requirements. For example, to achieve zero net energy consumption

© Springer International Publishing AG 2017   351
B.P. Zeigler and H.S. Sarjoughian, *Guide to Modeling and Simulation
of Systems of Systems*, Simulation Foundations, Methods and Applications,
DOI 10.1007/978-3-319-64134-8_18

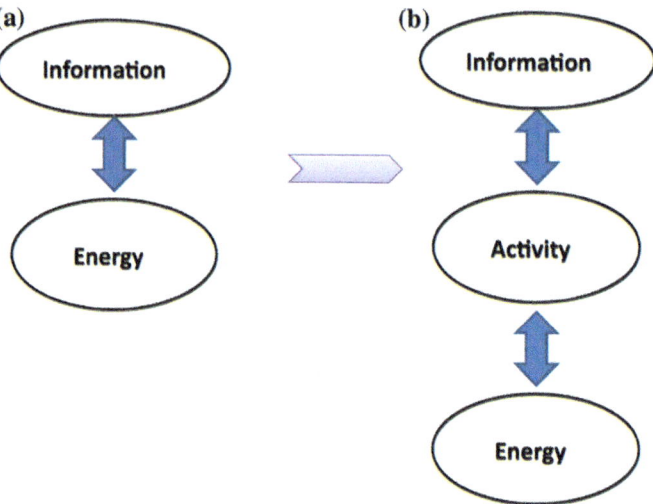

Fig. 18.1 Activity as the concept linking information and energy

without relying on the power grid, a building has to reduce its energy consumption and/or increase its capture of solar and other energy so that difference between the incoming and outgoing energy flows is not less than zero. Such a smart building has sensors to detect environmental conditions (e.g., where the sun is), decision-making systems to produce appropriate responses (to decide that more or less sunlight should be let in), and action systems to put decisions into effect (e.g., to open or close blinds). Timing requirements are manifest in that the building must respond fast enough to changing conditions so as not to lose or waste energy in transition. A DEVS-based hardware implementation of the information-technology SoS controlling the building can exploit the timing requirements and achieve lower power consumption than conventional approaches—which might make the difference between meeting the energy balance equation or not.

The energy required for sustainability—where the system consumes exactly the energy that it can acquire—is difficult to estimate without a more rigorous formulation of this relationship. We bring in the concept of activity (Fig. 18.1b) to enable us to link energy and information in a predictive manner.

Activity is a generic concept (like "information") and refers to the spatial temporal distribution of state transitions in the components of a system (Hu and Zeigler 2011). Activity concepts have been used to speed up simulation in the form of activity tracking which focuses computational resources on components based on their activity level—it arises naturally in DEVS models with space/time heterogeneity (e.g., crowds, fires) (Ntaimo et al. 2008). When you think of it, "information" is a useful abstraction for distinguishing system behaviors from their physical implementations—the same information may be represented in different physical manifestations, Likewise "activity" is a useful abstraction to relate system behaviors to their energy costs. Activity is a measure of system behavior that allows

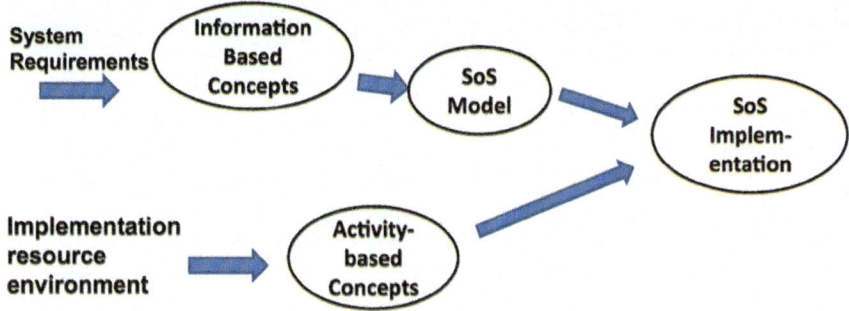

Fig. 18.2 Activity-based system design approach

estimating how much energy a behavior needs to consume. Intuitively, the more active that a component is, the more energy it requires to maintain its activity.

Figure 18.2 introduces activity-based/resource and energy considerations at the start of the system design process. Activity concepts allow a representation of the resource environment to be exploited earlier in the process. You will see how activity measurement and exploitation can be built into the implementation architecture to facilitate system of systems development.

18.2 Prototype System of Systems

To ground our discussion, let us consider a prototypical information technology-driven System of Systems sketched in Fig. 18.3. A specific example will be discussed later. The SoS is composed of a Sensor System, a Decision System, and Action System with message flow as depicted in the figure. The composed SoS is not meant to represent a specific system but can represent a

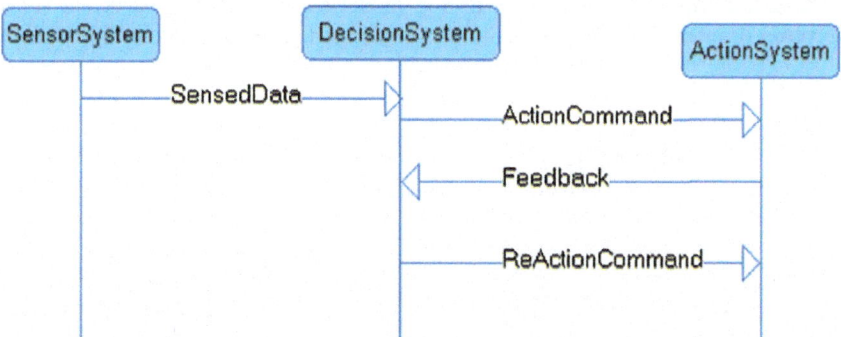

Fig. 18.3 Simplistic prototype of system of system

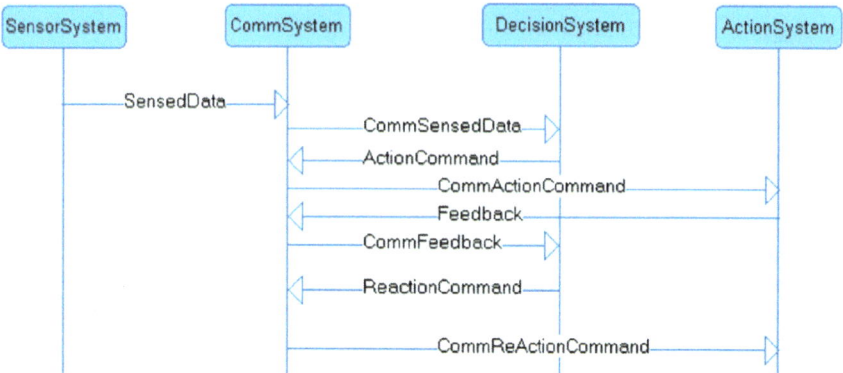

Fig. 18.4 Communication-augmented prototype of system of system

diverse range of systems of various scales. The component systems can be simple or complex systems in their own right. For example at a large scale, a defense system may have various airborne radars and cameras (the sensor system). The sensed data is sent for interpretation and decisions are made which initiate weapon launches or other actions. At a human scale, we have sensors such as eyes, the brain for decision making, and muscle driven limbs for action. Of course, scale is not necessarily significant in that the complexity and sophistication of micro-scale natural biological systems far exceeds those of macro-scale man-made technological systems.

For more realism, we add a communication system component to the SoS as shown in Fig. 18.4. All message exchange is shown mediated through the communication system. For example, sensed data from the sensors are transmitted to the decision system via the communication system in a coded form suggested by the prefix "Comm" (for Communicated). This accounts for example, for the data that are packetized for transmission in a store-and-forward data network.

As you have seen in earlier examples (Chaps. 13–17), Systems of Systems models may be of concern for a variety of reasons to a variety of stakeholders. An experimental frame interacts with an SoS model and embodies a particular set of purposes or interests for experimenting with the model. As depicted in Fig. 18.5, an

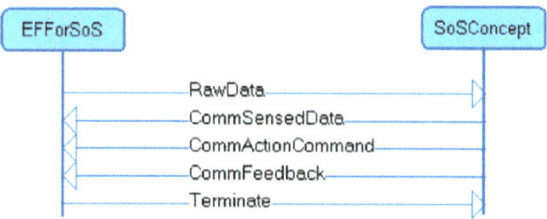

Fig. 18.5 An experimental frame coupled to the SoS

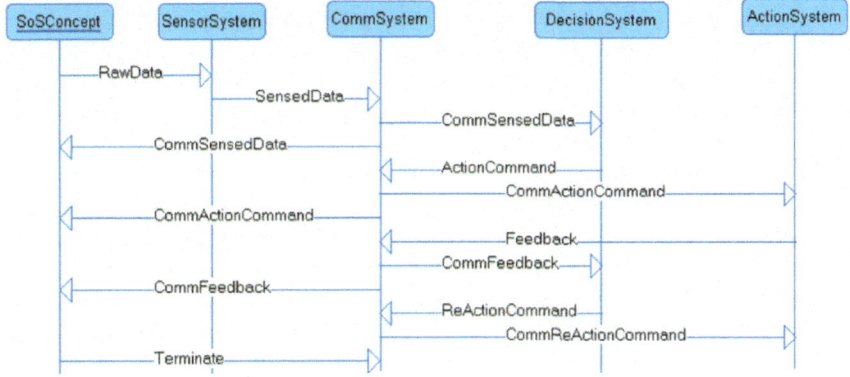

Fig. 18.6 The SoS conceptual model enhanced to interface with the frame

experimental frame is itself a model that is coupled to the SoS model (here called SoS Conceptual model or SoS Concept) and sends it a stream of data (called Raw Data). In turn, the experimental frame observes the sensed data, commands and, feedback messages that can be accessed by tapping into the communication system. The frame can also monitor the state of the model (as much as it can ascertain from the outputs it can observe) and issue orders to terminate the simulation when conditions of interest no longer prevail.

Let us expand the components in Fig. 18.5 using the Sequence Designer tool (as in Chap. 4). To interface with the Experimental Frame for SoS (EFForSoS), the SoS Conceptual model is enhanced so that the SensorSystem accepts raw data from EFForSoS. Also as in Fig. 18.6, the SoSConcept component exposes the outputs available from the communication system within it.

18.3 Experimental Frame and Timing Requirements

The experimental frame itself is expanded into generator, transducer, and acceptor components that interact as illustrated in Fig. 18.7 (see Chap. 4 and Zeigler et al. 2000). The overall results of simulation are available at the experimental frame output.

The experimental frame embodies system requirements in an operational form that can test whether a particular design meets these requirements. Considering the SoS example here, the system may be required to recognize certain situations in the environment and take action in response to them. The frame will test whether a model architecture satisfies these *behavioral* (also called *functional*) requirements. In a moment, we will also consider the *non-functional* requirements having to do with the cost of the implemented SoS. Testing for the behavioral requirements include tests of correctness (is the right response produced to a given input) and

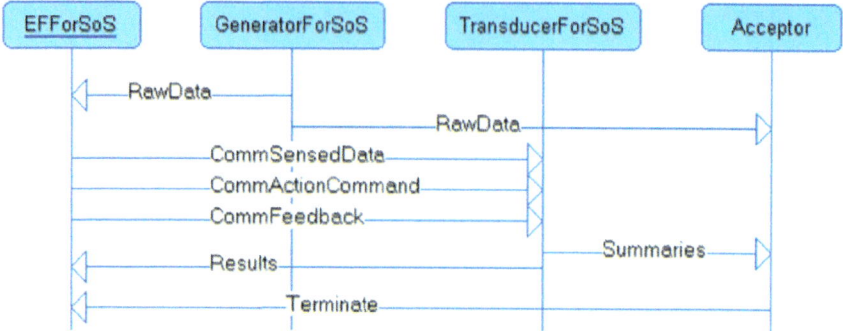

Fig. 18.7 Experimental frame for the SoS

timing (does the response get produced within the deadline or time specified). Correctness testing is particularly germane to systems of systems where pre-existing component systems may not "speak the same language" and need to be integrated and coordinated to properly work together at the syntactic, semantic, and pragmatic levels (see Zeigler and Hammonds 2007). In what follows, we focus on the timing requirements and relate them to activity and energy concepts along the lines of Fig. 18.2.

Recall that the frame, EFForSoS, can observe messages that are exchanged between systems through the communication system. This allows it to observe events such as called out in Fig. 18.8. Therefore, timing requirements can consist of *latency* constraints, which are upper bounds on durations of time intervals between pairs of such events. For example, a latency constraint might specify that the time between the arrival of an image (Event 1) and that of an action in response to it (Event 3) must be less than one second. Of course, the required behavior may not be

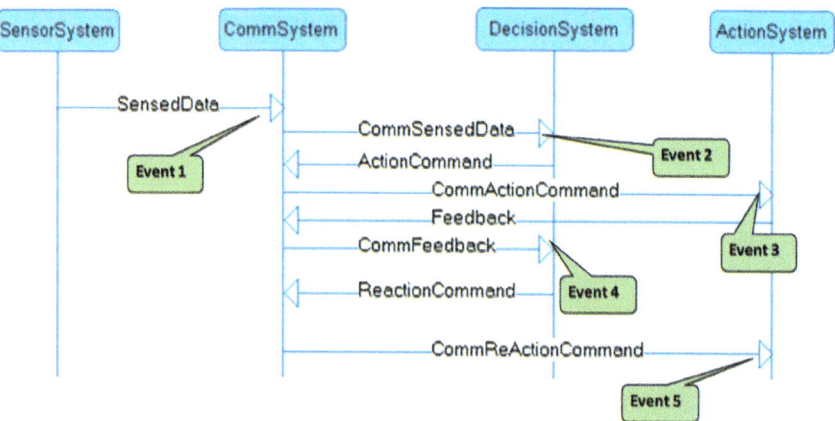

Fig. 18.8 Timing latency constraints

well represented by such simple stimulus/response pairs. This is why we have the possibility for more detailed observation of interaction between components, exemplified by Events 4 and 5. We can also label and time stamp events for unique identification and occurrence times. For example, successive image arrivals are uniquely identified and time-stamped.

18.4 Including Energy and Activity in SoS Models

As indicated before, we consider an implementation model of the SoS because it allows us to analyze the energy consumption of the implemented system. The implementation model, called the SoSConceptImpl, and a suitable experimental frame, EFForSoSImpl, are shown in Fig. 18.9. Here SoSConceptImpl outputs energy information to the frame which is concerned with testing whether the system meets its energy budget, an example of non-functional requirement. It also outputs the Activity measure which we assume is generated within the SoS model in the manner explicated in Fig. 18.10. Here each component system is assumed to be separately implemented and then integrated together with distributed simulation using the DEVS Simulation Protocol (Chap. 9).

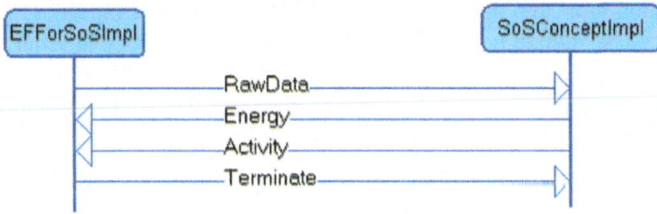

Fig. 18.9 Experimental frame for the SoS implementation

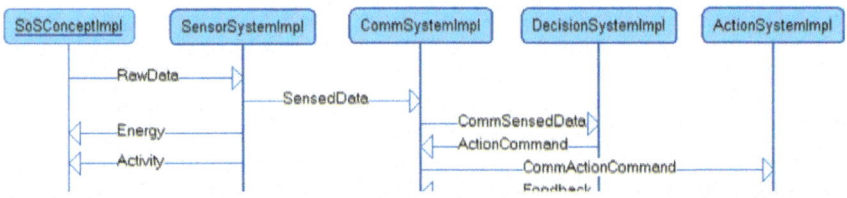

Fig. 18.10 Part of the implementation model of the SoS

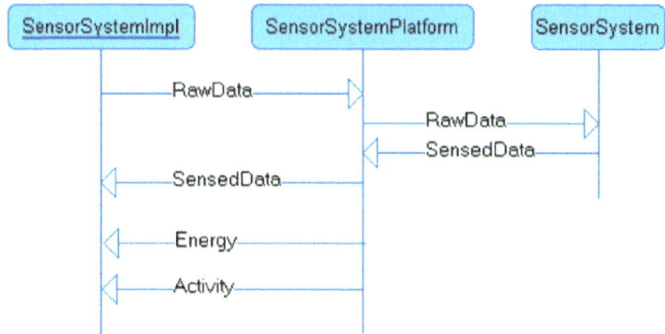

Fig. 18.11 Expansion of the sensor system implementation model

An example implementation model, the one for the Sensor System, shown in Fig. 18.11, represents the implementation as a coupled model in which the SensorSystem is coupled to a component called the Platform. This represents the concept of model continuity where the SensorSystem model is unchanged but the engine which executes it is switched to a real-time DEVS simulator (Chap. 9). Now, the real-time simulator can produce activity measurements since it can count the transitions of the model being executed directly. Also, as you will see later, energy can be measured with appropriate modeling of the underlying hardware. This accounts for the outputs of Activity and Energy from the Platform in Fig. 18.11. The output ports are coupled to EFForSoSImpl via external output couplings continuing up the enclosing SoS implementation model.

This formulation of system of system models and their implementation models will provide the backdrop for our discussion of hardware implemented SoS in a moment.

Exercise

Expand each of the other implementation components in the implementation model to send Energy and Activity to the experimental frame.

18.5   Review of Activity Concepts

Before proceeding to the consideration of hardware-implemented SoS, let us pause for some background on activity concepts and theory relating activity to energy. One of the unique properties of Discrete-Event System Specification (DEVS) is the intrinsic ability of the simulator to be aware of, and therefore, count internal and external state transitions in the model components. Let us measure information processing in a model by such state-to-state transition counts over some time interval, and call this the *activity* measure.

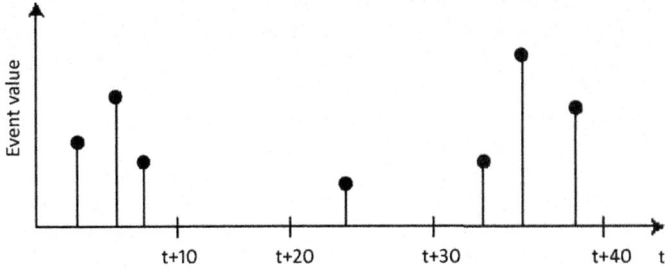

Fig. 18.12 Events occurring in time

As in Fig. 18.12, activity is defined in terms of the number of DEVS model events (internal and external transitions) in an interval, i.e.,

$$A(H) = |\{ev_i = (t_i, v_i)|0 < t < H\}|$$

where $A(H)$ is the activity level in time interval H. Accordingly activity rate is $A(H)/H$.

Intuitively, components with higher counts over an interval are more actively involved in the information processing than those with low counts. This makes the connection between activity and information. To make the connection with energy, we need to link transition counts with the actual cost of information processing in terms of energy

In application to DEVS simulation, consider simulating a coupled model with components and couplings. Here activity shows up as calls to the internal and external transition functions, handling of messages, and time coordination. In simulations using event management to handle time coordination, more generally, the activity rate will be reflected in the rate at which event notices are placed into the event list. The greater this rate of event notice processing, the greater the computational resources employed to handle the component sources of these events. Thus in DEVS simulation, the resources accorded to components vary in relation to their activity rates. Since our goal is to relate activity to energy, we will use energy to stand for resources from here on—although most consideration will generalize to resources as well.

In more detail, consider a distribution of activity rates across components as in Fig. 18.13. This is a snapshot of the distribution of activity over components (hence, in space) and represents a snapshot taken in time. Of course, this snapshot taken at different times could look different (representing variation of activity in time). For the moment, we will assume the distribution is constant in time.

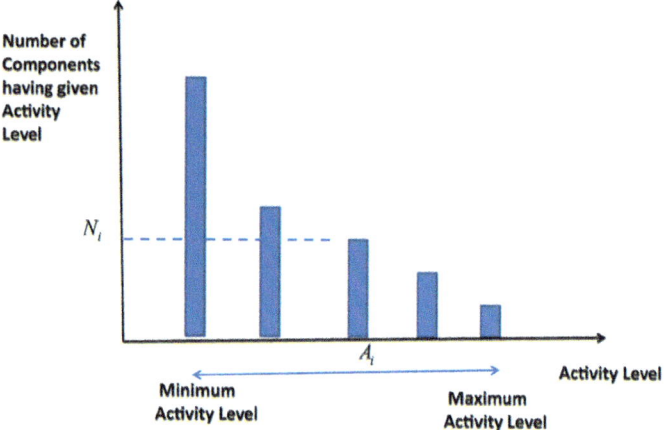

Fig. 18.13 Number of components having activity level versus activity level

18.6 Timing Requirements, Energy, and Activity

In the section, we relate timing requirements to energy and activity.

Given an SoSConcept model and timing requirements in the form of latency constraints, consider the set of implementation models, SoSConceptImpl that satisfy the latency constraints. Our interest is in characterizing the implementation models that minimize power consumption. To do this, we can gain insight by examining the distribution of activity in component systems. We make the assumption that power consumption is directly related to activity rate, or equivalently energy is directly related to activity level. We postulate the linear relationship:

$$E_i = aA_i$$

where E_i and A_i are the energy and activity of the component with subscript, i and a is the proportionality factor. Using this relationship, and given an implementation model and its distribution of activities, we can derive the total energy it consumes as follows:

$$Energy = \sum_{min}^{max} E_i$$

$$= \sum_{min}^{max} N_i aA_i$$

$$= a \sum_{min}^{max} N_i A_i$$

$$= aN \cdot A_{Avg}$$

where the total activity is

$$A_{\text{total}} = \sum_{\text{min}}^{\text{max}} N_i A_i$$

and the average activity is

$$A_{\text{Avg}} = \frac{A_{\text{total}}}{N}$$

and

$$N = \sum_{\text{min}}^{\text{max}} N_i$$

is the number of components.

Thus, the energy consumed by an implementation is proportional to the total activity (or average activity, for fixed number of components) of its system components.

Therefore, to minimize energy we are looking for an implementation that minimizes total activity. Consider such a least activity implementation and its activity distribution. We will assume that it is globally unique and therefore that it represents the intrinsic activity of the SoSConcept model required to satisfy the latency constraints. By "globally unique", we mean that no distribution with a component having a lower activity than its intrinsic level can satisfy the constraints. In other words, you can not decrease some activity (and perhaps raise another one to compensate) and still satisfy the constraints while achieving minimum total activity.

Exercise

Show that global uniqueness implies that no other distribution has a smaller total activity but the converse is not true. So global uniqueness is a more restrictive assumption than minimizing total activity.

We would like to exploit this intrinsic activity with an implementation that is optimal or as close to optimal as possible. However, as illustrated in DEVS simulation, achieving such a realization may require coordination of the component behaviors which has to be designed into the architecture. The right coordination policy will allow component implementations to achieve the intrinsic activity level of their components.

Consider an alternative policy, call it monolithic, that forces all components to run at the same activity level. Under the global uniqueness assumption above, this level can only be the maximum level since the latency constraints cannot be satisfied if components requiring the maximum level have lower activity. Let A_{max} and A_{avg} be the maximum and average activity levels for the optimal implementation. Then for the uniform implementation, the total energy is

$$MaxEnergy = N \times aA_{max}$$

The fractional difference between the energy required by the monolithic implementation and the optimal one is:

$$\frac{MaxEnergy - Energy}{MaxEnergy}$$

$$= \frac{aNA_{max} - aNA_{avg}}{aNA_{max}}$$

$$= \frac{A_{max} - A_{avg}}{A_{max}}$$

A rough measure of this reduction is the disparity in activity levels, i.e.,

$$ActivityDisparity = \frac{A_{max} - A_{min}}{A_{max}}$$

(Figure 18.13). This ratio is zero if all components have the same activity level and there is also obviously no advantage to partition energy according to activity. The closer this ratio approaches unity, the greater the spread in activity levels, the more we can expect to benefit from coordinating the components to allow them to attain the intrinsic activities required by the latency constraints.

Exercise

Show that for the case where there are just two components the energy savings is proportional to disparity:

$$\frac{MaxEnergy - Energy}{MaxEnergy} = ActivityDisparity/2$$

We conclude that to the extent that the intrinsic activity distribution required by a set of latency constraints shows some disparity, there is potential for reducing power consumption based on coordination of component systems.

18.7 SoS Example: Forest Fire Fighting

Information technology-based systems under development for fighting forest fires under the highly adverse conditions that have prevailed recently offer examples of systems of systems introduced early in this chapter. An architecture for such a SoS, illustrated in Fig. 18.14, consists of a component systems, along the lines discussed earlier: Sensor, Decision, Action, and Communication where:

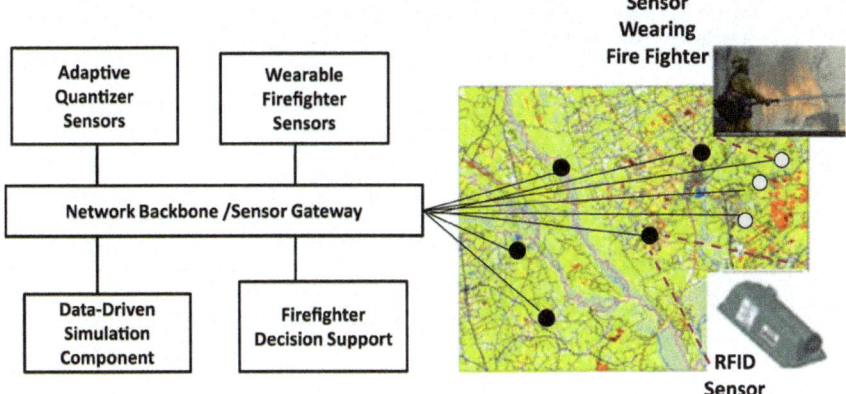

Fig. 18.14 Architecture for forest fire suppression SoS

- **Sensors** are of two types: fixed and wearable. The fixed sensors are spread throughout the area and measure weather variables such as temperature and humidity to indicate the state of combustion of their immediate neighborhood. Wearable sensors are carried on coats and hats of fire firefighters and measure their physiological state as well as the gas composition of the air in proximity to the fire. Sensors also can report identity and location information through radio broadcast (RFID) and global positioning (GPS).
- **Decision** components include a data-driven simulation system that assimilates the data collected by the sensors and predicts direction and intensity of the fire front, and a fire fighter decision support system that models fighters as agents and predicts optimal courses of actions to suppress the fire.
- **Action** components include fire fighters, the humans and equipment (including robots) executing the actions of controlled burns, application of water and fire retardants, and other fire suppression activities.
- **Network Communication** connecting the sensors together to report readings to decision component and reaching back from the decision system to provide adjustment and control of the sensors.

The sensor packages are based on the quantization principle illustrated in Fig. 18.15. As data values are sampled by the sensor, the quantizer only accepts a new input if it represents a significant change from the last value that was accepted. Significant change is determined by the size of the *quantum* which is the amount that the input has to differ by from last saved value to become the next saved value. When an input is saved it is also sent out for use by downstream consumers. Therefore, the output event time segment is a sub-selection of the input event time segment whose sparseness depends on the quantum size. The quantum size can be adapted by an external controller so that for example, it is increased when energy must be conserved or decreased when more fidelity is required. A FDDEVS model

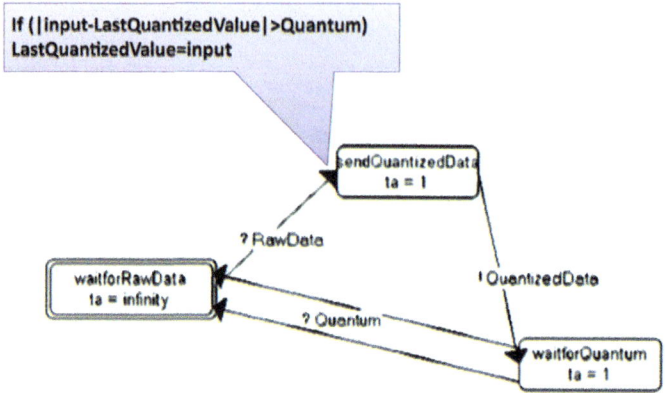

Fig. 18.15 Adaptive quantizer state diagram

of the quantizer is given in the Appendix. The theory of quantization is discussed in Hu and Zeigler (2011).

Exercise

Explain how increasing the quantum size can conserve energy and decreasing it can increase the fidelity of the output relative to the input.

The adaptive quantizer sensor package that is replicated and distributed throughout the forest is depicted in Fig. 18.16. The core coupled model contains the quantizer, quantum adapter, wireless transmitter and receiver. An experimental frame is packaged with the core to allow it to be tested during the long periods

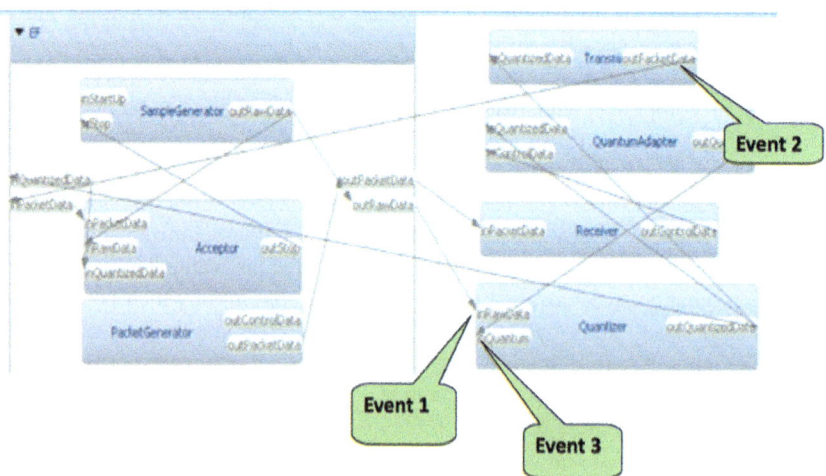

Fig. 18.16 Adaptive quantizer sensor package

between actual uses. The frame has two generators, one for raw data of the kind intended for measurement (e.g., high temperature values) and one to generate test data packets for the receiver. The acceptor tests for correct operation of the quantizer by comparing its input/output behavior.

Exercise

Design a straightforward test that the acceptor can do to check whether the quantizer is working correctly and implement it in an FDDEVS model. Hint: the acceptor gets raw data from the SampleGenerator and QuantizedData from the Quantizer with easy to relate timing.

Exercise

Develop a model for the Forest Fire Fighting SoS to study different patterns of placement of the sensors in the forest. Employ multi-aspects (Chap. 6) to represent the sensors and action components in an SES that can be pruned for numbers of sensors and selection of placement algorithm (e.g., random, mesh, etc.).

18.8 Relating Activity to Hardware-Implemented SoS

Sensors spread throughout a forest should last as long as possible on their batteries. Adaptive quantization contributes to reduce power drain but let us also see how hardware design can achieve additional savings. With this as motivation, we discuss a DEVS-based hardware design methodology that opens up the possibility of assigning energy to components in relation to the intrinsic activity levels associated with a set of latency constraints. The energy consumed in a hardware Field Programmable Gate Array (FPGA) is composed of static and dynamic segments. The static portion is related to the maintenance of the logic itself while the dynamic portion is related to the frequency of the clock driving the logic. Actually, for a circuit within the FPGA implementation, the dynamic power is proportional to frequency of the clock with the factor depending on the circuit. This empirical relationship underlies the linear relationship assumed between energy and activity in Sect. 18.4. Traditional hardware design typically uses a single clock and does not pay attention to activity levels so that it risks running at higher than necessary frequency and expending more energy than needed. In contrast, our design methodology can employ multiple clocks. These clocks can be organized to be active only when needed and to run at different frequencies allowing the potential to achieve the lower energy levels enabled by intrinsic activity-based coordination.

DEVS provides a robust formalism for designing systems of systems using event-driven, state-based models in which timing information is explicitly specified. Figure 18.17 depicts a high level workflow for DEVS-based hardware design, synthesis, and optimization methodology. This workflow translates atomic models

Fig. 18.17 DEVS-based
hardware design methodology

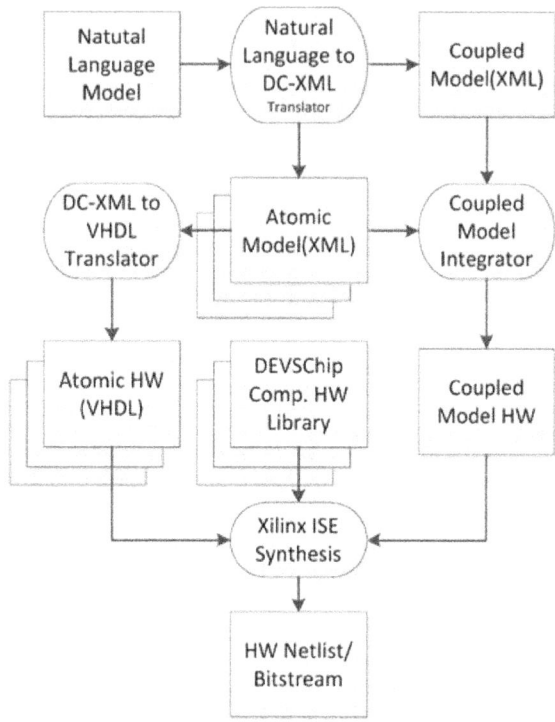

into Hardware Description Language (HDL) and uses coupling information to integrate them with coordination mechanisms to form a system model in HDL. The coordination paradigm is referred to as a *globally asynchronous locally synchronous* design approach. The resulting HDL is then mapped into the layout of a Field Programmable Gate Array (FPGA) or synthesized to Application Specific Integrated Circuits (ASIC) using vendor-specific synthesis tools.

Three coordination mechanisms to exploit the variation in activity in synthesis of atomic model components are *clock gating*, *handshaking*, and *clock frequency scaling* (differential frequency assignment).

Clock Gating circuits remove the clock signal from circuits that are not actively processing. They are controlled by enable and disable signals. The enable signals always have precedence over the disable signals to ensure proper functionality. The disable signal is explicitly determined from the DEVS model passive states. The enable signals are the incoming event requests and the timer signal, which ensure that the clock will be re-enabled when processing is necessary. The timer gate is disabled whenever the logic enters an infinite time advance and is re-enabled whenever the there is an external event to activate the model.

Handshaking enables communication across different frequencies, which allows each model to be run at the minimum functional frequency, and which reduces the power consumption. Handshaking components require no alteration to hardware description, they work from the event that the model generates then use asynchronous request and acknowledge signal that allows the event to be reliably propagated across different clock domains. Handshaking results in additional latency between events related to the two clock domains that are communicating. Each atomic model includes half of the handshaking hardware for a given event, whether the input event or output event.

Clock Frequency Scaling The coupled model synthesis is mostly straightforward, following the DEVS coupled model an HDL file instantiates each model and generate the necessary signals to make the connections. This is also the stage that atomic model frequencies are defined. Atomic models are specified in real time, but the hardware implementation uses a discrete-timer specified in clock cycles. The number of clock cycles to use is calculated based on the specified time and the specified frequency allowing the same model to run at different frequencies, but maintain the correct behavior.

Dynamic clock management modules (DCM) can be set to one of 256 frequencies that are evenly distributed. Model components are divided among available DCMs allowing groups of components to get the same clock frequency. Ideally, each atomic component gets its own clock and independent frequency assignment. Practically, DCMs are limited in availability and multiple atomic models are partitioned among the available DCMs. Details are provided by Pifer (2012).

18.9   Experimental Test

Experimental tests of the DEVS-based methodology are described by Pifer (2012). One test is an application to an adaptive quantizer sensor package such as in Fig. 18.16. The power consumption of the FPGA implementation of the package is determined by summing the energies of the clock domain groups using the known linear relation. Employing the natural board frequency of the FPGA implementation, the effect of using clock gating was found to reduce dynamic power consumption by approximately 80% (Fig. 18.18).

As discussed in Sect. 18.5, latency constraints are assigned to the timing requirements based on events 1, 2, and 3 shown in Fig. 18.16. The time between RawData arriving to the Quantizer at event 1 and the transmission of corresponding packet data (event 2) is required to be less than Latency 1 → 2. The latency between event 1 and event 3 (change in quantum) is required to be less than Latency 1 → 3. Further the ratio of Latency 1 → 2 to Latency 1 → 3 is set at 1:10 in line with the fact that for consistency the longer path should be allowed more latency. Two levels of constraints were experimented with: Latency 1 → 2 = 1 microsecond and 1 ms.

Figure 18.19 illustrates the search for assignment of frequencies to meet input/output latency requirements while minimizing energy consumption. Enumeration of alternatives (see Chap. 8) searches through of all frequency

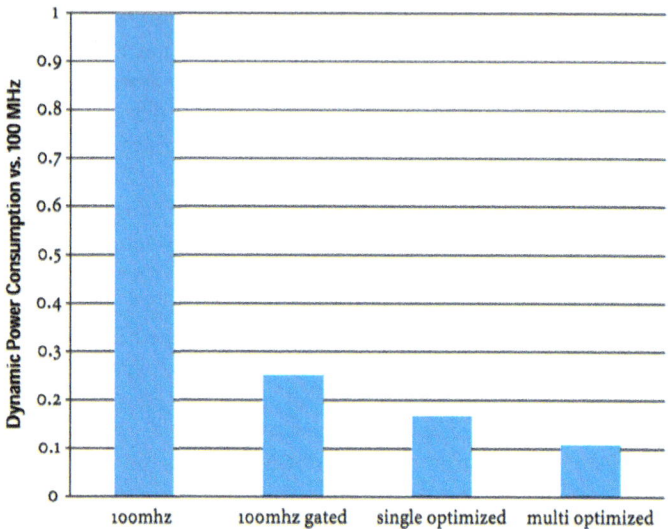

Fig. 18.18 Results for test case

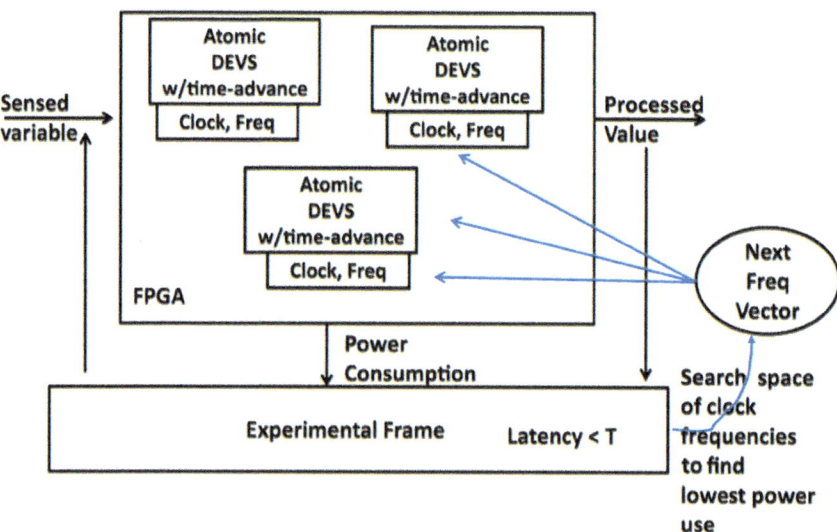

Fig. 18.19 Frequency search to find least power assignment

combinations, testing each one first, for constraint satisfaction, and then if satisfied, for total energy consumed which is estimated using the linear dependence of energy on frequency for each clock domain (Sect. 18.8). If the current energy consumed is lower than the existing best estimate, it replaces the latter as best estimate. Figure 18.18 shows that using a single frequency with clock gating and hand-shaking, the energy can be reduced by approximately 30%. Further, employing three frequency domains, the energy can be reduced by another 30%. Interestingly, the tighter the latency constraints the greater this reduction. The reason appears to be that tighter constraints require the faster response, and higher intrinsic activity levels causing greater disparity between maximum and minimum levels. According to the theory of Sect. 18.5, greater disparity offers the potential for increased energy reduction. The end result is two orders of magnitude reduction in dynamic power for tighter constraints using both clock gating and frequency scaling.

18.10   Summary

The environment imposes both behavioral and timing requirements on a system of systems. This chapter presented activity concepts as a means to bridge the gap between information-level requirements (behavior and timing) and energy consumption. This bridge enables implementations of SoS that minimize energy while meeting information-level requirements. In particular, we showed how hardware synthesis from DEVS coupled models can exploit disparity in activities of its components, giving rise to design for low-power optimization methods. The basic approach is a globally asynchronous, locally synchronous design pattern that enables efficient clock management and clock gating of individual design elements. Explicitly capturing timing requirements within the system model enables optimization to create a design that differentially assigns clock frequencies. This allows component clocks to run only when needed and at frequencies that may be much less then would be needed in the standard single clock design. A DEVS-based hardware implementation of an SoS can exploit the timing requirements and achieve lower power consumption than conventional approaches—which might make the difference between sustainability or not.

Appendix: Quantizer.dnl

```
RealDataSample has Value!
the range of RealDataSample's Value is double!
use LastQuantizedValue with type RealDataSample and default
"new RealDataSample()"!
use Quantum with type double and default "1"!
accepts input on RawData with type RealDataSample!
generates output on QuantizedData with type RealDataSample!
accepts input on Quantum with type RealDataSample!
to start passivate in waitforRawData!
when in waitforRawData and receive RawData go to
sendQuantizedData!
external event for waitforRawData with RawData
<%
```

```
RealDataSample val = messageList.get(0).getData();
if(Math.abs(LastQuantizedValue.getValue() - val.getValue())
  > Quantum){
    LastQuantizedValue = val;
    holdIn("sendQuantizedData",0.);
       }
else passivateIn("waitforRawData");
%>!
hold in sendQuantizedData for time 1!
after sendQuantizedData output QuantizedData!
from sendQuantizedData go to waitforQuantum!
output event for sendQuantizedData
<%
output.add(outQuantizedData, LastQuantizedValue);
%>!
hold in waitforQuantum for time 1!
from waitforQuantum go to waitforRawData!
when in waitforQuantum and receive Quantum go to
waitforRawData!
external event for waitforQuantum with Quantum
<%
RealDataSample val = messageList.get(0).getData();
Quantum = val.getValue();
%>!
```

References

Hu, X., & Zeigler, B. P. (2011). Linking information and energy—activity-based energy-aware information processing. *Simulation*.

Ntaimo, L., Hu, X., & Sun, Y. (2008). DEVS-FIRE: Towards an integrated simulation environment for surface wildfire spread and containment. *Simulation, 84*(4), 137–155.

Pifer, T. (2012). *DEVS-based hardware design, synthesis, and power optimization using explicit time specifications and deterministic path-based latency.* Masters Thesis, University of Arizona.

Zeigler, B. P., & Hammonds, P. E. (2007). *Modeling and simulation-based data engineering: introducing pragmatics into ontologies for net-centric information exchange.* New York: Academic Press.

Zeigler, B. P., Praehofer, H., & Kim, T. G. (2000). *Theory of modeling and simulation* (2nd ed.). San Diego: Academic Press.

DEVS Support for Markov Modeling and Simulation

19

19.1 Introduction

Markov Modeling is among the most commonly used forms of model expression. For background in Markov chains and other forms of Markov state-based modeling, you can consult many articles in Wikipedia. For example, the link https://en.wikipedia.org/wiki/Markov_chain lists examples of Markov chains from numerous disciplines and many other applications are also evident from searching the Web. Specific background for this chapter on exponential distributions, Poisson processes, and Markov basics is available in Appendix 1.

Besides their general usefulness, the Markov concepts of stochastic modeling are implicitly at the heart of most forms of discrete-event simulation. Indeed, such concepts are fully compatible with the DEVS characterization of discrete-event models and a natural basis for the extended and integrated Markov Modeling facility developed within the MS4 Me environment. The facility described here offers an easy-to-use set of tools to develop Markov models which are full-fledged DEVS models and able to be integrated with other DEVS models just like other DEVS models. From this point of view, the facility makes it much easier to develop probabilistic/stochastic DEVS models than was previously. It does this by automating a lot of the development tasks that you would otherwise have to do manually. Therefore, this facility raises the power of model development afforded by MS4 Me to a new level of speed and quality assurance that is unparalleled in all other commercial and academic tools on the market. Using it, you will be able to develop families of DEVS models for cutting-edge challenging areas such as Systems of Systems, agent-directed systems, and DEVS-based development of Web/Internet of Things.

Finite-state Markov model classes (Kemeny and Snell 1960; Feller 1966), with both discrete and continuous time bases, have been implemented in MS4 Me using the Finite Probability DEVS (FP-DEVS) capabilities (described below). The three available modeling classes are *Continuous Time Markov* (CTM) *model, Discrete-Time Markov* model (DTM), and the *Markov Matrix* (MM) class.

© Springer International Publishing AG 2017
B.P. Zeigler and H.S. Sarjoughian, *Guide to Modeling and Simulation of Systems of Systems*, Simulation Foundations, Methods and Applications, DOI 10.1007/978-3-319-64134-8_19

Continuous Time Markov models can represent complex systems at the level of individual subsystems and actors. Each system or actor can be represented as a CTM with states and transitions as well as inputs and outputs that enable them to interact as atomic models within coupled models using coupling in the usual way. Briefly stated, these atomic and coupled models are useful because:

- The DEVS simulator provides a Monte Carlo layer that generates stochastic sample space behavior.
- You can use DEVS Markov models to express probabilistic agent-type alternative decisions and consequences.
- Together with experimental frames, DEVS Markov models support queuing-like performance metrics (queue sizes, waiting times, throughput, losses).
- You can generate and analyze both transient and steady-state behavior.

Markov Finite Chain Matrix (MM) models are computationally much faster because they employ deterministic computation of probabilities interpreted as frequencies of state occupation of the corresponding CTMs. Such models are very useful because:

- They yield probabilities for ergodic CTMs in steady state.
- They yield probabilities for CTMs that reach absorbing states.
- They support computation of state-to-state traversal times for models where time consumption is of essential interest.
- They provide simplifications of CTMs that are accurate for answering certain questions and can be composed to yield good approximations to compositions of CTMs.

19.2 Markov Matrix Model

An example of a Markov model supported by MS4 Me is the Stock Market model taken from Wikipedia as shown in Fig. 19.1.

The section on Markov Modeling in the MS4 Me Users Guide shows how to use the state diagram menu to easily construct state diagrams like this. The dashed arrows signify transitions from one state to another. There are only six nonzero transitions. The one from BullMarket to StagnantMarket is labeled with the number 0.025. When interpreted as a Markov Matrix model, such numbers are taken as *transition probabilities*, e.g., the probability of transition from BullMarket to StagnantMarket is assumed to be 0.025.

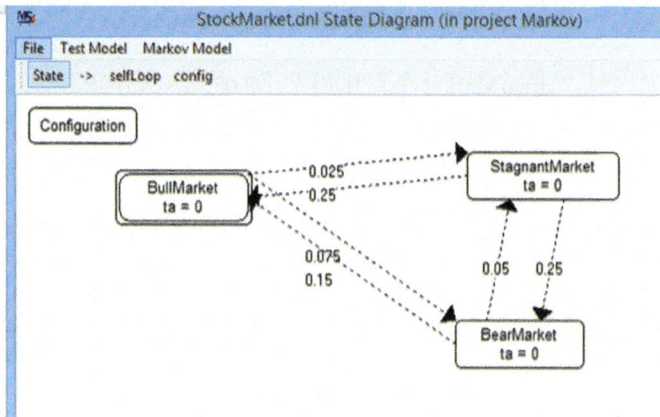

Fig. 19.1 Stock Market Markov model example

19.2.1 Steady-State Probabilities

One use of such a model is to predict the steady-state (also called equilibrium or long run) probabilities on occupation in the states. For example, the steady-state probabilities computed for the Stock Market model are given in the following table:

We see that Bear and Bull Markets are the most likely to occur over a long period of time while Stagnant Market is much less probable. To understand how this might be true, notice that the probabilities of transitioning to StagnantMarket from the other two states are much lower than the transitions between the latter. Also the transition probabilities for leaving StagnantMarket are quite large. So we can expect that the StagnantMarket is rarely entered and also does not persist very long, The quantitative computation done by the Markov Matrix model provides precise numbers to back up this intuition. Often, we go back and forth between model predictions and intuitive understanding until we are confident in the results. Having fast computations as given by the Markov Matrix model is a great asset in this kind of iteration.

In MS4 Me, you can create a model whose state is a vector with components that correspond to probabilities of state occurrence. For the StockMarket model, this takes the form:

$$\begin{bmatrix} \text{Probability of BearMarket} \\ \text{Probability of BullMarket} \\ \text{Probability of StagnantMarket} \end{bmatrix}.$$

Note that the entries are listed in alphabetical order. The state transition probabilities are placed in an array, called the transition matrix, with columns and rows that have the same ordering as the state vector:

[BearMarket BullMarket StagnantMarket].

$$
\begin{bmatrix} \text{BearMarket} \\ \text{BullMarket} \\ \text{StagnantMarket} \end{bmatrix} \begin{bmatrix} 0.8 \\ 0.15 \\ 0.05 \end{bmatrix} \begin{bmatrix} 0.075 \\ 0.9 \\ 0.025 \end{bmatrix} \begin{bmatrix} 0.25 \\ 0.25 \\ 0.5 \end{bmatrix}.
$$

For example, the probability of transitioning from BearMarket to BullMarket is 0.15. Notice that the probabilities within columns sum to 1 and that the probabilities of transitioning from a state back to itself lie along the diagonal. These self-transition probabilities do not have to be specified—the system computes them by subtracting the sum of all transition probabilities out of a state from 1. Notice that the layout of columns for outgoing transitions from a state differs from the usual one in which rows are used in this manner—however, it corresponds to the usual manner of matrix multiplication in which columns are mapped to columns. Indeed, the Markov Matrix model is given an initial state vector of probabilities and multiplies it by the transition matrix to obtain a next state vector of probabilities. It keeps iterating like this until the next vector equals the previous one (using an appropriate measure of closeness) in which case, the equilibrium or steady-state probability distribution has been reached. Under certain conditions, called ergodic conditions, the same final vector will be reached no matter which initial state is chosen.

Exercise

Follow the MS4 Me Users Guide to create a CTM model for the StockMarket of Fig. 19.1, and then, create a Market Matrix model called StockMarketMM. Notice that within the "Initialize variables" section in the StockMarketMM.dnl file, the following statement starts the model from the unit vector associated with BullMarket in the sense that its entry is 1 and all others are 0:

setInitialStateVector(mm,"BullMarket");

Run the model from this initial state using the Simulation Viewer and compare your results with those of the table in Fig. 19.2. Also, start the model in unit vectors associated with each of the other two states (replacing their names, respectively, in the setInitialVector () statement) and compare all the results. Are they all the same? Why do you think this model seems to be ergodic?

Exercise

Remove some of the arrows from the Stock Market model and rerun it from different initial states. Can you create versions whose final states depend on the initial states?

Fig. 19.2 Steady-state
probabilities for stock Market
model

State	Steady State (Equilibrium) Probabilities
BearMarket	.31
BullMarket	.63
StagnantMarket	.06

19.3   CTM and DTM Models

Summarizing, we see that the interpretation of a state diagram such in Fig. 19.1 as a Markov Matrix model is a very common one often associated with Markov chains —the numbers on the arrows are transition probabilities: And, these arrayed together form a transition matrix which generates a sequence of state vectors starting from a given initial one. In fact, such models are Discrete-Time System specifications (DTSS) with time step equal to 1 (although you can change this setting in the dnl file). Such models are also deterministic because the matrix transforms a vector of probabilities to exactly one next vector.

The interpretation of Markov state diagrams for continuous time and discrete-time models is very different. The reason follows from the fact that the state trajectories they generate are stochastic processes—starting from the same initial state, many different trajectories can be generated. The easiest way to think about this is that, interpreted as a continuous time model, the numbers on the arrows specify *rates of transition* from one state to another. In other words, the *inverse* of a number on an arrow is the *average time it takes to make the indicated transition.* For example, the average time to transition from a Bear Market to a Stagnant Market is $1/0.05 = 20$ years (assuming that the time unit being used is one year). The continuous time version becomes a discrete-event stochastic model in that it samples times from an exponential distribution with the given average and creates events separated by such times for its transitions. The discrete-time version is an approximation of the continuous time version in that it slices time into discrete steps and creates events at each time step. Clearly, the continuous time version is much more efficient and accurate so that we prefer using it almost exclusively.

19.3.1   Implementation of CTM and DTM in MS4 Me

Let us see how these ideas are implemented in MS4 Me. The transition system underlying this example is interpreted as either a CTM or DTM by taking the following approach (Soares et al. 2012). First, CTM, the **continuous time** interpretation employs the probabilities associated with internal transitions as specifications of their time advances. Indeed, let the transitions out of a state $(phase, \sigma)$ be

$$\{\tau'|\tau' = (phase, p', phase')\},$$

where p' is the probability of going to $phase'$. Then, the time advance for the state is

$$\sigma_{next} = min\{ \sigma'|\sigma' = -(1/p')ln(r)\},$$

where r is a random number between 0 and 1. The phase selected is the one whose sigma is the minimum (or one of this minimal set, if more than one exists). This implements the Markov assumption that transitions occur independently as events with Poisson distributions with rate parameters $\lambda' = 1/p'$. The model remains in the current *phase* for the computed time advance and transitions immediately to the selected *phase'*. Thus, the smaller a probability of transition is, the longer is the associated time to its next occurrence (on average) and the less likely it is to be selected as the transition to take. Notice that the self-transition is omitted as a contender to selection.

Exercise

Follow the MS4 Me Users Guide to create the CTM version of the model in Fig. 19.1 showing the graphical displays of elapsed times and probabilities. Check that the elapsed times spent in the states are in the same order as predicted by the MM model in Fig. 19.2, i.e., the model spends twice as much time in the Bull Market as in the Bear Market, and 10 times more than the Stagnant Market.

The probabilities in the CTM model are computed by normalizing the elapsed times at any point in time. For example, the elapsed times at time t = 400 for the states of the Stock Market model are shown in the first column of the table in Fig. 19.3. These values sum to 418, and the probabilities in column 2 are obtained by dividing column 1 by this sum.

Notice that the probabilities obtained from the CTM are close to those predicted by the Markov Matrix model in Fig. 19.2. This confirms the interpretation that probability of being in a state as the relative time spent in that state during a state trajectory.

Exercise

Explain why the sum of the elapsed times over all states at any time should be close to, but not necessarily equal to, that time. Hint: This sum is computed from time advances for events.

State	Elapsed Time at t=400	Estimated Probabilities
BearMarket	134	.32
BullMarket	257	.61
StagnantMarket	27	.07

Fig. 19.3 Elapsed times and estimated probabilities for Stock Market model

DTM, the *discrete-time* version is parameterized by a time step (or cycle length in the common Markov terminology). As with the basic FP-DEVS convention presented in the MS4 Me Users Guide, transitions occur with a time advance equal to the time step and with specified probabilities, in this case, determined by the given rates and the time step. For small enough time steps, the employed probabilities are given by the product of the corresponding CTM values and the time step. For larger time steps, a better approximation is given by employing probabilities equal to *1-exp(-h*p)* where *h* is the time step and *p* the corresponding CTM probability (this is the probability that the first event in the Poisson process happens in the time step interval). The approximation loses accuracy with longer time steps as more than one intervening events become likely.

Exercise

Follow the MS4 Me Users Guide to create DTM versions of the model in Fig. 19.1 showing the graphical displays with time steps of 1, 0.01, and 0.001, respectively. Compare the accuracy and speed of the models with the CTM version. Notice that to get acceptable accuracy with DTM seems to require unacceptably slow simulation.

19.4   Transient Behavior in Markov Models

We have seen in an example like the Stock Market model of Fig. 19.1 that many Markov models have long-run steady-state (ergodic) behavior which continues indefinitely. However, equally important are models in which the model reaches states in which it remains forever—the so-called *absorbing* states. In such models, the behavior of interest concerns the relative chances of entering absorbing states and the times it takes to reach them. This type of behavior is referred to as *transient,* as distinguished from steady-state behavior. In fact, life itself is transient, going from birth to death, and its processes often involve competing for resources in a time-based Winner-take-all manner. Consider for example, the following formulation of such a competition.

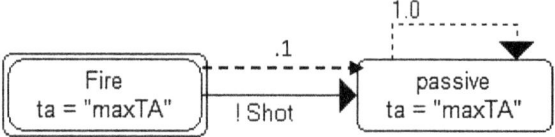

Fig. 19.4 Competer state diagram

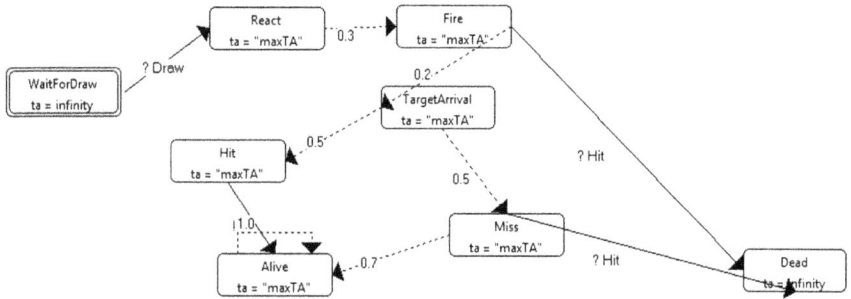

Fig. 19.5 Gun fighter state diagram

Contestants compete in a competition where time is of the essence. For example, in a race, the first to cross the finish line is the winner. Or as in Fig. 19.4, in a simplified shootout, the first to fire his gun wins. The Markov CTM model in Fig. 19.4 specifies that an output, shot, is produced in a time that is sampled from an exponential distribution with rate 0.1.

Given the rate of 0.1, we can infer easily that the mean time to shoot is 10 secs. However, since the model is stochastic in nature, the time it takes at each repetition will vary and when two or more competitors are active, the one with the minimum time to shoot will win.

A more elaborate example of this type of model is shown in Fig. 19.5 where a gun fighter can get an input to draw his gun, take time to react, and fire—where he may hit or miss the target with some probability depending on how accurate the shooter is. Now consider two such fighters who are facing each other—each now has the other one as target. Here, the one who fires first and hits the target wins—goes to the alive state—the other loses and goes to the dead state.

This is an example of transient behavior which shows that it is not so easy in general to get the probabilities of entering the absorbing states (alive or dead) and the times it takes to reach them.

Exercise

Following the MS4 Me Users Guide, create a Matrix model version of the CTM in Fig. 19.5. Run the model to get the probabilities of winding up in the alive and dead states. Experiment with varying the various transition probabilities to see how they affect the absorption state results.

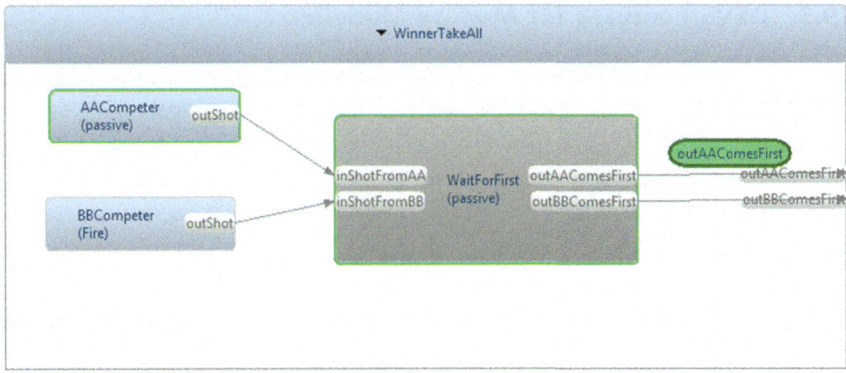

Fig. 19.6 Winner-take-all competition

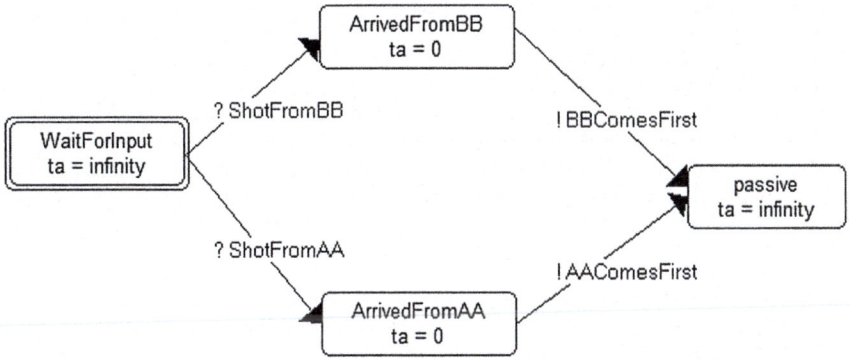

Fig. 19.7 Wait for first input to arrive

Also, you can use a function that estimates the average time to get from one state to another in state diagram without loops (directed acyclic graph) as illustrated in the following:

```
double          AvgTimeToHit = propagateSumOfTimes("React",
"Hit");
```

which you can place, for example, in the "Initialize variables" section of the MM model. Vary different transition probabilities to see how they affect the time it takes to hit the target.

Going back to the simpler version of Fig. 19.4, two such contestants, called AACompeter and BBCompeter, are competing to see who can shoot faster. In Fig. 19.6, they send their outputs to a referee component, WaitForFirst, which notes the first input to arrive and outputs the corresponding winner.

The state diagram for the WaitForFirst atomic model in Fig. 19.7 shows the simple logic for reacting to the first input to arrive. Note that this model is not a Markov model since it can easily be described with a deterministic behavior.

19.5 DEVS Features for Markov Modeling

So far you have seen MS4 Me provide facilities for Markov model creation and
execution. However, since the created Markov models are in fact DEVS models, all
the features of DEVS modeling also transfer to the Markov subclasses. In the
following, we discuss some of these features.

19.5.1 Individualizing Markov Models

As suggested in the preceding exercises, it is often of interest to experiment with the
parameters of models to see how their settings affect the behavior. For Markov
models, this relates to controlling the transition probabilities. Setting such values in
CTM and DTM models can be done by accessing and resetting the information
acquired from the XML file of the model using for example:

```
TransitionInfo    ti = ctm.getTransitionInfoFor("Fire",
"passive");
ti.setProbValue(0.6);
```

This can be done after the CTM[1] instance has been created, for example, at the
end of the "Initialize variables" section of the dnl file. For example, you can use a
part of the model name to set the probability value for the fire to passive transition:

```
if (getName().contains("Fast"))ti.setProbValue(0.6);
else    if    (getName().contains("Slow"))ti.setProbValue
(0.4);
```

Since the name of a model instance can be determined in model generation, this
allows different instances of the same model to have different transition probability
structures. For example, in the SES for the Winner-take-all-coupled model that
includes AACompeter, we can add the specialization for speed:

```
AACompeter can be Fast or Slow in speed!
```

Then, the pruning process can make different selections for the firing rate
probability for different model instances.

19.5.2 Dynamic Structure Markov Models

Since such access and control of the transition information can be done, any time
after initialization you also have the capability to dynamically alter the transition
structure during model operation to achieve *dynamic structure* change.

<hr>

Exercise

Extend the model in Fig. 19.4 to include a reloading state which returns the model
to the Fire state after shooting. Use the dynamic structure capability just discussed

<hr>

[1]The CTM model is created automatically and is referenced by the token, ctm.

to represent a situation in which the rate of firing slows down with continued repetition.

Hint: In the tagged code block for the internal transition back to the Fire state, place one or more transition altering statements such as in Sect. 19.4.

19.5.3   Multi-aspects and Statistical Considerations

Although the WaitForFirst model in Fig. 19.7 is deterministic, the inputs from the contestants are random processes and WaitForFirst takes the earliest arrival time of these inputs. Therefore, its output can be described as a random process whose average time is half that of the contestants (assuming each as the same transition probability). Thus, the winner as determined by WaitForFirst can vary with each repetition—from one such observation, it is not possible to tell which contestant is actually faster. Let us consider an expanded model, Winner-take-allMult (Fig. 19.8). It consists of a number of Winner-take-all components in parallel and sending output to another component that collects winner information called AggregationDecider. The latter waits for all winner reports to come in and decides the winner as the contestant with the largest number of wins.

Figure 19.4 shows a pruning and transformation of Winner-take-allMult with 3 Winner-take-all components. Recall Chap. 6 on the use of multi-aspects to generate multiple instances in this manner. A run of the model produced the result that AA won twice while BB won once. This might suggest that AA is the faster of the two even though they have been specified as equally fast on the average. Our confidence in this result should not be very high. This illustrates that we can get better statistical certainty by running many copies of the same component in parallel, but there will be some number that will give a confidence value that we are willing to accept. Standard statistical tests may be applied to determine this number, but we can also experiment directly to get a direct sense of the dependence of the winner

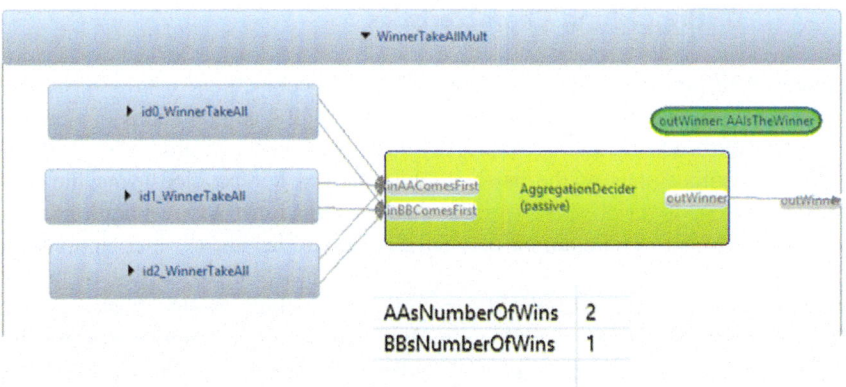

Fig. 19.8 Winner-take-allMult

Size of Group	Average of Difference in Wins/Group Size	Sampled Instance: #AA wins, # BB wins
10	0.3	6,4
100	0.1	47,53
1000	0.02	492,508

Fig. 19.9 Dependence of majority decision on size of group

decision on number of competitions. The table in Fig. 19.9 shows the results of 100 runs at each of group sizes 10,100, and 1000 taking the average of the difference in number of wins. You can see that this difference normalized to group size decreases with the square root of group size. This is consistent with sampling theory and design of simulation experiments (Kleijnen 2008).

19.6 Case Studies

Now that you have familiarity with the basics of Markov Modeling in the DEVS context; it may help to examine a few studies where such modeling can provide significant insights. First, we will discuss how DEVS Markov Modeling can support multi-resolution modeling in drug therapy applications to overcome limitations of current single-resolution-level approaches. Then, we will show how such modeling helps to understand how speedup using parallel processing can be catastrophically limited by the interprocessor connection network.

19.6.1 Markov Modeling of Populations with Multiple Distinguishing Characteristics

Figure 19.10 illustrates that providing each of the competitors with a speed specialization generates a uniform random selection of all 4 combinations of slow and fast speeds for each competitive pair. Any number of such specializations as well as further decompositions of the basic components can be specified using the SES, thus giving rise to a rich space of individual combinations. A direct application of this capability is to evaluation of cost-effectiveness of healthcare interventions. An ongoing controversy in evaluating the tradeoff of quality of life with cost in drug therapy relates to the use of Markov chain modeling versus what is called Discrete-Event Simulation (DES) in the drug effectiveness literature. Karmon and Afzali (2014) review a large number of studies in the area and discuss pros and cons of the use of the first vs the second approach. Basically Markov models are also called cohort models which follow patients as a group over time in aggregated

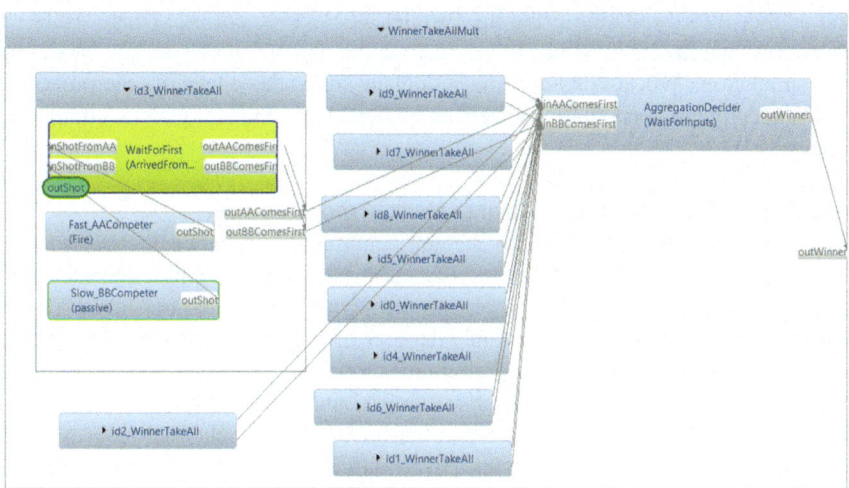

Fig. 19.10 Winner-take-allMult with multiple characteristics

form. Consequently, these models cannot accommodate patient differences. However, they are easier to develop and calibrate and also run very fast. In contrast, DES requires more detailed data, is much slower to execute and require numerous runs to achieve statistical validity, but can easily accommodate individual patient stochastic disease and treatment trajectories. Rather than either-or use of Markov and DES, the MS4 Markov modeling facility allows both approaches to be used in an integrated manner. The Markov model classes CTM, DTM, and MarkovMat support cohort-level models where aggregations of homogeneous patients are tracked. Moreover, the embedding of CTM models within multi-aspects in SES, as in Fig. 19.10, enables them to serve within patient models to produce the individualized stochastic and disease trajectories of DES.

19.6.2 Speedup in Multiprocessor Computation

Amdahl's law, or "model," states, in essence, that speedup cannot exceed the number of processors employed, where speedup is the ratio of the execution time of a program on a single-processor system to the execution time of the same program on a multiprocessor system. Numerous extensions of the model to account for overheads, failures, energy use, and memory bounds have been made (see (Nutaro and Zeigler 2017; Zeigler 2017) for background on Amdahl's law). However, they have all started from the same set of assumptions: a) the same program is executed in both single and multiprocessor systems and it has serial (non-parallelizable) and parallel (parallelizable) parts; and b) the parallel part can be made to run N times faster with N processors (Amdahl). The assumptions are made without proof although no unexplained violations have been uncovered. Zeigler (2017) developed a simple stochastic model that explains Amdahl's law from basic considerations and applies it to simulation using the Parallel DEVS Protocol (see Chap. 9). Here, we express the model in MS4 Me to illustrate the use of DEVS Markov Modeling and simulation. We also extend the model to study the effect of interprocessor communication on computation speed, an interesting problem of general computing interest.

19.6.2.1 DEVS Modeling Approach to Amdahl's Law

We outline a model that takes into account communication between processors by including a physical medium that constrains messaging to a single channel with waiting and access protocol. The access protocol could take on various forms such as a first-in/first-out queue and random selection of waiting processors. Our model allows us to get a handle on the communication time dependence on number of processors, N. We perform simulations as well as analysis to get an understanding of how the behavior depends on the parameters of the model. Each processor in Fig. 19.11 cycles between two states, *Active* and *Wait*. In *Active*, it takes an exponentially distributed time with mean *CompTime* to compute its current part of a job and upon completion issues a request for more communication services and waits to receive an acknowledgment to proceed. Upon getting a service response, it transitions to *Active* and the cycle continues until all processors have finished their parts of the job. We assume that a request from a processor to the controller (server) takes zero time but that once issued, a service takes *CommServTime*. The service can be sending of messages in distributed case or accessing a common memory in shared case.

We assume that each of N processors gets an equal part of the job to do so that $N * CompTime$ is the expected time taken in sequential processing. If all operate independently, the expected time taken for parallel processing is *CompTime*. Thus,

$$Speedup = sequential\ time/parallel\ time$$
$$= \frac{N * CompTime}{CompTime}$$
$$= N.$$

Indeed, this expresses Amdahl's law that computation can be sped up proportional to the number of processors if there is no interaction among the processors. Another way of expressing this is

$$Relative\ Speedup = \frac{Speedup}{N} = 1.$$

However, taking the communication service into account, we see in Fig. 19.11 that a processor must wait its turn in the queue while other waiting processors are served before proceeding to its active state. Thus, we must add *CommTime*, the average time that a processor experiences (including waiting and communicating), to the processing time attributed to each processor, *CompTime* + *CommTime*. Now, we have

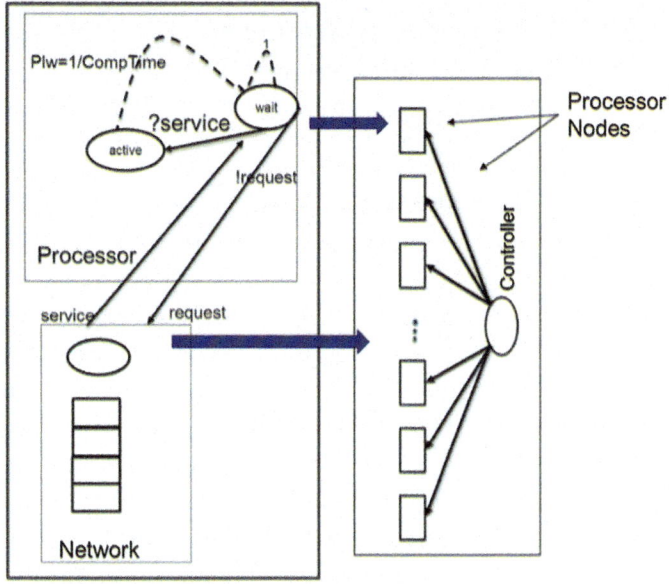

Fig. 19.11 DEVS Markov model of multiprocessor

$$Speedup = sequential\,time/parallel\,time$$
$$= \frac{N * CompTime}{CompTime + CommTime}$$

So that now

$$RelativeSpeedup = \frac{Speedup}{N}$$
$$= \frac{CompTime}{CompTime + CommTime/N}$$

(1)

and we see that speedup is reduced to the extent that the communication service per processor is a significant fraction of its computation time.

19.6.2.2 SES for MultiProcessorNComm Model

We now present the SES that sets up the simulation model family called MultiProcessorNComm to enable simulation to determine the dependence of the total service time, *CommTime* on number of processors. This will enable us to study speedup as a function of the number of processors and to compare the effect of different service protocols.

The natural language definition for the SES of Fig. 19.12 is as follows:

From the CommNetNsys perspective, MultiProcessorNComm is made of ProcessorGroup, Transducer, and CommNet!

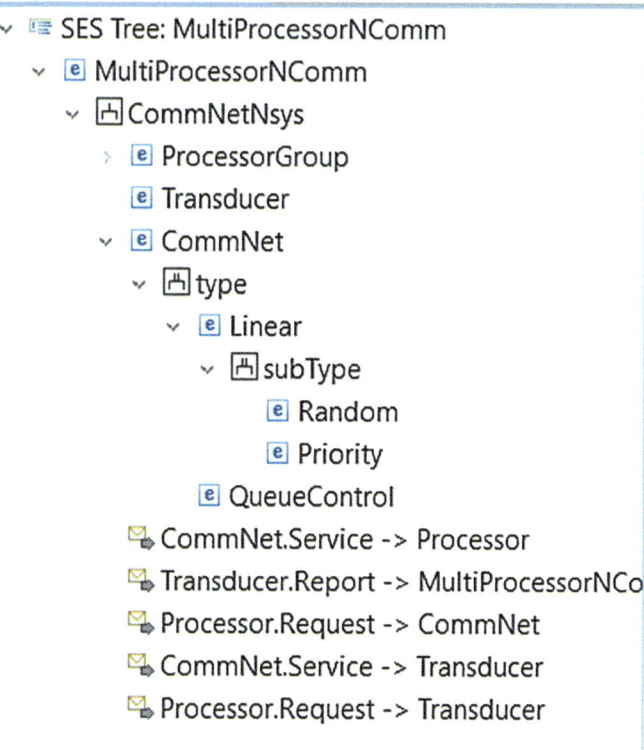

Fig. 19.12 Outline of SES for MultiProcessorNComm model

From the multiPrior perspective, ProcessorGroup is made of more than one Processor!

From the CommNetNsys perspective, Transducer sends Report to MultiProcessorNComm!

From the CommNetNsys perspective, all Processor sends Request to CommNet!

From the CommNetNsys perspective, CommNet sends Service to all Processor!

From the CommNetNsys perspective, all Processor sends Request to Transducer!

From the CommNetNsys perspective, CommNet sends Service to Transducer!

Processor can be id in index!

CommNet can be Linear or Queue Control in type!

Linear can be Random or Priority in subType!

The SES includes a multi-aspect called *multiPrior* to enable selecting any number of processors. These are coupled in all-to-one and one-to-all fashion to a network model, CommNet that provides the communication services. Requests from the processors contain their identity so that CommNet can remember their arrivals and provide service individually when the time comes. In addition, a transducer of the same type as discussed in Chap. 4 keeps track of such requests and their service satisfactions to determine the average time from request to satisfaction. The SES contains a specialization for CommNet to enable selection of alternative service protocols including first-in/first-out queueing, random selection among those waiting, or prioritized selection. A PES for selecting a composition of 4 processors with prioritized discipline for the communication service is exemplified by:

19.6.2.3   PES for Selecting 4 Processors and Priority

```
Set name of model as MultiprocessorNCommPriority !
   Pruned from MultiprocessorNCommPriority.ses !
   Mergeall from MultiprocessorNComm.ses !
   Select Linear from type for CommNet!
   Select Priority from subtype for Linear!
   Restructure multiaspects using index!
   Set multiplicity of index as [4] for Processor!
   Write class files !
```

19.6.2.4   SimView of MultiProcessorNComm

Figure 19.13 shows a SimView portrait of the MultiProcessorNCommPrior Model generated by the PES shown above.

19.6.2.5   Components in MultiProcessorNComm

The basic components that are coupled together in the simulation model are constructed using the Markov modeling facility in the State Designer tool. The CTM processor in Fig. 19.14 a holds in Active before issuing a Request stamped by its ID and transitioning to Wait. It passivates in Wait until receiving a Service input stamped with its ID and transitions immediately to Active. In contrast, the CommNet passivates in WaitForRequest and when receiving a Request transitions to AckRequest where it stays for an average of 1.0 before issuing a Service output responding to the Request with the same ID. Requests that arrive while the server is in either of these states are placed in a queue (not shown) and handled according to a selectable discipline as discussed above. Also selectable is *CompTime*, the mean time that a processor takes while active. Recall that this corresponds to a rate of *CompRate = 1/CompTime* for the transition from Active to Wait. Such a rate can range from the relatively low value shown (0.01) to higher values up to 1.0 where it equals the rate of the communication service (1.0). Intuitively, increasing the rate of transition from Active to Wait allows the processor to more frequently request communication service, thus placing more and more heavy workloads on the network server.

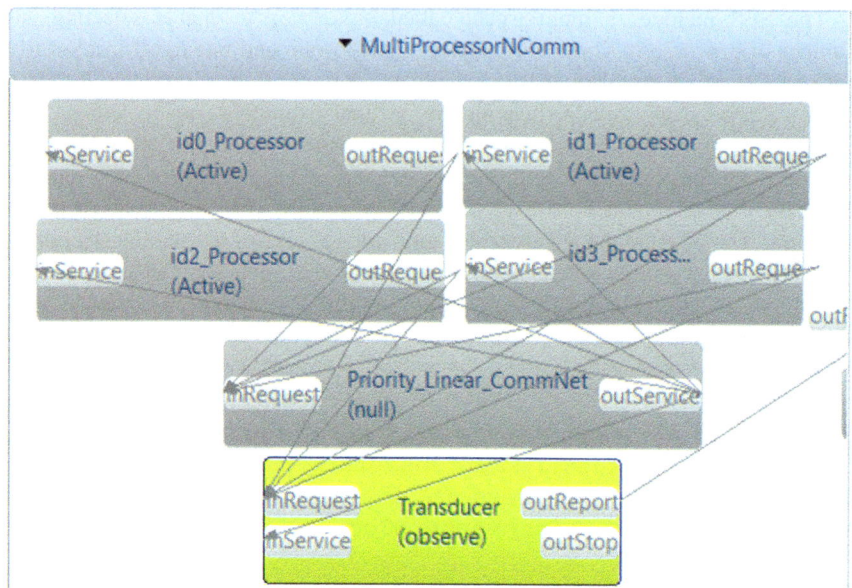

Fig. 19.13 MultiProcessorNCommPrior model generated by the PES shown above

Fig. 19.14 Processor and
CommNet DEVS CTM
models

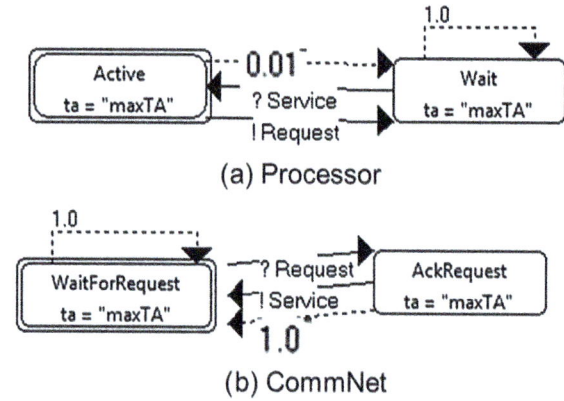

(a) Processor

(b) CommNet

Note in Fig. 19.14, the states for waiting ("Wait" and "WaitForRequest") are passive states with time advances equal to "maxTA" which stands for infinity. However, it also important to include the self-transition with probability 1.0 since every state requires at least one probability assigned to its outgoing transitions.

19.6.2.6 Simulation Results

The transducer in the simulation model measures *CommTime*, the average time between requests for service and their satisfaction. In other words, as in Chap. 4,

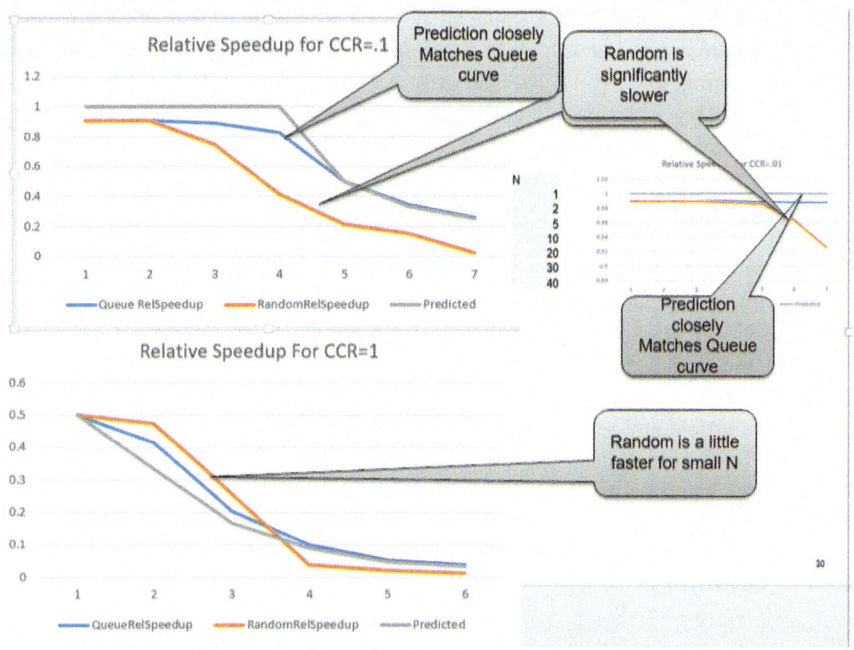

Fig. 19.15 RelativeSpeedup against processor number and for different ratios of processing to service rates

each request is stored together with its ID and time of arrival in a table. When after waiting its turn the request is satisfied, the server sends the ID to the transducer which can subtract the time of arrival from the current time to get the time taken for this request. These times are averaged over all requests to get the *CommTime*. Plugging this value into Eq. (1) allows us to compute the *Relative Speedup* as dependent on number of processors, *N* and mean computing time, *CompTime*. Recall that *CompTime = 1/CompRate* and in the Markov model, we set rates not times for transitions.

Figure 19.15 displays results of simulation for *RelativeSpeedup* against *N* under different values of *CCR = CompRate/CommServRate,* the ratio of computation rate to communication service rate. Note that CCR increases with increasing *CompRate* while *CommServRate* remains constant at 1.0 representing higher rates of processing demands and more queueing overload.

As expected, *RelativeSpeedup* decreases with increasing *N*. Speedup is generally higher for the FIFO queue discipline than when selection at random is employed (although random may be a little faster in queue the overload situation). We might expect random to be slower since a processor waiting in line is not guaranteed to ever get service, although on the average, the waiting time for random selection should be the same as in a FIFO queue since its wait is also proportional to the length at the time it has entered. We see a noticeable bend in the curve of

RelativeSpeedup versus *N* at a value of *N* close to the inverse of *CCR* (or since *CommServRate* is fixed at 1.0, close to the inverse of *CompRate*). You can see this break happening at $N = 1$, 10, and 100 for *CompRate* = 1.0, 0.1, and 0.01, respectively. This is where congestion sets in due to processor requests arriving faster than they can be managed.

Exercise

A recent article on public health spread of infectious diseases employed data on the Spanish flu epidemic in 1918 to compare differential equation models with an agent-based model expressed in DEVS (Özmen et al. 2016). Although the DEVS model in the article does not explicitly employ the Markov Modeling extension discussed here, it does lend itself to interpretation using the Markov concepts. Consult the article and reformulate the DEVS model given there in the form of the Markov DEVS model discussed above in Sect. 19.5.

19.7 Summary

This chapter, an addition to the second edition, demonstrates how the DEVS formalism supports Markov Modeling within MS4 Me. It does so by creating a subclass of DEVS models to express Markovian structural features such as transition probabilities and rates and uses DEVS behavior generation to compute their system-theoretic behaviors such as steady-state distributions and transient trajectories. Moreover, since the created Markov models are in fact DEVS models, all the features of DEVS modeling also transfer to the Markov Discrete and Continuous time subclasses. Markov models can be coupled with DEVS models (including other Markov models) to form interesting coupled models. Due to their transition structure, Markov models can be individualized with specific transition probabilities/rates which can be changed during model execution for dynamic structural change. Multi-aspects can be employed to simulate multiple randomized instantiations and designed experimental frames for garnering statistical confidence. Finally, we discussed case studies where such modeling can provide significant insights through multi-resolution modeling in drug therapy and how speedup using parallel processing is limited by the interprocessor connection network.

Appendix 1 Exponential Distribution and Markov Model Basics

This appendix provides a brief introduction to the probability distributions underlying Markov model construction before summarizing the properties of such models that are important to know when you come to construct them.

A1 Exponential Distribution Properties

The probability distribution function of the exponential distribution is expressed as $p(t) = \lambda e^{-\lambda t}$ for $t \geq 0$. The cumulative distribution function is expressed as $F(\tau < t) = 1 - e^{-\lambda t}$ for $t \geq 0$.

The mean of the distribution is $E(t) = 1/\lambda$

λ is called the *rate parameter*

$T_{avg} = 1/\lambda$ is called the average time and is the mean of the distribution.

Either T_{avg} or λ can specify the parameter, they are inversely related.

Some of the properties of exponentially distributed random variables are as follows:

1. The minimum of independently distributed exponential distributions is an exponential distribution with rate equal to the sum of the rate parameters.
2. The mean of a sum of independently distributed exponential distributions equals the sum of their means (but the distribution is not exponential).
3. The mean of the maximum of independently identically distributed exponential distributions is a multiple of the mean of one of them which increases as $1 + 1/2 + 1/3 + \cdots$.

A2 Poisson Process

A Poisson process is a sequence of event instants, t_1 t_2... i_i..., such that the inter-event times are independently and identically exponentially distributed:

$$p(t_{i+1}/t_i) = \lambda e^{-\lambda t_{i+1}}$$

The rate and mean parameters are the same as the underlying exponential distribution.

A3 Markov Modeling

Referring to the model in Fig. 19.16,

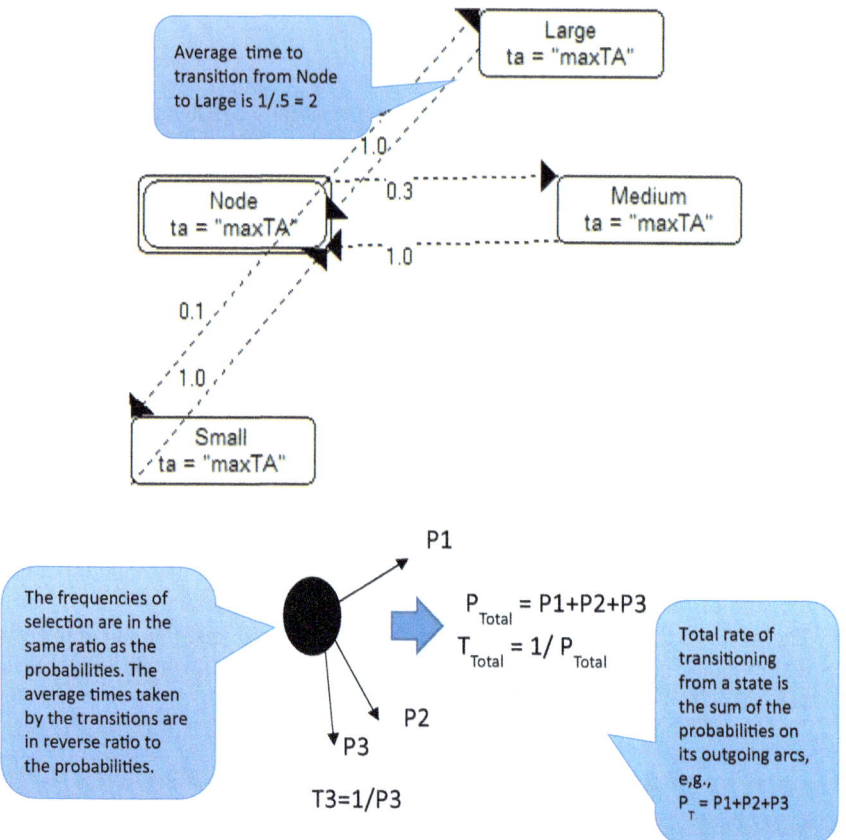

Fig. 19.16 ExponTest model for summarizing Markov Modeling

- A probability on a dotted arrow (state transition) is interpreted as the probability of transitioning to the target state (or the rate of making such a transition in time), e.g., 0.5 is the probability of transition from Node to Large.
- Each of the probabilities emerging from a state must ≥ 0 and must sum to ≤ 1. The remaining 1—sum is the probability of remaining in the state, e.g., the sum of the probabilities out of Node is 0.9, leaving 0.1 as the probability of remaining in Node.
- Given a state, the simulator independently samples an exponential distribution with each probability value as its rate parameter and takes the minimum to compute the resting time in the state before transitioning to the target state (one with the minimum time).

For example, for state Large, there is only one sample taken from the exponential with parameter 1.0; for state Node, samples are taken from distributions for 0.5, 0.3, and 0.1 with the smallest sampled value determining the result.

- The total rate of transitioning out of a state is the sum of the rates along its arcs. Mathematically, the distribution of the minimum of exponential distributions is exponential with the sum of the rate parameters as its rate parameter, e.g., the rate parameter for the minimum of the 3 distributions for state Node is 0.9.
- Since the mean of an exponential with rate r is $1/r$, the average residence time in a state (before transitioning to another one) is 1/ sum of outgoing probability values. e.g., for state Node, the average residence time is $1/0.9 = 1.11$ ... The average residence times for the other states are all the same $= 1$.
- Mathematically, the frequency with which a transition is selected for a state by the simulator is equal to the probability on its arc. e.g., for state Node, the frequencies of transitioning to Large, Medium, and Small are in the ratio of 5:3:1.
- The probability of being in a state is measured by the fraction of the time spent in the state during a run—this is the number of entries into the state times the average residence time in the state. In general, we need to run models to observe the number of transitions into a state (it is not analytically computable).
- The sum of the probabilities of state occupancy (probability of being in a state) equals 1. So if we compute all but one of the state probabilities, we also know the remaining one.
- The concepts underlying combining times of successive nodes are illustrated in Fig. 19.17. Note that average times of isolated transition of successive nodes add up, but this is not necessarily true for nodes that have more than one outgoing transition.
- Consider representing a node that has both an assigned residence time and outgoing probabilities that are not interpreted as rates. The node can be represented in a CTM by assigning it rates equal to the probabilities divided by the residence time. However, if the resulting rates sum to more than unity, scaling to meet this requirement is required (Fig. 19.18).

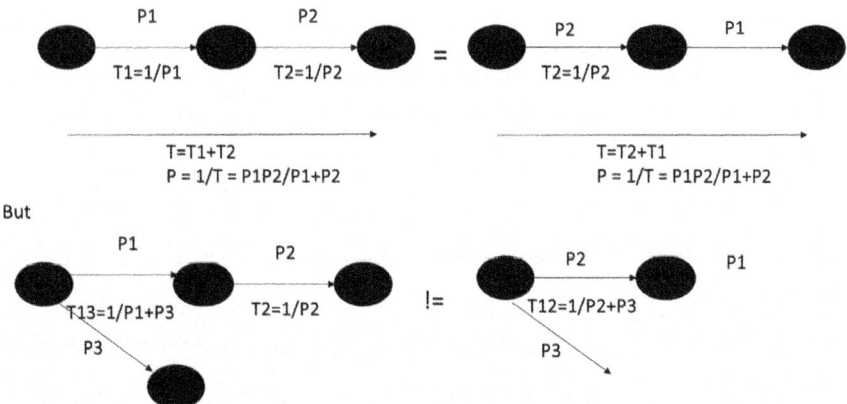

Fig. 19.17 Traversal time-based output rate analysis

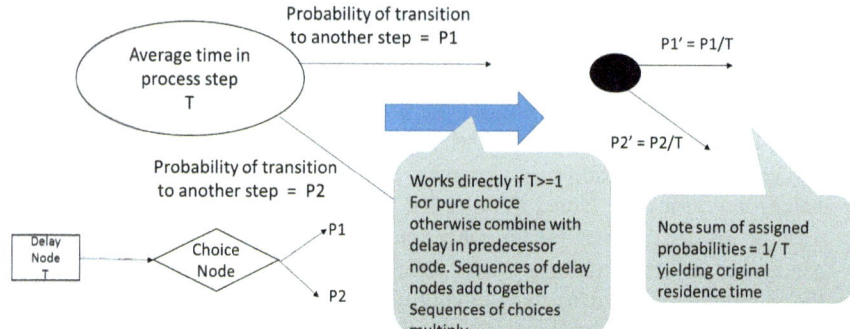

Fig. 19.18 Representing both residence time and probability in CTM

References

Feller, W. (1966). *An introduction to probability theory and its applications* (pp. 1–2), Wiley.
Karnon, J., & Afzali, H. H. A. (2014). When to use discrete-event simulation (DES) for the economic evaluation of health technologies? A review and critique of the costs and benefits of DES. *Pharmaco Economics, 32*, 547–558.
Kemeny, J. G., & Snell, J. L. (1960). *Finite markov chains*. v. Nostrand.
Kleijnen, J. P. C. (2008). *Design and analysis of simulation experiments*. Springer.
Nutaro, J., & Zeigler, B. P. (2017). How to apply amdahl's law to multithreaded multicore processors. *Parallel and Distributed Computing*. http://dx.doi.org/10.1016/j.jpdc.2017.03.006.
Özmen, Ö., Nutaro, J. J., Pullum, L. L., Ramanathan, A. (2016). Analyzing the impact of modeling choices and assumptions in compartmental epidemiological models. *Transactions of SCS, 92* (5), 459–472. Retrieved May 1, 2016, from doi:10.1177/0037549716640877.
Soares, M.O. and Castro, L.L.C. (2012) 'Continuous timesimulation and, discretized models for cost-effectivenessanalysis', *Pharmacoeconomics, 30*(12), 1101–1117, doi: 10.2165/11599380-000000000-00000.
Zeigler, B. P. (2017). Using the parallel DEVS Protocol for general robust simulation with near optimal performance. *IEEE, Computing in Science & Engineering, 19*, 68, 68–77. doi:10.1109/MCSE.2017.52.

Index

© Springer International Publishing AG 2017
B.P. Zeigler and H.S. Sarjoughian, *Guide to Modeling and Simulation of Systems of Systems*, Simulation Foundations, Methods and Applications, DOI 10.1007/978-3-319-64134-8

The manufacturer's authorised representative in the EU is Springer
Nature Customer Service Centre GmbH, Europaplatz 3, 69115 Heidelberg,
Germany. If you have any concerns regarding our products, please
contact ProductSafety@springernature.com

Printed and bound by CPI Group (UK) Ltd, Croydon, CR0 4YY
28/04/2026
02098457-0005